American West Collection

American West Collection

My Life Among the Indians
The Life of John Wesley Hardin
Days on the Road

By

George Catlin
John Wesley Hardin
Sarah Raymond Herndon

Pioneer Press
2018

Copyright © 2018 by Pioneer Press.

All rights reserved. This book or any portion thereof may not be reproduced or used in any manner whatsoever without the express written permission of the publisher except for the use of brief quotations in a book review or scholarly journal.

First Printing: 2018.

ISBN-13: 978-1719190688.

ISBN-10: 1719190682.

Contents

MY LIFE AMONG THE INDIANS
By George Catlin 7

THE LIFE OF JOHN WESLEY HARDIN
By John Wesley Hardin 176

DAYS ON THE ROAD
By Sarah Raymond Herndon 266

MY LIFE AMONG THE INDIANS

By George Catlin

THE FIRST INDIAN I EVER SAW was under the following circumstances.

I was born [July 26, 1796] in the beautiful and famed Valley of Wyoming, which is on the Susquehanna River, in the State of Pennsylvania. Not a long time after the close of the Revolutionary War in that country, a settlement was formed in that fertile valley by white people, while the Indian tribes, who were pushed out, were contesting the right of the white people to settle in it. After having practiced great cruelty on the Indian tribes and been warned from year to year by the Indians to leave it, it was ascertained one day that large parties of Indians were gathered on the mountains, armed and prepared to attack the white inhabitants.

The white men in the valley immediately armed, to the number of five or six hundred, and leaving their wives and children and old men in a rude fort on the bank of the river, advanced towards the head of the valley in search of their enemies.

The Indians, watching the movements of the white men from the mountain tops, descended into the valley, and at a favorable spot, where the soldiers were to pass, lay secreted in ambush on both sides of the road, and in an instant rush, at the sound of the warwhoop, sprang upon the whites with tomahawks and scalping-knives in hand, and destroyed them all, with the exception of a very few, who saved their lives by swimming the river.

Amongst the latter was my grandfather on my mother's side, from whom I have often had the most thrilling descriptions. This onslaught is called in history, the Wyoming Massacre. Some have called it treachery. It was strategy, not treachery; and strategy is a merit in the science of all warfare.

After this victory, the Indians marched down the valley and took possession of the fort containing the women and children, to whom not one of the husbands returned at that time. Amongst the prisoners taken in the fort was my grandmother and my mother, who was then a child only seven years old.

These several hundred prisoners, though in the hands of more than a thousand fierce and savage warriors, were not put to death, but kept captive for several weeks. When a reinforcement of troops arrived over the Pocono Mountains, the Indian warriors left the fort, with the women and children in it, having hunted for them and supplied them with food, and painted their faces red, calling them 'sisters and children,' and to the honor of the Indian's character, be it for ever known (as attested by every prisoner both men and women), treating them in every sense, with the greatest propriety and kindness.

These brief facts, which happened many years before I was born, with a thousand others which could be narrated, having become startling legends of that region, will account for the marvelous and frightful impressions I had received in my childhood, of Indian massacres and Indian murders, and also for the indelible impression made on my mind and my nerves by the thrilling incident I am about to describe.

Whilst my infant mind was filled with these impressions, my father, for the relief of his health, impaired by the practice of the law, retired some forty miles from the Valley of Wyoming to a romantic valley on the banks of the Susquehanna River, in the State of New York, where he had purchased a beautiful plantation, resolving to turn his attention during the remainder of his life to agricultural pursuits.

This lovely and picturesque little valley, called by its Indian name Oc-qua-go, was surrounded by high and precipitous mountains and deep ravines, being nearer to the straggling remnants of the defeated Mohawk and Oneida Indians, who had retreated before the deadly rifles of the avengers of Wyoming's misfortunes.

The ploughs in my father's fields were at this time daily turning up Indian skulls or Indian beads, and Indian flint arrowheads, which the laboring men of his farm, as well as those of the neighborhood, were bringing to me, and with which I was enthusiastically forming a little cabinet or museum; and one day, as the most valued of its acquisitions, one of my father's ploughmen brought from his furrow the head of an Indian pipe-tomahawk, which was covered with rust, the handle of which had rotted away.

At this early age, when probably only nine or ten years old, I had become a decent shot, with a light single-barreled fowling-piece which my father had designated as especially my own, and with which my slaughter of ducks, quails, pheasants, and squirrels was considered by the neighboring hunters to be very creditable to me.

But I began now to feel a higher ambition—that of killing a deer—for which the rifles of my two elder brothers were the weapons requisite, and which (they being absent, and pursuing their academic studies in a distant town) I began now to lay temporary claim to.

In my then recent visits to the Old Sawmill on the Big Creek—a famous place, to which my other propensity, that of trout-fishing, often called me—I had observed that the Sawmill 'lick' was much frequented by deer, and that I soon fixed as the scene of my future and more exciting operations.

The Old Sawmill was the shattered remains of a sawmill which had been abandoned for many years and consisting only of masses of timbers and planks, converted into piles by the force of the water, under and around which I always had my greatest success in trout-fishing.

This solitary ruin, about one mile from my father's back fields, was enveloped in a dark and lonely wilderness, with an old and deserted road leading to it, following mostly along the winding banks of the creek. Nearby it, in a deep and dark gorge in the mountain's side, overshadowed by dark and tall hemlocks and fir-trees, was the 'lick' to which my aspiring ideas were now leaning. The paths leading to it down the mountain sides were freshly trodden, and the mud and water in the lick, still riley with their recent steps, showed me the frequency with which the deer were paying their visits to it.

A lick, in the phrase of the country, is a salt-spring which the deer visit in warm weather, to allay their thirst, and to obtain the salt necessary for digestion. Most of the herbivorous animals visit these places and appear oftentimes under a sort of infatuation in their eagerness for them, in consequence of which they fall an easy prey to wild beasts, as well as to hunters, which lie in wait for them.

Stimulated by the proofs above named, and by my recollections, yet fresh, of the recitals of several of the neighboring hunters of their great success in the Old Sawmill lick, I resolved to try my first luck there.

A rifle for this enterprise was essential; a weapon which I never had fired, and as yet was not strong enough to raise, unless it was rested upon something for its support.

For this I foresaw a remedy, and I had every confidence in my accuracy of aim. But the greater difficulty of my problem was the positive order of my father that I was not to meddle with the arms of my elder brothers, which were in covers and hanging against the wall. This I solved, however, by a maneuver, at a late hour of the night, by extracting one of them from the cover, and putting my little fowling-piece in its place, and taking the rifle into the fields, where I concealed it for my next afternoon's contemplated enterprise.

The hour approaching, and finding the rifle loaded, I proceeded, with a light and palpitating heart, through the winding and lonely road, to the Old Sawmill lick; creeping along through narrow defiles, between logs and rocks, until, by a fair glance, at the lick, I found there was no game in it at the moment. I then took to a precipitous ledge of rocks in the side of the hill partly enclosing the dark and lonely place where the salt-spring issued, and where the deer were in the habit of coming to lick.

The nook into which I clambered and seated myself was elevated some twenty or thirty feet above the level of the lick, and at the proper distance for a dead shot. I here found myself in a snug and sly little box, which had evidently been constructed and used for a similar purpose on former occasions by the old hunters.

Having taken this position about the middle of the afternoon, with the muzzle of my rifle resting on a little breastwork of rock before me, I remained until near nightfall without other excitement than an occasional tremor from the noise of a bird or a squirrel in the leaves, which I mistook for the footsteps of an approaching deer! The falling of a dry branch, however, which came tumbling down upon the hill side above and behind me, in the midst of this silent and listless anxiety, gave me one or two tremendous shivers, which it took me some time to get over, even after I had discovered what it was; for it brought instantly into my mind the story which I had often heard Darrow relate, of killing the panther, which it had not occurred to me until that moment, took place, not long before, at the Old Sawmill lick!

JOHN DARROW, A POOR MAN LIVING IN THE NEIGHBORHOOD of my father, often worked for him in his fields, but was fonder of hunting, for which his success had gained him a reputation in that vicinity. He often supplied my father with venison, and as he took a peculiar fancy to me for my hunting propensities, one can easily see how I became attached to this charismatic man, and how I came to take my first lessons in deer-stalking and bear-hunting with him.

Well, Darrow had been in the habit of watching a great deal in the Old Sawmill lick, and of placing beyond the lick, at the height of the middle of a deer's body, a small bit of phosphorescent wood (a rotten wood which often occurs in those wildernesses, and called by the inhabitants foxfire, probably from phosphor) and which is always visible in the darkest night, looking like a small ball of fire. Then secreting himself before dark on the ground, on a level with his target, his rifle resting in a couple of crotches and aiming directly at his phosphor light, at any time of the night when he heard the stepping of the deer in the lick, and his light was obscured, to pull trigger was a certain death.

His story of the panther, which I was now revolving in my mind, he had told on arriving at my father's house one morning at an early hour from one of these nocturnal hunts, himself covered from head to foot with blood, and with a huge panther slung upon his back, with a bullet hole between its eyes, ran thus:

"I was watching last night, Squire (as he called my father), at the Old Sawmill lick, and it getting on to be near midnight, I fell asleep. Seated on the ground, and my back leaning against a beech tree, I was waked by a tremendous blow, like a stroke of lightning—'twas this beast, d'ye see; he sprung upon me, and landed me some ten or twelve feet, and dropped me, and made only one jump farther himself, as I knew by the noise when he stopped. I knew it was a panther, though I could see nothing, for it was total darkness. I was badly torn and felt the blood running in several places. My rifle was left in the crotches, and feeling my way very gradually with my feet, but keeping my eyes set upon the brute, for I knew exactly where he was lying, I at length got hold of the rifle, but it could do me no good in the dark. My knife had slipped out of the scabbard in the struggle, and I had now no hope but from knowing that the cowardly animal will never spring while you look him in the face.

"In this position, with my rifle in both hands, and cocked, I sat, not hearing even a leaf turned by him, until just the break of day (the only thing I wanted —it was but a few hours, but it seemed a long time, I assure you), when I could just begin to discover his outline, and then the wrinkles betwixt his eyes! Time moved slowly then, I can tell you, Squire; and at last I could see the head of Old Ben: there was no time to be lost now, and I let slip! The beast was about twenty feet from me."

One can easily imagine my juvenile susceptibilities much heightened by such reflections in such a place; and every leaf that turned behind me calculated to startle me. My resolve, of course, was not to trust myself in that gloomy place in the night, nor to wait much longer for the desired gratification, which I was then believing I should have to forego for that day at least.

The woodlark was at that moment taking its favorite limb in the lofty and evergreen hemlocks for its nightly rest, and making the wooded temple of solitude ring and echo with its liquid notes, whilst all else was still as death, and I was on the eve of descending from my elevated nook and wending my way home. Just then I heard the distant sounds of footsteps in the leaves, and shortly after discovered in the distance a deer (a huge buck!), timidly and cautiously descending the hill and approaching the lick, stopping often to gaze, and sometimes looking me, apparently, full in the face, when I was afraid even to wink, lest he should discover me.

My young blood was too boilable, and my nerves decidedly too excitable for my business. Successive chills seemed to rise, I don't recollect where from, but they shook me, each one of them, until after shaking my head, they seemed to go out at the top of it.

The deer kept advancing, and my shakes increasing, at length it entered the pool, and commenced licking; and the resolve that the moment had arrived for my grand achievement, set my teeth chattering. My rifle, cocked, was rested before me on the surface of the rock, and all things, save myself, were perfectly ready; after several useless attempts I got my aim, but before I could pull trigger, from another chill and a shake, I lost it again. I tried again and again, but in vain, and then more prudently resolved to lie still a few moments until I could get my nerves steadier, and at all events, until I could see more clearly the forward sight of my barrel, which seemed to be enveloped in a sort of a mist.

Just at this moment also popped into my head another idea that gave me one or two renewed shivers. I had fired my little fowling-piece hundreds of times without harm, but I never had fired a rifle. It may be overloaded, or so long loaded as to kick, or to explode! But never mind, I must run those risks. After checking my latter apprehensions for a few moments, and feeling again more calmed, I was getting my aim with tolerable accuracy, when away went another of those frightful chills, like a snake running through me from my feet to the top of my head, because I was just about to pull trigger!

The deer at this time seemed to have got enough of licking, and, stepping out of the lick, disappeared in the thicket. "Oh, what a loss! What a misfortune! What a chance is gone! What a coward, and what a poor fool am I! But if he had stopped, though, one minute longer, I am sure I could have killed him, for I don't tremble now."

Just at this cool moment the deer came gliding through the bushes and into the lick again, much nearer than before. One little chill began; but by gritting my teeth tight together I succeeded in getting a steadier aim, when—*BANG!* went the crack and the flash of a rifle, a little to the left of me!—and the deer, bounding a few rods from the pool on to an elevated bank, and tumbling upon the ground, quite dead, showed me that I was too late!

My head and the breech of my rifle were instantly lowered a little more behind my stone breastwork, and then—oh, horrid! what I never had seen before, nor ever dreamed of seeing in that place—the tall and graceful form of a huge Indian, but half bent forward, as he pushed his red and naked shoulders, and drew himself slowly over the logs and through the bushes. Trailing his rifle in his left hand and drawing a large knife with the other from its sheath in the hollow of his back, he advanced to the carcass of the deer, which had fallen much nearer to me than it was when it was shot.

His rifle he leaned against a tree, and the blade of his bloody knife, which he had drawn across the neck of the deer, he clenched between his teeth, while he suspended the animal by the hind legs from the limb of a tree to let it bleed. "Oh, horrid! Horrid! What a fate is mine! What am I to do?"

No length of life could ever erase from my recollection the impression which this singular and unexpected scene made upon my infant mind, or the ease, and composure, and grace with which this phantom seated himself upon the trunk of a large and fallen tree, wiping his huge knife upon the moss and laying it by his side, and drawing from his pouch his flint, and steel, and spunk, with which he lit his pipe, and from which it seemed, in a few moments, as if he were sending up thanks to the Great Spirit in the blue clouds of smoke that were curling around him.

Who will ever imagine the thoughts that were passing through my youthful brain in these exciting moments? For here was before me, for the first time in my life, the living figure of a Red Indian!

If he sees me I'm lost; he will scalp me and devour me, and my dear mother will never know what became of me!

From the crack of that rifle, however, I had not another chill, nor a shiver: my feeling now was no longer the ebullition of childish anxiety, but the awfully flat and stupid one of dread and fear; and every muscle was quiet. Here was perhaps death in a moment before me.

My eyeballs, which seemed elongated as though they were reaching half-way to him, were too tightly strained to tremble. An instant thought came to me, when his naked back and shoulders were turned towards me. My rifle is levelled, and I am perfectly cool; a bullet would put an end to all my fears. And a better one followed when he turned gently around, and moved his piercing black eyes over and about the ledge where I was sitting, and the blue streams were curling upwards from his mouth and his nostrils; for I saw then (though a child), in the momentary glance of that face, what infant human nature could not fail to see, and none but human nature could express. I saw humanity.

His pipe burned out; the deer, with its fore and hind legs tied together, he slung upon his back, and, taking his rifle in his hand, he silently and quietly disappeared in the dusky forest, which at this time was taking the gloom of approaching night.

My position and reflections were still like lead that could not be removed, until a doubly reasonable time had elapsed for this strange apparition to be entirely out of my way. He seemingly, at last view, to have taken the direction of the 'old road' by which I had expected to return, my attention was now turned to a different but more difficult route. By clambering the huge precipice still above me, which I did as soon as perfect safety seemed to authorize it, and by a run of more than a mile through the woods, scarcely daring to look back, I was safely lodged in my father's back fields, but without hat or rifle, and without the least knowledge of the whereabouts in which either of them had been deposited or dropped. The last of these, however, was recovered on the following day, but the other never came to light.

Such was the adventure, and such the mode of my first seeing an Indian.

Having seen him, the next thing was to announce him, which I did without plan or reserve, but solely with youthful impulse; exclaiming as I approached the vicinity of my father's house, and as pale as a ghost, "I've seen an Indian! I've seen an Indian!"

No one believed me, as no Indian had been seen in the neighborhood for many years. I related the whole of my adventure, and then they thought "the boy was mad." I was mad—I went to bed mad and crying; and my poor dear mother came and knelt by my bed, and at last comforted me a little by saying, "My dear George, I do believe you— I believe your story to be true—I believe you have seen an Indian."

I had a restless night, however, and in the morning, when I awoke, Johnny O'Neil, a faithful farm-laborer in my father's employment, was at the door, announcing that, "Jist in the toother end of the bag whate-field, where ye sae thit lattle smohk areesin, has kimmed thae japsies; sae ye may be lookin' oot for yer toorkies, an' yer suckin'-pigs, an' yer chahkins, for I tal ye ther'll be nae gude o' 'em!"

Poor Johnny O'Neil! He was not believed either; for, said my father, "That's almost a bull, Johnny, for there are no gypsies in this country."

"I bag yer parthen," said Johnny; and my father continued: "I'll be bound these are George's Indians!" and putting on his hat, and taking me by the hand, he and Johnny O'Neil and myself started off for the farther corner of the big wheat-field, where we found my Indian warrior seated on a bear-skin spread out upon the ground. His legs were crossed, his elbows resting on his knees, and his pipe at his lips; with his wife, and his little daughter of ten years old, with blankets wrapped around them, and their necks covered with beads, reclining by the side of him; and over them all, to screen them from the sun, a blanket, suspended by the corners from four crotchets fastened into the ground, and a small fire in front of the group, with a steak of venison cooking for their breakfast.

"There's the japsies!" said Johnny O'Neil, as we were approaching. "There is the Indian, father!" said I; and my father, who had been familiar with Indians, and had learned to sing their songs and speak somewhat of their language in his early life, said to me, "George, my boy, you were right! These are Indians."

"Yes," said I, "and that's the very man I saw."

He was smoking away, and looking us steadily in the face as we approached; and though I began to feel something of the alarm I had felt the day before, my father's stepping up to him and taking him by the hand with a mutual "How—how— how" and the friendly grip of his soft and delicate hand, which was extended to me also, soon dissipated all my fears, and turned my alarm to perfect admiration.

Understanding and speaking a little English, he easily explained to my father that he was an Oneida, living near Cayuga Lake, some one hundred and fifty miles distant, that his name was On-o-gong-way ('a great warrior'). He asked us to sit down by him, when he cleaned out his pipe, and, charging it afresh with tobacco, lighted, and gave it to my father to smoke, and then handed it to me, which, my father explained, was a pledge of his friendship.

My father then explained to him the story of my adventure the day before at the Old Sawmill lick, to every sentence of which I was nodding "yes," and trembling, as the Indian was smoking his pipe, and almost, but not quite, commencing a smile, as he was earnestly looking me in the face.

The story finished, he took me by both hands, and repeated the words, "Good, good, good hunter." He laid his pipe down, and very deliberately climbing over the fence, stepped into the shade of the forest, where he had suspended a small saddle of venison, and brought it, and laying it by my side, exclaimed, as he laid his hand on my head, "Dat you, you half; very good;" meaning that I was a good hunter, and that half of the venison belonged to me.

The saddle of venison, though very small, was no doubt a part of the animal I had seen in the lick, though it had appeared to me the day before, as I had represented it at home, a "buck of the most enormous size," and the Indian a giant, though on more familiar acquaintance, to my great surprise, he proved to be no larger than an ordinary man.

This generous present added much to my growing admiration, which was increased again as I listened to his narrative, made to my father and myself, of his history and of some of his adventures, as well as the motive which had brought him some hundreds of miles over a country partly of forest and partly inhabited by a desperate set of hunters whose rifles were unerring, and whose deep-rooted hostility to all savages induced them to shoot them down whenever they met them in their hunting grounds.

His father, he said, had been one of the warriors in the battle of Wyoming, and amongst them was afterwards driven by the white soldiers, after many battles and great slaughter, up the shores of the Susquehanna to the country where the remnant of his tribe now lived, between the Oneida and Cayuga Lakes.

During this disastrous retreat, he being a boy about my size, his father made him assist in carrying many heavy things which they had plundered from the white people, where they fought a great battle, at the mouth of the Tunkhannock; amongst which, and one of the most valuable, as one of the most difficult to carry, was a kettle of gold.

"What!" said my father, "a kettle of gold!"

"Yes, father," said he. "Now listen ...

"The white soldiers came through the narrows you see yonder," (pointing to a narrow gorge in the mountains, through which the river passes); "and on those very fields, which then were covered with trees," (pointing to my father's fields, lying beneath and in front of us), "was a great battle, and many were the warriors that fell on both sides; but at that time, father, another army of white men came from the north, and were entering the valley on that side, and the poor Indians had no way but to leave the river and all their canoes, and to cross these high mountains behind us, and make their way through the forests to Cayuga.

"In passing these mountains, my father, they followed the banks of that creek to its head (pointing to the creek on which the Old Sawmill was built, and which passed in a serpentine course through my father's farm to the river). On the banks of that creek many things were buried by the Indians, who were unable to carry them over the mountains; and amongst them, somewhere near that bridge, my father, where the road crosses, on the farther bank, I saw my father and my mother bury the kettle of gold with other things, in the ground.

"When my father was old and infirm, I was obliged to hunt for him, and I could not come; but since he has gone to the land of his fathers, I have made the journey a great way, to dig up the kettle of gold. But I see this day, from where I now sit, that there is no use in looking for it, and my heart is very sad.

"My father—we buried the kettle of gold at the foot of a large pine-tree that stood on the bank; but I see the trees are all gone, and all now is covered with green grass; and where shall I go to look? This, my father, I kept a secret for many years, but I see there is no use in keeping it a secret any longer, and this makes my heart sad. I have come a great way, my father, and my road in going back I know is beset with many enemies.

"These green fields, my father, which are now so beautiful to look upon, were once covered with large and beautiful trees, and they were then the hunting grounds of my fathers, and they were many and strong; but we are now but a very few—we live a great way off, and we are your children."

My father asked him many questions about the kettle of gold, and in answering these, he extended both arms in the form of a circle, his fingers' ends just touching each other. "There," said he, "it was about thus large, and just as much as I could lift; and must be of great value."

My father, after a study of a few minutes, turned to me, and said, "George! Run down to the house and ask your mother to give you the little brass kettle and bring it here as quick as you can." I never, perhaps, had run more nimbly (but on one occasion) in my lifetime, than I ran and scaled the fences on this errand.

While this conversation was passing about the 'kettle of gold,' it had occurred to my father that Buel Rowley, one of his hired men, had ploughed up a small brass kettle a few years before, on the bank of the creek, and at the identical spot designated by the forefinger of the Indian; and that kettle being brought by me from my mother's culinary collection, was now under the eyes of the child of the forest.

Whilst he was in silence gazing upon it, and turning it over and over, my father described to him the manner and place in which it was found, and that it was made of brass, which, to be sure, looked like gold, but was much harder, and of much less value. After a pause of a few minutes, and without the change of a muscle, but drawing a deep sigh, as if he recognized the long-hidden treasure, and trying his knife two or three times on the upper rim of it, he laid it down, and drawing a deep breath or two through his pipe, said to my father, that he had no doubt but it was the same kettle, but that two things troubled his mind very much—the first was, that the kettle should be so small; and the other, that he found it was not a 'kettle of gold.' The first error he attributed to his having carried it when he was quite a small boy, as it was then a heavy load for him; and the other, from having learned amongst the white people that a very small piece of gold was worth ten dollars; and having estimated from this standard the probable value of a kettle of gold, not having as yet learned enough from the white people to know the difference between gold and brass.

Poor ignorant child of the forest! He had learned from his teachers something of the value of gold before he knew what it was; and he had risked his life, and those of his wife and his little daughter, in wending his way for hundreds of miles through the forests infested with hunters whose rifles were levelled upon every Indian they could meet. His long journey had cost him no gold, for he had none to spend; his rifle had supplied him and his family with food, and he had thus far escaped his enemies, and in this wise accomplished his object; but his dangerous steps, which were to be retraced, were rendered tenfold more dangerous from the vague reports which had accidentally and unfortunately got into circulation amongst the hunters and brigands of the forests through which he had to pass, that he had dug up, and was returning with, a 'kettle of gold.'

My father and several of his neighbors paid frequent visits to his little bivouac; and I spent nearly all my time there, so completely were all my fears turned into admiration. My rusty tomahawk-head I brought to him, for which he made me a handle, and curiously carved it with his knife. The handle was perforated for smoking through, a mystery which no one of the neighbors could solve, as "there was no gimlet long enough to make such a hole," little thinking, as he explained the secret to me, that the handle was made of a young ash, the pith of which is easily burned away with a heated wire, or a piece of hard hickory wood.

The handle finished, my friend Johnny O'Neil laid the head and blade of it on the grindstone while I turned, until it was everywhere silvery bright, and its edge as sharp as a knife. This lighted the eyes of the child of the forest, and he gave a new gleam to mine, when he filled the bowl of it with tobacco (or k'nick-k'neck, an Indian substitute for tobacco)

And yet the great charm and mystery of the tomahawk was still to come—yet to be learned. My readers must know that the tomahawk (like the scalping-knife, which generally has the Sheffield mark upon it) is a contrivance of civilized invention and construction, too deadly and destructive to have been made by the poor Indian; combining the two essential requisites—of being capable of being used in war as the most efficient and deadly weapon, by throwing or striking with, and, when war is at an end, of being turned into a luxury, for which it is equally valued, the smoke passing through it when charged with tobacco.

The first of these characters of the tomahawk having been illustrated as above stated, to my inexpressible delight, and the tobacco all burned out; my good and confiding friend now arose with the tomahawk in his right hand, and raised my astonishment and admiration still higher, by throwing it at the trunk of a tree some rods distant, and burying its blade in the solid wood, explaining to me the certain fate of an enemy within an equal distance. I had not the power to draw it out; but under his practiced hand it seemed to leave the tree like a breath of wind.

He then stepped back again some ten or fifteen steps, with the end of the handle in his hand, when —chick!—it seemed to pronounce, as quick as electricity, and was there buried again! This he did more than twenty times, without failing once, to the astonishment of my father and others looking on; the weapon revolving many times in the air, and the blade, no matter what the distance, always entering the tree. Here I was left in one of the several inexplicable mysteries which I have met in Indian life, and never have been able to solve, even to the present day.

My flint arrowheads I brought to him, which he looked upon with an evident gloom. He made me shafts (which he feathered) to a number of them; and from a young hickory he made me a beautiful bow, and ornamented it with woodpecker feathers; and from the skin of the fawn (the 'huge buck,' which I would have killed) he made me a quiver, and, with the arrows in it, slung it on my back. What could more completely have capped the climax of my boyish ambition than this?

The honesty and childlike simplicity of these poor people gained them many friends in the neighborhood, and yet there were, no doubt, murderous enemies in disguise plotting and prowling around them. My father made them many presents, and my attachment to them laid my mother's pantry under daily and heavy contributions.

My father was under constant apprehensions for their safety, and while he was maturing a plan for sending them home by a different route, and at his own expense, it was discovered one morning that their smoke was missing in the corner of my father's 'big wheat-field;' and on the same morning was found hanging in my father's woodhouse, which was always open on one side, a fine saddle of venison, with one of the beautiful and well-known eagle quills from the head of On-o-gong-way fastened in it!

Poor, honest, and harmless man! He had left, to meet the chances for his life on his long journey home; and as an unmistakable evidence of his friendship and gratitude, he had left this silent parting gift, and with it, as he could not write his name, his choicest plume, to identify the giver.

"The Indians are gone! The Indians are gone!" was echoed everywhere, and through the neighborhood, in the morning; and poor Johnny O'Neil, when he looked upon the saddle of venison containing the eagle's quill, exclaimed, "Upon my word, squire, thase is nae japsies—an' I'll be shot if thot mon's not a gintleman!"

A few days after the departure of the Indians, two neighboring boys and myself were practicing with my tomahawk, by throwing it at the trunk of a tree; and when thrown by the hand of one of the boys, it glanced from the tree, by which I was standing too closely, when the sharp blade struck me on the left cheek, cutting deep into the cheekbone, and felling me to the ground, covered with blood; giving me a wound which was several months in healing, and a scar which any one of my readers may always know me by, if they have the opportunity of seeing me.

This was the first catastrophe growing out of the new and singular acquaintance thus recited, but not the saddest; that came to our knowledge a few days later, and in this lamentable form—that the dead body of poor On-o-gong-way was found, pierced by two rifle bullets, in Randolph Valley, a dark and dreary wilderness, some eight or ten miles from my father's plantation, which it was necessary for him to cross in order to reach his own country and friends.

What became of his poor wife and the interesting and innocent little daughter, no mortal was ever able (or willing) to say; and the 'kettle of gold,' which my father had confident hopes would have led to the detection of so foul a murder, notwithstanding his exertions from year to year, never furnished any clue to the villainy.

II

IN THE FOREGOING CHAPTER I HAVE SHOWN how I received my earliest impressions of the Indian character; and skipping over the intervening part of my life, from my boyhood to the age of thirty-three, when, as I have said, I entered the forests to learn more of it, we will now enter upon scenes that I witnessed in those pursuits, from which a more intimate knowledge of these people and their customs may be gleaned.

The great valley of the Mississippi and Missouri, containing nearly one-half of North America, with its vast prairies, and mountains, and lakes, was the first field of my roamings, which occupied some five or six years of my life; during which time I visited many tribes, and some of the finest races of mankind in America or in the world; the principal, and most numerous, and most interesting of these were the Sioux; the Blackfoot; the Crows; the Mandan; the Pawnees; Ojibbeways; Comanche; Osages and Choctaws; and in my subsequent travels west of the Rocky Mountains, a few of the numerous tribes, the Flatheads; the Apaches; the Shoshones; the Arapahos, and others; and in South and Central America, the Caribbees; the Arowaks; the Chaymas; the Gooagives; the Macouchis; the Guarani; the Tupi; the Botocudos; the Connibos; the Chiquitos; the Moxos, and fifty others.

A connected narrative of my wanderings amongst all of these remote people would require a very large and perhaps tedious book;

but, my readers, I will not fatigue you by traveling over the whole ground—I will take a shorter way. I will introduce you at once to the people themselves and their modes of living, and afterwards to their customs, which you will then be better able to appreciate.

We now take an immense stride of twelve hundred miles in a moment, from the scenes of my younger days just described, in the State of New York, where the Indian tribes have all disappeared many years since, to the center and heart of the great American wilds, where men and animals are still roaming in their native beauty and independence, on the great and almost boundless grassy plains of the Upper Missouri.

The Sioux is one of the most numerous and powerful tribes in North America, numbering about twenty-five thousand, divided into forty bands, each band having a chief at its head, which chiefs are again subordinate to one head-chief; and with him, in council, they form the government of the nation; and such is the custom amongst most of the other tribes.

There is no tribe better clad, who live in better houses (wigwams), or who are better mounted, than the Sioux. They catch an abundance of wild horses, which are grazing on the prairies, oftentimes in groups of several hundreds, and from their horses' backs, at full speed, they deal their deadly arrows, or wield their long and fatal lances in the chase of the buffaloes, and also in war with their enemies.

These people, living mostly in a country of prairies, where they easily procure the buffalo-skins, construct their wigwams with them, in form of tents, which are more comfortable than rude huts constructed of timber, are more easily built, and have the advantage of being easily transported over the prairies; by which means the Indians are enabled to follow the migrating herds of buffaloes during the summer and fall seasons, when they are busily engaged in drying meat for their winter's consumption, and dressing robes for their own clothing, and also for barter to the fur traders.

In one Sioux village, on the Upper Missouri, there were about four hundred skin tents, all built much in the same manner: some fifteen or twenty pine poles forming the frame, covered with one entire piece of fifteen or twenty buffalo-skins sewed together, and most curiously painted and embroidered, of all colors; presenting one of the most curious and beautiful scenes imaginable.

Inside of these tents, the fire is placed in the center, the smoke escaping out at the top; and at night the inmates all sleep on buffalo-skins spread upon the ground, with their feet to the fire; a most safe, and not uncomfortable mode. When you enter one of these wigwams you have to stoop rather awkwardly; but when you are in, you rise up and find a lofty space of some twenty feet above your head. The family are all seated, and no one rises to salute you, whatever your office or your importance may be. All lower their eyes to your feet, instead of staring you in the face, and you are asked to sit down.

A robe or a mat of rushes is spread for you, and as they have no chairs you are at once embarrassed. It is an awkward thing for a white man to sit down upon the ground until he gets used to it, and when he is down, he doesn't know what to do with his legs.

The Indians, accustomed to this from childhood, sit down upon and rise from the ground with the same ease and grace that we sit down in, and rise from, a chair. Both men and women lower themselves to the ground, and rise, without a hitch or a jerk, and without touching their hand to the ground. This is very curious, but it is exceedingly graceful and neat. The men generally sit cross-legged; and to sit down they cross their feet, closely locked together, and extending their arms and head forward, slowly and regularly lower their bodies quite to the sitting posture on the ground: when they rise they place their feet in the same position, and their arms and head also, and rise to a perfectly straight position, apparently without an effort.

The women always sit with both feet and lower legs turned under and to the right or the left, and, like the men, lower and raise themselves without touching the ground. When you are seated, to feel at ease your legs must be crossed, and your heels drawn quite close under you, and then you can take the pipe when it is handed to you, and get a fair and deliberate glance at things around you.

The furniture in these wigwams is not much, but it is very curious in effect, and picturesque, when we look at it. The first startling thing you will meet on entering will be half-a-dozen saucy dogs, barking, and bristling, and showing their teeth, and oftentimes as many screaming children, frightened at your savage and strange appearance.

These hushed, you can take a look at other things, and you see shields, and quivers, and lances, and saddles, and medicine bags, and pouches, and spears, and cradles, and buffalo masks (which each man keeps for dancing the buffalo dance), and a great variety of other picturesque things hanging around, suspended from the poles of the tent, to which they are fastened by thongs; the whole presenting, with the picturesque group around the fire, one of the most curious scenes imaginable.

In front of these wigwams the women are seen busily at work, dressing robes and drying meat. The skin-dressing of the Indians, both of the buffalo and deer-skins, is generally very beautiful and soft. Their mode of doing this is curious: they stretch the skin, either on a frame or on the ground, and after it has remained some three or four days with the brains of the buffalo or elk spread over the fleshy side, they grain it with a sort of adze or chisel, made of a piece of buffalo bone.

After the process of 'graining,' and the skin is apparently beautifully finished, they pass it through another process, that of 'smoking.' For this, a hole of some two or three feet in depth is dug in the ground, and a smothered fire kindled in the hole with rotten wood, producing a strong and peculiar sort of smoke; and over this a little tent, made of two or three buffalo-skins, and so closed as to prevent the smoke from escaping, in which the grained skins hang for three or four days. After this process, the dresses made of these skins may be worn repeatedly in the rain, and will always dry perfectly soft—a quality which, I believe, does not yet belong to dressed skins in civilized countries.

Drying meat is done by cutting it into thin slices and exposing it in the sun, hung upon poles, where it dries, and is successfully cured, without salt and without smoke.

It is proverbial in the civilized world that "the poor Indian woman has to do all the hard work." Don't believe this, for it is not exactly so. She labors very hard and constantly, it is true. She does most of the drudgery about the village and wigwam, and is seen transporting heavy loads, etc. This all looks to the passer-by as the slavish compulsion of her cruel husband, who is often seen lying at his ease, and smoking his pipe, as he is looking on.

His labors are not seen, and therefore are less thought of, when he mounts his horse, with his weapons in hand, and working every nerve and every muscle, dashes amongst the herds in the chase, to provide food for his wife and his little children, and scours the country both night and day, at the constant risk of his life, to protect them from the assaults of their enemies.

The Indian woman's life is, to be sure, a slavish one; and equally so are the lives of most women equally poor in all civilized countries. Look into their humble dwellings in all cities and towns, or in the country, in civilized communities, and see the industry and the slavish labor of a poor woman! She works all the days of her life, brings water, makes fires, and tends to her little children, like the poor Indian woman; and she may be a slave to an idle husband, who is spending his time and his money, as well as her own earnings, in a tap-room.

The civilized world is full of such slavery as this; but amongst the American Indians such a system does not and cannot exist; every man is a hunter and a soldier; he must supply his family with food, and help to defend his country.

The education of woman in those countries teaches her that the labors are thus to be divided between herself and her husband; and for the means of subsistence and protection, for which she depends upon his labors, she voluntarily assumes the hard work about the encampment, considering their labors about equally divided.

'Slaves to their husbands' is an epithet so often and so inappropriately applied to the poor Indian woman by the civilized world, and so frequently reiterated and kept alive by tourists who have happened to see an Indian woman or two at work when their husbands were asleep or smoking their pipes, that I cannot, in common honesty to you, my readers, nor in justice to the Indian, consent to pass it by in this place without some further comment.

One of the distinguishing natural traits of the American Indian, that stamps his character as mentally superior to that of the African and some other races, is his uncompromising tenacity for unbounded freedom. All efforts made (and there have been many) to enslave these people, have resulted in failures; and such an abhorrence have they of the system, that they cannot be induced to labor for each other or for white men for any remuneration that can be offered, lest the disgraceful epithet 'slave' should be applied to them by their tribe.

In the relationship of man and wife, in which, as amongst white people, 'both are one,' they can and do labor for mutual interests and mutual subsistence, without incurring this reproach; and I do not believe that, among the poorer class of any civilized people on earth, a better and a more voluntary division of the toils of conjugal life can be found than exists amongst the American Indians.

By the custom in all the American tribes, the person of every individual in society, either within the pale of the domestic relations or out of it, is considered sacredly protected from the lash or a blow, which in themselves imply degradation or servitude, and in all cases they may be revenged with death.

If this system should, by possibility, have its disadvantages, how much does it redound to the credit of the Indian's character, and to the honor of his race, and what a lesson is it for the civilized world, that there never was known to exist amongst them the unnatural brute that has beaten his wife or his little child!

But we left these poor women at their 'slavish work,' dressing robes and drying meat. Let us go back to them for a few moments yet, lest we should lose sight of a Sioux village before we know all about it, and of course be unable to appreciate some extraordinary and amusing Sioux customs, to be explained further on as we advance.

We here see the Indian women in the full enjoyment of their domestic happiness, with their little children and dogs around them, the villagers dressed in their ordinary costumes, and the little cupids taking their first lessons in archery, which is the most important feature in their education. This happens to be 'scalp-day.' The Sioux, like most of the other tribes, having several days in the year for 'counting scalps,' which are observed somewhat as holidays. The chief on those days passes through an aperture in the side of his wigwam, and erects over it a pole called the 'scalp-pole,' from which are suspended the scalps which he has taken, which is the signal for all the warriors to do the same; so that the chief and every person in the village can count them, and understand each warrior's standing and claims to promotion, which are estimated by the number of scalps he has taken.

Amongst the Indian tribes every man is a military man, a warrior, a brave, or a chief. All are armed and ready to go to war if necessary. A warrior is one of those who has taken one or more scalps; a brave is one who goes to war as a soldier, but as yet has taken no scalps, has killed no enemy.

Taking the scalp is practiced by all the American tribes much in the same way, and for the same objects, which, with the mode of taking it and using it, will be more fully described hereafter.

From the Sioux mode of constructing their villages, which I have thus briefly explained, and to which we shall have occasion again to return, we will now take a glance at some other modes practiced by other tribes living at great distances from them.

The Assiniboine, the Crows, the Blackfoot, the Omaha, the Cheyenne, the Comanche, and yet several other tribes living near the herds of buffaloes, build their wigwams, and live much in the manner of the Sioux. All of these I would denominate 'skin-builders.' There are also the grass-builders, the dirt-builders, the bark-builders, and the timber-builders, and yet other builders, all of whom will be noticed in their proper places.

How curious it is that these ingenious people, who have invented so many ways of constructing their dwellings, never yet have adopted the mode of building with stone. This is probably not the result of ignorance or want of invention, but from their universal policy of leaving no monuments. All the American tribes are migratory; and when they move, they destroy all their marks, by burning their wigwams, if they cannot take them with them, and 'smoothing over the graves of their parents and children.'

The Pawnee-Picts (in their own language Tow-ee-ahge), a numerous tribe living on the head waters of the Red River, in Western Texas, build their wigwams by a sort of thatching of long prairie grass, over a frame of poles fastened in the ground and bent in at their tops; the structure, when completed, having much the shape and appearance of a straw beehive.

This singular mode, which is only practiced by that tribe, and partially so by the Kiowa and Waco, smaller tribes subjugated by the Pawnee-Picts, is very convenient; they are comfortable dwellings, easily constructed, and easily demolished when they are left, by putting a firebrand to them.

The tribe of Mandans, on the Upper Missouri, the Pawnees of the Platte, the Minatarees, and the Riccarrees, are the only dirt-builders, and they all seem to construct their wigwams much in the same manner.

These tribes, unlike the Sioux and other tribes living in skin tents, and who are constantly roaming about the country, live in permanent villages, and construct their wigwams with more labor and more strength, and uniformly fortify them against the assaults of their enemies, by the bank of a river on one side, and a stockade on the other. These wigwams are always made by excavating, in a circular form, some three or four feet into the ground, for a foundation, from which they make a superstructure of round timbers lying against each other, the butt ends placed in the bottom of the excavation, and the smaller ends concentrating near the top, and supported within by beams resting on upright posts; the whole is covered with willow boughs, to preserve the dryness and soundness of the timbers; and covered again with a foot or two in thickness of a concrete of tough clay and gravel, permitting the whole family, dogs and all, to recline and gambol on the top of it in pleasant weather.

In the Mandan village I measured several of these, and found the smallest to be forty-five feet, and many of them sixty feet in diameter. The fire is always built in the center, with the smoke escaping at the apex.

These, then, are the only modes of construction which are confined to any uniform shapes; the wood-builders, and the bark-builders, and others, like the timber-builders and palm-builders in Central and South America, using a thousand different shapes in constructing with those materials.

So much for the various modes in which these curious people live. We will now take a little further view of their personal appearance, and then proceed to their actions and usages, from which I intend you shall draw more amusement, and obtain important information in support of the character of these abused people, which, I have fearlessly said, entitles them to a high position amongst the families of the world.

III

NOW, MY READERS, WE ARE SOON COMING to scenes and events that will be more exciting; skip over nothing, but read every word as you pass along, for we are so far getting a foundation for what is to follow. Don't get impatient for the description of scalps and scalping, for the buffalo-hunts, the dog-feasts, the stone-man medicine, the Thunders Nest, etc.,

Every Indian tribe is a separate community, surrounded by other tribes with whom they are generally at war, owing to several causes which don't exist to the same extent amongst civilized nations. They have no settled (but always disputed and imperfectly defined) boundaries, over which their fierce hunting excursions often lead them, exposing them to the attacks of their enemies. Another, and more frequent cause of warfare, is the popular ambition to signal themselves, which is felt amongst all Indian warriors, who have but the one mode to rise to enviable distinction in their tribes, that of being a great warrior.

War dress and war paint is something very curious. It is the invariable custom of the warriors of all Indian tribes in America, to go to war in war dress and war paint; the first consisting in a mode of dressing the person just as each individual may fancy for himself, so as to afford the greatest facility for the free use of his weapons; and, in fact, most generally amounting to (nearly) no dress at all. And the second, his limbs being chiefly naked, consisting of a thick daubing or streaking of red and white clay, vermilion, and charcoal, mixed with bears' grease, covering various parts of his body and limbs, as well as his face, sometimes half black and half red, and at other times the whole face black, in such a manner as even to be disguised, oftentimes, from his own familiar friends.

Each warrior has some peculiar and known way of painting, by which he is recognized by his fellow warriors, at a distance at which they would not distinguish him from his comrades from the natural differences, so great is their resemblance in the open air when naked and in action.

It was one of the curious and unaccountable facts that I met with in my travels, that I never in any instance was able to get a warrior to stand for his portrait until he had spent the requisite time at his toilette (oftentimes from sunrise until eleven or twelve o'clock) to arrange himself in his war dress and war paint. And I also everywhere learned that all warriors apprehended through life, with the greatest solicitude, the possibility and the misfortune of losing their lives when they are not in their war paint.

The principal arms (or weapons) of all the American tribes are their bows and arrows. Their bows are short and light, for easy and effective handling on horseback; but they have great power, being mostly covered on the backs with layers of buffalo sinews, giving them great elasticity. Their arrows are mostly pointed with flints, broken in so ingenious a manner, with a point and two sharp edges, as to enable them to enter the flesh of the buffaloes or their enemies, on whichsoever they may use them.

These arrows are carried in a quiver slung on the back, and generally made of the skins of animals adapted in shape and size to hold them. When not in service, their arrows are carried in the quiver with the points downwards, for protection; but when they are going into battle, the arrows are reversed, leaving the points standing out, being thus readier to be drawn suddenly and without obstruction.

Besides the bow and arrow, the tomahawk, already explained, and war clubs of various shapes and materials, and lances, are used in warfare, and shields carried on the left arm for protection. These shields are carried by every horseman, completing his dress and equipment, completely in the classic style of the ancient Roman and Grecian cavalry.

These shields are invariably made of the skin of the buffalo's neck, the thickest part of the hide; tanned and hardened in such a manner with the glue remaining in them, that they are proof against arrows, and even against a gunshot when held obliquely, which they do with great skill. They paint and ornament these shields in a great variety of ways and add to their picturesque appearance by suspending eagle quills and other beautiful plumes from them, and oftentimes painting the representation of their medicine bags upon them. ('Medicine bags' you will understand in a few moments.)

"Smoking the Shield"—Have you ever heard of Smoking the Shield? I believe not. Why, it is one of the grandest and most imposing ceremonies to be seen in the Indian countries. Let's see.

An Indian lad is old enough to go to war—he is sixteen or eighteen years old—he wants a shield— must have one —can't go to war without one. Can he buy one? He might, perhaps, but "it won't protect him if he does"—he must make it for himself—and how? He must kill the buffalo bull with his own hand. With a gun? No; a smaller boy than he can do that: he must kill it with an arrow, and take the hide off with his own hand; and then—Well, then what? Why, he has got to make his shield. Can he do this privately, and at his leisure? No; Indian soldiers are counted by their shields. Indian warriors are the property of their nation. Can any Indian lad secretly enlist, and make himself a warrior? Have they any newspapers to announce their enrolments? No: the making of a warrior is a public act, and must be made in a public way: the warriors help in this.

IN THE GREAT COMANCHE VILLAGE, IN 1836, I was invited to go and see the 'Smoking a Shield.' An immense crowd was assembled a little out of the village, within which a circle, of a hundred feet or more in diameter, was preserved by a line marked on the ground. In the center of this circle a young man had dug a hole in the ground, and over it, stretched horizontally, a little elevated above the surface, the bit of bull's hide, of which he was to forge his shield, tightly strained by a great many pins driven into the ground, and a fire burning in the excavation underneath, while the glue extracted from the buffalo's hoofs, and spread over the skin, was frying and roasting into it, to give it the hardness and stiffness required.

To witness this ceremony, which they call 'smoking (or roasting) the shield,' in order to insure its success, and legitimately to publish its owner's change from the phase of boyhood to that of warrior, all the warriors of the village had assembled at his invitation, in full war dress and war paint, with their shields on their arms, who formed in rings within rings, and danced in circles around the roasting shield; and each one passed it brandishing their war clubs, their tomahawks, and shields over it, vaunting forth the wonderful efficiency of their own, and invoking the 'fire-spirit' to give strength and hardness enough to that of the young warrior, to guard and protect him from the weapons of his enemies. Was he then a warrior? No; his shield finished, he was a brave—a soldier; and this ceremony his enlistment—no more. He can go to war, as you have been told. If he can take a scalp, he then becomes a warrior.

All the American tribes may properly be said to be warlike. I have explained the principal causes of their wars, and a book might yet be written on their modes of conducting and ending them. Their arms, as I have shown, are not numerous, nor so destructive as those used by civilized nations; and consequently their wars are not so devastating.

Warfare amongst those people is generally conducted by small parties who volunteer under a war-chief, to avenge some wrong or cruelty inflicted by their enemy; and when a few scalps are taken, sufficient for retaliation, they generally return, make a great boast, and entertain the villagers with the scalp dance and other ceremonies.

As these people have fewer and less efficient weapons, they depend somewhat more upon strategy to gain advantages than white men do; and in these they are beyond all conception ingenious and inventive.

In the warfare waged between these people and civilized forces, the Indians are often condemned for their strategy, as 'cowardly,' because they prefer secret ambuscades and surprises, instead of coming out into the open field and 'taking a fair fight' (i.e., coming out and standing before the cannon's mouth, and being shot down like pigeons). This is wrong; the poor Indians know the advantages which white men have, with their rifles, and revolvers, and cannons, in the open field; and their refusal to stand before them and be cut down, under such circumstances, should be called prudence rather than cowardice.

There are no people on earth more courageous and brave than the American Indians, if they can only be assured that they are contending with an enemy with equal weapons. Their sagacity in tracing or reconnoitering an enemy, and evading pursuit if necessary, is almost beyond the reach of comprehension for those not familiar with their modes.

Their signals in war are many, and very intelligent as well as curious. The worldwide notorious (but partially appreciated) war-whoop (or war-cry) is one of these, and is given by all the tribes, both in North and South America, precisely alike, when rushing into battle. It is a shrill and piercing note, sounded long, and with a swell, on the highest key of the voice, with the most rapid vibration possible, made by the striking of the flat of the hand or the fingers against the lips.

There is nothing so very frightful in the sound itself, for many sounds can be produced by the human voice, in themselves far more terrifying than the war-whoop; but none other, perhaps, that could be heard so far, and so distinctly in the din and confusion of battle. It is the associations of those who know its meaning and its character, that give it its terror; its being known to be the infallible signal for attack—the war-whoop never being sounded until the rush is made, and weapons are raised for shedding blood.

A person not accustomed to Indian modes might listen to the war-whoop as the Indians were rushing on to him, without alarm, when others, aware of its meaning, would shudder at its sound. No Indian is allowed to sound the war-whoop in time of peace, except in the war-dance and other ceremonies countenanced by the chiefs, lest it should be echoed by their sentinels on the hill tops and their hunting parties through their country, raising an unnecessary and disastrous alarm.

Another signal is the war-whistle, which is very curious. Every chief leading in war carries a little whistle of six or eight inches in length, made of the bone of a turkey's leg, the two ends of which have two very different sounds, so shrill and so piercing, and so different from the mingled war-cry and other din in battles, that they can be distinctly heard an immense distance; blowing in one end is the signal for "advance —on—on;" and in the other for retreat. No chief goes into battle without one of these little war-whistles suspended from his neck and hanging on his breast; and no warrior goes to war without knowing the distinction and meaning of these sounds.

Flags also are used as war-signals. The white flag is in all tribes a flag of truce, an emblem of peace, and a red flag the challenge to combat. How curious is this! All savages are found using the white flag, and advance with it even into their enemies' ranks, in the midst of battle, their lives sacred and protected under it, the same as in civilized nations. How strange (not that the Indians should use it, for civilized nations have brought the custom out of savage life); but how strange that the native races of all the world should use the same color as the emblem of peace; and as sacred and inviolable, even in the din and rage of battle! Has an American Indian ever been known to violate the sacredness of the white flag in time of war? No. Have Christian nations ever done so in their wars with the Indians? We shall see. Such a disgraceful act would be strategy? No; its better name would be 'treachery.'

But then the 'savage cruelty of scalping!' Savage, of course, because savages do it; but where is the cruelty of scalping? A piece of the skin of a man's head is cut off after he is dead; it don't hurt him; the cruelty would be in killing; and in the Christian world we kill hundreds of our fellow beings in battle where the poor Indians kill one! Cutting off a small piece of the skin of a dead man's head is rather a disgusting thing; but let us look. What better can the Indian take? He must keep some record. These people have no reporters to follow them into battles, and chronicle their victories to the world; their customs sanction the mode, and the chiefs demand it.

The scalp, to be a genuine one, must be from an enemy's head, and that enemy dead, and killed by the hand of him who carries and counts the scalp.

An Indian may have sufficient provocation to justify him, under the customs of his country, in slaying a man in his own tribe; but he would disgrace himself in such case by taking the scalp.

Scalps are the Indian's badges or medals, which he must procure by his own hand; he can neither buy nor sell them without disgracing himself; and when he dies, they are buried in his grave with him; his sons can't inherit them; if they want scalps, they must procure them in the same way as their father got his.

Prisoners of war are made in savage warfare as well as in civilized nations. The cruelty of savages to their prisoners is sometimes terrible, but this has been much exaggerated. Their modes of torturing prisoners of war, in the few instances that we know of, have been cruel and diabolical, almost beyond the reach of imagination; but these occurrences have been but very rare at any time, and for the last half-century have not been heard of at all.

All tribes exchange prisoners, precisely as is the practice in civilized nations, as far as equal exchanges can be made; the remainder of those not exchanged are adopted into the tribe, where they are captives; and as far as there are widows of warriors who have been killed in battle, these prisoners are compelled to marry them and support them and their children; the surplus are adopted into the tribe, with all the rights and privileges of other citizens, and go to war with them, and make reliable and efficient warriors, even against their own nation.

The torturing of prisoners is therefore nowhere a general custom, nor a frequent mode, as the world has been led to believe. In the isolated cases which have been known, the relations of persons who have been cruelly tortured by the enemy's tribe, have demanded of the chiefs one or two of the prisoners taken, to wreak their revenge upon; and the chiefs, after a long deliberation and hearing of the grounds of the claim, have handed over the prisoners demanded, to the women related to the person or persons who have suffered; and their modes of cruelty have, in some cases, no doubt, been as cruel and fiendish as the accounts we have heard of them.

Wars are ended, and treaties of peace made amongst the Indian tribes, much in the same manner as amongst civilized nations; but from the causes above named, peace establishments amongst them are less solid, and of less duration.

The chiefs and warriors come together in treaties under the white flag, and take their seats in two semicircles on the ground, facing each other, each warrior having his head decorated with two eagle's quills, one white, and the other blood red, informing their enemies that they are ready for war or for peace. In these treaties the calumet (or pipe of peace) is used. The calumet is strictly a sacred pipe, differing in appearance and in its uses from all others. It is public property, and always kept in the possession of the chief, and only used on such occasions.

For this purpose, in the center of the circle formed by the chiefs and warriors seated in treaty, the calumet rests in two little crotches, charged with tobacco, and ready to be smoked when the treaty stipulations are agreed upon; when each chief, and after him, each warrior of the two tribes, in turn, draw one whiff of smoke through the sacred stem, as the solemn engagement to abide by the terms of the treaty. These treaties are all verbal, of course, as they have no means of recording them; and the smoking through the sacred stem is equivalent to the 'signing' of a treaty, which they are unable to do in writing.

IV

INDIAN LIFE HAS MANY PHASES, and here we suddenly enter upon a new and a different chapter.

The American Indians are all more or less superstitious, and all have their physicians, who deal in roots, and herbs, and other specifics, and also pretend to great and marvelous cures by mysteries, or a kind of sorcery, which they practice as the last resort with their patients, when all the other attempted remedies have failed.

These Indian doctors were called by the Frenchmen, who were the first traders on the frontiers, Medecins, the French word for physicians; and by a subsequent frontier population, 'Medicine Men;' and all mysteries, 'Medicine' as synonymous with mystery. We shall have, therefore, Medicine Men, Medicine Drums, Medicine Rattles, Medicine Dances, Medicine Rocks, Medicine Fire, and a great many other medicine things to deal with before we are at the end of this book.

Whilst residing in the American Fur Company's Factory at the mouth of the Yellowstone River, on the Upper Missouri, I had an opportunity of witnessing a Blackfoot doctor's display, in costume (the skin of a yellow bear), over a dying patient, whom he had placed on the ground, and was hopping over and over, and pawing about with his hands and his feet, in the manner that a bear might have done, and who breathed his last under his strange and even frightful gesticulations, and growls, and groans.

The day after this pitiable farce, upon which some hundreds of his tribe were looking, and crying with their hands over their mouths, I painted his portrait, and also purchased, at an extravagant price, the extraordinary dress, with all its appendages, which has formed an interesting object in my Indian Collection, and been examined by hundreds of thousands of persons in London and in Paris.

Every tribe has its physicians; and all physicians deal (or profess to deal) in mysteries (or medicine). There is nothing but what they will attempt to do by the powers of their medicine; and if they fail, they have generally not much trouble in making so superstitious a people believe that something was wrong in the time of day—in the weather—or (what is more probable) in their want of faith, to interfere with their complete success.

Each one of these Indian physicians, during his lifetime of practice, conjures up and constructs some frightful conception for his medicine dress, strung with skins of deformed animals, reptiles, and birds —the hoofs of animals—the claws and toenails of birds—the skins of frogs, of toads, of bats, and everything else that he can gradually gather to consummate his ugliness, and the frightfulness of the sounds made by their grating and rattling as he dances, with his face hidden underneath them; adding to them the frightful flats and sharps of his growling and squeaking voice, and the stamping of his feet, as he dances and jumps over and around his dying patient.

The doctor never puts on his frightful dress until he goes to pay his last visit to his patient, and when he moves through the village with this dress on, it is known to all the villagers that the patient is dying; and from sympathy, as well as from a general custom, they all gather around in a crowd to witness the ceremony; and all, with the hand over the mouth, commence crying and moaning in the most pitiable manner.

All persons in Indian societies breathe their last under the operation of these frightful mysteries, if a doctor be near; and all the crowd seem to have more or less faith in the efficiency of this dernier resort. From what I have seen and learned (as they are said in some instances to cure), these ingenious jugglers sometimes put on the official garb of monstrosities, and call the villagers together to witness the miraculous cure of a patient whose disease they alone have previously discovered to have taken a favorable change.

One such success in presence of the whole village is enough—it gains him presents to last him his lifetime, and a renown that nothing can shake. And on the other hand, if his patient dies, which of course is generally the case, he gets along by condoling with the relations, and assuring them that for some purpose which they are not allowed to know, the Great Spirit has called their friend away; and that when such is the case, his medicines are of no avail.

These jugglers, I have said, exist in every tribe, and are invariably looked upon by the people as oracles, as sorcerers, as soothsayers, as high priests. They officiate in all religious ceremonies, of which they have many; and are entitled to a seat with the chiefs in the councils of the nation. Their influence, therefore, is very great, and for the traveler passing through their country, it is as necessary to have the good will and countenance of these dignitaries, as it is to have his passport to travel on the continent of Europe. They are a sort of octroi to every village, and at one's first entry, after conversing, and smoking a pipe with the chief, the next important inquiry should be for the great medicine man; with a little present given expressly in compliment to "his great fame, which you have heard of at a long distance."

The results of this little prudence, at first interview, will be sure to be a kind and friendly welcome everywhere; and most likely, as the author has several times experienced, a regular and formal installation, in a convocation of medicine men, as Doctor (or Fellow) of Mysteries, by the presentation of a shi-shi-quoin—a mystery rattle, the usual badge of that enviable Order.

Some unaccountable cure, or other effect, it matters little what, first entitles an Indian to the appellation of mystery or medicine; and once lucky enough to gain the public confidence in this way, it requires no very great degree of tact and cunning, amongst those ignorant people, to keep it up through the remainder of life.

Medicine men are perhaps more often made by some mere accident, than by any long and labored design, which often costs them great pain, with the danger of a great failure, resulting in a disgrace as lasting as their fame would be in case of success. For instance, when I was residing in a large Sioux village on the Upper Missouri, I was one day attracted by a great crowd surrounding a man who was endeavoring to show his people that he was great medicine. The custom which is often practiced amongst them, and which he was trying, they call "Looking at the Sun."

Here was a man, naked, with the exception of his breech-cloth; with splints about the size of a man's finger run through the flesh on each breast, to which cords were attached, and their other ends tied to the top of a pole set firmly in the ground, which was bending towards him, by nearly the whole weight of his body hanging under it as he was leaning back, with his feet slightly resting on the ground. He held his medicine bag in one hand and his bow and arrows in the other, and in this position was endeavoring to look at the sun, from its rising in the morning until it set at night; moving himself around the circle, inch by inch, as the sun moved.

His friends were gathered around him, singing, and reciting the heroic deeds of his life, and his many virtues, and beating their drums and throwing down for him many presents, to encourage him and increase his strength; whilst his enemies and the skeptical were laughing at him, and doing all they could to embarrass and defeat him. If he succeeds, under all these difficulties, in looking at the sun all day, without fainting and falling, "the Great Spirit holds him up," and therefore he is great medicine, and he has nothing else to do to make him, for the rest of his life, a medicine man; and compliments and presents are bestowed upon him in the greatest profusion. But if his strength fails him and he falls, no matter how near to his complete success, shouts and hisses are showered upon him, and his disgrace not only attaches to him for the moment, for having dared to set himself up as a medicine, but the scars left on his breasts are pointed to as a standing disgrace in his tribe, as long as he lives.

It is easily seen that this is a somewhat dangerous experiment to make, and is therefore more seldom resorted to as the mode of making a doctor than many others that might be named.

WHILST I WAS RESIDING AMONGST THE TRIBE OF PUNCAHS, living farther down, on the bank of the Missouri, I witnessed another mode of the self-creation of a medicine man, which one will easily conceive to have been much more agreeable, and no doubt equally efficient in its results.

Hongs-kay-de, a gallant little warrior of eighteen years, and son of the chief, took it into his head (when his father had told him he was a man, and old enough to marry, and gave him nine horses, and a handsome wigwam to live in, and other presents to start him in the world) to marry four wives in one day. Major Sanford, the government agent, and myself were lucky enough to be present; on the merry occasion, and to witness the exciting scene which took place on a little hill just back of their village, where he had assembled the whole tribe to witness the plan which he contrived, and which they as yet but partly anticipated.

It seems he had gone to one of the subordinate chiefs, who had a very pretty little daughter of thirteen or fourteen years of age, and made arrangements for her hand in marriage, for which he was to make him a present of two horses and other things, and the chief was to meet him exactly at noon on the top of that little hill, on a certain day, with his daughter, where the horses would be ready, and the exchange made, according to promise; but the condition of this was to be profound secrecy until he asked for the hand of the girl at that place.

He then went to a second chief, who also had a beautiful daughter about twelve years old, and made with him a similar arrangement, and also on the same condition of secrecy. He then went to a third, and afterwards to a fourth chief, each of whom had a beautiful daughter, and for whose hands he stipulated precisely in the same manner as with the first, enjoining in each case profound secrecy, and appointing the same hour and the same place for the ceremony, having thus disposed of eight of his horses, keeping one for his own riding.

The appointed day arriving, he invited the whole village to attend his wedding, which was to take place at noon, on the top of the little hill, back of the village, where all the villagers assembled. It was a beautiful scene, the hill was completely covered. The chiefs were all seated around on the ground, leaving a little space in the center, where the ceremony was to take place.

At the moment appointed the gallant young and new-made chief (for his father had that day abdicated in his favor) presented himself with his waving plumes, in the center; and addressing himself to the chief whom he had first arranged with, and whose little daughter was sitting by his side in a very pretty dress—"My friend, you promised me the hand of your daughter in marriage this day, and I was to present you two horses; was this so?" "Yes," replied the chief. "The horses are standing here and are ready. I now demand the hand of your daughter."

The chief rose and led up his little daughter, placing her hand in that of the young chief, which was followed by a great shout of applause by the multitude, who were then about to disperse.

The proud little fellow then said to the crowd, "My friends, be patient;" and, turning to the second chief with whom he had arranged— "My friend, you agreed to give me the hand of your beautiful daughter in marriage on this day and at this place, and I was to give you two horses; was this so?" "Yes," replied the chief." "Then I expect you to perform your promise—I demand the hand of your daughter in marriage." The chief then arose and led up his little daughter, and, like the first one, placed her hand in that of the young chief; and precisely in the same manner he demanded and received the hands of the daughters of the other two chiefs whom he had last arranged with, and, taking two in each hand, he said to the chiefs, "This day makes me medicine?" "Yes." "My father has this day made me chief of the Puncahs! Am I not a medicine chief?" to which the whole tribe shouted with one voice, "How, how!" (Yes, yes!)

Hongs-kay-de then descended the hill triumphantly, leading off to the village his four beautiful little wives in their pretty dresses, two in each hand, the crowd all following, to his own wigwam, which was thenceforth the wigwam of the medicine chief.

I have before said that the medicine men will undertake to do anything and everything by their mystic operations, however impossible or ridiculous it may be. But in these efforts where the results are in the least uncertain, the constituted medicine men take especial care not to run any risk by making a second attempt; but they superintend and manage the preliminary forms, leaving younger aspirants to run the chances of failure or success.

In the Mandan tribe I found they had "Rain-makers" and also "Rain-stoppers" who were reputed medicine men, from the astonishing fact of their having made it rain in an extraordinary drought, or for having stopped it raining when the rain was continuing to an inconvenient length.

For this purpose, in a very dry time, when their maize and other vegetables are dying for want of rain, the medicine men assemble in the Medicine Lodge (a large public wigwam built expressly for medicine operations, councils, etc.), and sit around a fire in the center, from day to day smoking and praying to the Great Spirit for rain, while the requisite number of young men volunteer to try to make it rain. Each one of these, by ballot, takes his turn to mount on the top of the wigwam at sunrise, with his bow and arrows in his hand, and shield on his arm, talking to the clouds and asking for rain—or ranting and threatening the clouds with his drawn bow, commanding it to rain.

One of these young men, who flourishes throughout the whole day in this manner, in presence of the crowds gathered around him, and comes down at sunset without having succeeded, can never, on any occasion, again pretend to medicine: "his medicine is not strong."

After several days of unsuccessful attempts have passed off in this way, with a clear sky, some one more lucky than the rest happens to take his stand on a day in which a black cloud will be seen moving up, it is reported through the village that "his medicine is better," when the whole tribe will gather round him to hear him boast, to see him strut and bend his bow upon the clouds, commanding it to rain; and when he sees the rain actually falling in the distance, to see him let fly his arrow (which by his dexterity, as the string snaps, is turned into his hand with the bow), and pointing with his finger, "There! my friends, you have seen my arrow go, there is a hole in that cloud, we shall soon have rain enough." The rain begins to fall in torrents, the gaping multitude are hidden in their wigwams, but this successful debutant in mysteries still stands, sawing the air and commanding it to continue raining, until he is completely drenched, that the Mandans may have no further cause to complain. When he comes down he is a medicine man, the doctors give him a feast and a great ceremony, and a shi-shi-quoin (a doctor's rattle).

These maneuvers are very wonderful, and there are two things about them that are curious—the one, that when the doctors commence 'rain making' they never fail to succeed; for when the ceremony is once begun, they are obliged to keep it up from day to day until rain begins to fall; and the other, that those who once succeed in making it rain, in presence of the whole village, never undertake it a second time. "The whole village have seen me make it rain, they all know what I can do, and I would rather give other young men a chance."

Every Indian village has its medicine (or mystery) lodge, a sort of town-hall, strictly a public building, in which their councils are held, and all their religious ceremonies performed. These sacred places, which are closed most of the year, were generally granted to me as the place to paint my portraits in, which they always looked upon and treated as great medicine, and myself as the greatest of medicine men, for painting their chiefs and warriors, in whose portraits they often discovered "the corners of the mouth and the eyes to move," considering, therefore, that there must be life, to a certain degree, in them.

Amongst the Mandans I was soon the talk of all the village, from the portraits I had made of the war-chief and the great doctor. My wigwam was filled with the chiefs and warriors from day to day, and the whole village assembled in crowds around it. I was styled the greatest of all medicine. I received the doctor's badge, a beautiful shi-shi-quoin, and was regularly named, 'Te-hee-pe-nee Washed' (the Great White Medicine).

The wives of several of the chiefs brought their beautiful and modest little daughters to the door of my wigwam in splendid, pretty costumes, and the interpreter to explain, to know if I should like to marry; all of which complimentary and tempting offers I was obliged, from various reasons, to decline. My reasons seemed to be sufficient, and my answers, though a disappointment, to give no offence.

My gun and pistols, with percussion caps, which they had not seen before, were great mysteries, and no one was willing to touch them. The remaining half of a box of lucifer matches I had, was also great medicine, and was soon exhausted by one of the medicine men, who turned it to great account after I had given it to him, by a mode he soon discovered, of igniting the matches by drawing them between his teeth, and "making fire in his mouth," which he did with wonderful effect, amongst the astonished villagers, until the box was unfortunately exhausted. His medicine was much improved for the while by this little lift, but he told me he lost it all when his matches gave out. The poor fellow seemed losing caste by the unfortunate exhaustion of his matches, and I presented him a little sun-glass which I carried in my pocket, by which he could light his pipe anywhere when the sun shone, and which, I explained, he could never wear out. This, therefore, was a greater wonder to him than the other, and more highly valued. He gave me a very beautiful pair of leggings for it, and until the day that I left them he had crowds about him to see him "draw fire from the sun!"

Medicine Bag. This is one of the most important and extraordinary medicine things in all Indian tribes. This curious appendage to the person pertains not only to medicine men, but to every male person in Indian society, whether warrior or brave, over the age of fifteen or sixteen years, the usual time of life when it is first instituted.

A lad of that age is said to be "making his medicine" when he absents himself from his father's wigwam for several successive nights and days, during which time no one makes any inquiries about him; it is enough to know, or to suppose, that he is "making his medicine." During this absence he is fasting the whole time, and the first animal, reptile, or bird, that he dreams of, he considers the Great Spirit has designated, and introduced to him in his dream, to be his mysterious protection through life, his medicine.

He returns home, relates his dream to his parent who make him a choice feast, to which he invites his relatives and as many of his friends as he chooses, who all compliment and congratulate him on his success. After the feast he starts out and traps or hunts for the animal or bird until he kills it, and obtains the entire skin, which he prepares and preserves as nearly in the size and shape of the living animal as possible. This he carries about his person the most of his life as his talisman, a charm that protects him from all harm, and to which he attributes all the good luck of his life; and which he confidently believes is to accompany and protect him in the world to come; it always being buried with him with the greatest care.

To go to battle without his medicine bag would be to go with a "faint heart," and under the conviction that he would be killed. To lose it in battle is to live in disgrace in his tribe, as "a man without medicine" until he can procure another, in battle, by adopting that of an enemy whom he has slain; his medicine is then reinstated; but by no means can he ever institute a second medicine if he loses his first, no matter by what means.

No money therefore could purchase an Indian's medicine bag, though such things have in several instances been presented to me by warriors who had taken them in battle, together with the scalps of their enemies.

These talismans are of all sizes, from the skin of a mouse, hidden under the dress, to the size of a duck, a loon, an otter, a badger, and even sometimes to the skin of a wolf, and therefore exceedingly awkward to carry. I recollect that when I was painting the portrait of a Comanche chief, I inquired his name, which another chief, sitting by, gave me, as Ish-a-ro-yeh ('he who carries a wolf'). I expressed my surprise at his getting such a name, and inquired if he had ever carried a wolf? To which he replied, "Yes, I always carry a wolf," lifting up his medicine bag made of the skin of a white wolf, and lying by the side of him, as he was sitting on the ground.

Medicine men and mysteries I need say no more of in this place. I shall therefore end this chapter here, and have something more to say of them and their doings in future pages.

V

IN THE MIDST OF THOSE VAST PLAINS DENOMINATED THE VALLEY OF THE MISSOURI, let us take a little further look yet at the numerous tribes and their modes, and the country about us, before we sweep off across the Rocky Mountains, or into the evergreen valleys of the Essequibo and the Amazon, in South America.

Besides the Sioux and the Mandans, there are the fierce and terrible Blackfoot, and the beautiful Crows, with their long and glossy-black hair trailing on the ground as they walk; the Knistineux, the Assinneboins, the Ojibbeways, the Shiennes, the Pawnees, the Omahas, the Ioways, the Saukies, the Winnebagos, the Osages, the Comanches, and yet many other tribes, all of whom I have lived amongst, and studied their looks and their modes.

In general, in their ways of life, in the chase, in war, and in their amusements, of which they have many, they bear a strong resemblance to each other, as well as in their color and features.

Their color, which has often been described as red, as yellow, and more often as copper color, is not exactly either; but more correctly described as cinnamon color, the exact color of cinnamon bark; sometimes a little more dark, and at others more light; but that may with truth be said to be the standard of color amongst the American tribes. Their forms are generally very perfect and handsomely proportioned, much more so than those of any civilized people, owing chiefly to the facts that they are so constantly exercising their naked limbs in the open air, free from the enervating and weakening effects of heavy costumes, and also the rigid manner in which all American Indian infants, without exception, are reared in cribs (or cradles), their backs lashed to straight boards for the space of six months or a year, giving straightness to the spine and the limbs, which last them through life.

All the American Indians have straight and black hair, and generally (though contrary to the opinion of the world), exceedingly fine and silky. Their eyes (though their effect is black) are of a deep and reddish-brown, and their teeth, almost without exception, uniform and regular in their arrangement, and white and sound, even to old age.

These people have probably got the appellation of 'Red Indians' from their habit of using so much red ochre and vermilion, their favorite colors, in painting their bodies and faces, rather than from their natural color, which I have already said is not red.

The habit of painting is much the same in all the various tribes. They mix their colors with bears' grease; and, with the aid of a little bit of broken looking-glass, which they buy off fur traders, they daub the paint on with their fingers used for brushes. Paint is considered by them as a part of their dress; and few Indians allow themselves to be seen in the morning until they have spent an hour or so at their toilette, oiling and arranging their hair, and painting their faces and limbs, after which they consider themselves in full dress, and ready for society.

This would seem to be a great deal of trouble, and to occupy much of their time uselessly; but then it will be borne in mind that these people have little else to do, and time is not so valuable to them as it is to other people. They are excessively vain of their personal appearance, and well they may be, for, as I have said, their fine and manly figures, reared in, and used to, the open air, without the flabbiness and emaciation which overclothing generally produces, have a roundness and beauty which the civilized world cannot produce.

The tribes which I have above named, living chiefly in a country stocked with buffaloes and wild horses, also hunt and go to war much in the same manner.

The wild horses, which were no doubt first introduced into America by the Spanish invaders of Mexico, have in time wandered away and spread over the prairies as high as the fifty-first degree of north latitude, affording the Indians, who catch and convert them to their use, the means of killing the buffaloes and other game with more ease, and also of carrying on their warfare with more effect; and what is best of all, a pleasurable and healthful mode of exercise in the open plains, so conducive to strength and manly beauty.

The buffaloes, we have a right to believe, have been created for the use and happiness of the Indian tribes, who exist almost entirely on their flesh, clothing themselves and constructing their dwellings with their skins, and converting almost every part of these useful animals to the supply of their various wants and comforts. Their tongues, when cured, are amongst the greatest of luxuries, and equally so the hump (or fleece, as it is familiarly called) on the shoulders; the rest of the flesh is about equal to the best of beef. Of their skins their comfortable dwellings are made, and their beautiful robes, as already explained. Their sinews are used for strings to their bows, and many other purposes; the bones of the shoulders form the trees for their saddles; their brains are used for dressing their skins; the bones of their legs are broken up for their marrow, which resembles and equals the richest of butter; and their hoofs are boiled up for glue, which they use in the construction of their beautiful bows and other weapons.

These noble and useful animals roam over the same vast and boundless prairies of green grass where the wild horses graze, and are often seen in herds of many thousands together. One can easily imagine that here is the easiest and most independent region for the Indians to live in; and it is here, and from these causes, no doubt, that the healthiest and most beautiful races of men are found that are to be met with in America, or perhaps in the world.

It is over these interminable carpets of green, dotted with flowers of all colors—where the Indian gallops on his wild horse, his wants all supplied, and his mind as free as the air that he breathes—that man, in the unshackled freedom of his nature, extends, and has extended his hand in friendship, to all strangers in his country, before he has been ensnared by the craft and cunning of the mercenary white man.

A FEW WORDS MUST BE SAID OF THE PRAIRIES, the dwellings of savage steeds and savage beeves.

If we could together leap from the deck of a steamer upon one of the grassy banks of the Upper Missouri, and clamber up the sloping sides of the bluff, on our hands and feet, knocking the bowing lilies of yellow, and blue, and of red, and the gay sunflowers, from our faces; and leaving the purple violets and gushing ripe strawberries under our feet till we come back, and take a glance from its rounded top over the vast expanse of green and of blue beneath and around us—of the serpentine windings of the river above and below us, with its vast alluvial meadows alternating on one side and the other; and, back of them, the thousands of shorn and green bluffs sloping down like infinite ranges of grass-covered ramparts and redoubts—and, back of them again, in the east and the west, an ocean of green, enameled with all colors at our feet, but terminating in a horizon of blue—you would get in that glance, a partial knowledge of an American prairie.

But if at this point we could mount our horses together, and gallop to the east or to the west; here a covey of grouse fluttering from under our horses feet; next, the swift antelope bounding over the surface; the frightened deer rising and springing from its lair; and farther on, the huge white wolf, with a dogged sauciness and reluctance, licking his hungry chaps as he walks slowly out of our way, with the bristles raised on his ugly back as he stands and scans us as we pass, to smell and follow in our track behind us—we should then be gathering further knowledge of the prairie. But we go on; the noble elks have "taken the wind," and are sweeping away to the right or the left; the stately moose, under his long and unbroken trot, and his mighty horns, passes out of sight; the funny little prairie dogs in myriads, barking from the tops of their mounds of dirt, dart into their burrows, and our horses are brought to the ground by breaking into their vaulted underground villages; and the huge and frightful rattlesnakes are seen coiled and ready for a leap—we are still wiser.

And yet farther on, a band of wild horses, with their rising manes and tails, and starting eyeballs glaring upon us, put off for a five-mile heat before they stop; and on—on—on—again, and far beyond, a straight black line forms all the western horizon! And over it, to the right, a cloud of smoke is rising from the ground! That can't be a fire? No, my friends; we are now in the midst of a great and level prairie—we are out of sight of land; the black streak you see is formed by the backs of a large herd of buffaloes, and the cloud of dust which you see, is raised by their feet, which shows us they are in motion, with a party of Sioux Indians with arrows and lances pushing them up on the flanks and in their rear.

On—on, farther yet; and at length the black streak disappears, they are all out of sight; but the cloud still rises—and rises yet, as on we go. And at last we discover, like mere specks in the distance, here and there, individual objects moving in various directions, and evidently nearing us, as we move on. Next we find the greensward under our horses' feet cut to pieces, and looking, in the distance, much like a newly-ploughed field; the herd has here passed; and in the distance we discover here and there black specks lying upon the surface, and horsemen galloping to them and dismounting. We will rein up our horses to them—don't be afraid: put on a bold and calm front (the Indians always admire a bold and daring man), and offer them your hand.

Smiling and exulting, as they shake their heads to part their falling locks from before their eyes, come dashing up from different directions, on their puffing and snorting little horses, with inflated nostrils and shaggy manes, a hundred warriors astride their horses' naked backs, with bows and lances in their hands; they rush up with the friendly hand extended; but our horses, like civilized people, have a dread of the savage—and we must dismount, or be dismounted. We are all upon our feet, Indians and all, and our horses held; a shaking of hands takes place. Next moment we are seated on the ground, and the pipe is lit and passed round. Here is a pause and a rest for all, for all are tired. A conversation takes places; and in the midst of this, what do we see? In the distance, a moving, unintelligible mass, of all colors. It approaches; and, at last, we see it is a phalanx of several hundred women and children, with three or four times that number of dogs, coming out from their village to skin the slaughtered animals, and cut up the meat and transport it to their village. We see no more, for the refreshed hunters have invited us to their village; and remounted, we fall in their wake, leaving the women and children to do the rest.

Their village, as I have described, is built of skin-covered wigwams. We are taken to the chief's tent—we smoke the pipe with him, seated on beautifully-garnished robes and rush mats spread upon the ground; we feast with him and the hunters in his hospitable dwelling, and lodge in it during the night. Our horses have been well taken care of by the chief's sons and relations, and brought to us in the morning when we are ready to start back.

But where are we? Only one day in the prairie! And so we might go on from day to day, for a month of days, before we should find its end. We have yet to return; have we seen all? Not quite—we take a different route.

VI

WILD HORSES, I HAVE SAID, ARE THE SHYEST ANIMALS OF THE PRAIRIES, and oftentimes run in immense herds. The wild horse will generally run from the approach of a man at a mile distance, without "getting the wind," such is the power of his eye in distinguishing his enemy man from wild animals, when the elk may be approached within half-a-mile, and the buffalo and deer oftentimes within dead-shot distance for a rifle, before they take to flight.

The Indians have a hard struggle in capturing these animals, which they generally do with the lasso, thrown from the back of another horse, while they ride at full speed. The lasso is a strong cord made of raw hide, with a noose at the end of it, which being open some four or five feet, the loop is dropped over the horse's neck, and being drawn tight chokes the animal; and the Indian, checking his own horse gradually, and drawing on the lengthened cord, at last brings the animal to the ground, which falls for want of breath.

The horse is then completely at its captor's mercy, who proceeds to secure his prey, and then to tame it. For this he hobbles the animal's two fore-feet together, and then fastens a short halter with a noose around the horse's under-jaw, back of the teeth, while its mouth is wide open and it is gasping for breath.

At this moment the lasso is loosened, allowing the animal to breathe; by which, in a few moments, as it is getting strength to rise, it finds the Indian at the end of the halter, prepared to prevent its rising on to its feet. The horse makes a struggle to rise, getting only on to its fore-feet, which are fastened together, and it still remains in a sitting posture.

Before it can rise on its hind feet, it requires to throw its head quite back, which the Indian, standing in front of the animal, prevents it from doing, by leaning back, with the weight of his body on the halter. By a great many useless struggles to rise, the horse remaining yet in its sitting posture, and the Indian approaching nearer and nearer (inch by inch) to its nose, on the shortened halter, and yelling as loud as he can, the animal's fear is increased to the highest degree. The Indian still advances nearer on the tightened halter, and at length begins patting the horse on the nose, and gradually slipping his hand over its eyes, begins breathing in its nostrils, their noses being together.

After a few breaths exchanged in this manner, the relaxation of the horse's muscles and its other motions, show that its fears are at an end—that it recognizes a friend instead of a foe, in its captor; and this compromise being effected, the Indian is seen stroking down its mane, and otherwise caressing it; and in fifteen or twenty minutes he is seen riding it quietly off!

From the moment of this unaccountable compromise, the animal seems to make no further effort to escape, but becomes attached to its master, whom it recognizes by the breath: which it always seems fond of exchanging from that moment.

I have witnessed these exciting scenes on a number of occasions, and always have viewed them with great surprise. It requires a severe effort to catch the horse in the first place, and then a struggle ensues which is cruel, and painful to look upon; but the excess of fatigue, of fright, and actual pain, followed by soothing and kindness, seems to disarm the spirited animal, and to attach it at once, in a mysterious way, to its new master.

You have all read of Mr. Rarey's wonderful mode of breaking and taming vicious horses, which I believe, in some respects, is very similar; but Mr. Rarey has not the wild horse to catch. It is very likely that an Indian could not break a vicious horse as well as Mr. Rarey; and at the same time it might be equally, if not more difficult, for Mr. Rarey to take the lasso from an Indian's hand when he has got it over the neck of a wild horse, and stop its career, and conquer and break it, as an Indian does.

The judgment of man in guiding his horse enables him, on an animal of less speed, to get alongside of a wild horse, though he seldom is able to overtake the fleetest of them. But here is something more surprising yet—the Cheyenne, who capture more wild horses than any other tribe, catch a great proportion of their horses without the aid of a horse to ride; they overtake the wild horse on their own legs; which is done in this way:

Plunging into a band of wild horses while on the back of his own horse, the Indian separates some affrighted animal from the group, and forcing it off to the right or to the left, he dismounts from his own horse, and hobbling its feet, or leaving it in the hands of a friend, he starts upon his own legs, his body chiefly naked—a lasso coiled on his left arm, a whip fastened to the wrist of his right hand, and a little parched corn in his pouch, which he chews as he runs; and at a long and tilting pace, which he is able to keep all day, he follows the affrighted animal, which puts off at full speed.

Throwing himself between the troop and the animal he is after, and forcing it to run in a different direction, the poor creature's alarm causes it to over-fatigue itself in its first efforts, and to fall a prey to feebler efforts, but more judiciously expended. In the beginning of the chase, the horse discovers his pursuer coming towards him, when he puts off at the greatest possible speed, and at the distance of a mile perhaps, he stops and looks back for his pursuer, who is coming at his regular pace, close on to him! Away goes again the affrighted steed, more alarmed than ever, and at its highest speed, and makes another halt, and another, and another; each time shorter and shorter, as he becomes more and more exhausted; while his cool and cunning pursuer is getting nearer to him. It is a curious fact, and known to all the Indians, that the wild horse, the deer, the elk, and other animals, never run in a straight line: they always make a curve in their running, and generally (but not always) to the left.

The Indian seeing the direction in which the horse is "leaning," knows just about the point where the animal will stop, and steers in a straight line to it, where they arrive nearly at the same instant, the horse having run a mile, while his pursuer has gone but half or three-quarters of the distance. The alarmed animal is off again; and by a day's work of such curves, and such alarms, before sun-down the animal's strength is all gone; he is covered with foam, and as his curves are shortened at last to a few rods, his steady pursuer, whose pace has not slackened, gets near enough to throw the lasso over the animal's neck. One must imagine the rest; what kindness and caressing through the night (for they encamp upon the ground), and what compromise is effected, for the Indian rides his captured horse into the village the next morning, having attached his lasso with a noose around its under-jaw, and having taken up his hobbled horse in his way.

I have said that the horse and other animals "generally turn to the left." How curious this fact, and from what cause? All animals 'bend their course.' Why bend their course? Because all animals have their homes, their wonted abodes, and they don't wish to leave them: but why bend to the left?

I never have forgotten one of the first lessons that I had from my dear friend Darrow, in deer-stalking in the forest. "George," said he, "when a deer gets up, if the ground is level, never follow him, but turn to the left, and you will be sure to meet him; he always runs in a curve, and when he stops he is always watching his back track."

But man 'bends his course;' man, lost in the wilderness or on the prairies, travels in a curve, and always bends his course to the left: why this?

While ascending the Upper Missouri, some years since, on a steamer, the vessel got aground, and there was no prospect of getting it off until the water rose, which might not be the case for some weeks. I was anxious to reach a Sioux village on the bank of that river, about one hundred miles above where we were detained, in order to be using my brushes amongst them. I left the steamer with one man to accompany me, and with my rifle in my hand, and my sketchbook on my back, we started to perform the journey on foot. In our course we had a large prairie of some thirty miles to cross, and the second day being dark and cloudy, we had no object by which to guide our course, having no compass with me at the time.

During the first day the sun shone, and we kept our course very well—but on the next morning, though we started right ('laid our course') we no doubt soon began to bend it, though we appeared to be progressing in a straight line. There was nothing to be seen about us but short grass, everywhere the same; and in the distance a straight line, the horizon all around us. Late in the afternoon, and when we were very much fatigued, we came upon the very spot, to our great surprise, where we had bivouacked the night before, and which we had left on that morning. We had turned to the left, and no doubt travelled all day in a circle. The next day, having the sunshine, we laid (and kept) our course without any difficulty.

On arriving at the Sioux village, and relating our singular adventure, the Indians all laughed at us very heartily, and all the chiefs united in assuring me that whenever a man is lost on the prairies he travels in a circle; and also that he invariably turns to the left; of which singular fact I have become doubly convinced by subsequent proofs similar to the one mentioned.

The Indian having taken his wild horse in the manner above described, and broken it for the purpose, we see in the chase, by which means he supplies his family with food, and in the same manner also he contends with his enemies in battle.

The horse being the swiftest animal of the prairies, the rider on its back is able to come alongside of any animal; and at the little distance necessary to throw his arrows, the first arrow is generally fatal; being sent with such force as to penetrate the heart of that huge animal the buffalo, and oftentimes (as I have myself witnessed) sent quite through the animal's body, leaving a wound resembling that of a gunshot.

The bow used for this purpose is very short, being more convenient for handling on horseback, and generally not more than two feet and a half in length, but made of great strength, and with much ingenuity: the main part frequently one entire piece of bone, but more often of wood, and covered on the back with buffalo's sinews, so closely glued together as seldom to come apart.

Besides the bow, a long lance is often used, and perhaps with more deadly effect in the chase than the arrows; for the Indian, with his horse trained to 'approach,' easily rides near enough to the side of the animal to give the fatal lunge of his lance, which seldom fails to reach the heart, tumbling the animal instantly to the ground.

In battle and in the chase, the Indian always has dragging behind his horse a long cord of raw hide, which is attached to its neck; a different thing from the lasso. The object of this cord is, in case he is thrown from his horse, by the horse falling or stepping into holes, that he may grasp hold of it and recover his horse, and be again upon its back. This is called by the French, l'arret (the stop), and by some travelers and writers, larriette.

NOW, SPEAKING OF BUFFALOES, I must be allowed to say a few words of myself, and some of my own exploits, amongst buffaloes in the prairie country.

The reader will recollect that I commenced my early career with a strong passion for guns and fishing-poles, and will scarcely believe that my hunting propensities lay dormant during the gap that I have mentioned, from the affair of the 'kettle of gold,' to the age of thirty-three, when I started on my Indian campaigns; he will easily believe that during that period, surrounded as I was with all the temptations, and with my old Nimrod companion, John Darrow, as my teacher, I was making constant progress in the slaying art, and in rifle-shooting; and that I had greatly increased, instead of diminishing that passion which first led me to the Old Sawmill lick, and which eventually had its weight in leading me into the great prairies of the Far West.

Poor Darrow! He was good for nothing else but hunting; but what a veneration I had for him! How he could trace a deer or a bear; and how deadly the crack of his rifle! What music it was to my young ear when I heard it sing amongst the lofty forest trees; and how happy were those days when John Darrow and I, in our white hunting shirts and white caps, with our rifles trailed, entered the deep and lonely forests to spend the day in a good 'tracking snow!'

But to fight off from these scenes in my native valley and my boyhood, and to come back to where I left you, in the buffalo range, and ready for my first buffalo hunt, on the prairies of the Missouri. At the mouth of the Yellowstone River, on the banks of the Missouri, two thousand miles above St. Louis, where the American Fur Company has a large factory, or trading house, I was residing with Mr. M'Kenzie, the chief factor, when it was announced one morning by one of his men, that a large herd of buffaloes had arrived during the night, and were then grazing on a beautiful plain across the river, and but two or three miles distant.

M'Kenzie instantly resolved that he "wanted some meat," and invited me to join the hunt, for which he turned out some five or six of his best hunters, on horseback, and himself took the lead, with a small and exceedingly light and short single-barreled fowling-piece in his hand.

They furnished me with a tremendously tall horse, called 'Chouteau' (for what reason I never knew), said to be a very good animal in the chase. Several others of his men were ordered to follow at a proper distance, with one-horse carts, to bring in the meat, and we all moved off, somewhat like a regular caravan.

When we had arrived within half-a-mile or so of the unsuspecting animals, we were called to a halt, to decide upon the best mode of attack: that decided, all hands started off upon a gallop, at the signal given, ready to make the dash as soon as the animals took the alarm. This done, the dust was rising, and we were in the midst of them!

M'Kenzie, Major Sanford, and Chardon were the most experienced, and consequently the most successful in the melee. The repeated flashes of their guns I distinctly saw, as they seemed to be buried in the moving mass of black and dust. These men were hunting "for meat," and of course were selecting the fattest and the sleekest of the young cows for that purpose; but I had quite a different ambition; I saw in the crowd the back and horns of a huge bull towering so high above all the throng that I resolved upon his scalp or nothing.

I made several desperate lunges with old 'Chouteau' into the various openings which seemed to afford me a chance of coming near to him: and as often was closed in and jammed along with the moving mass, no doubt with a most imprudent risk of my life; for hundreds on hundreds were plunging along behind me, and ready to have trampled me to death in a moment if I had lost my balance.

I at length saw my way clear, and made a desperate rush for his right side, that I might get my shot from the proper point.

My gun was a double-barreled fowling-piece. My first shot seemed to have no effect, but the second one brought him down upon his knees, and the herd passed on. I was swept along a great distance before I could extricate myself from the throng, having no further ambition than the capture of this overgrown, and, in fact, giant of the band.

When I got relieved from the herd, I reloaded and rode back to my noble prize, who had risen up and stood balancing his huge carcass on three legs, one of his shoulders being broken. His frightful mane was raised, and his eyes bloodshot with madness and rage, as he was making lunges at me, and partly tumbling to the ground at each attempt.

Here was just the subject I wanted, for all the world: and having my sketch-book with me, I sat upon my horse, in perfect safety, and made my model change his positions as I wanted them. It is impossible to describe the demoniacal looks of this enraged animal when he bristled up and was just ready to spring upon me.

While I was engaged in this operation, M'Kenzie and Sanford came riding up to me, and laughing most excessively at me for attacking a poor old bull which scarcely the wolves would eat. I claimed a great victory nevertheless, and was perfectly satisfied with my first exploit, which, however, had a little drawback to it when Sanford asked me how it was that my horse's head was covered with blood, which I had not observed, and which was found to be issuing from a round hole through one of old Chouteau's ears, near to his head, where my first ball had undoubtedly passed.

My sketches completed, I finished the old bull with another shot in the head: and joining M'Kenzie and Sanford, who were looking up and claiming their victims left upon the ground they had run over, I was astonished to find that the former, with a single-barreled gun, and with a flint lock, had selected and shot through the heart, six fat cows in the run, which was probably not over a mile distance, in which time he must have reloaded his gun five times at full speed! The carts were soon up, in the rear, and conveyed the meat, with the head and horns of my venerable bull, to the factory's larder.

I said at the end of the last chapter, that we had not seen the whole of the prairies—that "we should return by another route." We are a great way from home, so we will leave our horses and take a canoe.

VII

SEATED IN A LIGHT AND FRAIL CANOE in front of the American Fur Company's Fort, at the mouth of the Yellowstone River, Ba'tiste, Bogard, and I took leave of M'Kenzie and his little colony, for a voyage to St. Louis, which, by the winding course of the Missouri, was but about two thousand miles; and the whole of that way without other habitations than the occasional villages of the wild Indians; and without inhabitants, excepting wild men and the wild animals that roamed over and through it.

Jean Ba'tiste, a Frenchman, and Abraham Bogard, a Mississippian, were two discharged hands who had been for eight or ten years in the employment of the Fur Company, trapping beavers and other furs at the base of and in the Rocky Mountains, and were now returning to St. Louis; and of myself, more will be learned hereafter.

We three, then—the two first of whom with good rifles, and knowing well how to use them; and myself with a good double-barreled fowling-piece, for ducks, and geese, and prairie hens, and a first-rate rifle for long range, and a belt with two side pistols for nearer quarters—took our seats in our little bark; the first in the bow, the second in the center, and myself in the stern, with my steering-paddle, with which I steered it in safety, but not without some accidents, amid snags, and sandbars, and sawyers, and rocks, to the wharf in St. Louis, whilst the boiling current swept us along, and Ba'tiste and Bogard, and most of the time all three, paddled.

We had powder and ball in abundance laid in, and our fishing tackle; some good robes to sleep upon and under; a tin kettle, a coffee-pot, a frying-pan, plenty of ground coffee, of sugar, and salt; each man a spoon, a knife, and a tin cup; and though we had no bread or butter, the reader, whose imagination is strong, will easily see we had a tolerable chance for enough to eat, and that there was a glorious prospect for the indulgence of my sportive passion, as well as the gratification of my Indian propensities, ahead of me; and he will be just about as much disposed to skip over the next part of this book, as I would have been inclined to have left my little outfitted canoe and the beautiful shores of the Missouri, to have taken a nearer cut, and footed it over land.

There are now ten thousand things of curious interest before us, and I must needs again be brief; for we shall have other rivers, and a great many other things to speak of.

At our starting, we had another compagnon du voyage, which I had almost forgotten to mention. Mr. M'Kenzie had made me a present of a full-grown, domesticated war-eagle, the noble bird which the Indians so much esteem for its valor, and the quills of which they so much value to adorn the heads of chiefs and warriors. I had a perch erected for it some six or eight feet high, over the bow of the canoe, on which it rested in perfect quietude, without being fastened, silently surveying all that we passed above and below; thus forming for our little craft the most picturesque and appropriate figurehead that could be imagined.

From day to day we thus passed on, surveying the beautiful shores; the grassy and rounded bluffs rising in groups, sometimes hundreds on hundreds, appearing in the distance as if green carpets of velvet were spread over them; sometimes speckled with herds of buffaloes grazing on their sides, which the crack of a rifle would set in motion: the scattered herds grouping together and running in little and winding paths, seemed in the distance like black snakes drawing their long carcasses over and around the hillsides.

The sandbars in the distance sometimes seemed as if they were covered with snow, from the quantities of pelicans and white swans that were grouped upon them. The white wolves that were looking at us from the banks got an occasional pill from one of our rifles, and sometimes the terrible grizzly bears, that trace the water's edge for the carcasses of dead fish, and the buffaloes often left fastened in the mud, where large herds have been crossing the river.

We went ashore every afternoon a little before sunset, where we could discover dry wood enough to make a fire with, cooked and ate our supper; and then, leaving our fire, paddled on till sometime after dark, hauling our buffalo-skins out, and, scarcely knowing what was around us, quietly spreading our beds upon the grass, lest prowling war-parties might be attracted by the smoke of our fires, and strike a blow upon us in their sudden way, mistaking us for their enemies or for some of the fur traders, against more or less of whom these people have long and just causes of complaint, and for which we are, in such cases, liable to pay the forfeit.

We were generally off again at daybreak, and usually stopped at eight or nine in the morning, to make and to take our breakfast.

At one of these delicious breakfasts, after we had been some days on our voyage, when we had just finished, my two men, observing a herd of buffaloes grazing on a hill at a short distance, took up their rifles and went for some meat.

I remained by the fire, and while making a sketch of a very pretty scene in front of me, I resolved that I would have another cup of coffee before we started, and placed the coffee-pot on the fire to make it hot. The sound of their rifles soon announced to me that they had got some meat (for they made it a rule never to lose a charge of powder for nothing), and the next moment came the throng dashing down the hill nearby me. I seized my rifle and ran to a deep and narrow defile where the whole herd were aiming to pass, and placing myself in the bed of the stream then dried up, and behind a small bunch of willows, I stood unobserved, and probably unheard by them (such was the thundering of the throng as they came plunging down one side, and clambered up the other, of the deep ravine), and reloaded and fired until I had shot down some twelve or fourteen of them, each one tumbling down within a few paces from where he was struck, and several thousand passing by me within gun-shot.

This wanton slaughter, which I always regretted, was easy, was simple, and wicked; because Ba'tiste and Bogard had got meat enough to last us for several days. Not even the skins, the tongues, nor the humps, of these poor creatures were taken, but were left for the wolves to devour.

My two men joined me, having heard my firing and when we went to our little bivouac, I found my coffee all boiled away, and the seams of my poor coffee-pot all unsoldered, and the fabric falling to pieces. Was not this retribution? I shot not for meat, nor in self-defense—and I never shot for the mere pleasure of killing after that.

Our tin kettle having fallen overboard a few days before, I made a sort of coffee a few times in the frying-pan, but this was excessively awkward, and proved a decided failure; and Bogard, who had a rabid taste for coffee, had the privilege of filling his pocket with ground coffee and sugar, which he daily ate from the hollow of his hand, while it lasted; and thus was our luxury of coffee, with that of delicious soup, which had vanished with the loss of our tin kettle, for the rest of the voyage at an end.

Our noble and beautiful pet was a picture to look at: he held to his perch, and could not have been made to leave us. He was well fed with fresh buffalo meat, and sometimes with fish. His eagle eyes gazed upon all around him, and he seemed to be owner and commander of the expedition. We always found him on his stand in the morning; and during the day, as we were gliding along, when he became tired of his position, he would raise himself upon his long and broad wings, and spreading them over us, would hover and soar for miles together, a few feet above our heads, and in precise progress with the canoe, looking down upon us, and fanning us at times with fresh air, and at other times shading us from the rays of the sun!

Birds of all kinds and wild fowl, as they flew over, this monarch of the air would gaze at from his perch; and whenever he discovered one of his own species soaring in the sky, or even in the clouds, which was sometimes the case, he commenced a chattering of recognition which no other excitement could bring forth, and which they invariably answered. He knew them, and could easily have gone to them in a moment, but the perch that he clenched in his feet he preferred, for there he was sure of his daily food.

ONE DAY, WHILE WE WERE PASSING THROUGH what is called the Grand Detour, a deep gorge through which the river passes, with precipitous clay banks, some hundreds of feet in height, on each side, our royal guest rose suddenly, and unusually high from his perch, and flapping his long wings, flew back some distance, and kept rising, when we all of one accord exclaimed, "He has gone! He has taken final leave!" But he made a circuit or two in the air, and then a stoop, just grazing the side of the ragged clay bluff, from which he lifted a huge snake, that was writhing and twisting in his deadly grasp as he was coming towards the boat. "Sonnette! Sonnette!" exclaimed poor Ba'tiste, as the snake, when the eagle was on his perch, was to hang right over his head!

It happened, luckily perhaps, not to be a rattlesnake, but a harmless reptile, probably better known to eagles than to us, which the eagle's eyes had discovered basking in the sun as we had passed, and which he had gone back for, and now on his perch, directly over poor Ba'tiste's head, was regularly making a delicious meal of. Ba'tiste soon got over his fright, and admitted that "it was all right,— that we were all hunters and adventurers together."

Annoyed to agony, and sometimes almost to death, by the mosquitoes that infest the shores of that river in some places, we generally selected a barren sandbar or sandy beach as the place of our bivouac, for they generally fly only as far as the grass extends.

Having one night selected such a beach, and drawn our canoe well on to it, we spread our robes on the soft sand, and got a comfortable night's rest; and a little after daylight in the morning, I heard Ba'tiste exclaim, "Voila, Mr. Catlin! Voila Caleb!" (as the trappers of these regions habitually call the grizzly bear). "Regardez, Mr. _____!" I raised myself up, and found Bogard and Ba'tiste rising gradually, with their hands on their rifles, and their attention fixed upon a monster of a grizzly bear, sitting a few rods from us on the slope of the prairie, regularly reconnoitering us; and at a little distance farther, the female with her two cubs; about enough altogether for us three to have furnished a comfortable breakfast, for which they were no doubt, with some impatience, waiting.

The time had passed heavily with them while they had been waiting for us to wake up, for it is a curious saying of the country, and probably a true one, that "man lying down is medicine to a bear"— that grizzly bears will not attack a man when he is asleep, although they are sure to attack him if they meet him on his feet. We all alike knew the motto of the country, yet I believe none of us were quite disposed to go to sleep for our protection.

A council of war was the first thing that was necessary; and as we discovered, on looking around, that these terrible beasts had been in our canoe and hauled every article out of it onto the beach, and pawed them open, and scattered them about; and that our poor eagle was gone, and swallowed, no doubt; and knowing the danger of attacking them, we agreed that our canoe was the first thing; the scattered remnants of our property (if we could have time to collect them) the next—preferring to have our battle afterwards. We simultaneously arose, moved our canoe into the water, and got our paddles into it, and our guns safe in our hands.

The animals made no move towards us in the meantime, and we began to gather our robes and other things which were strewed in all directions. Some packages were carried several rods from the canoe, and everything excepting a couple of large portfolios of drawings which they could not untie, and a roll of canvas which had stood the test, but was sadly pawed about in the mud, were as regularly unrolled and looked into (and smelled) as they would have been in passing a custom-house in France or in Brazil, with a doubtful and suspicious passport.

We had three or four days' supply of fresh meat laid in, and some delicious dried buffalo tongues, and a quantity of pemmican, all of which were devoured. My paint-box was opened, and nothing left in it—the brushes were scattered over the beach, and many of the bladders with colors tied in them, chewed, and the contents scattered and daubed, in strange mixtures of red, and green, and all colors, over everything. Two packs of Indian dresses, safely tied with thongs, were as regularly untied as if done by human hands; and shirts, and leggings, and headdresses, and robes, were daubed in the mud and spread out upon the beach as if to dry, or to be disposed of in lots at an auction sale. What an unprincipled overhauling this!

In taking up our sleeping robes, the enormous footprints sinking two or three inches into the hard sand, showed us that these stupid and terrible beasts had passed many times around and between our beds, which were not more, perhaps, than two or three feet apart. Was not here enough to shake one's nerves a little?

Our things thrown in confusion into our canoe for a better arrangement at a more agreeable place, we pushed out a little from the shore, and felt again at ease, knowing that the grizzly bear will never enter the water for anything.

The moment our canoe was afloat, with the accustomed flappings of his wings, the long and yellow legs of our illustrious passenger were reaching down for their perch, whilst he was drawing in his long wings, and seemingly shrugging his shoulders with satisfaction at being back to his old stand, and out of danger, as he was casting his piercing eyes around and over the gathered wreck, which he seemed to be aware of. From what hilltop or ledge this noble creature descended, or where he got his night's lodging, no one had the least knowledge.

Now we were ready for the attack—we were brave—we could flourish trumpets. Bogard and I levelled at the male—he being the nearest to us—Ba'tiste reserving his fire, which he gave to the female as she came, in all fury and with horrid growls, to the water's edge; she received his ball in her breast, and, galloping off, followed her companion, which had got our two rifle balls, and entered a thicket of high grass and weeds.

We were now floating down stream again, and though I urged my two companions to go back with me and complete the engagement, they both had fears, and most likely very prudent ones, of following those creatures into a thicket; so we left them to die, or to cure their wounds if they could, in their own way.

VIII

WE ARE NOW AT THE VILLAGE OF THE KIND AND HOSPITABLE MANDANS (or, as they call themselves, See-pohs-ka Nu-mah-kah-hee, People of the Pheasants), two hundred and fifty miles below the mouth of Yellowstone, from which we started: a tribe of two thousand, living in a village of clay-covered wigwams, on the west bank of the Missouri. My canoe and all my things are carried up by the women to the chief's wigwam, where they are to be kept in safety until I want them, and I a welcome guest while I stop—not a sixpence to pay.

The Mandans I considered one of the most interesting tribes that I visited, inasmuch as their language and many of their customs, as well as personal appearance, were so decidedly different from all other tribes in America.

As they were not a roaming, but a stationary tribe, they all lived in one village, which was effectually protected against Indian assaults by a high and precipitous bank of the river on two sides, and a stockade of large timbers set in the ground, on the back part.

This tribe, not following the migrations of the herds of buffaloes, like the Sioux and other tribes, secured themselves against want by raising considerable fields of maize (which they always kept hidden) in sufficient quantities to answer them when the buffaloes might for a time leave their vicinity.

The most striking singularities in the personal appearance of these people were those of complexion, and the color of their hair and eyes. I have before said that black hair, black eyes, and cinnamon color were the national characteristics of all American savages; but to my great surprise I found amongst the Mandans, many families whose complexions were nearly white, their eyes a light blue, and their hair of a bright, silvery grey, from childhood to old age!

This singular appearance I can account for only by the supposition that there must have been some civilized colony in some way engrafted on them, but of which neither history nor tradition seem as yet to furnish any positive proof.

From having found several distinct Welsh words in use amongst them; their skin canoes round like a tub, and precisely like the Welsh coracle, and their mode of constructing their wigwams like that in use at the present day in the mountainous parts of Wales, I am strongly inclined to believe that this singularity has been caused by some colony of Welsh people who have landed on the American coast, and after having wandered into the interior, have been taken into this hospitable tribe.

The Mandans I found to be a very peaceable people, not engaging in warfare except to defend their village and preserve their existence, for which they have had many hard struggles with the Sioux and Crow Indians.

When I was with the Mandans, there were living amongst them two chiefs of great distinction, the Wolf chief, head civil-chief, and Mah-to-toh-pa (the Four Bears), head war-chief of the tribe. I painted the portraits, at full length, of these valiant and proud men; and the latter, who became very much attached to me, I shall always consider one of the most extraordinary men who has lived amongst the American tribes.

He was in every way graceful, elegant, civil, and polite, and at the same time most gallant and invincible as a warrior. After I had painted his portrait, with which he was much pleased and astonished, he presented me his robe, with all the battles of his life painted on it, his wife being allowed time to make him an exact copy of it.

On this extraordinary robe he was represented, at full length, in fourteen battles in which he had been victorious, and for which he had the scalps as proofs which no one could deny. When he gave me the robe, lest it should be unappreciated by me, he spread it upon the ground, and inviting me to sit down by the side of him, he proceeded to explain to me each group, the place where the battle was fought, and the manner in which he gained his success; and for each battle he showed me and placed in my hand, the scalp.

Several of his most celebrated warriors, who were familiar, of course, with his military exploits, were listening to his explanations, and nodded assent to every scene which he described, and which I wrote down, word for word, in my notebook; and amongst those fourteen achievements there was one which he described in this way:—

"This spear," said he, taking it up from the ground behind him, and laying it on the robe—a spear of some eight feet in length, and ornamented with a number of red and white eagles' quills, and with a long blade of steel, "this spear once belonged to the war-chief of the Riccarrees (a tribe about equal in numbers to the Mandans, and living two hundred miles below them on the same bank of the river). The Riccarrees have always been making war upon us, and in one of their cowardly midnight attacks upon our village, when a great many of our young men, as well as women and children, were killed, my brother, younger than myself, was missing; and three days after the battle, in which we had driven our enemies away, I found the body of my brother amongst the willows, with the blade of this spear remaining in his body. I recognized the spear as belonging to the treacherous war-chief of the Riccarrees, having seen it and handled it when we had sat together and smoked the calumet in a treaty of peace but a few months before; many of my warriors also recognized the spear. I preserved it, with the blood of my brother's body dried on its blade, and I then swore to avenge my brother's death with my own hand.

"I kept this spear for three years, and no opportunity occurring, and unwilling to spill the blood of the innocent by bringing the two tribes into conflict, I resolved to get my revenge in another way. For this purpose I put my body and face into war paint, which a chief, by our custom, is not in the habit of doing. I took parched corn in my pouch to last me several days, and without other weapon than this spear in my hand, I started off, unknown to my people, for the Riccarree village, traveling over the prairies by night, and lying secreted during the day.

"In this manner I came near to the Riccarree village on the sixth day. I secreted myself during the last day, and when it was dark I approached and entered the village without danger of being detected. Knowing the wigwam of the war-chief, I loitered about it, and often peeped in and saw him seated by the fire smoking his pipe.

"His wife at length went to bed; and after he had sat and smoked out another pipe by himself, he went to bed also. The time for me had then arrived; the fire was almost out, and the wigwam quite dark. I gently opened the door and walked in with the spear in my hand, and sat down by the fire. There was a pot hanging over the fire with some meat in it, which I commenced eating, as I was almost starved to death. Whilst I was eating I heard his wife ask him what man that was eating from the pot in their wigwam; to which the chief replied, 'No matter; I suppose the man is hungry.' After I had satiated my hunger, I very gradually stirred the fire a little with my foot, until I just got light enough to see my way to my enemy, when I arose and drove the lance to his heart. I darted from the wigwam with the lance in one hand and his scalp in the other, and made my way as fast as possible towards the Mandan village, without their knowing where the enemy was from, or which way he had gone.

"I travelled fast all that night, and lay secreted during the following day, and so travelled night after night until I entered the Mandan village in triumph, with the scalp of the war-chief of the Riccarrees resting on the point of his own spear. 'This, my friend,' said he, 'is the scalp of that enemy, and this is the spear which I drew from the body of my brother, and with which, I believe, it was the will of the Great Spirit I should avenge his death. You see, my friend, that I have done it, and the blood of both is now dried upon its blade.'

"This, my friend, was unlike the deeds of Mah-to-toh-pa; but I went to slay a dog, who died as he deserved. Though he was a war-chief, and had many scalps, he was not an honorable man; he hung about our village like the sneaking wolves in the night, and even scalped our women and children when they were bathing on the shore of the river. If he had been an honorable man, Mah-to-toh-pa would have given him a chance for his life in equal combat; but as his life had been that of a coward, it would not have been just that he should die the death of a brave man."

Now, the rest of this book might be filled with the exploits of Mah-to-toh-pa; but I will describe one more, and then we will pass on. While sitting upon the robe, Mah-to-toh-pa showed me the scalp of a brave man—a celebrated chief of the Crows; and, pointing to the illustration on the robe, dictated while the interpreter described in this way:

"The Crows have long been our enemies; their war-parties have often attacked our village and our hunting-parties when they have been upon the plains. A few years since, many hundred Crow warriors appeared on the prairies, not far distant from the Mandan village, when Mah-to-toh-pa, with his warriors, went out to meet them. When the two war-parties were coming near to each other, on a level plain, and just ready for battle, they halted, and the war-chief of the Crows sent a white flag to the Mandans, with this message: 'Is Mah-to-toh-pa, the war-chief of the Mandans, there? He is a brave man. If he leads the Mandan war-party today, let him come out alone, and he and I will decide this combat, and save the lives of our brave warriors. Hora-to-ah, war-chief of the Crows, sends this message.'

"To this Mah-to-toh-pa replied—'Hora-to-ah is a chief and a brave warrior, and worthy of Mah-to-toh-pa. Mah-to-toh-pa leads the Mandan war-party this day. Mah-to-toh-pa is glad to meet the war-chief of the Crows, and save the blood of his brave warriors. It is Mah-to-toh-pa, war-chief of the Mandans, who sends this reply.'

"After the messenger had returned, the Crow chief was seen galloping out upon the plain, on a milk-white horse, with a shield on his arm and a gun in his hand.

"Mah-to-toh-pa was not slow to meet him. They passed each other twice, and fired with their guns without effect; but Mah-to-toh-pa's powder-horn was shot away; he held it up, and showing that he had no more powder, the Crow chief drew his powder-horn from his neck, and flung it to the ground and his gun also, and drew his bow, his shield and quiver being slung upon his back. Mah-to-toh-pa did the same, and the combat was now with bows and arrows. Many were the passes that were made, and many the arrows that were shielded off. Each chief was wounded in the legs, and the horse of Mah-to-toh-pa fell, with an arrow through its heart. Mah-to-toh-pa was on his feet, but his bow and his shield were before him.

"The Crow chief was a gallant and brave warrior and was worthy of Mah-to-toh-pa; he sprang upon the ground, and driving an arrow through the heart of his horse, stood before his antagonist. The battle here began again, but was near its end, for at last the Crow chief raised and shook his empty quiver, and throwing it to the ground, drew and brandished his terrible knife. Mah-to-toh-pa's quiver was also hurled to the ground, and he said 'Yes!' as both were rushing on. His knife was not in his belt! But it was too late, they were in each other's arms! The wounds of Mah-to-toh-pa were several; the two-edged blade of his antagonist's knife was twice drawn through his hand, but he at length wrested it from his enemy's hand and plunged it to his heart. Thus fell Hora-to-ah, the war-chief of the Crows. The scalp of that chief and his war knife, with his own blood dried upon it, belong to Mah-to-toh-pa, and here they are; and the right hand of Mah-to-toh-pa, as you see, is crippled for the remainder of his days."

The women in the Mandan tribe, like those of most of the neighboring tribes, were comfortably, and oftentimes very beautifully, clad with skins, extending from the throat quite to the feet. They were generally modest and timid, and observed exceeding propriety in their conduct. Some of them were very beautiful, of which the Indians seem to have a correct and high appreciation.

Amongst the Mandans, the reputed belles when I was there were Mi-neek-e-sunk-te-ca (the mink), and Sha-ko-ka (mint), daughters of two of the subordinate chiefs; amongst the Riccarrees, Pshan-shaw (the sweet-scented grass); and amongst the Minatarrees, a few miles above the Mandans, Seet-see-be-a (the mid-day sun). These were all very beautiful and (then) unmarried girls. I painted their portraits full length, in their soft and white dresses, made of the mountain sheep-skins, and fringed, not with scalp-locks, but with ermine, and beautifully embroidered with porcupine quills.

How curious their names, and how pleasing! The sweet-scented grass is a sort of grass with a delicious odor which these little girls gather in the prairies, and which they wear in braids amongst the strings of beads on their necks.

And also amongst the Assinneboins, Chin-cha-pee (the fire-bug that creeps, or glow-worm). Amongst the Shawanos, Kay-te-qua (the female eagle); of the Ioways, Ru-ton-ye-wee-me (the strutting pigeon); and among the Puncahs, Hee-la-dee (the pure fountain), and Mong-shong-shaw (the bending willow). Among the Pawnee-Picts, Shee-de-a (wild sage); and amongst the Kiowas, Wun-pan-to-mee (the white weasel).

The Mandans related to me a very curious and distinct tradition they have of the Deluge, teaching that all the human race were destroyed by the rising of the waters, excepting one man, who landed his big canoe on a high mountain, not far from their village, and was saved, and that all the present human family have descended from that man.

The name of this "first, or only man," was Nu-mohk-muck-a-nah; and they held an annual religious ceremony, lasting four days, in commemoration of the event, lest it should happen again. This strange ceremony they called O-kee-pa, and have an immense wigwam kept solely for this purpose, called the Medicine Lodge. This strange man, Nu-mohk-muck-a-nah, professes to come every season (about the middle of June) and open the Medicine Lodge, and to commence the celebration by appointing a medicine man, whom they then call O-kee-pa-ka-see-ka (the conductor of the ceremonies), and then returns over the prairies to the high mountains, where he professes to dwell, telling the people they may be sure he will reappear the next year, to open the ceremonies again.

The appearance of this personage is very grotesque and curious; he, no doubt, is a medicine man who goes out upon the prairies the night before, and enters the village at sunrise, from the mountains in the west, where he tells them he has resided from the time that he landed in his big canoe. He wears a robe made of four white wolf-skins, his head-dress is made of two raven-skins, and his body, otherwise naked, is covered with white clay, and his face and his cheeks painted, apparently, to personate a white man.

I was fortunate enough to be present during the four days' ceremony, in which the young men were suspending their bodies by splints run through the flesh on the shoulders, and breasts, and arms, and otherwise torturing themselves in various ways, as a religious penance, almost too shocking to describe, and entirely too long to be fully explained in this place. I consider it altogether the most extraordinary and curious of all the customs I have met in the savage countries.

It was pitiable to see so kind, so hospitable, and apparently so happy a people, under the influence of ignorant superstition, practicing such self-inflicted cruelties; but it was a part of their religion, and, like all religious customs, would have required time and patience to have corrected. But, poor unfortunate people, they are all gone, and their errors are done away with!

The second summer after my visit to them, one of the American Fur Company's steamers, [how many steamers did they have?) ascending the Missouri River to trade with the various tribes, and to supply their trading establishments with rum and whisky, and other articles of commerce, imprudently stopped in front of the Mandan village while there were two of their men sick with smallpox on board. The disease was soon taken into the Mandan village, and, in the space of three months, the two thousand Mandans were reduced to the exact number of thirty-two. This I give to the world on the authority of a letter in my possession, written by a Mr. Potts, formerly of the City of Edinburgh, in Scotland, and at that time a clerk in the Fur Company's factory at the Mandan village, and who says, "At the moment I am writing, there are but thirty-two of these poor people in existence, and they mostly women and children."

What an illustration is this of the wickedness of mercenary white men, who push their commerce into the Indian country, calling these poor people up to trade under the cannon's mouth, and selling rum and whisky to them, as these poisons were sold at the Mandan village at that time, at eighteen dollars per gallon, and other articles of extravagance and luxury at similar ruinous prices!

There was a government Indian agent on board of the steamer when this unfortunate occurrence took place, a staunch and honorable man—Major Dougherty—who remonstrated against the steamer's advancing to the Mandan village with the smallpox on board, and ordered the commander to turn it back; but he was two thousand miles beyond the reach of the laws, in a country where brute force was the law of the land, and what could he do? He could do nothing against the weight of a solid cargo of rum and whisky, and so the poor Mandans suffered; and the disease went to the Blackfeet, of whom twenty-five thousand perished, and how much farther towards the Pacific, and how many other thousands perished, no one knows, for newspapers are not received from those regions, and fur-traders are not the most reliable sources for information.

The last I saw of my friends the Mandans, was at the shore of the river in front of their village. My canoe and all my packs were brought down in safety to the water's edge—my canoe placed in the water— the whole tribe upon the beach. My friend, Mah-to-toh-pa, the Wolf chief, and the Great Medicine, all successively embraced me in their arms; the warriors and braves shook hands with me, and the women and children saluted me with shouts of farewell; and Ba'tiste, and Bogard, and myself were again afloat, and on our way for St. Louis.

At this exciting moment, when we had got too far into the current to stop, and well under way, a gallant young warrior whom I recognized followed opposite to us, at the water's edge, and, leaning over, tossed safely into the canoe a parcel which he took out from under his robe; and seeing me attempting to unfold it, he waved his hand and shook his head, and made a sign for me to lay it down in the canoe, which I did. All now was done, and we were off.

After we had got a mile or so from the village, I took in my paddle and opened the parcel by untying a great many thongs, and, to my great surprise, found the most beautiful pair of leggings which I ever had seen, fringed with a profusion of scalp-locks, and handsomely garnished with porcupine-quills.

These I instantly recognized as belonging to the son of a famous chief, the 'Four Men,' and the identical pair I had been for some time trying to purchase, and for which I had offered the young man a horse, but got no reply, excepting that "he could not sell them, as the scalp-locks were so precious as trophies, and his fellow warriors would laugh at him if he sold them."

What a beautiful trait this! Having parted with me without the least prospect of ever seeing me again, he compels me to accept as a present what he could not sell to me the day before for the price of a horse! And envelops it in an intricacy of thongs which he had intended I should not be able to untie until the current had wafted me beyond the possibility of my making him any compensation for them! And how much like the gift of the saddle of venison left in my father's wood-house, containing the eagle plume, by the unfortunate On-o-gong-way, and which so opened the eyes and the heart of poor Johnny O'Neil!

IX

ON—ON—STILL GLIDES OUR LITTLE BOAT, as Ba'tiste and Bogard paddle and I steer; the unceasing banks of greensward, enameled with beautiful wild flowers, and the countless sloping hills and knolls, with their verdant sides, are still before, around, and behind us. The river still winds in its tortuous course, and at every turn a new and cheerful landscape is presented, with here and there beautiful meadows, with tufts and copses of trees, and many of the hillsides dotted with solitary oaks; the whole presenting a continued and never-ending view as of an old and beautifully cultivated country greensward, instead of ploughed fields, with the houses and hedges removed.

Such are yet the American prairies, and more must still be said of them before they will be fully understood. Night after night, and for weeks of nights, our little craft is hauled ashore, and our robes spread upon the grass or upon the barren sandbars, while the silvery, but discordant notes of the bands of howling wolves are hourly serenading us as we are getting our night's rest.

The great tribe of Sioux are below us, and there are probably some days yet between us. Our larder was low, and a lazy little herd, quietly sleeping and grazing on the right bank, tempted us ashore, where we silently landed our canoe, and nicely approaching in a deep ravine, we soon got our three buffalo tongues and our three fleeces (or humps) without the slightest trouble, and continued on; I having stopped a few minutes to make a sketch of the snug little box in which the band were luxuriating.

Whilst we had enough to eat, and our paddles were constantly at work, it was natural to sing, and to whistle, and to tell stories for amusement; and whilst Ba'tiste and Bogard were relating to me some exciting and amusing stories about the Crows and the Blackfeet, in whose countries they had been trapping and trading, *BANG!* went a gun on the shore opposite to us, and skipping, skipping, came a bullet across the water, a rod or so ahead of our canoe! An Indian was standing at the water's edge, alone, and making signs and calling to us to come ashore.

The shot fired ahead of us was the usual friendly mode of inviting parties ashore on that river, but is generally the second invitation, the first being by signals and by calling. Bogard was anxious to go ashore, but I did not exactly like the mode of invitation, nor the position of things; for this man could scarcely be supposed to be there alone; and he had placed himself on the shore just above the sudden bend in the river, where the current running in very swift, would bring us in quite near to a rocky shore, in case we drifted with it. In this place his companions, if he had any, would naturally conceal themselves in case they had any unfriendly design upon us, as they might easily have; there being then existing many unsettled feuds between some of that tribe and some of the fur-traders, for which I or any other traveler might be liable to suffer.

The river was very wide where we were, and I steered the canoe nearer to the opposite side, to prevent floating with the current into the bend. Bogard, who was a drunken fellow, and I believe thought it might be an opportunity for getting something to drink, said in rather an authoritative tone, "We will go ashore," and Ba'tiste said, "Oui, oui," and I said, "No; the canoe is mine, and I won't go ashore —I don't like the look of things ashore;" when both drew in their paddles and violently threw them down in the bottom of the canoe, and were evidently looking over their shoulders for their rifles, which were lying under a buffalo robe between them and me.

I instantly seized my double-barreled gun, and cocking both barrels, laid it across my lap, having their backs, luckily, towards me. They perfectly understood the meaning of this movement, and, from my looks, what would have been the instant consequence if either of them had reached for his gun. I then commenced paddling the canoe myself, and succeeded, by a violent effort, in not allowing it to fall into the current near the shore, and in forcing it towards the opposite side. Just at this time, and when the two men were snarling and growling at me for "being afraid of one, poor, solitary Indian," some twenty or thirty naked warriors, seeing that we were not coming in, rose from behind the rocks where we should naturally have landed if we had gone ashore, raising the war-whoop, and running down the shore to meet us below the bend.

"Il faut combattre!" exclaimed Ba'tiste, as he seized his rifle.

"No," said I, "on ne combattre pas. Il faut ramer! Ramer!"

"On rame!" said Ba'tiste, laying down his rifle and taking up his paddle, and all three paddled with all our might.

Bogard, who was a desperate and sullen fellow, said, "We must knock over some of those fellows." I said, "No; we have nothing to do but to row, and every man to ply his paddle." I kept the canoe about in the middle of the river, in order to take advantage of the strongest current, and the Indians were running on the beach and sounding the war-whoop, which showed us beyond a doubt what their object was.

Notwithstanding all our exertions, they were in a little time some distance below us, when some eight or ten of them sprang into the water and came swimming towards us, holding their bows and arrows in the left hand above the water.

Seeing them thus ahead of us, and nearing the boat, I then said to my men, "Now, take up your rifles, but don't fire unless I give the word." We all took in our paddles, and with our rifles in our hands, and cocked, I beckoned to them to go ashore; but still coming nearer, and some of them within a few rods, I raised my rifle as if to fire, when they sunk almost entirely under the water, and commenced returning towards the shore. Those on shore were still running and yelling, and setting them on us again, when several of them approached us a second time; but in a similar manner were turned back. Seeing that they were armed with only bows and arrows, though they use these with great effect in the water, I felt no further alarm, and resolved not to use any unnecessary cruelty upon them. If they had begun upon us, however, we should have been obliged to fire, and could easily have killed every one of them as they approached our boat.

Getting ashore, the whole party followed opposite to us for several miles, but finding the chase unprofitable, they turned back, and we paddled on till after dark, and bivouacked on the opposite side of the river without further molestation.

Who these people were, whether Sioux or Riccarrees, or what was their design, I never was able to learn; but it has been a source of continual gratification to me that we had the forbearance not to fire upon them.

A few days more of paddling brought us to Fort Pierre, a large trading establishment amongst the Sioux, with fifteen hundred skin wigwams of Sioux Indians grouped upon the plains around it. Hundreds on hundreds of horses were grazing on the prairies, and as many children and dogs guarding them.

I have shown you how the Sioux Indians build and ornament their tents, and you can easily imagine now how picturesque and beautiful a scene was around us. My canoe, as amongst the Mandans, was carried by the squaws (as they call their women); a tent was prepared for my painting operations, and I was soon at work with my brushes, and plenty of picturesque subjects to paint.

Ha-won-je-ta (the One Horn), head civil-chief of the Sioux, was the first whose portrait I hit off, the size of life, in a beautiful costume. All had been quite silent about my wigwam, and my advent but little cared about or known, until this private operation, known only to the chief and his doctor, was finished, and his portrait, held by the corners of the frame, was elevated above the heads of the crowd by the great medicine, crying to the gathering multitude in front of my tent: "Look, my friends! We have now got two chiefs—when the one is dead the other will live—look at him and be ashamed! He smiles upon you and is alive; tomorrow you will see me. Be patient, my friends! I am but a little boy." (I had made a dead coloring of the old doctor, and set it by to dry.) "Mine is put in a box, to grow overnight; tomorrow, my face will shine upon you. This is the wonderful work of a great white medicine man; he is now sitting and smoking with the chief; you cannot see him, but perhaps he will sometime walk through our village, and then you can look at him. The Great Spirit has shown him how to do these things, and you must make but little noise. He says I can do the same thing, and I think so, my friends!"

The doctor's harangue was long and very curious, and, through some little crevices in my tent, the astonished multitude was one of the most curious sights I ever beheld—an interminable mass of red and painted heads, of eagles' quills, of ermine-skins, of beads and brooches, spears, lances, shields, and quivers. Some were mounted on horses, and others raised upon the shoulders of their friends, and all gazing in wonder and astonishment at the one object—the chief "that had a little life" (as they said); the corners of whose mouth many of them could see to move, and the eyes of which actually turned and followed all as they changed their positions. Oh, for a photographic lens! What a picture or two I could have got!

"My friends," said the doctor, "you see the chief's eyes move! If any doubts that, let him walk round and look at the chief again. My friends, our chief is a great chief! But here is a chief whose eyes are on you all at the same time; he sees you all at one time alike. What chief can do that? My friends, put your hands over your mouths and be silent; tomorrow you will see me!"

Mr. Laidlaw, the factor at that fort, in whose house I was made welcome, brought into my wigwam several of the most distinguished chiefs and warriors to be painted, and I had full employment. The chiefs and warriors were seated round the sides of the wigwam and smoking their pipes while I would be at work at one, and each one waiting patiently for his turn to come.

This time they seemed to while away very merrily, relating all the anecdotes, creditable or otherwise, of his life, whilst he was under the operation of the brush, with his mouth shut, and unable to deny anything that was said. The scene was one of continual merriment and laughter, and the laughing and fun was increased when the operation was over and the portrait placed before them, when they were not sparing in criticisms on its good looks and in anecdotes of his life, which "it reminded them of."

In the meantime the door of my wigwam was guarded by a warrior with a lance in his hand, a sort of police placed there by the chief, with orders not to allow anyone to enter except those whose rank entitled them to admission; and the facetious old doctor had enough to do outside, magnifying my wonderful powers, and the importance of medicine, whilst he was keeping back the women and children and dogs, and hushing them into respectful silence.

Thus progressed the mystery operations inside and outside of my wigwam from day to day; and I had but one difficulty which I could apprehend before me, which was this:

It had been represented to these chiefs and warriors that I was a great chief in my own country, that I had heard they had some very distinguished chiefs and warriors amongst them, and had come a vast distance to see who they were, and to obtain their portraits to hang on the walls alongside of the great men in the civilized world. This made it necessary that they should be painted in order, according to rank. I had begun with the head chief, and gone on until I had painted nearly the number that I cared about painting, and from necessity, some of the ugliest looking men I ever saw; and finding new subjects waiting in my wigwam every day in full dress, and ready to take their turn as decided by the chiefs, and knowing that the Sioux tribe contained forty bands, with forty chiefs, and ten times that number of medicine men and great warriors, I began to apprehend a serious difficulty approaching. Some remonstrances were also being raised by several of the jealous chiefs, as to the right of the great medicine being painted next to the head chief; but that was a fait accompli, and the chief decided that it was all right.

In the midst of these growing difficulties, and amongst these jealous spirits, Mr. Laidlaw brought into my wigwam a fine young man in his war dress and war paint, and fully armed and equipped, and said, "Mr. Catlin, I have brought in a friend of mine for you to paint—Mah-to-chee-ga (the Little Bear); he is not a chief, but he is a young warrior of such distinction, and of so good a character, that I am sure the chiefs will agree that he shall be painted." To this the chiefs all agreed, and he taking his position, I put a canvas on my easel and commenced immediately. His first attitude was beautiful, and what I wanted. He was looking off, towards the sides of the wigwam, as if gazing over a boundless prairie; the face was, therefore, what we painters call a "three-quarter face," one-half of it thrown into shadow.

While I was painting, and had the portrait pretty well advanced, one of the secondary chiefs, by the name of Shon-ka (the Dog), and whose portrait I had painted some days before, rather a surly-looking fellow, and somewhat sarcastic, crept round behind me, and for a while overlooked the operation of my brush, having a full view of the portrait. Being an evil-disposed man, disliked by most of his fellow-chiefs, and jealous of this rising warrior, he addressed to him this insulting remark—'I see that you are but half a man.' 'Who says that?' said Mah-to-chee-ga, in a low tone of voice, and without the change of a muscle or the direction of his eye. 'Shon-ka says it,' replied the Dog. 'Let Shon-ka prove it,' replied Mah-to-chee-ga. 'Shon-ka proves it in this way; the white medicine man knows that one-half of your face is good for nothing, as he has left it out in the picture.' Mah-to-chee-ga replied, 'If I am but half a man, I am man enough for Shon-ka in any way he pleases to try it.'

Here a sharp repartee took place for a few minutes, the Dog keeping his eyes upon the portrait, and those of Mah-to-chee-ga still stretching over the distant prairie. In this dialogue, which was carried on to the great amusement of the chiefs, Mah-to-chee-ga seemed to have the advantage of his adversary, who sprang upon his feet, and wrapping his robe violently around him, suddenly darted out of my wigwam, evidently in a rage.

The chiefs seemed, from the change in their manner, to be apprehensive of the result, while my subject still stood without a change or apparent emotion, and so stood until the portrait was finished, when he deliberately took off from his legs a beautiful pair of leggings, fringed with scalp-locks of his own earning, and asked me to accept them as a present.

After sitting down and smoking a pipe with the chiefs, and hearing their comments on his portrait, with which they were all well pleased, he got up, shook hands with me, and went out, passing into his own wigwam, which was but a few paces from mine.

Apprehensive of what might happen from the last expressions of the Dog, as he had left my wigwam, he took down his gun and loaded it in a hurried manner, which excited the apprehensions and inquiry of his wife, to which he made no reply, but set his gun aside, and prostrating himself upon the ground, his face to the dirt, according to their mode when danger is near, he prayed a moment to the

Great Spirit; and during that moment, to prevent mischief, his wife extracted the ball from his gun without his knowing it, and set it down; and at the next moment, the voice of the Dog (who had gone to his own wigwam, and returned with his gun in his hand) was heard in front of his door, "If Mah-to-ohee-ga is man enough for Shon-ka, let him come out and prove it."

Like a flash of lightning, Mah-to-chee-ga was upon his feet, his gun in his hand, and the instant he rushed out, the two guns, lapping over each other, were fired! Mah-to-chee-ga fell, weltering in his blood, that side of his face entirely blown away which had been 'left out' in the painting, and decided by the Dog to be "good for nothing" and the Dog, with his face a little blackened, and the thumb of his left hand carried away, fled to the outer part of the village occupied by his band, where he called upon the warriors of his band to protect him.

At the firing of the guns, the chiefs all rushed out of my wigwam, each one raising the tent behind where he sat, and disappearing in an instant. I was left alone; not a word for some time, but footsteps running and leaping were heard in all directions. I peeped through the crevices in my medicine house, and saw women, and children, and men running in all parts; the horses were caught and brought in at full gallop from the prairies, the twilight was approaching, and the dogs were howling.

I was slipping my pistols into my belt, and examining the caps of my double-barrel, when Laidlaw dashed into my tent. "Now we shall have it!" said he; "for the pictures! That splendid fellow, the Little Bear, is dead! All that side of his face you left out in the portrait is shot off! Hang the pictures! I have been afraid of them. I have urged these people to sit for these pictures, and they are saying everywhere that you are the cause of the Little Bear's death. The warriors of the Little Bear's band are all arming, and, if they can't kill the Dog, they have said they will look to you for satisfaction."

At this moment guns were heard firing in the outskirts of the village.

"Leave your tent as quick as lightning," said Laidlaw, "and come into the fort; you know it is all open; it is but half-finished, and we may all be cut off before morning." I followed with him, leaving all behind me excepting my arms and ammunition. Most of Laidlaw's men were off on the prairies at the time, and our position therefore was extremely critical.

One of Laidlaw's clerks, by the name of Halsey, and myself, took possession of one of the unarmed bastions, a small log building, barricading the windows and doors as well as we could, and receiving from the Company's stores some two or three dozen of muskets, which we loaded, and stood listening and waiting results during the greater part of the night in almost breathless anxiety. We kept our quarters darkened, and could hear the constant trampling and running in different parts of the village, and now and then the flash of a gun or two, and at last a rapid succession of flashes on and over the prairies, convincing us that the Dog was retreating, protected by his warriors, whilst the warriors of the Little Bear's band were pursuing him into the country.

On the following morning all was quiet, but the village and fort had assumed quite a different appearance. All was silent, and seemed sullen. Several fine young men on both sides were reported killed, and the Dog, though wounded, was still retreating, and pursued. My wigwam was found solitary and unentered, just as I had left it. My paintings and all things were speedily packed. We joined together in burying the remains of the fallen warrior, raising an honorable monument over his grave; and made liberal presents to his widow and all of his relations, which saved us perhaps from violence.

The chiefs treated me with friendship afterwards, apparently satisfied that I was in no wise to blame; but the medicine man was of a different opinion, notwithstanding all his kindness and attachment to me. He had "just learned that my medicine was too great," and that I "must have known that that side of the warrior's face was good for nothing, or I would not have left it out in the portrait; and if I had not left it out there would have been nothing said about it, and that therefore the Little Bear would still have been alive." There was no metaphysics amongst these people to rebut such conclusive reasoning as this; and though we had mended the breach as well as we could, I thought the safest way was to be on the water again as quickly as possible; which it is easy to imagine I lost no time in effecting.

Thus ended one of the most exciting and lamentable affairs growing out of my interviews with these curious people; strongly illustrating, from its beginning to its end, the high and chivalrous jealousy existing in their society, and a striking instance of the extent and certainty to which they are sure to carry their revenge.

Another brief anecdote, growing out of the unaccountable process of my portrait painting amongst these people, will help to show further how far their superstitions will sometimes carry them, and may be worth relating.

While ascending the Missouri River on a subsequent occasion, and stopping in the tribe of Omahas, after having painted several of the chiefs and warriors, I painted the portrait of a fine young man, who was not a warrior, but a brave. The portrait was recognized and approved by all; but I had observed him for several days afterwards, coming in and sitting down, and looking at his portrait a while, and going off, apparently in a somewhat surly and melancholy mood. One day he brought in the interpreter, and said "he did not like his picture; it was not good; it looked ashamed, because it was looking the other way."

The portrait was a three-quarter face, and the eyes looking off. He said "I had painted all the others right, looking straight forward. He had been always in the habit of looking white men in the face; but here they would all see him with his face turned the other way, as if he was ashamed." He requested me to alter it, and make his eyes look straight forward. The chiefs were all pleased with it, and advised me not to do so.

He had learned a few days afterwards that I was not going to change his eyes in the portrait, and the interpreter came into my wigwam, and said I had got to fight; that the young man was in front of my wigwam, and ready, and he believed there was no alternative.

I went out with my palette in my hand, and to be sure, here he was, entirely naked and ready. I explained to him that I was very much surprised, and that I loved him too much to fight him; and also, that I had not thought he was so much offended with his portrait, which the chiefs all liked so much; and if to alter the eyes of his picture was all that he wanted, I would do it with the greatest pleasure the next day. This prevented all necessity of our meeting; and the next day, with some water colors mixed on my palette with some dry white lead, and he sitting a few minutes, I painted him a new set of eyes, staring in a prodigious manner across the bridge of his nose, which pleased him exactly, as they were looking straight forward. He shook hands with me, seeing what I had done, and made me a present of a pair of leggings as an evidence of his satisfaction.

On my return to St. Louis, a year afterwards, a piece of sponge with some clean water took off the new pair of eyes, and the portrait now stands as it was originally made, one of the most interesting in my collection.

X

BUT, READERS, WE NEED NOT GO ON ALL THE WAY TO ST.LOUIS; it is a long distance, though Ba'tiste and Bogard and I did jog on, through smoke and through fire, for the fall season was approaching, and the broad prairie meadows, with their waving grass eight or ten feet high, were now in flames; and our long beards in constant danger, for my razors were lost in the unfortunate affair of the tin kettle, and for six months our beards had had their own way.

My poor little canoe, so safely taken care of by the Mandans and the Sioux, was stolen from me at the wharf at St. Louis within two hours after our arrival; and my beard being thoughtlessly shaved off, so that my friends might know me, rendered me a laughing-stock for the space of two or three weeks, until the sunburnt redness of the upper half could be made to harmonize with the death-like paleness of the nether portion of my face.

From the Sioux, on the Missouri, it is but a step of two or three hundred miles to the Platte River, on the banks of which dwell the numerous tribe of Pawnees. Oh, what a terrible, and yet beautiful-looking set of warriors they are; their heads all shaved, and painted blood-red, and surmounted with the beautiful red crests! When a war-party of them, on their war horses, are prancing along over the prairies in the distance, with the blades of their long lances glistening in the sun, they look like a bed of red poppies mingled with the silvery heads of barley, bowing and waving in the wind.

These are the gentlemen who catch such vast quantities of wild horses, their country abounding in countless numbers of them, and also in the most numerous herds of buffaloes.

Shon-ha-ki-hee-ga (the Horse chief), oftentimes called Wee-tar-ra-sha-ro, is the head chief of this tribe, a very dignified and hospitable man. It was in this man's wigwam that the Hon. Charles Aug. Murray was entertained, protected, and made welcome on his visit to the Pawnees in 1833. Mr. Murray, for several subsequent years, was Master of her Majesty's Household. (Have you read his Prairie Bird and his Tour on the Prairies?)

WE ARE NOW NEAR THE BASE OF THE ROCKY MOUNTAINS, but the smoke is getting too bad here too. All is gloom; the fires are all around us; the prairie hens are flying in all directions; the deer are all in motion; the frogs and reptiles are looking for their burrows; the black and smoking plains are strewed with bleaching bones, and shrouded nature has lost its charms.

Imagination (how lucky) can waft us in a single moment to the falls of St. Anthony, on the Upper Mississippi; the distance is but a thousand miles, where perhaps there is a clear sky. This dashing, foaming cataract, second only to Niagara, which was discovered and christened after his patronymic saint by the good old Father Hennepin in 1860, has been a dividing boundary line, and consequently hostile ground, for centuries past between the Sioux and the Ojibbeway tribes, and the vicinity around is strewed with human bones, which indicate the destructive scenes which have been enacted there.

With Corporal Allen, seated in a beautiful birch-bark canoe, he paddling while I steered, I started from this beautiful scene, in the summer of 1834, wending our way amidst the towering cliffs and grassy plains of the mighty Mississippi to St. Louis, a distance of nine hundred miles, drawing our light little craft upon the beach at night, and supplying our little larder from day to day with rock bass taken from the rocky eddies, and wild fowl and deer, which we killed with our rifles.

The Indian tribes which we saw on the banks of this river were the Sioux, the Winnebagos, the Menomonies, the Saukies, the Foxes, and Ioways. My paintings were made, and we were treated by them all with kindness. My little bark canoe, which was beautifully painted, was always taken care of by them while we stopped, and placed in the water when we were prepared to proceed on our way.

When we arrived at the wharf at St. Louis, our luggage was lifted and sent to my hotel, and, for the sake of safety, with the captain's permission, I had my pretty little canoe lifted on to the deck of his steamer lying at the wharf, to remain for a few hours until I could find a place to store it; and when I came for it – it was gone. I never again could hear of it.

In the next succeeding summer, with an English gentleman, Mr. Wood (now residing in Philadelphia), I ascended the Fox River, from Green Bay to its source, also in a bark canoe. At the head of that river, in making the portage to the head of the Wisconsin, which we were to descend to the Mississippi, we had but a distance of two miles over a level prairie.

My companion said, "But what are we to do here?"

"Well," said I, "we have got to take turn about with our little canoe; it has carried us a great way, now we have got to carry our canoe."

"Oh, but, my dear sir, what shall I do with my dear little wife?" (meaning his beautiful little guitar, which he played with great taste). "Never fear," said I; "if you will carry the pack which I have now made up, I will take the canoe on my shoulders and your guitar case under my arm." Turning the canoe bottom upwards, raising it upon one end, and getting the middle beam on my shoulders, I very easily carried it the distance, and laying it on the clear waters of the Wisconsin, there but a few yards wide, we took our seats, and, paddles in hand, commenced our descent of some hundreds of miles to the Mississippi, encamping at night upon its grassy and picturesque shores.

After we entered the Mississippi we had some hard work against its boiling current before we reached Prairie du Chien; and from that to the Falls of St. Anthony, a distance of four hundred and fifty miles, some 'uphill work' again. Men in these regions sometimes have to use their arms as well as legs in traveling.

'Uphill work' we all know the meaning of, and I have had much of it to mar my progress in life; but 'upriver work,' with a somewhat similar meaning, is a term less perfectly understood. The difference between them is, that the one may be very hard work, and the other is sure to be; but in the latter, like the boy who drags his sled with hard labor up the hill, we are encouraged by the pleasure we anticipate in riding down.

FROM THE FALLS OF ST. ANTHONY WE ASCENDED THE ST. PETER'S RIVER one hundred miles, to visit the red pipe-stone quarry on the Grand Coteau des Prairies, where the Indians procure their red stone for making their beautiful pipes. This place we found to be one of great interest, not only from the Indians' traditions about it, but from the peculiar features of the country, and the singular character of the pipe-stone, a species of steatite, but differing from any other sort found in America, or perhaps in the world.

Many of the contiguous tribes have no doubt been in the habit of visiting this place to procure the red stone for their pipes, protected from the weapons of their enemies, under the belief they all have that the Indians were made from the red stone, it being precisely their own color—"that it is a part of their flesh—that the Great Spirit gave it to them expressly for their pipes, and it having been given to them all alike, the Great Spirit would be angry if they raised their weapons against their enemies going to or returning from the red pipe-stone quarry. The Great Spirit told them it was their own flesh, and must be used for no other purpose than the bowls of their pipes."

The Sioux, in whose country this quarry is, stopped and detained us several days, and made great resistance to our going there, asserting that no white people had been there, and that none were permitted to go, because it was a sacred place. They said they believed we were sent by the government to see what it was worth, so as to try to buy it from them, and they did not wish to sell it.

Assuring them, however, that we were but two private persons, who had only curiosity to see it, and that we would respect all their feelings, they permitted us to go and see it, provided twenty of their warriors could accompany us; probably to see that we committed no sacrilege about the place.

While at the pipe-stone quarry the Indians told us we were within twenty miles of the "thunder's nest!"

"Thunder's nest! Why, what on earth is that?"

"Why," said one of the medicine men, "it is the place where the thunders are hatched out."

"The thunder comes out of an egg, then, does it?"

"Certainly."

"It must be a pretty large bird to lay such eggs?"

"No, it's very small."

"How large?"

"Why, about as large as the end of your little finger; most of the medicine men of the Sioux have seen it."

"Well," said my friend Mr. Wood, "we must go and see that by all means. I have heard a great deal about it, and I venture to say it must be something very curious to see."

Our interpreter and guide, a half-breed, told us that this strange place was on the highest ridge of the coteau, and the Indians believed that in the very hottest days, previous to the thunder-showers, the bird was sitting on her eggs, and when they hatched out it made the thunder. He told us that on our way to the thunder's nest he would take us a little to the west, and we would see the "stone man medicine."

"This," said he, "is a great curiosity—a place where every Indian who is going—"

"Never mind," said Mr. Wood, "don't tell us all about it; that will spoil it all; let's go and see it."

So we took an early start the next morning, on our way to the "thunder's nest" and the "stone man medicine."

We rode off at an early hour with three of the Indian party, and spent the day in looking at these wonderful places, the last of which we found on the top of a high and rounded bluff, covered with short grass, and from the top of which no tree or bush could be seen: all around was a mass of rolling and sloping hills of green stretching off to the horizon. On the top of this mound, which has, perhaps, a couple of acres of slightly rounded surface, lay the "stone man medicine." It was the figure, in tolerably good proportions, of a man lying on his back, his arms and his legs distended, of some three or four hundred feet in length, composed entirely of flat stones, which had been brought by Indians, probably through centuries, and deposited there; and, what was singular, I could not discover another stone the size of a pigeon's egg for several miles on either side of it.

Whatever led to the beginning of this strange monument no one knows; but the Indians tell us that no Indian going on a hunting excursion, or on a war-party in that direction, has any confidence in success unless he stops at the "stone man medicine" and adds a flat stone to the figure; no matter how far it be out of his way, or how far he has to carry the stone.

There is nothing of the character of a barrow in this strange mass, no one stone lying on the top of another, and the number may well be said to be countless; exhibiting, by size and different colors, the features of the face, and even the fingers and toes of a human figure.

Our Indian companions having each deposited their stone offering, and explained all they could to us, we started for the "thunders nest." This terrible-sounding mystery we reached after a hard ride, and found it, like the other, on the top of a high prairie mound, where we observed a small bunch of hazel bushes, thickly matted, and as high as a man's waist, occupying some two or three rods of ground.

The leader of our little party at this time was a very droll old fellow, called the Blue Medicine, extensively known to the officers of the United States army in the vicinity of the Falls of St. Anthony; and when we were ascending the side of the mound, and near to the wonderful place, the doctor requested us all to dismount and wait a little. The Indians took all the plumes out of their heads, and placing them under their robes, smoothed down their long glossy-black locks, and with their little looking-glasses took a squint at their own faces, to see if the paint was all right, and then, with their robes wrapt around them, and the doctor leading the way, all marched slowly towards the bunch of bushes, leading the horses by their halters.

Within some two or three rods of the bushes the Indians halted, and each one tossed a plug of tobacco into the grass, which, forward of us, showed no sign of human trespass; but, under our feet and behind us, seemed much trodden down by the frequency of passing visitors.

I gave the reins of my horse to my companion, and with my gun in both hands, as if to shoot upon the wing, I started to walk into the hallowed ground and see if I could put up the little bird; and hearing a deep groan behind me, I looked back, and seeing the poor Indians all with their hands over their mouths, and evidently in great distress, I retreated and came out without seeing anything excepting some hundreds of bits of tobacco, lying in the grass, that had been thrown by the poor superstitious children of the forest as sacrifices to the Spirit they there invoke—'The Thunder Spirit' in dread of whom they always live.

These are but two of the numerous shrines to which the poor Indians travel out of their way, and at which they throw their hard earnings as propitiatory offerings.

AT THE 'TRAVERSE DE SIOUX,' at the base of the coteau, Mr. Wood and myself left our horses, and seated ourselves again in our little canoe, and downstream (not downhill, but a little like it) we were wafted off, and oh how happy! For we could paddle when we pleased, or fish when we pleased, or alternately sleep when we pleased; or listen to the sounds of his 'dear little guitar,' accompanied with his rich tenor voice, which he told me had echoed for many years on the stage of the Italian Opera-house in London. And our canoe was still going on—on —on—as the hills resounded and echoed with 'Away to the Mountain's Brow,' etc.

Thus we descended the St. Peter's River, to its junction with the Mississippi at the Falls of St. Anthony, and then the mighty Mississippi again, as Corporal Allen and myself had descended it the summer before; spreading our robes upon the grass, and supplying our larder in the same manner; often bivouacking on the identical spots, and as often lifting our beautiful rock bass from the same eddies, and from under the same rocks.

The day before we reached the city of St. Louis, being fatigued with paddling nine hundred miles, and having a strong wind against us, we hailed a steamer descending the river, and with ourselves had our little canoe and its contents lifted on board.

I related to the captain my former misfortunes in losing my canoes at St. Louis, and told him I should take more care of this. He laughed at me heartily, and said, "You have been very unlucky, but you shall at least be sure of one." We arrived at St. Louis too late in the evening to remove my canoe, and in the morning I was saved the trouble; and on this occasion, with it had departed for ever a large package which I had left in the cabin, with my name on it, containing several very beautiful articles of Indian costumes, pipes, etc. For the loss of these things on his vessel I remonstrated with the captain, and severely so, for the parcel taken from the cabin of his steamer with my name on it. For this he laughed at me in the face again, and said, "Why, don't you know, sir, that if you leave a box or a parcel in any steam-boat on the Missouri or the Mississippi, with George Catlin marked on it, it is known at once by all the world to be filled with Indian curiosities, and that you will never see it again unless it goes ashore with you?"

This accounted for the losses I had met with on former occasions of boxes and parcels sent by steamers and other boats, from various remote places in the Indian countries, to St. Louis, containing one-third at least of all the Indian manufactures I ever procured, after I had purchased them at exorbitant prices; and oftentimes the poor Indians had stored them, and carried them over rivers, and transported them over long distances in safety for me. What a comment is this upon the glorious advantages of civilization!

But we are yet at the Falls of St. Anthony; the Indians are many around us, and their modes are curious, but much like what we have seen. The prairies are yet here, they are everywhere. Everything here is gloom; the country is everywhere steeping in smoke and ashes, and let us be off to something new; more fresh and more congenial. Where shall we go?

In the Rocky Mountains there are the funny little fellows, the Root Diggers, who burrow amongst the rocks, and live by digging roots and killing rabbits and pheasants with their short clubs (beng-twas), which they throw very dexterously; they have no guns and no horses, and therefore never venture out upon the plains, nor can the horsemen overtake or injure them amongst the rocks and crags in which they live.

Beyond them are the Banaks, the Kayuses, the Kayules, the Paunches, and the Snakes, on the Snake River; and below them, on the Columbia, the Flat Heads, who squeeze the heads of their very young infants between boards until an unnatural and distorted shape is given, and their eyes stand out like those of a rat caught in a deadfall.

I can show these, and the Nayas, who wear great round blocks of wood, several inches in diameter, passed through their under-lips 'to add to their good looks.' I can show you the terrible Apaches, with their long lances, and their lasso always in hand, before whom the Californian gold-diggers are constantly trembling; the Arapahos, the Navahos, and half-a-dozen other 'hos' living west of the Rocky Mountains. Shall we take a look at these? No, not at present. If we have space, we may take them on our way back; their countries are all prairies, and like those we have just seen, are probably, at this season, fuming in smoke and cinders.

I know of a country that is always fresh and green, that has no smokes, no fires, no winters; whose birds and insects always sing, and fruits and flowers are always growing.

America has two hemispheres; we have seen the wild people and their modes in the one, why not take a peep into the other? Allons!

XI

BUT STOP! WE ARE TRAVELING VERY FAST. There are yet the bold and daring Comanches, who hang on the sides of their horses on their fields of battle; the tall and manly Osages, with their shaved and crested red heads (like the Pawnees); the Konzas; the Pawnee-Picts (who, I have before said, build their wigwams of grass, in the shape of straw beehives); the Kiowas; the Wicos, and a dozen other o's and wa's in Western Texas.

And then the Senecas, the Oneidas, the Onondagos, the Mohawks, the Mohigans, the Delawares, the Potowatomies, the Kickapoos, the Kaskaskias, the Weeahs, the Peorias, the Shawanos, the Muskogees, the Chocktaws, the Cherokees, the Seminoles, and yet others, all of whom I have lived amongst, and of some of whom I must say a few words before we wander too far away from them.

In the spring of 1836, a regiment of mounted dragoons, under the command of Colonel Henry Dodge, was ordered to start from Fort Gibson, on the Arkansas River, seven hundred miles west of the Mississippi, on a visit to the Comanches, the Pawnee-Picts, and other wild tribes on the western borders of Texas, to make a first acquaintance with those tribes, and to put a stop to border difficulties, which were at that time becoming very alarming on those parts of the frontier.

This favourable opportunity of seeing those remote and hostile tribes I took advantage of, by obtaining from the Secretary-at-War the privilege of traveling under the protection of the regiment, with my faithful friend, Joseph Chadwick, of St. Louis, a young man who was strongly attached to me, and willing to give his time and risk his life for me, for the pleasure of shooting, and of seeing the Indians and their country.

Armed and equipped, Joe Chadwick and myself were on the spot, at Fort Gibson, and ready. We had proposed to travel and maintain ourselves quite independent of the regiment, only asking for their protection. We had, therefore, supplied ourselves with a mule to carry our packs and our culinary and other requisites, and with our own weapons and horses.

For this expedition I had purchased the finest horse then known in that section of the country, belonging to Colonel Birbank, an aged officer of the garrison at Fort Gibson, who had become a little afraid to ride him on parade, where he attracted the attention and admiration of all the officers; but by his flourishing gaiety and prancing, he had too much excited the nerves of his rider, who was willing to sell him for the price of two hundred and fifty dollars, which I gave for him.

"Charley" (the name he answered to) was an entire horse, a mustang, of cream color; his black tail sweeping the ground, and his black mane nearly so. He had been taken and broken by the Comanche Indians, who take great care never to break the spirit of those noble animals.

I rode and galloped Charley about, gradually beguiling him into the new relationship, for some weeks before the regiment was ready to commence the march; and my friend Joe, on his nimble, slender-legged little buffalo charger, which he had bought of an Indian hunter, was everywhere my companion.

Colonel Dodge had employed two famous Delaware Indians, semi-civilized, with several of other tribes, as hunters and guides for the regiment; and while resting in the encampment for the regiment to start, they amused Joe and me by the ingenious preparations they were making for their different modes of decoying and entrapping game.

Amongst these there was one that attracted our particular attention, a sort of whistle, made of the bark of a young sapling, of two or three inches in length, and which they carried in their pouch, by blowing in which they would precisely imitate the bleating 'ma!' of the young fawn; so that whenever they discovered a deer on the prairies at too great a distance to shoot, by sounding this, and lying secreted in the grass, they would invariably bring the deer up to them, led to their certain death by the natural sympathy which that animal has for the calls of the young, and the perfect imitation produced by that curious instrument.

Joe and I, from our impatience for the pleasures ahead of us, became exceedingly fatigued with the delay of the dragoons, and to shorten weary time, we resolved to shorten one day at least, by taking a day's amusement at deer-stalking on the Maple Ridge, a range of hills and heavy-timbered country, some eight or ten miles from the garrison, which was said to be full of deer and turkeys. So the next morning, at an early hour, we mounted our steeds and galloped off, rifles in hand and our luncheons in our pockets. Leaving our horses with a half-breed Indian who lived at the foot of these mountains, we entered and traversed these dark and solitary haunts, laying out and carrying out our numerous drives and meets, and other schemes for the accomplishment of our designs.

We drove, we approached, and we met, many times, and without success; we saw their white flags a number of times, but had got no shot, and about the middle of the day, having for a long time lost sight and knowledge of Joe, I came to the edge of a small prairie, and stepping a little into it, I heard the sudden bleating of a fawn, which was several times repeated 'ma—ma—ma!' From its direction I was sure the little creature was in the shade of a small copse of bushes farther in the prairie, and at too long a distance for a dead shot, so I dropped myself upon my knee in the grass, resolving to wait a while until it might come out.

I kept my eye fixed upon the place, and presently it called again, and I then began to creep slowly and carefully, on my hands and knees, towards the bushes, and getting near, it called again, and at last again; and believing that one or both of its parents was with it, I felt sure that I was going to get a shot.

I kept creeping on, but with greater and greater caution, until I got quite close to the copse, with my rifle cocked and drawn to my shoulder, when, to my inexpressible surprise, the poor little thing called out 'ma!' right behind me, and on turning my head slowly around, but without changing my position, I beheld, within ten feet of where I had passed, lying concealed in the grass, and heartily laughing at me, the two Delaware Indian hunters.

My hunting pretensions were a good deal cut down by this little occurrence, but I sat down with these good-natured fellows, and learning from them that there was not the slightest use in stalking at that hour, as "no game at that time of day was moving," we spent an hour or so in the shade, and I then entered the timber again. I often sounded my whistle for Joe, but heard nothing of him.

I travelled on and on, and saw no game; but descending a gently-sloping hill, through an open but dark and gloomy forest of large timber, I espied Joe sitting on a large log, with his back towards me and his rifle standing by his side, while he was engaged eating his lunch, which he had brought in his pocket.

As I had had my shock, and there seemed little chance of getting any game, I thought jokes would be better than nothing; so I resolved on giving Joe a little shock. I started in a straight line towards him, and as slowly and cautiously as I could step, not to make a noise in the leaves to startle him, and thus advanced with my rifle in my left hand: and after creeping in this manner for some thirty or forty rods—gradually and carefully setting one foot and lifting the other, until I had got very near to him, and laughing at the jump he was to make if I could only get a step or two farther without his hearing me—which accomplished (as he was chewing away), I let my right hand fall upon his shoulder with a "BOOH!" at which instant came a heavy red paw on my own shoulder, with a "BOOH to you too!" Poor Joe! He made his leap near twenty feet, and I made mine nearly as far in a different direction. And in the very tracts that I had left, stood smiling at me, a huge Osage Indian, with his rifle in his left hand, and his right still remaining in the air where my shoulder had left it.

We all straightened up, and the good-natured expression of the Indian's face set us all right; but when he related to me, that, knowing my object, he had stepped his foot into every one of my tracts in the whole of that distance the instant that my foot was lifted out, I felt more ashamed of my hunting abilities than I ever had felt before in my life.

The Osage was a good-natured and harmless Indian, and spoke a little English, and having shared our lunch with him, and a little canteen of brandy which Joe had in his pocket, he related several of his hunting feats, which amused us very much.

I told him that notwithstanding my friend and myself had killed nothing that day, we had sometimes had better luck, and that we had hunted many days together. "One day last winter," said I, "when this young man and I were on a steamboat, going from the mouth of the Ohio to St. Louis, on the Mississippi, one of the wheels got broken and they stopped the boat at the shore, by the side of a great and dark forest of cotton-woods, and the captain told us it would take all day to mend the wheel.

"My friend here and I both had our rifles with us, and we went ashore into the woods to hunt; there was a fine tracking snow, about four or six inches deep, and there were a great many signs of deer. My friend and I separated after we got a little way into the woods, and took different directions. The day was very gloomy and dark, and after I had travelled a long distance without getting a shot, I fell into the track of a man who had just gone along ahead of me, with a large dog following him: 'That can't be my friend Joe? No; he had no dog with him.' I followed on, and walked pretty fast, in order to overtake him.

"After a long walk I stopped, and brushing the snow from a large log, I sat down, but the forest being so dense, and the day so thick, I began to think I had missed my bearing and was lost. I then started on again, resolved to overtake the person on whose track I was following, who could, probably, put me on the right course.

"After walking a long distance farther, and following the track, I at length found another man's track coming into it. 'That's Joe! Very likely; he is lost perhaps, and he is following that man with the dog, as I am; I'll push on and overtake him. But stop; this can't be my friend Joe, for he has got a dog also. Never mind, I'll push on and overtake him, for I know I am lost and going wrong.' I continued on, and at length came to a large log where the snow was brushed off. 'The man has been sitting down! Yes; and this is the very log I brushed the snow from and sat upon half-an-hour since! It can't be—it must be—and that is my own track! I am lost!—I am walking in a circle! But that dog? He steps in my track—he is stalking me! I have no dog! A panther's track is like a dog's!' I was at this moment sitting upon the log, and had leaned my rifle against it by the side of me. I took it deliberately into my hands and cocked it, to lose no time if there should be need for it behind me; and rising slowly, and looking back on my back track, at the distance of some six or eight rods I discovered the head of a huge panther raised over the top of a log, as he rested his fore-paws upon it, and was staring me in the face, without winking or moving a muscle!

"One of my old, boyish 'shivers' began to rise as I was raising my rifle to my shoulder; 'But,' said I, 'that won't do—it won't do to miss this time.' And by the time I had got my barrel levelled, my nerves were perfectly steady, and the little black wrinkle between the gentleman's eyes so snugly took the bead, that when he fell behind the log, I just walked up as confidently as I would have walked up to a target, knowing exactly where the bullet had gone. This fellow made no more tracks.

"With his heels tied together, and slung on my back, I was able to walk under his weight, heavy as it was; and hearing the carpenter's blows on the boat at this time, I was enabled to lay my course to it. I met Joe near the boat, coming in with a saddle of venison on his back, and he told me he had dressed and hung up two more, for which he was just sending two men from the boat, on his back track, to bring in.

"My panther was laid upon the deck of the steamer, and its length, from the end of the nose to the end of its tail, was measured, and found to be nearly nine feet. Both Joe and I were complimented by the officers of the boat, and also by the passengers, for our day's work."

My story pleased the good-natured Osage Indian very much, and we shook hands and parted. Joe and I got back to our horses, and galloped home. So ended that day of our amusements.

The dragoons were at length on their march, stringing off over the prairies and through the timber two by two, their usual mode of marching; and Joe and I, with our little pack horse, were hanging on one or the other wing, and so encamping at night; our buffalo robes spread upon the grass, our saddles for our pillows, and our horses picketed by our heads.

After a week or two of days and nights thus passed, we had forded the Little Blue, and swam the 'Canadian,' and were now creeping along on the dividing ridge between the Canadian and the Red River, and near to their sources. Bands of wild horses were running from us, and from herds of buffaloes the rifles of our Delaware hunters were supplying us with a daily abundance of fresh meat.

While moving on and on in this manner, from day to day, Joe and I espied one day, at too great a distance to the right to be frightened by the dragoons, a band of wild horses grazing, and placing our pack-mule in the leading of one of the soldiers, we galloped off towards them for a nearer reconnaissance. On nearing them we discovered a ravine, near the banks of which they were grazing, and throwing ourselves into this, we rode till we supposed we were near their vicinity, and dismounting, we fastened our horses to some alder bushes, and commenced our ambuscade march on foot. We successfully approached behind some tufts of hazel bushes on the brink of the ravine, to within a fair rifle-shot of them without being discovered, notwithstanding their exceeding shyness.

I had always in my pocket a powerful opera-glass, which gave us, as we lay concealed, a perfect view of them, displaying all their blemishes and all their beauty. There were perhaps some two or three hundred in the group, and, like a kennel of hounds, of all colors, from jet and glossy black to snow white. Some were chestnut, some were iron, and others silver, grey; others were pied and spotted and striped, with two, and sometimes three, different colors intermingled. Their tails generally dragged on the grass, and their long and shaggy manes, which seemed generally to cover their eyes, fell from both sides of the neck, and oftentimes were under their feet, and dragged on the grass as they were feeding.

Poor Joe and I saw no way of encompassing or appropriating this noble and beautiful stud; nor had we approached them with the least mercenary view; but a thought instantly suggested itself. We both had heard of the mode which the Spaniards and other frontier hunters often use, who cannot take them in the usual way with the lasso, that of 'creasing' them, which is done by shooting them with a rifle through the fleshy (or rather gristly) part of the neck, on the top of the shoulders, by which the animal is stunned for the moment, and falls; and the hunter having advanced and fastened the halter upon it, and hobbled its feet together, it rises again, to be subjugated by its cruel master. "Let's crease one!" whispered Joe. "Well ..." said I. But here was a difficulty again: to travel light and handy, both Joe and I had left our heavy rifles at Fort Gibson, and armed ourselves with light and short single-barreled fowling-pieces, as better adapted for our daily support, by throwing shot as well as ball, and being more easily carried and reloaded on horseback than our rifles.

There was no certainty of sufficient accuracy with them, at that distance, for creasing, but we resolved to try; and one of the handsomest and noblest of the troop, a beautiful silver grey, turning himself round to a fair broadside, I fired, and he tumbled down, as the herd were off, as if by a blast of wind. "Beautiful! beautiful!" said Joe, as we arose and approached the animal, to find, as we did to our horror and shame, that the ball had fallen from my aim, and passed through the animal's heart! Poor Joe! His heart was too tender and too noble to stand this; he was younger than I, and had more tears to shed, and he wept bitterly over the fate of this noble creature, which we did not mean to injure, and leave for the wolves to eat. We had the best of reasons for keeping this adventure a profound secret, and it was never known to any of the regiment.

Joe and I were soon remounted, and alongside of the dragoons again; and though in our long, long travels over the prairies and through the oak openings we had many a fine chance for a rifle-shot, our light little fowling-pieces, which were easy to handle and deadly in the chase from our horses' backs, were but a poor reliance, and it became a motto in such cases, "Crease him, Joe," or "Crease him, Cat."

About this time began to be heard through the regiment, "Indians! Indians! Indians about!"

Their signs were fresh; and at last their waving plumes and the glistening blades of their long lances began to be seen, now and then dodging about over the tops of the grassy hills, announcing to us that we were under the gaze and reconnoitering of a war-party of Comanches.

Most of the men in the command, and probably many of the officers, never had seen an Indian, and were now undergoing something like the pulsations and vibrations which a certain little boy once underwent at an Old Sawmill lick.

THE COMANCHES—ONE OF THE MOST POWERFUL AND WARLIKE TRIBES IN AMERICA, and undoubtedly the most bold and efficient warriors on horseback, and heretofore considered hostile to the whites— were now hovering around us, and their villages, evidently not a great distance ahead of us. For several days' march, and as many uneasy nights of bivouac, these hordes of mounted horsemen were gathering around us; and during the daytime, constantly more or less in full view, in squads of flying cavalry, in front and in rear of us, reconnoitering us at a distance, and disappearing over the hills as we approached them. With ray-glass, which brought them nearer to me than they thought for, they were beautiful to behold; the fierce and manly expression of their faces, the grace and elegance of their movements, and the fierceness and elasticity of their horses, were altogether one of the most beautiful sights I ever beheld.

We kept moving on, and bivouacking in the nights in the open prairies, the companies forming into hollow squares, the men laying their knapsacks and saddles on the ground, close by the side of each other, for their pillows, with their horses picketed inside the square, and each within its owner's reach, in case of a sudden surprise.

A picket, in that country, is a small stake of iron or of wood, made to be driven into the ground, to which the horse is fastened, and is generally carried during the day attached to the saddle or crupper, to be always ready when the encampment is to be formed.

'Stampado'—Did you ever hear of a *stampado*, my readers? No; well, then, we'll have it. *Stampado* is a Spanish word, meaning 'a trampling,' or (what is much the same, and perhaps more intelligible), a tremendous scrambling and scampering, when a party of some hundreds of bold and furious Indian warriors, mounted on their darting war-horses, with brandishing lances and war-clubs in hand, in the stillness and darkness of midnight, when wearied soldiers and their horses are fast asleep, dash at full speed, like a flash of lightning with the thunder following, into and through an encampment, mingling the frightful war-whoop with the unearthly sound (not unlike theatre thunder) of their parchment robes shaken in the hands to frighten the horses.

The instant flash of a few guns begins the frightful melee, and in the confused escampette, the affrighted horses, en masse, dash against and over each other and their owners, and are off like a whirlwind upon the prairies at the highest speed, with their enemies behind them; leaving the scientific warriors with broken arms, with broken legs, and broken guns, upon their hands and knees, gazing through the dark in vain for some moving object to draw a bead upon.

Such is a *stampado*. It is like a tornado that's passed on. And where is it?—did it stop?—is it coming back? No. No scalp was taken, and none was looked for; none was wanted or thought of;— horses were wanted; and where are they? Why, twenty miles off— run and pressed to the last breath, and by the daylight next morning an easy prey, and a play spell for the Comanches' lassos before breakfast.

A stampado had been apprehended and feared for several nights past, from the surrounding appearances—as we learn from the dark and gathering clouds and their electricity that a storm is gathering and preparing to break forth. All were talking of stampados, all preparing for them, and every precaution in the regiment was made for the event. Every man slept with his rifle in his arms, and his horse picketed within his reach; and poor Joe and I, notwithstanding we were invited to sleep in the officers' quarters, in the center, preferred spreading our robes, and laying our own saddles a little outside of all, and on the uphill side, for reasons which the world will never guess.

These were trying times for Joe and me, for I knew that the Comanches were thirty thousand, and had at least ten thousand of the most desperate mounted warriors in the world; and we resolved whatever deaths we might die, not to be trampled to death, nor to lose our horses if we could help it. We therefore drove their pickets close to our heads, and hobbled them at the same time, and took the precaution while on dangerous ground, to spell each other in our sleeps during the night—one sitting straight up and awake, whilst the other was taking his nap.

My lorgnette was a pretty good night-glass, and we doubtless had, therefore, a better sort of clairvoyance of the vicinity of the bivouac than anybody else in it.

About midnight, on one starlight night, a few days after the Indians had ceased to show themselves on the hill-tops, and the whole caravan, excepting my friend Joe and I, had begun to think they had left the vicinity, and therefore to relax a little in their nocturnal discipline; Joe happened to be ogling with the spy-glass, and I was fast asleep—when flash and *BANG!* went a gun, close by a little bunch of hazel bushes, within a few rods of where we were lying, and where a sentinel had been walking his rounds, instantly followed by a struggling and rustling in the bushes, from which came a deep and frightful groan! And in the camp, oh, awful! The snapping of cords, the trampling of hoofs, the sounds of grunting, of groaning! Now and then the flash of a gun, but no war-whoops nor rattling of parchment skins, only a vanishing of steeds, that carried terror and confusion as they fled and disappeared, with their elevated tails and manes, like a fleet (but swifter) under full sail disappearing in a mist!

In the camp all were *à genou*, or 'lying close,' cocked and ready, or groaning with their wounds. When I awoke, my friend Joe had Charley's halter in one hand, and that of his little charger in the other. Charley stood, when I arose, with his mane and his tail spread—a picture in himself to look at; his eyeballs glaring and his nostrils raised, as he was trembling and alternately glancing his eyes over the flying mass, and turning his head to smell my breath, to know if I was frightened. A moment of silence ensued, and then said Joe, "Here, Cat, hold my horse; it's that fool of a fellow yonder who has done all this—he has shot a poor horse there, in the bushes." Saying this, Joe walked into the camp amidst pointing and aimed rifles and fixed bayonets, exclaiming, "Don't shoot! Don't shoot me! There are no Indians!"

Poor Joe, at some risk of his life notwithstanding, succeeded in arriving at the officers' quarters, where a sort of council of war was held, and Joe made his report, to wit, that a sorrel horse, belonging to the commissariat, had got loose, and after he had observed the poor creature feeding about for some time, it presented its head and breast out of a little bunch of hazel bushes near to one of the sentinels, who took it, of course, for a Comanche Indian, and after not learning 'Who's there?' and getting no countersign, blazed away and shot the poor brute through the heart.

The sentinel was put under arrest, and also three or four others, whose guns had gone off accidentally or otherwise in the melee, and also Corporal Nugent, who fired at Lieut. Hunter and missed him, as he was holding on to his horse, because he wore a fur cap, and was mistaken for a Comanche Indian.

Joe and I soon after, and our horses, went to sleep, and the rest of the caravan, excepting those whose wounds were being dressed during the rest of the night by the surgeons and their assistants. Here, of course, a halt for some days was ordered, and it lasted for some weeks, as well as I can remember, and that from necessity; for the horses, though not all gone, were so reduced in numbers that they must be recovered or replaced before the regiment could proceed.

The poor affrighted creatures had taken the direction of their back track in their flight. Some were retaken within twenty miles, some within fifty miles, some were never taken; and a great many were brought in by the Indians, taken with the lasso, and carefully and most honestly brought to the camp, and delivered to their owners, by the very people whom we had been sleeping, and even marching, in dread of, and who knew by the flight of our horses what had taken place, and that we stood in need of friendly assistance.

XII

THE READER CAN EASILY IMAGINE, from the close of the last chapter, that there was little difficulty in making acquaintance with the Comanches after this; for it was soon learned that there was a mutual good feeling, and a wish on both sides to 'shake hands,' which was done in a few days, with two or three of the secondary chiefs who were sent out to meet us with a hundred or more of their most beautiful and celebrated warriors, all mounted on fine horses, and fully equipped and painted for war. As they came galloping and dashing up, with their long lances in hand, and their beautiful white shields on their arms, they presented one of the most thrilling and exciting scenes that I ever beheld.

After a general shake of the hand with the officers, they invited us to the great Comanche village, some three or four days' march, to which they conducted us, and showed us daily, as we passed along, their astonishing feats in slaying the buffaloes, by which they furnished the regiment with daily food; and, in the meantime, they gave also to the officers and men, what they never before had seen, an exhibition of their powers of taking and breaking the wild horse.

Arrived on the summit of a hill, overlooking an extensive and beautiful valley, they requested the regiment to halt, and pointing, showed us the great Comanche village, at the distance of three or four miles, with eight or ten thousand horses and mules grazing on the plains around it. They then led us into the valley, and at the distance of a mile or so from the village, requested us to halt again, for the chief and the cavalry of the tribe were coming out to meet and welcome us.

Colonel Dodge formed his regiment in three columns, himself occupying the front, with his staff; and after resting an hour or so in that position, two or three thousand horsemen were seen, in real military order, advancing towards us. The chief was in advance, with his bodyguard around him, and his colors flying on each side—the one a white flag, a flag of truce, and the other blood red; showing that he was ready for either war or peace, whichever we might propose.

The white flag was seen waving in the hands of each of our ensigns, and the red flag was lost sight of. The chief now advanced, shook hands with Colonel Dodge and the rest of the officers, and then formed his army in a double column of nearly a mile in length, dressed and maneuvered with a precision equal to any cavalry maneuver I ever saw, himself and his staff taking their position in the center, and facing the officers of the dragoons.

After an exchange of friendly feelings between Colonel Dodge and the chief, the whole Indian force passed in review, each one extending his hand to Colonel Dodge, and then to all the other officers as he passed.

The chief then indicated a suitable spot for our encampment, and we were soon settled for a residence of two weeks, which afforded the writer of this and his faithful friend, Joe Chadwick, amusement enough, and plenty to do, in studying their manners and customs, in a beautiful village of twelve hundred skin tents, on the banks of a clear stream.

Here was material enough for the remainder of this book—horse-racing, ball-playing, dancing, buying and selling horses, councils, etc., but we must go on.

Everlasting peace and commerce with the United States was agreed on, and the pipe of peace was smoked, and we went to the Pawnee-Picts, their allies, eighty miles farther on, where I have said their wigwams were made in the form of straw beehives, and thatched with long grass. Peace was made with them also, and the officers were embraced in the arms of the venerable chief Wee-tar-ra-sha-ro. We saw also the Kiowas, the Wicos, and the Arapahos; all were friendly, and peace with all was easy, and was established, as with the Comanches, "to last forever." The mission of the dragoons was accomplished, and also the far more important designs of the author; for under the treaty of friendship and commerce came rum, and whisky, and a thousand abuses, the consequences of which were, that in one year after, the whole ground that we travelled over in peace and friendship became hostile ground, and has remained so ever since; whilst the works that I did have not faded or changed, but remain as fresh as the day they were made.

Back to Fort Gibson was a long and yet an interesting journey, but its incidents need not be recounted here— sufficit, that Charley was as fat and sleek on our return as he was when we started, though I had rode him more than two thousand miles; and our familiarity and mutual attachment, from a great variety of circumstances, had grown to a perfection which but few horses or few men have felt, or could probably fully understand.

I at this time was taken extremely ill with bilious fever, and went to bed, and Charley went to pasture in a large field overgrown with white clover and other delectables.

During my illness of two months, and until I was in a convalescent state, my ever faithful friend and companion, Joe, was constantly by me, and afterwards left for the Mississippi, where his business called him. Charley I could not see during this siege of two months; but I heard reports of him often, and learned that he was doing well, and that he had got so wild and so independent that no one could get near him.

I was anxious to take Charley to St. Louis, but to send him down the Arkansas seven hundred miles, and then up the Mississippi nine hundred, by steamer, would be a heavy expense, and I resolved that just as soon as I should be able to ride, Charley and I would start for St. Louis by a shorter route, by crossing the intervening country of prairies, which are entirely wild and without roads, a distance, in a straight line, of five hundred and forty miles.

I knew the point of compass, and with a little compass in my pocket, and a clear sky, and plenty of ammunition, I felt no apprehensions whatever for the result. So one morning in the beginning of September, feeling sufficiently strong to mount Charley with a little aid, and having prepared my little outfit, I sent for Charley to be brought up and saddled; but the answer was soon brought back, that "Charley couldn't be caught, and that no one could get near him."

An old schoolmate of mine, from the Valley of Wyoming, Dr. Wright, then surgeon of the port, and who had attended me through my illness, started with me to the field where Charley was busily grazing, and on entering the field I called "Charley!" at which the noble animal, evidently recognizing my voice after two months' separation, raised his head, and also his beautiful black tail and mane, and with his mouth full of grass, which he forgot to chew, instantly replied with a "eegh-ee-e-hee!" and started walking towards me, and soon increasing his pace to a trot, and then to a gallop, came up to me with another "eegh-ee-e-hee!" etc., and with the grass still hanging out of his mouth, commenced smelling my breath, which had always seemed a pleasure to him, and held his head down, and opened his mouth for the bridle which I put upon him, and with which I led him to my quarters.

In half-an-hours' time, with a couple of buffalo robes for my bed, a small coffee-pot and a tin cup tied to my saddle, with plenty of ground coffee and sugar, and about the half of a boiled ham, and some salt, my pistols in my belt, and my fowling-piece in my hand, I was ready to mount Charley and be off; but here were the Cherokee, the Choctaw, and the Creek (Muskogee) chiefs assembled to take leave of me. What have I told you of them? Nothing.

The Cherokees, of 25,000; the Creeks, of 21,000; the Choctaws, of 15,000; and the Seminoles of 12,000; are located in this vicinity, 700 miles west of the Mississippi, and 1200, and 1400, and 1800 miles from their former localities in the States of Georgia, Alabama, and Florida. These people are semi-civilized—in their own countries many of them were owning large plantations, and were raising extensive fields of cotton and corn, and lived in comfortable houses, built school-houses and churches, and printed and published several newspapers in their own language and English. But how came they here, in this wild and desert region? There's medicine in this. No, not at all; all is easily explained, but is too long to be detailed in this place.

These people owned and occupied vast tracts of the best cotton-lands in Georgia and Alabama, and were therefore rich. "These lands were too valuable for Indians to possess, and the Indians were bad neighbors." General Jackson was elected President at that time; he decided that all the Indian tribes should be removed west of the Mississippi, and it was done. It took a long time, and was cruel; they were forced to leave the graves of their parents and their children, and their houses and lands, and their crops growing in their fields, for a country given to them here, with a boundary line on the east, and the north, and the south, but none at the west; meaning, that they must not trespass on their white neighbors on the east, but that they might, with their rifles, destroy as many of the buffaloes and wild Indians to the west of them as they pleased.

With the Seminoles in Florida, the process of moving them was a very disastrous one on both sides. The draft of a treaty for the chiefs to sign, by which they were to agree to exchange their lands for a country west of the Mississippi, was laid before the chiefs in council, who all refused to sign it, assigning as their reason that their parents and their children were buried around them, and that the country was their own, given to them by the Great Spirit, and that they would therefore never remove from it.

The treaty was several times urged upon them without success; but it being announced to the eleven subordinate chiefs one day, that Charley Omatla, the head chief, had agreed to sign the treaty the next day—which they could not believe—they all assembled, and went to the Government agent's office, where it was to be done, with their rifles in their hands, to see if their chief was going to do so treacherous an act. With these chiefs came Osceola, whose name you all have probably heard; he was not a chief, but a desperate warrior, and of great influence in the tribe. The treaty was spread upon the table, and Charley Omatla, according to his promise, supposing the other chiefs would follow him, stepped forward, and leaning over the table, made his signature to the treaty, and as he was rising up from the table, the bullet from Osceola's rifle, and then six others from the chiefs, were through his body before it was to the ground, where he fell a corpse.

This treaty was sent by an express to Washington, "signed,"(!) to be ratified by the Senate (then in session) before the news of the manner of signing should reach there, a distance of 1800 miles, and no railroad or telegraph in those parts at that time. The treaty was ratified; and though it was subsequently proved on the floor of the Senate that the chief Charley Omatla had been bribed with 7000 dollars, still the tribe was removed by force under the treaty, as we shall see.

Osceola fled into the wilderness, the chiefs following him as their leader—for, by the custom of all American Indian tribes, he who kills the chief in his own tribe is, de facto, chief, as long as they allow him to live: if his act is approved, no one can object to his lead; and if it is not approved, he is at once destroyed.

One hundred United States troops were then sent into the forest to commence a war upon the Seminoles, and to move them, by force of arms, under the treaty. Major Dade, a very meritorious officer, had command of this invading force; and in a few days the news arrived that Dade and his whole force, with the exception of one man, had been destroyed by the Indians, who had lain in ambush, and gained an advantage by springing upon them before they could use their rifles; much in the manner of the Wyoming Massacre mentioned earlier.

This was echoed through all the newspapers in the United States, and of course across the Atlantic, as a 'horrid massacre,' and so was every successive battle for six years afterwards when the Indians had the best of the fight; and whenever, by an equal or more cunning stratagem, a number of the Indians were killed, the announcements were headed 'glorious victory!'

The gallant Osceola, at the head of his Spartan band of warriors, retiring before some 10,000 disciplined troops, kept them at bay for six years, bravely disputing every foot of ground. He was at last captured, however (or rather kidnapped), with four of his principal chiefs and 200 of his warriors, by a stratagem too disgraceful to have ever been practiced by an Indian tribe. They were called up by a flag of truce, and as Osceola advanced, with a white flag in reply in his own hand, and their weapons left behind them, they were encompassed by an order from the officer in command, and, pinioned and fastened on horses' backs, were made prisoners of war, and sent to Fort Moultrie, at Charleston in South Carolina.

Here, my readers, we have arrived at last to a definition of 'Treachery in Warfare.' This disgraceful act was condemned by every officer in the United States army, and it is probable that the shame and repentance of the one who was guilty of it, have sufficiently punished him for it. The Administration discountenanced the act, but the chiefs were too valuable a prize to be released, notwithstanding; and all were sent, as Prisoners of War, through the States, to the wilderness frontier, where we now find them.

Thus was broken the spirit of the Seminoles, and thus ended the Seminole war, after an expense to the Government of 32,000,000 of dollars, the lives of 28 officers and 600 soldiers, as many Indians, and 2000 innocent and defenseless men, women, and children, living exposed on the borders of their country, whose lives are always known to be imperiled when an Indian war is waging in their vicinity.

From the city of New York to Charleston, a distance of 1500 miles, I travelled with my canvas and brushes to paint the portrait of this extraordinary man, Osceola. Though a humble prisoner in the fort, I found him an easy, affable, and pleasant man, but broken-hearted. He was a half-caste, and spoke English enough to describe to me many of the interesting events of the war, and the shameful manner in which he had been entrapped. I painted his portrait full length, and also those of Mic-e-no-pa, Co-a-ha-jo, Cloud, and King Phillip, the four chiefs captured with him.

There were at Fort Moultrie at this time 250 men, women, and children, who were taken with Osceola, and all held as prisoners of war.

One of the young men of this party, and one of the handsomest men I ever saw, was one morning accused by a white man, a producer of poultry and vegetables, living in the vicinity of the fort, of having stolen a chicken from him the night before. The complaint was laid before the chiefs, who took cognizance of it, hearing the proofs advanced by the accusing party, which he made out to be very conclusive, while the young man accused had no evidence to give, only asking the chiefs, "Did any Seminole ever know Chee-ho-ka to steal?" However, the white man's evidence was so strong that he was convicted, and the sentence of the chiefs, though prisoners of war (they being partly civilized), was, by the custom of their country, that he should be publicly whipped the next morning at nine o'clock. At seven o'clock, however, the next morning, his body was found suspended from a spike in the side of the wall of the fort, by a thong of raw hide, with a noose around his neck, and quite dead. And a little time after, while the officers of the garrison and the Indians were in a group around him, the fiend came up who had sworn against him, with the chicken under his arm, and alive, and confessed that it had not been stolen!

This wretch was standing right by my side at the moment, and from an impulse quicker than thought, I seized him with both hands by the throat with an iron grip, that I never was capable of before or since; and lynching, without waiting, must have been expressed in my face, for several of the officers stepped forward and begged me to use no violence; and what had ten times more effect, the soft and delicate hand of Osceola was laid lightly on my shoulder, when he whispered, "Don't, don't, my friend, don't hurt him; don't strike a dog!" I let the monster go, and the women and children hooted and hissed him out of the fort, and gave him his chicken to carry home.

After these events I returned to New York, and to my great surprise on my arrival in that city, I learned that Osceola was dead. The news, by express, had passed me on the road. He died the next day after I left the fort, and his disease was announced as a sudden attack of the quinsey.

BUT THIS IS AN AWFUL LONG TIME TO KEEP POOR CHARLEY waiting under the saddle, for, like myself, when he was ready, he was always impatient to be off. Well, I took leave of my old friend, Dr. Wright, the officers of the post, and the chiefs who, I said, had gathered to bid me good-bye. These good-byes were forever, and therefore were sorrowful—but my farewell to the country was quite the reverse—for the officers and men of the garrison were dying at the rate of six or eight per day, and of the Indian tribes in the vicinity almost an equal proportion, from a deadly fever raging at the time.

Charley and I mounted the grassy hills back of the fort, and soon disappeared. The country for five hundred and forty miles ahead of us (about twice the breadth of England), of hills and dales, of meadows and grassy plains, with brooks, and rivers, and oak openings, was vast, and apparently tedious; but as my departure from the deadly atmosphere of Fort Gibson was a sort of escape, and myself in a state of convalescence, with the bracing air of autumn around me, I entered upon it with a pleasure that few can appreciate who have seen and felt but the monotones of life.

Charley and I, though heretofore the best of friends, had always before had too much company with us to know how much we loved each other; we both required the solitary and mutual dependence we were now entering upon to fully develop the actual strength of sympathies that had long existed between us, and the extent to which such sympathies may be cultivated between an animal that works for an object, and another that labours without one.

There was another advantage we had that took much of the apparent hardships of our coming campaign from our shoulders; that arising from the fact that Charley and I were old campaigners together, and knew exactly how to go at our work. And there was yet another advantage that cheered the way very much. Twenty-five days is a long time to be entirely mum, without the power of speaking to any one, or hearing the cheering sound of any one's voice; and from a long familiarity and practice, Charley and I had established a sort of language which was at times very significant—at all events better than none—and therefore very cheering in breaking the awful monotony of a solitary campaign on the prairies. As, for instance, when I went to the field to catch Charley, as I have before mentioned, after a separation of two months, when I said, "Charley, is that you?" he instantly replied, "Eegh-ee-e-eh" (yes); here was an affirmative, distinctly; some might call this gibberish, but still it had its meaning; and if he sometimes used it in a wrong sense, he was nevertheless sure to be right, provided I put him the right sort of questions; and certainly he had one agreeable peculiarity which by no means belongs to all traveling companions in those desert countries, that of answering immediately either night or day, to any question I put him. But we shall see.

I said we had set off; we were now wending our way over the prairie hills and knolls, crossing beautiful green fields, passing through forests of timber, leaping and wading brooks, and, when night overtook us, bivouacking in the grass. By the sun, while it shone, we easily kept our course; and when it was obscure, our little pocket compass showed it to us.

I was feeble, having just risen from a bed of sickness, but meeting a cool and bracing autumnal wind, I was every hour gaining strength, though I had every alternate day an ague chill and fever, and for these, as I felt them coming on, I dismounted from Charley, and lay in the grass until they were over.

Charley profited by these halts, as his saddle and packs were taken off, and he had an hour or two to luxuriate on the prairie grass, of which he was very fond. He got a good roll or two in the grass in the meantime, which seemed to be a great luxury to him; and these rolls he took a peculiar pleasure in performing as near to me as he could without rolling on to me. The shake and the fever, the bait and the roll all over, and Charley saddled again, we would start on our course.

Carrying one of my barrels always charged with shot, ready for grouse or other small game, and the other with ball, our larder was easily supplied from day to day with fresh food without the trouble of dismounting, except to tie it to my saddle for my supper and breakfast where I encamped. Grouse were many times a day rising under Charley's feet, and now and then a fine fat doe was gazing at us, little thinking that in five minutes the choicest part of her rump-steaks would be suspended from Charley's saddle-strings.

With the exception of one night in the twenty-five I managed to bivouac on the bank of some little stream or river, where there was water to make my coffee, and wood to make a fire. We generally halted a little before sundown, so as to give Charley abundance of time to get his supper before I took him up; that is, before I took up his picket and brought him in. The moment his saddle was off I drove down his picket where the grass was plenty and fresh, and gave him the full length of his lasso to feed around.

I would then gather my wood and make my fire; and that well going, I would dress my prairie hen or prepare my venison steak, erecting them on little sharpened stakes before my fire, and get my coffeepot on the coals, and spread out all my little traps, such as a tin cup, a bowie-knife, an iron spoon, a little sack of salt, some sugar, and a slice or two of cold ham.

I was in the habit (and this was a habit of long standing with Charley and me) of leaving my little bivouac just at such times and going to Charley with a little treat of salt, of which he was very fond, and which he no doubt took with an additional relish from the fact that I always stood by him, while he licked it out of my hand. This might perhaps have been one of the causes of Charley's affectionate attachment to me; and on this occasion I had taken care to lay in enough to keep up friendly feelings between us during our campaign, Charley was in the habit, also, of receiving this little attention at that particular time when his meal was about half enjoyed and mine about ready; and he had learned the time so well, that if I was not ready at the moment, his head was up and his tail spread out like that of a turkey-cock, while he would stand gazing at me. I did not ask him on these occasions what he wanted, for he might have been perplexed to answer emphatically, but I would say to him, "Charley! Do you want your salt?"

"Eegh-ee-e-eh!" (yes).

He never failed to answer me in the affirmative on these occasions, and I never failed to carry it to him.

After finishing my supper, and just at dark, having brought in and driven his picket close by the side of me, I was in the habit of spreading one of my robes upon the grass, and using my saddle for a pillow, with the other robe drawn over me, head and all; thus sleeping soundly and comfortably until daylight, when Charley became restive; getting up and moving his picket, I generally got another good nap of an hour or so before rising for the day. Fire built, breakfast eaten, and Charley saddled, we were jogging along again.

In one instance we crossed a large prairie of many miles in extent, without a tree or a bush in sight, all the way covered with a short grass of some six or eight inches high, and the country all around us, when we were in the middle of it, perfectly level, and the horizon a perfect straight line, "out of sight of land," as it is termed in those regions. Night overtook us in the midst of this, and we were obliged to bivouac without water, but not without fire. We had no coffee, of course, that night; but a venison steak I cooked very nicely with a fire which I made of dried buffalo dung, which I gathered on the prairie.

I was awoke in the middle of the night by thunder and lightning approaching in a terrible thunderstorm. I got up and drove Charley's picket doubly strong, and folding up my nether robe to keep it dry, and laying it on the saddle, I took my seat upon it, and spread the other one over my head; it falling to the ground all around me in the form of a tent, sheltered me and all my things perfectly from the rain. The rain fell in torrents, and the flashes of lightning seemed to run like fiery snakes over the surface of the prairie, as if they were hunting for something to strike; and I feared at every flash that Charley and I might be snapped up for that purpose.

The rain continued until morning, and I got some sleep, but not of the most satisfactory kind, as I was obliged to keep my upright position all night.

The monotony of these broad and level prairies sometimes became exceedingly tedious, and even doleful. I repeatedly fell asleep while riding, and waking, I always found Charley not only going along, but keeping on the course. Sometimes for hours together, creeping along, without a moving bird or beast in sight, while both were in deep thought and contemplation, I have said, "Charley! A penny for your thoughts."

"Eegh-ee-e-eh!" Charley would reply; both bracing up our nerves, and evidently moved along with a new life, and consequently increased speed.

One day, while we were thus jogging along, each one wrapped up in his own thoughts, suddenly sprang up from his lair, right before us, and within eight or ten rods, a stately buck, with a pair of horns that looked as if he had a great chair on his head! Charley raised his head suddenly and stopped, and was gazing at him, while I was getting my left barrel to bear upon him, and he was trembling so from fear or anxiety, that I had difficulty in getting my aim. When I fired the deer staggered back a little, but recovered, and bounded off, but without "showing his flag," by which I knew I had struck him right. A few rods took him over the top of a little hill, and he was out of our sight. I pushed Charley up to the spot where he had stood, and I saw a profusion of blood on the grass, showing me that all was right. While I sat reloading, Charley had his nose to the ground surveying the bed where the animal had been lying, and also smelling of the blood upon the grass.

I then guided Charley along on the track, which I could easily follow by the traces of blood. Getting over the hill, the deer had gone into a meadow of high grass which came quite to the top of Charley's back. We entered the high grass on the animal's track, and observing the extraordinary excitement that Charley was under, which I could feel by his motions as well as see, and observing also his disposition to trace the deer, I had curiosity to slacken the rein and let him take his course. He went on in an unnaturally fast walk, snuffing and smelling along at the blood, keeping the exact track as precisely as a hound would have done, and so followed it for half-a-mile or more; and finally breaking out of the high grass at the foot of a small hill, he suddenly turned his elevated head to the left, and his ears pointing forwards, exclaimed, "Eegh-ee-e-eh!" (here he is, evidently); for I looked in the direction, and at twenty or thirty rods from us, on the side of the hill, lay our noble buck, with his frightful horns, quite dead!

I never straightened the rein even then; but Charley started upon a trot, with his head and tail up (oh, I wish I had a picture of him!), and brought me within a few paces, and stopped. I then pushed him up, and he smelled of the animal's nose and the bleeding wound. "Are you sorry," said I, "Charley?"

"Eegh-ee-e-eh."(yes).

"Oh, no," said I. "Charley, you are not. I put the question wrong; didn't I, Charley?"

"Eegh-ee-e-eh."

"That's right." I dismounted, and Charley looked on while I cut out a nice steak, and looked and smelled back at me as I was tying it to his saddle, and knew, no doubt, as well as I knew, that he was going to carry it, and that I was to cook it for my supper.

The almost incredible attachment of this noble animal, and the rest of the curious incidents of this journey from Fort Gibson to St. Louis, enough for a book of themselves, have been written, and must be omitted in this place.

The greatest difficulty Charley and I had apprehended on our route was the Osage River, which it was absolutely necessary to cross. We came to it— it was half-a-mile wide, its banks full with a freshet, and its muddy and boiling current pouring along at the rate of five or six miles an hour. Here poor Charley and I both looked chapfallen—give it up we can't, we cannot go round it, and cross it we must.

I got Charley's packs off, and put him out to graze with his picket, and then, laying down my gun, I followed up the river-shore for full a mile, picking up driftwood that I could find near it, and laying these at the water's edge. Having gathered enough in that way to form a raft sufficiently large to carry my saddle and other things dry above the water, I began following the shore down; accumulating and floating these as I advanced along, and getting them all together, I formed them into an awkward raft. I then took up Charley's picket, and leading him to the water's edge and taking off his lasso, I said, "Do you know what you have to do, Charley?"

"Eegh-ee-e-eh."

There was no mistake about this, as it was a thing he was used to.

I pointed to the other bank and drove him in, and off he started for the other shore. The current swept him down a considerable distance, but he got to the bank and out upon the prairie, and then he turned about and looked at me with a tremendous eegh-ee-e-eh! meaning this time, no doubt, "I am safe over, and I wish you the same." Charley then went to grazing, and I went to work, arranging my things on my raft; laying my saddle on it first, and then my robes, and my gun, and my clothes, which were all taken off.

I moved my raft into the stream, and swimming behind it, with one hand on it I propelled it, but very slowly, as the stream wafted us down. I labored steadily and hard, however, and was at length nearing the other shore, but with two alarming apprehensions: the dried logs and sticks with which my raft was constructed were many of them rotten, and, absorbing the water, were sinking so low as to bring some of my things into the river; and the shore where I was to land was lined with logs and tree-tops extending into the water.

But I had no alternative; "I must force it against them and hold it from pulling to pieces, and get myself, at all events, and, if possible, my things ashore." Some of the long timbers of my raft, as I had no axe to make them of equal lengths, caught in the limbs of a tree lying in the water, whirling it round, and thereby threatening to pull it to pieces, and throwing me out again quite into the stream. A second effort, however, brought me to a little better place for landing, and at length I got my feet upon the ground and my traps all safely landed.

I was then in front of a dense forest, and full a mile below where I had lost sight of Charley standing with his head and tail up, and watching me as I disappeared behind the point of timber. Getting my clothes on and all things ashore, and preparing to start through the woods for Charley, I was startled by a cracking noise in my rear, and as I turned round, "Eegh-ee-e-eh!" said Charley, as he was crowding through the thick weeds and nettles behind me.

I have said that Charley was a "noble animal," and that "he loved me." Was he a noble animal? And for what? Could I repay Charlie for such affection? I gave him a double ration. "Ration! Of what?" Of salt, of course.

XIII

NOW FOR THE FIELDS AND FORESTS OF EVERLASTING AND NEVER-ENDING GREEN, of all Nature's uninterrupted joy, of bloom, of gaiety, and song! Where dreary winter's blasts are not known, and leaves are dropping, and buds and flowers are growing at the same time! I have said that I knew such a place as this. Who has breathed the delicious air, seen the gaudy colors, and heard the sweet notes of this flower-garden, this music-hall, this aviary of the world—the grand and boundless valley of the Amazon—and who will not, if his life and his purse be long enough, go there and see it?

But we are not quite in it yet—Caracas is not in the valley of the Amazon, nor is it the beginning, exactly, of South America, but it is not a great way from it. It is in Venezuela, on a sandy, scorching coast. It was there that I first landed, and it is there we will begin.

From some unknown accident in the giant furnace that is burning underneath that region of country, a terrible shock and a shake were given in the beginning of this century, destroying ten thousand inhabitants; and, back of the town, and for a long distance on the coast, you may still see the frightful chasms which were opened at that time.

Natural things are on a large scale in the country now ahead of us. What is forged in the mighty furnace underneath us, and how long it has been worked, nobody knows. It formerly threw out its smoke and its cinders at the top of Chimborazo, only 19,000 feet high. Chimborazo (Tchimboratho) is 'laid up;' the chimney now at work is Cotopaxi, of equal height; its groanings and bellowings can be heard only 600 miles off! And a block of granite of 327 cubic feet it was able to project a distance of only nine miles!

THE ORINOCO IS A LARGE RIVER NOT FAR FROM US—the Amazon is much larger—larger than the Missouri, but not quite so long; at the head of tide water it is but thirty miles wide; it has but about 1500 islands, and the largest of them, occupied by individual nabobs, contain only 50,000 head of horses and cattle! Naval engineers who have surveyed the bed of the Amazon at the expense of the United States Government report that the Pennsylvania, a 140 gun-ship, built in Philadelphia, could go only as high as Tabatinga in low water; that is, only 1800 miles from its mouth! And ordinary passenger steamers could go only 1000 miles higher, without being liable to get aground, if the water was low! These distances are not very great! The valley of the Amazon is rather large; but it could not possibly hold with comfort more than the populations of England, France, Belgium, and the United States put together: for putting more than that number in might make some men's farms rather too small!

The precipitous wall of rock just back of the town of Caracas is only 6000 feet in height! And in the 'shakes' it "shook and shuddered so that the stones and trees were tumbling down from its reeling sides in all directions." Can one climb it? No. But by a hard day's work you may get to its summit by going a great way round. And then, where is the town and where the ocean? If the day is perfectly clear and sunny, you can see neither. If the weather is thick and overcast, you may see a little strip of white sand and some little red patches at your feet, if you can venture near enough to the brink; but the sky and the ocean are one, and you can't divorce them; and on the top—the cloud-capped summit—what's here? Here is a pebble! A sea-shore pebble! Worn round by the waves on the sea-shore; not in the bottom of the ocean, for there are no waves there, the waters lie still in that place. What bird could have brought this here?— But stop, here's another, and another, and then thousands of others!

These pebbles are flint—they contain silicified zoophytes! Everything has a life and a death; these have lived—zoophytes live and grow only in the sea; their beds have been cretaceous. We are only 6000 feet above the sea, and looking into it at our feet. When were these pebbles rolled by the waves of the sea? Where, for thousands of years, to be rounded as they are? In what cretaceous bed lay they for thousands of years, and perhaps for thousands of centuries, to be changed from the living animal, with all their curious and intricate tentaculae, into silex before they were rolled? And how long have they lain here? And then, how came they here? Or where has here been? But don't let us go mad; let us get down from this place, we are too high. No; it's too much trouble to get back again; we are now on the top of the 'Scylla,' the grand plateau that sweeps off to the Orinoco. There are Indians on these plains, and I, of course, must cross them. Have any Indian tribes ever escaped me? Yes. Shall I ever see them all? I don't believe so.

The prairies in this country are pampas; in shape and distant appearance they are much like those which Charley and I passed over between Fort Gibson and St. Louis, rolling and sloping about in all directions, with beautiful clear streams winding through them, and copses and bunches of timber and bushes on their sides and along the banks of the streams.

But those bunches and copses when we come near to them, oh, how lovely! There are the beautiful bananas, the pennated, lofty, and dwarf palms, and, at their feet, palmettoes; acres on acres of geraniums in flowers of all colors and of various odors; of wild roses, and fifty kinds of flowering plants. The meadows are filled with lilies of various hues; the hedges are bending with wild plums and wild grapes. The orange and fig-trees are on every little hillock, and yellow with fruit, and still white with sweet blossoms. Pinks of a hundred colors and patterns, and violets of all hues are under our feet, and now and then a huge rattlesnake!

The busy little humming-birds are buzzing about us, and ten thousands of beetles and other clumsy flyers, that no one stops to inquire about, are knocking and butting against us. Spathes of palm-flowers are opening, and these swarm in myriads about them.

The sun looks as it does at home, though perhaps a little smaller, and more over our heads; we have to bend our necks more to look at it. Man begins here to feel less than he does in England, his shadow is shorter, it don't follow him so exactly, and so far behind him.

The Indians; are there any? Yes; but not many. Smallpox, and rum, and whisky have destroyed the most of them. Here are the Chaymas and the Gooagives, semi-civilized, mostly mixed with Spaniards. Some full-bloods; color and character much like the Ojibbeways in North America; rather small and slight in stature, but quick and powerful men, beautifully formed, and no deformities amongst them.

Who is the happiest man in the world just at this time? Why, Doctor Hentz, while he is gathering these beautiful plants and lovely flowers, and packing them in his large books, which a Chayma is employed to help to carry to Angostura. And who the next happiest? Why, I, of course, who am putting these beautiful scenes into my portfolio; and yesterday, that beautiful dance! What dance? Why, the mach-ee-o-a ('handsome' or 'glad' dance), glad, or thankful, because the Indians are pleased with us, and perhaps have received some valued present, and also because the medicine man has told them that I am great medicine.

What! Medicine men here too? In South America? Yes, exactly the same as in North America. The chief's portrait was held up by the corners in the same way, and the medicine men had a grand dance around it. And then the warriors danced the war-dance, and gave the war-whoop. What! The war-whoop here too? Precisely the same. And then; and then, what? Why then came the handsome dance.

The young women dance in this country, but not often. Three young and beautiful women were selected by the chief to give this dance; it was an extraordinary compliment paid to my medicine; for many years it had not been seen. Was it beautiful? The most beautiful thing I ever saw. How were these girls dressed? Each one had a beautiful tiger-skin spread under her feet, upon which she danced; their hair, fastened by a silver band passing around the head, was falling down in shining tresses; long pins of silver were run through their under lips, and strings of blue and white beads were dangling from them; large and small beads hung in great profusion around their necks, and polished brass bands were worn, with strings of blue and white beads on their slender wrists and ankles; their cheeks were painted red, and their bodies were colored white with white clay.

Did they raise their feet from the ground when they danced? No, not quite, their toes were always on the tiger-skins. Did they separate their big toes? Not an inch. Did they dance to music? In perfect time to the beat of the drum and a chant of the chiefs. Were they graceful? Yes.

NOTHING CAN BE MORE BEAUTIFUL OF THEIR KIND than the rolling plains between Caracas and the Orinoco. They are abundantly stocked with wild horses and wild (not buffaloes, but) cattle, which answer all the same purposes for food to the Indians as well as to white men. These are taken both by the Indians and the Spaniards, not with the bow and arrows or lance, but with the deadly bolas.

The bolas is a cord of raw hide, branching three ways from the center, each branch being some eight or ten feet in length, with a leaden ball of half-a-pound or so in weight at its end. One of these balls the rider holds in his right hand, while his horse is at full speed, and the other two are swinging around and over his head until he is in the right position, when he lets go the ball in his hand, giving them all a sling at the same time. The three balls keep their respective opposite positions as they are whirling about in the air, till one of the cords strikes the neck of the animal, around which and its legs the cords instantly wrap themselves, and the animal falls upon its head and becomes an easy and certain prey to its assailant, who, with a long lance from his horse's back, or with his knife, by dismounting, does the rest.

This mode is used only for 'killing.' The wild horses are killed in this manner for their skins and their hair, and the wild cattle for their flesh, their skins, and their horns.

In taking wild horses for their use, this mode would not answer; for in nine cases out of ten the fall of the horse while at full speed, and entangled in the folds of the bolas, would break the animal's neck, or disable it for life.

For catching the wild horse, therefore, the lasso is used by these people much in the same way as it is used by the Indians in North America, which has been described; only with the difference, that when the horse is arrested by the lasso, and its speed is stopped, they strike it with a short baton loaded with lead, on the back part of the head, which stuns the animal, and it falls to the ground. The captor then places a bandage around its eyes, and gets upon its back.

The horse, recovering from the blow, and rising, soon yields to the wishes of its cruel master, not daring to run with its eyes blinded.

By the effects of this mode of breaking, which I have seen and closely studied, I believe the natural spirit of the animal is irretrievably lost, to such a degree as greatly to diminish its value.

At the small town of Chaparro, about sixty miles from the Orinoco, we learned that a large armed force of insurgents in the civil war at Venezuela, which had suddenly broken out, was marching on Angostura; and by the aid of mules which we employed of the Gauchos, we got posted on to San Diego, and from that to a point thirty miles below Angostura, to the banks of the Orinoco; a canoe took us to Barrancas, and from that we got a steamer to Georgetown, Demerara, in British Guiana.

But stop; we did not come to Demerara in a moment, we could not, and why should we? What did we see, and what did we do? Why, we saw from our little dug-out the stately and dark forests overhanging the shores of the Orinoco. Is there anything like them on earth? I don't believe it.

"Stately," did I say? Yes, and lofty. The towering mora, the miriti, with its tall and elegant shaft, the tough hackea, the green-heart, the ebony, the copal locust, the beautiful hayawa, and the olow, with their sweet gushing resin, and the graceful banana, the queen of the forest, and twenty others, mingled and intermingled with cordage and ropes of creeping, and climbing, and hanging vines; with clumps and bouquets of beautiful flowers of all colors and at all heights; and chattering monkeys leaping from branch to branch, with their little ones on their backs, cunningly ogling us as we passed.

The solitary tocanos bowing to us from the withered tops of the lofty moras, and saluting us— "Tso-cano, tso-cano! No, no, no! Go on there, go on there!" The beautiful white swans by hundreds, and pelicans also, as white as the snow, were flapping their long wings and on the air before I could get 'Sam' to bear upon them. "Sam! who's Sam?" Why, Sam Colt, a six-shot little rifle always lying before me during the day, and in my arms during the night, by which a tiger's or an alligator's eye, at a hundred yards, was sure to drop a red tear—but don't interrupt me. The last of these were everywhere basking in the sun and plunging off from their slimy logs as we approached. The timid turtles were shoving down from the banks of sand, and the tortoises, with their elevated heads, came pacing out of the forest where they roam, taking shelter under the waves whilst their enemies passed.

It is easier to fly over the water and between these hundreds of islands, with their matted, and twisted, and almost wedged foliage, than through them; and these crooked avenues, for birds and wild fowl, are what the Strand and London Bridge are to the Londoners.

There are all sorts, and all sizes, and all colors on the wing; some slow and some fast; some actually loungers, and some evidently expresses, as they dart through the crowds like a shot. Many are gossipers, for they chatter as they travel So there is din as well as motion; and in the midst of this, once in a while, a flock of wild geese must pass (an omnibus!); the crowd must give way! They fly in a triangle; their leader is a 'conductor' and distinctly cries, "Get in, John! Get in, John! Paddington! Paddington!" While the beautiful tocano turns his head sideways, and rolls his piercing eye down from the tops of the mora, as he echoes, "Go on, John! Go on, John! Go on! Go on!"

"Here's a swarm of bees ahead of us," said Dr. Hentz. "We shall be stung to death!"

"No, Doctor, it's only the opening of a spathe; and you know what a spathe is better than I; that's in your line, Doctor."

"Well," said the Doctor, "that's true, and I'll tell you."

"There are over two hundred different varieties of palm-trees in this country, and each sort has its blossoms and its fruits in its own shape. The fruit of all palms grows just where the leaves and branches start out from the trunk; and before the fruit comes immense large sacks or spathes, containing the flowers, are visible for weeks, and sometimes for months, before they are sufficiently perfected to open. These spathes on some palms are large enough for the back-loads of three or four men, and, when opened, present from ten to one hundred thousand fragrant and honey-bearing flowers of purple, of pink, and other colors, perfuming the atmosphere for a great distance around them.

"The honey-sucking birds and insects generally get a few days' previous knowledge of these important approaching events, and gather in myriads around them, ready for the onslaught, when a bright and clear morning shows them their feast opened and spread before them. That is the scene now before us. You see in the midst of that whirling cloud of insects the spadix of a palm in full bloom, and here is now just going on the 'set-to,' and pell-mell for honey. There's no danger of being stung now, I admit. These busy little creatures, though most of them with stings, are all at work; they have their little ones to feed, and no time now to sting; let's step and look at them a while."

Thank you, Doctor. This was a short lecture in botany; the Doctor had given us many.

We stopped our canoe, and looked at the busy group. Through my opera-glass the scene was indescribably curious. Whilst thousands of honeybees, of bumblebees, of beetles, and humming-birds, and other honey-sucking insects were whirling around it, like all other riches and luxuries of the world, it was easily seen that these were divided amongst the lucky few. The surface of these clusters of flowers seemed chiefly engrossed by the swift-darting and glistening little humming-birds, of all sizes and all hues, whose long and slender bills entered every approachable cell, as they balanced on their trembling wings, ready to dart away when danger comes. These seemed masters of the feast. But there were others apparently even more successful; the busy, fearless, little bees and others, that crept between and through the winding maze of flowers, and culled their choicest, freshest sweets, where others could not enter; but then, where were they? Like too many of the world who enjoy the sweetest things, the nearest to eternity.

The sharp claws of the bright-eyed little bee-hawk suspended him from these mats of flowers; he loves honey, but sucks it not; he gets it in a shorter way; he picks up these little laborers as they come out with their rich loads, and puts them in his crop. His feast finished, he flies, but heavily, with his plundered prey, and knows the gauntlet he too has to run; his enemies are of his own kin, but stronger and fleeter on the wing. They sit like silent sentinels on the dry limbs of overhanging trees, and stoop upon him and snatch him up as he passes through the open air.

Amidst these incongruous masses of contending and jealous insects, with their deadly weapons, many conflicts and many deaths ensue; and many such, with their accumulated treasure, drop to the ground beneath, in the grass, and there—("Let's go ashore," said the Doctor, "and I'll show you") and he did show me. "There, do you see that little green snake, and that white one too? They are both of one species, though their colors are different; they both are honey-eaters, though the world don't believe it. They know just as well as these insects when a spathe of flowers is opened, and here they are. They take the honey-loaded carcasses of the unlucky combatants that fall."

"How did you learn this curious fact, Doctor?"

"From the Indians."

"Doctor," said I, "next to the Indians, the thing I wish most to see is a cocoa-nut tree, and to hear your description of it."

"I don't think there are any near here," said the Doctor; "the cocoa-nut is not a native of America, but it has been introduced, and we shall probably see many of them before long; but I have not met one yet."

WELL, WE WERE JOGGING ALONG ON THE ORINOCO, WERE WE NOT? Look, next time you go to the Museum, for the beautiful cotingas; there are several sorts of them, a size larger than the humming-birds, and equally beautiful in plumage. They are all here, and in great numbers are darting about amongst us.

And the campanero (strange bird!), their notes exactly like the tinkling or tolling of a bell. They give the forest the most singular character. They are solitary birds, I take it, for we never see them. We hear their strange notes, and then, from some mystery in sound not yet explained, we can't tell which way they are; if we go one way or the other to look for them, it's all the same; the sound is equally near, and all around us; it seems a mile distant, but it may be within a few yards; it tolls only just at night, when it is too late to see it, or just at daybreak, when the difficulty is the same. There's medicine in this! It's like the thunder-bird of the 'thunder's nest.' I never could see one, though I am a 'medicine man.' Is it a bird? Or is it some sort of mirage of sound? Is it not a distant cow-bell? It's not a phantom; phantoms 'fly before us;' this does not fly; it's all around, before, and behind us, and travels with us; but we'll drop it, and perhaps hunt for it again.

Though these forests and these lovely river-shores are constantly ringing with song, still one-half of animal nature seems to sleep during the day; for when one set of songsters are done, another begins; but how different! The songs of the day are all joyous and cheering, if we could understand them, characteristic of the glow and warmth of sunshine; but in the dark, how emblematic of the gloom and loneliness about us, and characteristic of that stealth with which the animals of the dark steal upon their sleeping, unprotected, prey! The frequent roar we often hear of the hungry jaguar; the doleful howlings of the red monkeys; the hooting of owls; and every night the inquisitive goat-sucker, who lights upon a limb as nearly over us as he can in safety, and shocks our nerves, in his coarse and perfectly masculine and human voice, "Who are you? Go away! Go away!"

Well, we'll go away; we'll jog on; we are stopping too long in this place; but then, one word more before we start. What great ugly beast is that I see yonder, hanging under a branch of that hayama tree? That? That's a sloth, sir, the laziest animal of all the world, and perfectly harmless; it hasn't the energy to stand upon its legs, but hangs all day without moving, and, fast asleep under the limb of a tree, hangs by his long toe-nails. What! Hangs and sleeps all day? Well, that's easier than to stand and sleep; it's like sleeping in a hammock. What a gentleman! Sleeps all day! But he is a fat looking fellow. I believe he is up all night; and if you have a hen-roost I advise you to beware of him, he seems well fed; the world is full of such gentlemen. He can't move—ha! Hand me 'Sam.' I'll prick him up a little, and see what he's made of.

BANG!

He falls into the river! But he swims! And now upon the bank! And at one leap upon the side of a tree! And at another of forty feet, upon another tree! And the next, out of sight! That's your lazy gentleman, ha! Why, no alligator could catch that fellow in the water; no dog could catch him on the land; and amongst the trees, few monkeys would be a match for him. I believe he is a great rascal.

We are at Barrancas now; Barrancas is a large town; but what are large towns to us? London is considerably larger. This steamer goes to Demerara; just where our little canoe can't go, and where we must go. "A good chance to overhaul and air your plants, Dr. Hentz."

"First-rate, Mynheer."

"This is a strange looking place, captain. What a vast number of islands there are ahead of us! We are at the mouth of the Orinoco?"

"Not quite."

"It has a hundred mouths, I am told?"

"No; only fifty."

"How grand and magnificent the forests around us! Those thousands and tens of thousands of lofty palms, their trunks standing in the water, actually! Why, they seem like a grand colonnade, or portico of some mighty edifice!"

"Yes, they are truly so; but they don't look exactly so in low water. The tide is getting well-nigh up now. I see you are an Englishman, sir?"

"No, captain, not exactly; I am an American; that's not far from it."

"Give us your hand, stranger; you know who I am; we'll have a long talk after a while."

"But, captain, before you go below, what sort of birds' nests are those in those trees on the shore, and on that island ahead of us? They are too large for rooks, I think."

"Well, don't now! You'll make me smile, sir, if you don't take care. They are a large sort of bird, sir, and you'll see them hovering about us in a little time. These birds fly upon the water, sir; not in the air; they live upon fish and oysters; and I expect some fresh supplies from them by-and-by.

"These, what you call birds, sir, are Indians, Guaroanes (Caribbees); they build their houses in the trees, and go up to them by a ladder from their canoes, and never venture out except when the tide is up, and that always in their canoes; when the tide is out, all is deep mud and slime about them, which nothing can walk through."

"Captain, I would give almost anything if we could stop near some of these for a little time."

"That's quite easy, sir, for I've got to lie-to a little till the tide gets high enough to take us over the bar, and you may have a first-rate opportunity to see them, and visit them too, if you wish, for I am going to send the yawl to one of them with that Spanish gentleman and his two daughters sitting in the bow yonder, who are going to them."

"Splendid, Captain! Splendid!"

XIV

GEORGETOWN, DEMERARA, IN BRITISH GUIANA, is a large and very flourishing town, where coffee and cotton and sugar are raised in great perfection, and in great abundance.

One could stop a long time, and, in fact, spend his life here, with pleasure; but, as I have said, we are not traveling to see large towns and cities—we have no time, and everybody knows what they are; but it is not all the world who knows what's before us. And no better key to that can be given at this place than the following extracts made from a series of letters written at Para, in Brazil, by a fine young man of the name of Smyth, who (like my faithful friend, Joe Chadwick, in North America) accompanied me across the Acary (or Tumucumaque) Mountains to the valley of the Amazon. These letters were written to his brother in Berkshire several years since; and, since my return, I have been permitted to make these extracts, which so graphically and correctly describe scenes and country we passed, that I consider them well deserving of this notoriety.

"PARA, BRAZIL, 1854.

"DEAR BROTHER, You will have thought, perhaps, from my long silence, that I had been killed by a tiger, or swallowed by an alligator before this. I arrived in Georgetown, Demerara, one year since, and I am sorry to say I found it not to be the thing it was said to be. I lounged about there for six months without making a sixpence. My tin was about all out, without my knowing what to do, when I fell in company with an old acquaintance of London, Mr. Catlin, whom you will remember, whose Indian Collection we went often to see in the Egyptian Hall.

"I one day espied a crowd in the street, amused at the red heads of some Caribbee Indians, looking out of a chamber window. I ventured in, and finding myself at the top of the stairs, I got a peep in and saw what was going on. There was a great crowd in the place, and at the farther end of the chamber I recognized the old veteran, with his palette and brushes in his hands, painting the portrait of an Indian chief, who was standing before him. He didn't observe me, and I backed quietly out.

"An hour or so after, when the crowd had cleared chiefly away, and the chamber was pretty much empty, I entered again, and advancing, offered my hand. I said, 'You won't remember me, sir; it is over six years since you saw me;' but he called my name in an instant.

"There was a German Doctor with him, and they had just arrived from Angostura, on the Orinoco River, their noses and faces tanned and burnt almost to the color of Indians. A large table in the room was loaded with plants and skins of animals and birds, and the sides of the room around lined with Indian portraits and views of the country.

"I soon learned they were going to start in a few days for a journey across the Tumucumaque Mountains into the valley of the Amazon, in Brazil, just the place precisely where I wanted to go of all others. I proposed to the gentleman, that if he would pay my expenses and furnish me with powder and ball, as I had a first-rate Minié rifle with me, I would go with him, hunt for him, and protect him, at the risk of my own life if it was necessary. This offer saved him the expense of hiring a worse man, and suited him exactly, and the arrangements were soon concluded.

"You know the 'old Minié' well, and what she can do; and you may easily imagine there was enough now preparing for her. He spent some little time in painting some tribes in this neighborhood and in Dutch Guiana, at Paramaribo, and then we were prepared to cross the mountains, and at last set out, after I had got pretty tired of waiting, in a large canoe, with a family of Indians who had come down to Georgetown to make their trade. Our course was up the Essequibo, and our party consisted of Mr. Catlin (or governor, as we called him); the German Doctor and his servant; an Indian half-breed, whom the governor had hired as a guide; a Spaniard, our interpreter; and myself.

"We ascended this magnificent river for a hundred or two miles, to near the great falls, and then took off to an Indian town, where we were told we could get horses and mules to take us onto the base of the mountains.

"The banks of this noble river, lined with its stately palms and other evergreen trees, are beautiful beyond anything that can be described or imagined. The river is alive with wild fowl and alligators, and the shores abound in wild animals as we pass along. The old Minié was almost constantly in my hands, and the lead which she hove ashore was curious, I assure you.

"The Indians in this country use no guns, and the Indian party in our boat were constantly amused and astonished at the distance at which I would knock the alligators off their logs, and the manner in which the scales would fly when I struck them.

"The whole shore on both sides was lined with one immense forest of palms and other trees overhanging the river, and many of these, from the ground to their very tops, were covered with white and pink flowers. Their branches were constantly shaken by squeaking monkeys looking out at us and leaping from tree to tree, keeping opposite to us as we passed along; and parrots were chattering and scolding at us as if we had no right to be there. Peccaries, a sort of wild pig, were running on the banks in great numbers; they are fine game, and good eating.

"At night the Indians always slept in their canoe, but we stretched our hammocks and slept upon the high banks amongst the trees, lighting a strong fire, and keeping it up all night.

"There is a sort of monkey that howls in the night, making the most hideous noise that ever was heard, and they seemed to gather around us every night. As soon as it was nightfall, it was curious to see the bats come out and sail about over the shores of the river. Some of these were as large as a leather apron; and the mosquitoes, oh, horrid! They were the worst enemy we had; the old Minié couldn't touch them. There was no such thing as getting to sleep until ten or eleven o'clock at night, when they always disappeared.

"When we left the canoe and our Indian party, and took to the land, we had a hard siege of it; each one had to carry his share of the luggage, and we were all loaded down. We left in the morning, and our guide brought us to a small Indian village just before night, through swamps and quagmires, with nothing but a footpath to follow. The Indian town, however, was upon an open plain, very beautiful, with small palms in groups standing out upon it.

"The huts of these people were all thatched over with palm-leaves, and there were a great number of horses and mules grazing around them; and amongst them some of the handsomest mules I ever saw.

"The guide led us to the chief's hut, who received us very kindly; he was an oldish man, and was seated on the ground. Some skins were placed for us to sit upon, and, through the interpreter, the governor soon commenced a conversation with him; telling him where we were going, and what our object was. The chief was sitting cross-legged, and was smoking a long pipe; his head was cast down, and he now and then gave a sort of grunt, and I saw that the governor began to show a little concern.

"The conversation went on for some time, without much change, when the governor commenced making some sort of masonic signs with his hands to the chief, who raised his head a little, very suddenly, and after watching them closely for a minute or so, he laid down his pipe, and striking both his hands quickly together, he began making signs in reply. The governor began to smile, and the chief, seeing they mutually understood each other, jumped upon his feet as nimbly as a boy. The governor arose, and the chief embraced him in his arms, calling him his 'brother!'

"A further conversation then took place between the two for some time, while the old chiefs limbs trembled with pleasure and excitement. The governor then explained to him that he had come from a great many tribes of red people exactly like himself, living three or four hundred days' march to the north (in North America), who all understood the same signs, and smoked the pipe in the same manner: to which the chief replied, 'These people are our brothers, and you are their father.'

"The governor told the chief what our views were, and that we wanted to hire some horses and some of his young men to take us to the base of the mountains. At this, the chief turned to the interpreter, who it seems had been giving him a different interpretation, and told him he was a great scoundrel to deceive the white men who had employed him, and to try to deceive him also.

"The Spaniard, seeing himself detected, was in a great rage, and demanded his pay for three months, for which time he was employed. The governor refused to pay him a sixpence, when he advanced up suddenly in front of the governor, and placing his hand upon the handle of a large knife which he wore in his waistband, demanded his money again; but observing the muzzle of the old Minié about that instant near his short ribs, and a click! (a sort of a hiccup she has when she is just about to speak), he drew a little back.

"The chief then said to him, as he had acted the traitor in his house, it was for him, and not for the white man, to pay him; that he was known to many of the young men of the tribe to be a great scoundrel, and the sooner and the more quietly he got out of the way the better. The scamp then walked off, and we never heard of him afterwards.

"All was now friendly and cheerful; the pipe was passed round several times for us all to smoke; the old chief holding the long stem in both hands, as he walked round and held the pipe to our mouths. The old man introduced us to his two sons, young men about my age; they were almost entirely naked, like most of the tribe; but I only wish that I had limbs so round and beautiful as theirs. I often thought how beautiful a racecourse of such young men would be.

"The chief told us that his house was small, and not very good, but he would do all he could to make us sleep well, and we should be welcome. We were placed, with all our things, in a small adjoining hut, and passed the night very comfortably.

"The governor commenced the conversation the next morning, by telling him he was going to show him and his people how the red-skins looked in North America, where he had come from, which the good old man could not at all comprehend, until the governor opened a large portfolio with a hundred or more portraits of Indians, buffalo hunts, etc., all in full blazing colors. Perhaps few men on earth were ever more suddenly amused and astonished than this old veteran was at that moment.

"We were seated at that time by the side of him, and all upon the ground, with the German Doctor and his man, and no other Indians in the hut. The old man looked at them all, but very fast; and when he was done, began to howl and sing the most droll song I ever heard in my life, which seemed at last to be the signal for a strange-looking being to enter, whose visage was filled with wrinkles, his face most curiously painted, with a fan in one hand, and a rattle in the other, which he was shaking as he entered.

"This, I learned, was an Indian doctor, who took his seat by the side of the chief, and after they had hastily looked over the pictures, the old chief got up and took down from quite up under the roof of his hut a little round roll of bark, like a paper scroll some eight or nine inches long, which had several yellow ribands tied around it, and in the middle a string of blue beads hanging down. He handed this to the old doctor, who took it in his hands, and raising it near his mouth, spirted upon it from his lips at three or four efforts, at least a pint of some liquid as white as milk, covering it from one end to the other. Where on earth this was concealed, or what it was none of us could tell. The chief then laid it on the fire, which he sat by, and kindled up until it was entirely consumed, while he in silence gazed upon it. This done, both he and the doctor got up, and smilingly gave us their hands in a hearty shake.

"The governor never could learn what was the meaning of all this ceremony, but supposed it was some offering to the Great Spirit.

"The whole village was by this time assembling outdoors, where we went, and the rest of this day was spent in looking at the pictures, and also in examining our guns. You know the old Minié and the governor had always in his hand one of Colt's six-shot rifles; this he had nicknamed 'Sam.'

"These people had but three or four light and short guns in their village (and good for nothing), their weapons being bows and arrows, and lances, and the bolas. The governor's gun, therefore, was the greatest of curiosities to them, as they never had heard or thought of a revolver; and I having given out that the governor's gun would shoot all day without stopping, made an exhibition of its powers necessary.

"For this I took an old cow-skin, which was stretched on a hoop, and had been the door of a hut, and placing it at some sixty or eighty yards, with a bull's-eye in the center, the governor took his position, and let off one! two! three! four! five! six! By an understanding, I at that moment touched him on the shoulder, till we could learn from the chief, who was standing by the side of us, whether that was enough; at which, on having appealed to the crowd, they were all perfectly satisfied. While this little parley was going on, the governor, without their observing it, had slipped off the empty cylinder and placed another one on, which he always carried in his pantaloons pocket, charged and ready with six shots more. His rifle was raised and levelled at the target, and he was about to proceed, when the chief advanced and said it would be wrong to expend more powder and ball, as we might want it all on our journey, and that his people were now all convinced that his gun would fire all day.

"The target was brought up, and the shots all in the space of the palm of one's hand: they were still more astonished, and myself a little so amongst the number.

"Next came the old Minié. I was anxious to show them what she could do. And I carried the target and set it up at about two hundred yards, and when they saw me strike it the first shot, though it could not fire so fast, my gun was an equal curiosity, for hitting the target at such a distance. They were both considered great mysteries, and there was not a man in the tribe who was willing to touch the triggers of either of them.

"But the funniest part of this scene now took place. Some of the little boys standing near the governor having discovered in his belt a revolver pistol, which he always carried, had reported it to some of the young men, who came up to him very timidly to ask him if he hadn't a young rifle. The governor not having thought of his pistol during the excitement, began to smile, and drawing it out, said, 'Yes.' Here the squaws, who had all along been in the background, now began to come up, but very cautiously, all with their hands over their mouths as they gave a sort of a groan and a 'ya, ya.' This was really amusing.

"The governor held the pistol by the side of the rifle, and the exact resemblance, except in size, convinced them that the pistol was a 'young one' and if it could have said 'mamma' it would not have created greater sympathy amongst the women than it did.

"The governor explained that it was very young, but notwithstanding, at a shorter distance, it had got so as to do pretty well. At this he levelled it at the trunk of a palm-tree, standing some six or eight rods off, and fired a couple of shots, to their great amazement. For these, the boys were cutting and digging with their knives for several days, but the report was they had not got to them before we left.

"All satisfied, the governor placed his pistol in his belt, and wrapping his capot around him, the squaws all raised a shout of approbation, 'Keep the poor little thing warm.'

"The report of the medicine gun, that could fire all day without reloading went ahead of us to all the tribes we afterwards visited, and the moment we arrived, all were waiting to see it. If these poor people had had the shillings to give, I could very soon have made all the fortune I ever wanted, by exhibiting old Sam and 'the young one.'

"The governor having painted some portraits, and his friend the German doctor having busied himself in collecting his roots and plants, we were prepared to move on. The doctor, however, who was a feeble man, and was getting weak, and I think a little afraid of the Indians, resolved, with his man, to go back from this place, and we never heard anything further how they got on. Here our party was split, just half the number we started with gone back.

"The chief gave us one of his sons and a nephew, a fine man, and horses to ride until we reached the base of the mountains, and we had yet the faithful half-breed, who knew the route. The chief knew him well, and told the governor he was a first-rate and honest man. The governor bought a strong mule to carry our packs, and we started off.

"The country we now passed over was beautiful and delightful; most of the way rolling prairies, with here and there little patches of timber. We visited several villages of Indians, who all were much like those we had left, and the chief's son seemed to be acquainted with them all, and conversed with them, the language being pretty much the same.

"Immense herds of wild cattle were seen grazing, and of all colors—red, black, white, and striped, and as wild as deer or any other animal. In one place the governor was induced to go about thirty miles out of our way to see the 'hill of the shining stones' that he had heard of from the Indians. We came to a little village on the bank of a small lake, and on the other bank, about a mile, were the 'shining stones.' They were glistening in the sun, and, to be sure, were very beautiful to look at; but when we got to them the governor said they were crystals of gypsum, sticking in the clay, and of no value. They were in myriads, and in a hundred different shapes, and very beautiful, perfectly transparent as water; but one could cut them with a knife, they were so soft.

"At another village much farther on, and nearer to the base of the mountains, we stopped for several days in a large town better built, on the bank of a lake some four or five miles long. The western shore of this had a broad beach of rounded pebbles, resembling exactly the sea-beach, which I should think it once had been. These pebbles were flint, and of all colors, and some of them, when broken, the most beautiful things I ever beheld. Many of them were beautifully transparent, with figures of a thousand shapes in them, some of which were exactly like the rays of the setting sun.

"We gathered and brought away some ten or fifteen pounds' weight of the most beautiful of them, difficult as it was to carry them.

"The governor was in the habit of going along this beach every morning and collecting these pebbles; and the little Indian children skulking about in the bushes and watching him at a distance, and not fully understanding what he was doing, but seeing him picking up the stones and breaking them with a little hammer which he always carried, and then wetting them with his tongue to see the colors, and when he found a right handsome one, putting it in his pocket, ran back and told their parents that here was the strangest man in the world; declaring that they had seen him every morning making his breakfast on stones, and putting others into his pocket for his dinner! The Indians gave him the name of the 'Stone Eater.' I forget the Indian for it.

"Not long after we left this village, when we halted to encamp one night in a beautiful little valley filled with wild flowers and vines, and handsome enough for the lawn of an English gentleman's house, after we had taken our supper, and it was approaching nightfall, and we were preparing our beds, I went for my saddle to make me a pillow, having left it on the bank of the little stream a few rods off. I took up the saddle, and reaching down for what I took to be the girth lying on the ground, it beginning to be a little darkish, I lifted up a huge rattlesnake. He made a grand pass at my arm, but just missed it as I flung him down; and then coiling himself up in a circle, he commenced buzzing his rattle, and was ready for a spring! My outcry brought up all the party, and I must say I never beheld so frightful a beast before in all my life. We heard the rattle of its mate, at a few rods' distance, which was soon looked up by the Indians, and both were knocked on the head.

"As we were nearing the base of the mountains we discovered ahead of us an unaccountably strange appearance—a streak of bright red, many miles in length, and perfectly straight. The governor thought it must be from some mineral substance, and we steered towards it. Our Indians knew without doubt what it was, but they had no word for it which we could understand, and were obliged to wait till we got to it for an explanation, when we found it to be an immense bed of wild poppies about as high as the stirrups of our saddles, and so thick that no vegetables whatever grew between them; their red heads being so thickly grouped, that in looking over them at the distance of thirty feet from us, the flowers formed one complete mass of red, without another color mixed with it.

"It took us a mile or two to go through it, and the quantity of deer that were jumping up and trotting off through it was really surprising. We could only see their heads and horns above the flowers as they were moving along, when they looked as if they were swimming in a lake of blood!

"At the base of these mountains the two Indians, with their horses, went back, and we then took to our feet, with our mule to carry our packs; but before we started, the governor and I sat down and looked over our pretty little stones, and selecting a dozen or so, left the rest to be called for."

XV

"THESE IMMENSE MOUNTAINS, which rise in a number of ridges, one after another, very rugged and barren, took us at least one hundred miles to cross, and we often wished ourselves back again; our pack-mule, poor beast, gave out about the middle of them, and we had to leave it. We left behind the heaviest of our articles, and took the rest on our own backs and got on much better than before. Horses' legs are not made for these mountains of rocks; two legs are far handier and better managed, and we can creep along almost anywhere now.

"We got at length the first glance into the great valley of the Amazon as we came out of a deep chasm we had followed for many miles. When we struck off into the valley, we had, I do think, the most beautiful scene in the world before us—the beautiful rolling prairies, covered with grass and wild flowers, and herds of wild cattle and wild horses grazing on them; and the deer that were springing up from the shade of every little bunch of palm-trees were tilting along for a few rods, and then standing to look at us, in fair range for a dead shot, never having heard the report of a gun. I am sure that in some places I could, with the old Minié, have easily killed some forty or fifty per day, by regular stalking. It seemed a pity to kill them, for one feels in shooting them as if he was shooting in some nobleman's park.

"We crossed here a large stream, and followed it down some miles, the bed of which, it being nearly dry, was filled with countless numbers of round stones, some of them two feet across, which, when he broke them open, were filled with the most beautiful quartz crystals of various colors—some were purple, some were yellow, and others as pure as water: these the governor called geodes. There were also wagon-loads of others shaped like rams' horns; some of these as large as two men could lift, and many of them filled with beautiful crystals.

"We struck at last upon the Rio Trombutas, where we found some very hospitable villages of Indians; and finding a couple of half-breeds and several Indians loading a large canoe with hides and other things for Para, we got a chance to go down with them. This canoe, some forty or fifty feet long and five feet wide, was made from a solid log, dug out, and had its sides built up a foot and a half higher, with ribs interwoven with palm-leaves, so as to keep out the waves when heavily loaded, and would carry some four or five tons with ease.

"On the head of this river we were exactly under the equator; the sun right over our heads. There is no winter in this country: it is one perpetual summer and spring-time here. Everything out in full blossom all the year round. All the trees are evergreens, and ripe fruit and fresh flowers we see on the same trees at the same time.

"Frost never was known here, and the governor got himself quite into disrepute in one of the small villages, where he stopped a few days to make his portraits, by endeavoring to explain to these people how different the country was that he came from. He tried to describe hail and snow to them, but there seemed to be no words in their language for them, and they could not understand him at all. And when he told them of ice—of our rivers freezing over, and becoming so hard that we could walk and run, and even drive our horses and wagons over them, they became entirely incredulous, and laughed at him excessively. And an old man (it seems, one of their doctors), who had been strongly opposed to the taking of the portraits, got up and began spouting in a most violent manner against him, telling his people it was very silly to be listening to such stories, and they were rapidly beginning to haul off."The governor sent for me—I was on the boat at the time—and got me to testify to the truth of what he had stated, which I easily did; but this only made the trouble worse, and the facts no easier to be believed, for the doctor told them, 'It only made the lie stronger.'

"We had no other means of proof to offer; and the old doctor wrapped his tiger-skin around his shoulders, and walked off in quite a huffy mood towards the village, at a few rods' distance. We were sitting under the shade of some palms on the bank of a river at the time, where the greater part of the village were assembled to witness the operation of painting the portraits.

"The greater portion of the crowd got up and followed the doctor to the village, and some of the squaws clapped their hands over their mouths, and began to howl and cry, believing that the insult given by the doctor was such as the governor would feel bound to resent, and there would soon be a fight.

"The chief, however, who was a very pleasant and dignified man, remained seated by the governor's side, and said the old doctor had behaved very foolishly; and so the affair dropped, the governor getting only a hard name—the squaws called him Hard Water, by which name he will, no doubt, be spoken of for a long time to come.

"After we had got a little recruited, the canoe loaded, and the governor had laid in a goodly number of sketches, we all set off towards the Amazon, perhaps then some three hundred miles off; and you can well imagine that the old Minié had plenty to do again. All the animals, and birds, and trees, and plants seemed much the same as on the Essequibo; but tigers and monkeys were at least three to one.

"The tigers live chiefly along the shores of the river, for their favorite food is the soft-shell turtles that come out of the river to lay their eggs in the sand in the night. The tigers watch them, and rush upon them at that time, and turn great numbers of them on their backs with their paws; and after eating as much as they want, and digging up their eggs out of the sand as a sort of dessert, they just creep up on to the top of the bank in the shade of the timber, where they lie until they are hungry again, when they have only to slip down and eat; by this means they keep so fat that their hair glistens as if there was oil upon it.

"When they hear us talking and rowing, they creep up to the edge of the bank, and are discovered looking at us, showing only their heads above the grass and weeds. We steer our canoe near enough to the shore for a dead shot, which we never miss. The governor counts five skins, one a beautiful black tiger, very scarce here, and I have eight, every one of which shows the bullet-hole as exactly between the eyes as you could put your finger.

"There is, in fact, no sport in killing these fellows in this way, for it is only like shooting at a target at some thirty or forty paces (this you will say is child's play). We might find sport, however, if we should go ashore for these chaps; but we had no time nor much inclination for that, and took good care not to go ashore where we saw fresh signs of them. We generally know where they are by the carcasses of turtles on the sand-beaches, and in such cases we are all on the lookout.

"We were in the habit of making a halt and lying by a couple of hours every day at noon in the heat of the day. In one of these rests we had landed by the side of a high bank, where we saw no signs, the Indians were asleep in the canoe, and the governor and the half-breed and myself were a-top of the bank—the governor and I had built a large fire, and were roasting a fat pig which I had shot from the boat, and while the governor was sitting down on one side and I squatting down on the other, and he was with a wooden spoon ladling some rich gravy over the pig from a short-handled frying-pan which I was holding underneath, I observed his eyes staring at something over my shoulder, in the direction of our half-breed guide, who was lying a couple of rods from us, and fast asleep, under the shade of some small palms.

"The governor said, 'Smyth! Be perfectly calm and cool; and don't spill the gravy; and don't move an inch; there is a splendid tiger just behind you!' I held onto the frying-pan, but gradually turned my head around, when I saw the beast lying on all fours alongside of the half-breed, who was lying on his face, and fast asleep! He was lifting up with his paws one of the half-breed's feet, and playing with it apparently as carefully and innocently as a kitten.

"The governor who had left his hat behind him, was at this time sliding down the grass-covered bank backwards, and feet foremost, to the boat, where our rifles were left. The next moment he had one foot upon its deck and his rifle in his hand. I was in hopes he would have taken up the old Minié, but he preferred his own; and getting it to bear upon the beast, he was obliged to stand a minute or so for it to raise its head high enough not to endanger the man's body, which was in front of the tiger, and over which he must shoot very close. Not succeeding in this, he gave a sudden whistle, which directed the attention of the animal to him, and caused it to raise its head and its eyes towards him, when he let fly.

"At the crack of the rifle the tiger gave a frightful screech, and leapt about fifteen feet into the air, falling perfectly dead. The Indian leapt nearly as far in the other direction; and at the same instant arose and darted into the thicket, the male, secreted in a bunch of weeds about fifteen feet behind the governor's back, when he had been sitting at the fire.

"After our pig was roasted, and this beautiful animal was taken on board, we pushed out a little into the stream and waited a couple of hours, in hopes the male would show himself again; but we waited in vain, and started on our course, losing our game.

"When we had gone ashore one day, on a broad sand beach lying between the river-shore and the timber, we were startled by a loud hissing, and we discovered a huge alligator coming at full pace towards us, from the edge of the timber towards the water. We were about springing into the boat, but our daring little half-breed, better acquainted with these beasts than we were, ran, without any weapon, towards it, meeting it face to face. When they had got within ten or twelve feet of each other, the brute pulled up, and lay stock still, with its ugly mouth wide open, the upper jaw almost falling over on to its back, and commenced the most frightful hissing!

"The little half-breed kept his position, and called out for a block of wood, one of the men, running a little way up the beach, brought a log of driftwood the size of a man's thigh, and six or eight feet long. The half-breed took this in both hands, and balancing it in a horizontal position, advanced up and threw it, broadside, into and across the creature's mouth; when, as quick as lightning, and with a terrible crash, down came upon it the upper jaw, with all its range of long and sharp teeth deeply driven into it.

"The little half-breed then stepped by the side of the animal and got astride of its back, and we all gathered round, turned the stupid creature over and over, and kicked and dragged it, but nothing would make it quit its deadly grasp upon the log of wood and nothing ever could while it lived, for the Indians all told us it would live some eight or ten hours, but not longer.

"The noise of a gun I don't believe was ever before heard on this river, for one has no idea of the fuss it makes when the old Minié speaks. I have sometimes fired in the middle of the day, when all was silent, and not a leaf on a tree in motion, and in one minute a thousand voices were going; and looking up and down the river, at one view you may see in the tops of the overhanging trees five hundred (not monkeys, but) little bunches of boughs and leaves shaking, where they and the parrots are peeping out to see what is going on, without your seeing hide or hair of them.

"In one of our noonday halts, when we were taking our lunch under a grand forest of lofty trees, and not much underwood or vines, we found the monkeys assembling in vast numbers over our heads, and chattering with an unusual excitement, as they were leaping around from tree to tree. The governor and I began to get alarmed for fear they were going to attack us. They kept coming up and increasing every moment, and there was no knowing where the crowd and the bedlam were to end.

"Our little half-breed smiled at our alarm, and said they must have stolen something from the canoe to have kicked up such a rumpus. I ran down to the canoe, where all hands were asleep at the stern end, and soon discovered that two beautiful feather head-dresses, which the governor had that morning purchased of some Indians we had passed, and the governor's powder-flask, which we had left on the deck, had been carried off; and returning, I soon saw the proof of the theft by the hundreds of feathers that were falling over our heads.

"These thievish little creatures had taken the two head-dresses into the tops of the trees, and whilst some were engaged in pulling them to pieces, others were leaping around with bunches of the quills in their mouths, and others with them as regularly stuck behind their ears as the pens of counting-house clerks are carried; and the powder-flask we could hear knocking about amongst the limbs of the trees, though we could not see it.

"One of the half-breeds from the boat had come up the bank in the meantime, and became so enraged, that he took the old Minié before. I observed him, while it was leaning against a tree, and aiming at a large monkey which he said was the leader of the fracas, he fired and brought him down, with his backbone shot off.

"The screams of this poor creature's distress being understood by the throng, they were all silent in a moment, and in less than one minute they were all out of sight, but the powder-flask never came down. Though it had been agreed by all parties at our start that no one should kill a monkey, it was impossible to cure the wound of this poor brute, and it was knocked on the head.

"The snakes on this river are very numerous, and some of them very large. The anacondas and boa constrictors, the Indians told us, had been killed here of immense size, but we were not able to see either of them. Rattlesnakes we killed several times, as we met them swimming the river.

"While passing along close to a high bank one day, where there seemed to be no timber on the top, the governor got the men to land him a moment, as he was anxious to climb the bank and see what was in the distance. The canoe came to the shore, and I held it fast by grasping to some bushes at the water's edge. The bank was fifteen feet or so in height, and covered with grass and flowers to the top.

"The governor stepped ashore, and after ascending a step or two, drew himself back a little, and with his eye fixed on something before and above him which I did not see, he said in a quick tone, as he was reaching his hand back, 'Smyth! Hand me my rifle!' 'Take old Minié?' said I. 'No! Be quick as lightning! I prefer Sam!' I handed him his gun, which was instantly at his face, and cracked. I saw a huge snake leap from the top of the bank, much higher than his head, right towards him, and fall at his feet; the governor sprung at the same time, at one leap, quite onto the boat, with his rifle in his hand, and as pale as a ghost. This was quick work, I assure you. He said that he had fired at a rattlesnake and had missed it; that he saw the creature coiling up for a jump, and by the rattling he knew there was not an instant to lose when I handed him the gun. He said that he had missed the snake and it had struck him on the breast, but that luckily he was not bitten; and how he could have missed the snake he could not tell, unless the ball had been lost out of the cylinder. 'The snake's head was raised high up,' said he, 'and perfectly still, and looking me right in the face, and at sixty yards I could not have missed such a mark.'

"The governor wore a stout brown linen frock, tied across the throat and breast with strings, and just where he represented he had been struck I saw a spot of blood the size of a half-crown piece, and I said, 'You are bitten!' All hands gathered around him then, Indians and all. We untied and opened the frock; the blood was still more upon his shirt and also upon his flannel worn under it, which were ripped open, and on the breast a spot as large as the palm of my hand, on the skin, was covered with blood. The blood was washed off, and the faithful little half-breed was down upon his knees, and prepared to suck the poison from the wound, by which means the Indians are in the habit of extracting the poison; but looking a moment for the wound, he got up, and with a smile of exultation, he said, 'There's no harm! You'll find the snake without a head.'

"One of the Indians then stepped ashore near where the governor had stood, and pushing some weeds aside with his paddle, showed us the monster, regularly coiled up where he had fallen, and with his headless trunk erect and ready for another spring! Its head was shot regularly off, as 'Sam' had designed, and the creature, being at the instant so near the spring and so ready, with its aim made, that it leapt and struck the governor probably in the spot where it would have struck him and have made him a corpse in ten minutes, provided he had missed his mark.

"The bleeding trunk had printed its mark with blood where it struck, and driven the blood through the dress to the skin. A blow with the edge of a paddle finished the battle. The length of this brute was four feet, and its thickness about that of my arm above the elbow.

"How curious it is that if you cut off the head of a rattlesnake its body will live for hours, and jump at you if you touch it with a stick; when, if you break the spine near the tail, with even a feeble blow, it is dead in a minute! This we proved on several occasions.

"Farther down the river, one day we had a great alarm by the yelling and singing of two hundred or more Indians, men, women, and children, coming down the river in canoes behind us at a rapid rate —a party, as they proved to be, from one of the friendly villages we had passed going a little farther down the river to a famous beach, where they often go on a turtle hunt! They invited us to join them, and we kept company with them, and encamped all together a little before night.

"These people told us the scene of their operations was a long sand-beach just around the point, below where we were landed; and they, knowing the shape of the ground, were aware of the time of night and the mode in which the attack was to be made. These turtles have soft shells, and are excellent eating; and at certain seasons of the year come out in vast numbers from the river, generally about midnight, and creeping up the sand-banks some five or six rods from the shore, dig holes in the sand a foot or more deep, and lay, each one, some fifty or sixty eggs, about the size of a barn-fowl's egg, perfectly round, and with soft shells; they are all yolk, and quite as good as barn-fowls' eggs to eat.

"It seems curious that these creatures are never seen in the day time, if you go the whole length of the river; nor can you see them in the night before midnight—the time that they come out to lay their eggs to be hatched by the heat of the sun.

"The Indians, aware of this, had encamped half-a-mile or so distant from the sandbar above, and made sorts of tents with mattings made of palm-leaves, which they had rolled up in their canoes. Their fires were built, and a great deal of merriment passed off, but no feasting nor dancing before the hunt, which would take place a little before midnight. The governor said he would not miss these scenes for fifty pounds. He tried to get some of the men to give him a dance, but they said their bellies were too empty, they had eaten nothing for four or five days, neither men nor women, so that the turtle feast might taste good; after that there would be plenty of dancing.

"During this time the women were all at work making torches, which they construct from a sort of palm-leaf that burns like pitch pine. There was a doctor, a sort of a conjuror, who was performing some sort of witchcraft to make the turtles come; he had told them he was afraid they wouldn't come up that night, and many believing him, made the party rather desponding and dull.

"However, about a quarter-past eleven, the men all started, leaving the women behind to bring up the rear with the torches; but they were all ordered not to speak a loud word from that moment.

"One of the men, who seemed to be the leader of the party, was one whose portrait the governor had painted while stopping in his village a few days before. He took the lead of the party through the point of timber we had to pass, perhaps a quarter of a mile, and had a small torch in his hand to see the way; he held a long cord for the governor and me to hold on to, that we might not lose the way; the rest of the men all followed in each other's tracks, Indian file, and without a word spoken.

"Coming up to the edge of the timber opposite to the sandbar, and finding there was nothing on it yet, our friend and two or three others, with the governor and myself, were seated behind some palmetto bushes, which had been arranged before night for the purpose, and the rest of the men, perhaps a hundred, were all lying flat, in a row parallel to the shore of the river, but a few paces back of us.

"From behind the screen of palmettoes we had a fair view of the sandbank, which looked white; and when the turtles appeared on the sand, the signal was given by the cord which extended from the conductor to the rear rank, who passed on the signal by touching each other. Nothing was seen for half or three-quarters of an hour; at length, when I was just falling asleep, I felt a pinch on my leg, and looking through the screen, the sands for a great distance seemed, near the water, to be black with these creatures coming up out of the water. They seemed to come up like an army of soldiers. They kept moving up farther and farther, and the Indian kept pinching my leg till I was almost ready to holloa out.

"The signal had been given to the rear-guard, and all knew what was on the beach though they couldn't see, but all lay as still as death. These creatures having got up some five or six rods from the water, went to heaving up the sand with their paws, making the holes and laying their eggs. This was very quick work, and they could not have lost much time; for in the space of half-an-hour the holes were all smoothed over, and the black mass was seen moving towards the water. The signal was then given, and as quick as the wind, the Indians were upon them and turning them upon their backs. Such a scrambling as this I never saw or thought of before! Some hundreds of them were upset in this manner, and some thousands plunged into the water, and many of these were dragged out again by the Indians, who plunged in after them.

"All this onslaught was completed in less than half-a-minute, and no noise but laughing and grunting heard. The chief then sounded a loud whistle, which was for the torch-bearers to come, and in five minutes came down the beach, at full speed, the women and children, each one carrying a blazing torch, when they joined the party with the lights, overlooking the field of battle, and counting the number of their victims lying on their backs.

"This scene, with the wild figures, the blazing torches, and the magnificent forests lighted up, the governor said was the most magnificent thing he had ever beheld. I am sure no picture could ever do it justice.

"The squaws now selected a dozen or so of the finest of the turtles for their feast, and with their torches lighted, the party went back to the encampment, leaving the prisoners on the field of battle till the next morning.

"When we got back to the encampment, where all the pots were boiling, it was equally astonishing and amusing to see how handily and how quickly these animals were cut up and cooked, and how quick the soup was made, and then how fast and how long it was devoured. The soup and the meat were delicious, and if we had had the empty bellies that these people had, we should easily, like them, have eaten ourselves into stupidity.

"The governor and I slept in our canoe that night, and got up at an early hour to see the maneuver on the battlefield, but, to our surprise, no one moved towards it before ten or eleven o'clock, for all were asleep as if they had been in a drunken carouse. In fact they had been up all night, and then eaten so much that they could scarcely move.

"About noon, after they had all feasted again, they started in a mass and went to the sands; here their victims lay. The women brought large baskets, and the men went around with large knives, and slicing off the under-shell and opening the carcasses of the animals, the women approached, and tearing out the yellow fat from their intestines, threw it into their baskets. After the fat was all obtained, and some more of the best animals selected for food, the women and children went in for the eggs!

"This was one of the scenes most curious of all. With the paddles brought from their canoes, they went into the hidden treasures like so many Irishmen into a field of potatoes; and in much less time the surface of the ground was more completely covered than ever was seen by the heaviest crop in an Irish potato field.

"As this part of the business required no knife, nor any other weapon, it was a woman's task, and beneath the dignity of a warrior: the men sat and smoked their pipes whilst the women accomplished it.

"It was really incredible the quantity of eggs that were in the sand; and then how they were deposited so quick! These, however, were not only the eggs laid by the animals killed, but by the whole party, and there might have been hundreds that got back to the water to one that was taken.

"These eggs, the Indians assured us, were all laid while we were secreted and watching. This the governor didn't believe; it was impossible that they should deposit so many in that time; and it would be unnatural that they should all be ready to lay on the same night and at the same moment. But the Indian doctor told him it was true, and that he could always tell the very night they would come out.

"The governor, however, saw that all this thing was under the control of the doctors or mystery men, and he said it was best not to question it.

"The women and children for the most part of the afternoon were taking up the fat, the carcasses, and the eggs, and packing them in their canoes. The fat is taken to their villages and put into large troughs, where they pound out the yellow oil or grease, which is very rich and like the best of butter, and is taken to Para in earthen jars which they manufacture, and sold at a high price.

"It was too late for us to start off that day, and we stayed overnight again. The governor tried again to set them dancing, but the old doctor told him that now their bellies were too full; and on inquiring how long before they would be ready for a dance, he said it might be several days, for they were going to remain there some days expressly to eat, and while they were feasting it was difficult to dance.

"So at an early hour the next morning, with three or four fine large turtles, and full a bushel of eggs laid in, we started off.

"Our turtles were a great luxury to us, and for me, the eggs more particularly so; for I never before enjoyed any food so much; and in the eating of them, there was a thing that bothered the governor very much—there was not a stale egg among them, but all fresh, as the Indian doctor had told us.

"After striking out into the mighty Amazon at Obidos, we had a journey of some six or eight days from that to Santarem, which is at the head of tidewater, and a place of, maybe, two hundred houses. From that we got a chance down to Para, several hundred miles nearer the coast. Para is a large and flourishing seaport town, where a great business is done.

"The governor was here a while, and left some three months since in company with a member of the Brazilian Parliament, on a steamer up the Amazon.

"Your ever affectionate brother, "J. S."

XVI

THE ABOVE RATHER LENGTHY EXTRACTS I have ventured to make because they so graphically describe scenes and events which we witnessed together; and because, at least, such an acknowledgment is due to the talents, as well as fidelity and attachment, with which this young man volunteered to accompany and aid me through a wild and difficult country. Smyth narrates well and correctly; but he travels fast—too fast. He has brought us to Para; Para is a great way. He has left out many things; he has forgotten my friends the Indians, and also the 'story of the pigs.' "Pigs?" "Yes." "What! Pigs in that wild country?" "Yes, pigs: and I'll tell you more about them by-and-by."

Before leaving Demerara with my little outfit, I visited the neighboring tribes in that vicinity; the Caribbees and Macouchis, the Accoways and the Warrows, in Dutch Guiana, in the neighborhood of Paramaribo and New Amsterdam; and the Arowaks on the Rio Corontyn; and on our way, on the headwaters of the Essequibo, the Tarumas and Oyaways, which, with those on the plains of Venezuela, are, in fact, but the names of different bands or sections of the great Caribbee family, which occupy one-fifth at least of the Southern hemisphere.

This numerous tribe also occupied all the Lesser Antilles at the time of the discovery of those islands by Columbus, and have since been destroyed, or fled from the islands, to evade the slavery endeavored to be fixed upon them by the Spaniards, to the coast of South and Central America, where they are living.

These people are generally rather small in stature, and inferior to the North American races, but not inferior to some that may be found there; and enough like them in features and color, as well as in customs, to stamp them, without a doubt, as a part of the great and national American family.

These tribes in this vicinity, which show a strong resemblance to one another in complexion and customs, also speak a kindred language, showing them to be a family group. Their skin is a shade darker than that of the North American races, and their modes of dress very different; the latter of which is undoubtedly the result of the difference of climate. The weather in the tropics admits of but little clothing, and these tribes are almost naked, both women and men; yet they have and support a strict sense of decency and modesty at the same time, for which these poor creatures deserve great credit.

Their naked limbs and bodies are rubbed over with some soft and limpid grease every day, and though often reputed filthy, they are nevertheless far more cleanly and free from filth and vermin than any class of people equally poor in any part of the civilized world, where they are, from necessity, loaded with a burthen of rags that don't have a daily (and oftentimes not a weekly, nor a monthly, and sometimes not an annual) ablution.

WE ARE NOW IN THE GREAT AND VERDANT VALLEY OF THE AMAZON! What shall I say first? The Acary (or Tumucumache, or Crystal) Mountains which we have passed over, forming the boundary line between British and Dutch Guiana and Brazil, are truly sublime; not unlike the Rocky Mountains in North America in some respects, and very much unlike them in some others.

The descent from these mountains, and their graceful slopes off into the valley of everlasting green, were, as my friend Smyth has said, truly grand and magnificent.

Let us sit down a few moments; we are weary— our mule died ten days ago, and our packs are now heavy. We have come out from that gorge I that awful ravine! It is frightful to look back or to think back! Why should we, when here is the blue sky, and the sun, and the ocean again before us! How warm and how cheering!

And what a curious cloud! What a straight line it makes across the sky! Yes, it must be. And what a boundless ocean of green and blue we are looking over, and not a vessel to be seen! But stop! That can't be. That can't be the ocean! We are on our course! Give me the pocket compass. There! That's south—there's no ocean there. We are steering into the valley of the Amazon; and here it lies before us—we are right! And what's at our feet? Green grass and beautiful flowers? Not at all—yellow and blue clay, and nothing else. And what beyond, beneath us? Clay. And what those thousand winding, twisting channels, that seem to soften into blue in the distance, down, down, so far below us? Clay, clay, and nothing else.

Yes, something else; they glisten in the sun; they have specks that sparkle like the Bude light; they may be diamonds? No, they are crystals of quartz, but they are very beautiful—let's fill our pockets. But here are some that are quite yellow, and others that are purple; oh, how beautiful!—Let's throw away those we have got. These are topaz and amethyst, and far more beautiful; and now and then there is one of carmine. And still more lovely! These are smaller and more scarce—they are rubellites. These are washed down from the mountains? Undoubtedly. And it just now occurs to me that some of the Spanish writers call these the 'Crystal Mountains.' Gold-mines were worked in these mountains two hundred years ago. There is gold, then, under our feet? Not a doubt of it; but we can't wash; there is no water within some miles, and our tin kettle is of no use.

But we begin to see more clearly; we see streaks of light green running down between these crevices and ravines, stretching off into the ocean, as it were, they become a solid mass of green, and then of black, at last.

The first of these are the rolling prairies, and then the level valley, with its dark and boundless forests of palms. But where's the end of it? It has no end. It is infinite. Take the glass and look; it's all the same; it rises up, up, and up, until it forms that blue line we see in the clouds! It can't be so! It must be so! And that black streak we see on the left beneath us, is the timber skirting the Rio Trombutas, to which we have got to wend our way. Shall we reach the timber today? I don't think so.

We feel like boys here, don't we? Exactly so. Our shadows are all under our feet; how awkward to step on one's own head! We are now exactly under the equator. At noon; where is the south? Which is the north? No one but our little compass can tell. How droll! But this clay is not so hot? No, the rays of the sun are straight down, and there is little refraction.

Like ants, we wandered and crept along over the winding gullies of clay; and, at length, met tufts of grass and sage, and afterwards, patches and fields, and, at last, an ocean of grass, speckled, and spotted, and spangled, with all the beautiful colors of the floral world. Clumps and bunches of palms, and palmettoes, and geraniums, each little group like a peep into the glass-house at Kew, though more beautiful, and filled with gay and chattering birds and insects.

And on and over these beautiful plains, immense herds of wild cattle and horses of various colors were grazing, and flying before us as we approached.

A fine fat cow was here felled by the old Minié, and we were again happy. We had plenty of good beef, and raw hide for soling our moccasins, and a clear and running brook for bathing and for washing our shirts; what could we want more? Some three or four days' rest put us on our legs and on our route again.

The Indian trails, and at last the feeble smoke of their distant wigwams, showed us we were again in the land of the living, though we were worn almost out of it. We were kindly received and treated by all the tribes on the Trombutas, which we were now to descend. These Indians— Warkas, Zurumatis, Zumas, Tupis, and several others, are very different from the Caribbee races living on the other side of the mountains. They are a taller and a heavier-built race, and somewhat lighter in color. They belong to the great family of Guarani, which may be said to occupy the whole of Eastern and Northern Brazil, and often called Tupi, but for what reason I cannot tell. Tupi is the name of a band (or section) only, of the Guarani, speaking the same language, with very little variation, and no doubt from the same stock. It is matter of little consequence, however, whether they are all called Guarani, or all called Tupi, for whichever they are, there never has been, and never will be, any boundary fixed between them.

From the early Spanish history of South America we learn that there were somewhere in the valley of the Amazon, a nation of Amazons; and the river and the valley seem to have taken their names from this tradition. The Spaniards and Portuguese have pushed their conquests and subjugations of the Indian tribes as far as they have been able to do, and not, as yet, having found the Amazons, their more modern historians have placed them on the banks of the Trombutas, where the Indians have been successful in keeping their invaders at a distance, and where it was natural to infer that the Amazons resided, as they certainly were nowhere else.

At the same time, it was easy to suppose, as they reported, that these people were cannibals, and ate foreigners who ventured amongst them. I had all these frightful reports to contend against, and it will easily be imagined how my nerves were excited. This required a stronger nerving up, if possible, than the approach to the Thunder's Nest!

But see how many marvelous things vanish when we come close to them!

I SOON FOUND THAT THERE WERE NO AMAZONS ON THIS RIVER, nor Dianas, nor Bacchantes, but hosts of Gladiators, of Apollos, and Fauns. Their young men and boys are all Fauns. Castor and Pollux, and old Silenus, with his infant Bacchus in his arms, may be often seen amongst them.

The nearest thing I could discover or hear of to the Amazons, were the women in some of the tribes, who were famous for mounting their horses, and, with the deadly bolas, could bring down the wild ox or the wild horse as easily as their husbands. And on inquiring amongst the various villages for the cannibals, I was laughed at even by the women and children for asking so ridiculous a question; a thing, apparently, that they never had heard of before.

One said they had not got to be quite so poor as to have to eat each other yet, but they might perhaps be reduced some time or other to the necessity of doing it. And in the midst of this conversation, a diffident young man stepped forward and said, "Yes, tell the white man, there are some such persons farther down the river. He will find some white men living in two or three wigwams on the left bank of the river, who eat the flesh of their own relations, and, what was worse, they sell their skins!"

This created a great laugh amongst the Indians; and, on descending the river, some distance above Obidos, at its mouth, we found these cannibals, several Frenchmen and Americans, killing monkeys, and sending their skins to Paris for the manufacture of ladies' gloves; and living, as they told us, entirely on the flesh of those poor brutes!

This was the nearest approach to cannibalism that I have discovered in my travels amongst North or South American Indians. Books are full of it, but the wilderness is without it! I have travelled and lived fifteen years amongst Indians, and I have not yet found it; and I don't believe that any man has seen anything nearer to it in these countries than what I have above described.

Cannibalism may have been practiced, and still may be, under certain circumstances, in some of the South Sea Islands, and in some parts of Africa. We have frequent reports of such practices from travelers, and those very respectable men; but these reports don't prove the fact. None of these travelers tell us they have seen it. No doubt they tell us what they have heard, and what they believe. But how do they get their information? Not from the savages; they can't speak with them. Every savage race on earth has its foreign traders amongst them. These are generally the interpreters for travelers who come, and jealous of all persons entering these tribes, to overlook their nefarious system of trade and abuse.

These traders have an object in representing the savage as ten times more cruel and murderous than he is; and amongst other things, as a cannibal, who is sure to kill and eat travelers if they penetrate farther into their country.

It is the custom with most savage tribes (and this in America as well as in Africa) to apply the term cannibal to their enemies around them as a term of reproach; but when we enter these tribes the cannibals are not there, they are in the next tribe, and then in the next, and so they fly, like a phantom, before us.

The leaders of war-parties also apply the epithet of cannibals to their enemies, in order to inflame their warriors going into battle: "You go to fight a set of cannibals; to conquer or to be eaten!"

Some of the most recent travelers in Africa (and the most recent ought to be the most reliable) assure us that several of the tribes they were amongst were cannibals, and that they eat the very aged people, "killing them to eat them, and eating those who die of old age." Grandfathers and grandmothers I should scarcely think would be very good eating. If these people eat each other for the pleasure of eating, one would suppose that they would take the middle-aged or the young and tender.

If these travelers would merely tell us that these people eat each other, we might believe it possible; but when they qualify their statements by telling us that they only eat the very aged ones, they weaken their own evidence. They leave us as history, assertions without proof, relative to the existence of a custom both against nature and against taste; raising presumptions formidable enough to stand against very strong positive proof.

As a ceremonial, in the celebration of victories, religious rites, etc., human flesh is sometimes eaten; and the practice, by custom, observed as a necessary form; but this is not cannibalism.

That savage tribes may sometimes eat their enemies whom they have slain in battle, one can easily believe. Savages always go to war on empty stomachs; and at the end of a battle, after many days' fasting and under great exhaustion, and having no commissariat to supply them with food, it would be easy, and almost natural, to use their enemies for food.

But that any race of human beings, with humanity enough to treat unprotected strangers amongst them with "kindness and hospitality," and to "help and to protect and feed them" in traveling through their country, will kill and eat their own people for the pleasure of eating, I don't believe.

The poor Indian's remark above quoted ("We have not got to be so poor as to have to eat each other yet; though we may sometime be reduced to that necessity") is not without its significance.

White men have in some instances been reduced to the dire necessity of eating each other, and have cast lots to decide which of the party should be first killed for food; but this is not cannibalism. If this were cannibalism, it might with truth be predicted, that by the system of robbery and abuse practiced on the American frontiers, thousands of the poor Indians will soon be compelled to become cannibals.

Some very respectable and accredited early travelers and explorers averred that they saw the Patagonians on the Atlantic coast, seven, eight, and even ten feet high! But modern travelers who go and live amongst them find the tallest of them to be but a little over six feet. It is evident that the atmosphere, under certain circumstances, has a magnifying power, and becomes a very uncertain medium, and particularly so when persons are frightened. The first Indian I ever saw, my readers will recollect, was a giant; but a little familiar acquaintance made him much smaller.

Some writers (who take a peep into an Indian's wigwam without knowing the meaning of things around them, see little balls of clay piled away, which every Indian stores up for cleaning his dresses, and painting his body and limbs, and of which he sometimes swallows a small pill to cure the heartburn just as my good old mother used to make me do when I was a boy) have reported some of the tribes as 'dirt eaters' asserting that "when they are in a state of starvation, they live for some time upon dirt; eating a pound of clay per day." What!—a pound of clay per day on a famished stomach? What an absurdity! And what a pity the revealers of such astonishing facts should not live a while in some of these poor people's wigwams, and learn what the Indians do with these little balls of clay, before they prepare such astounding information for the world's reading.

But stop; dirt is much more digestible than stones! I was a 'stone eater' a little way back— both are 'giants'—and one story has just as much truth in it as the other.

WE WERE NEAR THE HEAD OF THE TROMBUTAS—on it beautiful and grassy plains? Yes. Well, let us sit down here too, a while in the shade of these beautiful bananas—but no; these are not bananas, the pride and grace of the forest, such as we saw on the banks of the Essequibo and the Orinoco. No, but they are palms, nevertheless;

and oh, how charming and elegant, with their leaning, bending stems and pennated foliage! The graceful banana of Guiana, I think, has not yet made its way over the Tumucumache; I don't see it anywhere. All the rest seem to be here.

How beautifully and gracefully these bespangled prairies wind and roll their sloping sides down to the river shore! What a beautiful lawn for a nobleman's mansion, with this very clump of trees for its center, with these myriads of wild flowers, and all these gay and cheerful songsters in it! But look! What snake is that? That's not a rattlesnake, with a white ring around its neck. Oh, no; it's quite a harmless creature; it never bites; it's only a pilot. A pilot? I don't understand. Why, it's the rattlesnake's pilot, always with him, looking out the way. What a gentleman! Then the rattlesnake is close by us? Undoubtedly; most likely behind us: they always lie in the shade during the heat of the day. Let's move off; I can't say that I fancy the company of such gentlemen.

Our little boat rolls and glides along from day to day, and palms, and enameled rolling prairies, and gay and chirping birds are everywhere. The river enters the deep and shady forests, and we enter with it. Who knows what we shall see when we turn that next point? And the next? And the next? Each turn is new, each is beautiful, and more and more grand.

The dense and lofty forests, into which the sun's rays can never penetrate, are before us. Twining and twisting vines, like huge serpents, are rising to their tops; some clinging to their trunks, others hanging suspended in the air like broken cordage, and on them, in clumps and bouquets, the most beautiful parasitic flowers. Crowded out from these thickets of trunks and branches, leaves and vines, so thickly grouped that neither sun nor wind can penetrate, we see the strangled palms and other trees pushing their heads out, and bending over the river for a breathing-place.

And through and above these matted forests, the tall and straight trunks of the lofty palms are seen in the distance, like the columns of vast and boundless edifices, and spreading over and above all, their pennated heads show us a forest above a forest, the one apparently growing out of the other. How sublime!

These, with all their grandeur, are reflected in the mirrored water; and thus we have four forests all before us at one view, the one just as distinct in form and color as the other. How grand the mirage! The touch of the oar upon the boat comes back from these solitudes with a redoubled sound; every cough and every 'whoop' is echoed back, and with them 'who, who!' from the wilderness; but we don't know from whom. Every crack of the rifle sets a hundred squeaking and chattering voices in motion. A hundred monkeys are shaking the branches in the tree tops ahead of us, and taking a peep at us, and the sleeping alligators tumble from their logs into the water, leaving their circular waves behind and around them.

But these solitudes are not everywhere. We turn another bend, and before us we have, on one bank, a vast and beautiful meadow, and on it a forest in miniature. The grass, some six or seven feet high, and filled with twisted and knotted vines, and dotted with wild flowers; and above and through it, like the stately palms in the forest, the tall and straight shafts of the sunflowers, with their graceful yellow and leaning heads, forming a forest of black and gold above the green, and red, and pink, and blue below.

What myriads of bumblebees, and humming-birds, and butter-flies are working here! But, this path! This path? Why, it's the tigers' walk! Let's go on; push off.

We sleep in hammocks here. Not in these prairies? No, but always in the timber. We sling our hammocks between two trees, and build a fire on each side of us. The fire protects us from animals and reptiles; both are afraid of it.

We stopped our boat one day for our accustomed mid-day rest, in the cool shade of one of these stately forests, where there was a beautifully variegated group of hills, with tufts of timber and gaudy prairies sloping down to the river on the opposite shore. Our men had fallen asleep, as usual, in the boat, and I said to my friend Smyth, who, with myself, was seated on the top of the bank, "How awfully silent and doleful it seems—not the sound of a bird or a cricket can be heard! Suppose we have some music." "Agreed," said Smyth, and raising the old Minié, he fired it off over the water. 'Sam' followed with three cracks, as fast as they could be got off!

The party in the boat were all, of course, upon their feet in an instant, and we sat smiling at them. Then the concert began—a hundred monkeys could be heard chattering and howling, treble, tenor, and bass, with flats and sharps, and semitones, and baritones, and falsettos, whilst five hundred at least were scratching, leaping, and vaulting about amongst the branches, and gathering over our heads, in full view, to take a peep at us. We sat in an open place, that they might have a full view of us, and we rose up to show ourselves at full length, that their curiosity might be fully gratified. With my opera-glass, which I took from my pocket, I brought all these little inquisitive, bright-eyed faces near enough to shake hands, and had the most curious view of them. I never before knew the cleanliness, the grace, and beauty of these wonderful creatures until I saw them in that way, in their native element and unrestrained movements. Where on earth those creatures gathered from in so short a time, in such numbers, it was impossible to conceive; and they were still coming. Like pigeons, they sat in rows upon the limbs, and even were in some places piled on each other's backs, and all gazing at us.

To give the inquisitive multitude a fair illustration, I fired another shot, and another, and such a scampering I never saw before! In half-a-minute every animal, and every trace and shadow of them, were out of sight; nor did they come near us again. The woods were ringing at this time with a hundred voices—"Tso-cano! Tso-cano! Go on, John!"—came from the tops of the highest trees; the hideous roar of a tiger was heard, not far off, and when done, another answered on the other side of the river. The howling monkeys, who only open their throats at night, gave us a strain or two; the white swans were piping in the distance, and the quacking ducks and geese were passing to and fro in flocks up and down the river. The gabbling parrots and parroquets and cockatoos, with their long, and red, and blue tails, were creeping out and hanging on to the outer branches to get a look at what was going on.

So far we heard but the notes of alarm, of fear, and they were soon done—there was little music in these. But then the songsters came—the joyous, merry pipers (when fear was over, and curiosity not satisfied); they now began to venture out from the thickets and the towering forests, and in hundreds were seen sailing over the river from their shady retreats in the copses and little groves on the hillsides, and lighting on the trees around us. Curious and inquisitive little strangers, with your red breasts and throats, your white cockades, your blue jackets, and purple tufts, and piercing eyes, and turning beads, I wish I knew your hundred names!

All yet were silent. As we sat still, gazing and ogling were the first impulses—they with their piercing little sharp eyes, and I with my opera lens; but a chirp or two opened the concert. One song brought on another, and another, as an announcement that danger was passed; and no aviary that ever was heard could produce such a concert and such a chorus of sweet sounds as was here presented.

They swelled their little throats to the highest possible key in the din of their concert; and after it gradually died away, some hangers-on gave duets, and others solos, each little warbler hopping nearer and nearer to us, and dropping his last notes with a bow of the head and a "There, there! They can't beat that!—mine is certainly the most beautiful!"

"But hark!" said I, "Smyth; music is contagious." The crickets and grasshoppers were singing in the grass, and at length, 'P-r-r-out! P-r-r-out!' said a huge frog, whose snout and ears were raised a little above the surface of the water, amongst the water-lilies and rushes near the shore; and then, another, a smaller one, 'Peut! Peut!' and another, a big fellow, 'El-der-gin! El-der-gin!' and then a terrible bull-frog, his mouth the size of the clasp of a lady's reticule, 'Kr-r-r-ow! Kr-r-r-ow!' and at least five thousand more, on both sides of the river; for, by the custom of frogs, when one sings, all must join in, large and small, no matter what time of day or night, as far as their voices can be heard by each other.

All animals and birds sing in this country—it is the land of song. Music is the language of happiness and enjoyment—what a happy community this is!

Now for the 'pigs.' Pigs, in this country, are peccaries, a species of wild hog, resembling, in color and in proportion, as well as in character, the wild boar of the continent of Europe. They are not more than one-half the size, but have all the ferocity and sagacity of that animal, and are equally pugnacious. An individual one is not able to cope with the strength of a man, but when in groups they are able to tear a man to pieces in a little time.

Immense numbers of these animals are found throughout the whole valley of the Amazon and the Essequibo, living chiefly on the great quantity of mast that falls from various trees. They often run in groups of several hundreds, and unite in terrible conflicts with man or beasts for their own protection.

We had taken our dinner one day on the bank in a large and open forest, when Smyth took his rifle in his hand, and said "he was going to take a walk down the river, and see what he could murder." His passion was for shooting; and it seemed to be little matter with him what it was, if he could hear the 'old Minié speak' (as he called it), and see his game fall. He strolled off down the river bank, and after he had been gone a quarter of an hour or so, I heard the crack of his rifle; and in the half of a minute another—and in the quarter of a minute another!— and after the lapse of two or three minutes he commenced firing again!

I began to fear that he had met hostile Indians or some other dangerous enemy, and seizing up my rifle, and taking one of the Indians of the boat, with his quiver of poisoned arrows slung, we started for his assistance; at this time the firing stopped, and we heard him calling out at the top of his voice for help. We then ran as fast as we could, and getting near the place, we began to advance with caution, and I at length discovered him standing on the trunk of a fallen tree, the branches of which had lodged against others, preventing it from coming quite to the ground; his rifle was in his left hand, and by the other he was holding on to a branch to balance himself, and underneath and around him a dense mass of some two or three hundred peccaries, with the bristles all standing on their backs, as they were foaming at their mouths and whetting their white tusks, and looking up at him.

Smyth saw us approaching, and called out to me to take care of my life. These sagacious little creatures knew, from the direction that he was giving to his voice, that he had help coming in that quarter; and a hundred of them at least began to turn their attention to us, and were starting to come towards us without having seen us, and without our having spoken a word to notify them of our approach.

The only shelter for us was the trunk of a large mora tree, behind which we took our positions. I stood so as to look around the tree, and getting my rifle to bear, and my position to be right for firing, and the Indian with his bow drawn behind me, we waited till the foremost of this phalanx of little warriors came advancing up slowly, and whetting their tusks, not having yet seen us. When within some seven or eight rods, I began upon the nearest—and the next—and the next—and having shot down four of the leaders, the sagacious little fellows, seeing their foremost and bravest falling so fast—and thinking perhaps, like the Indians, that this was to last all day, they gave a grunt and made a wheel, which seemed to be a signal understood by the whole troop, for in one instant they were all off at full speed, and were soon out of sight, leaving the four I had shot, and some eight or ten of the leaders which Smyth had killed, on the field of battle, when his powder had given out and he was obliged to call out for help.

He told me that he had discovered some parts of the group whilst they were scattered about and hunting nuts; and having no idea of their numbers, he had shot one, when the others, from all quarters, gathered around him, and that if he had not luckily found the fallen tree close by him, or that if his foot had slipped after he got on to it, he would have been torn to pieces in a very few minutes.

I had not a doubt of this fact when I saw the manner in which they had cut and marked with their tusks the log on which he had stood, and also the mangled bodies of those he had shot; which, by their custom, they had fallen upon and torn to pieces in their fury.

XVII

LET US NOW FOR A WHILE LEAVE BEASTS, and birds, and reptiles, for a subject of far greater interest and importance. The studies of my wanderings have been the looks, condition, character, and customs of native man; and these their incidents or accessories merely. These are not without their interest and importance, however, but they can be seen in the wilderness alive, and in our museums, hundreds of years to come, as well as now; but native man, with his modes, is soon to disappear from the American forests, and not even his skin will be found in our museums.

The hand of his fellow-man is everywhere raised against him, whilst the grizzly bears, the tigers, and the hyenas are allowed to live—and why? Because he is unfortunately a landowner, and has the means to pay for rum and whisky.

Much the same system of traffic and dissipation, which I have before alluded to, is destroying these poor people in this country, but without the devastation which it carries with it in some parts of North America; because there are no immigrating masses here to push forward a frontier so rapidly, dispossessing the Indians of their country.

A sort of civilization has been longer established in this country, and more generally and more gradually infused amongst the savage races, without so completely destroying them. By this process, a greater mixture of races and languages has been produced; and though there is little high civilization, and seldom extinction, there is yet an immense extension of demi-races, and very seldom full bloods. The true original looks and customs of the Indians in this country are therefore, most generally, very difficult to see.

From the warmth of the climate, the Indians in these regions, semi-civilized or not, go almost naked. Their character and customs are nevertheless equally full of interest; and in this country, as in North America, I have aimed at gathering everything pertaining to a full and just account of them. In doing this, the reader can imagine that I have had many long and tedious journeys by land and by water; some of which have been already briefly told, and most of the others (though we may journey together yet a little farther) must be left for a larger book.

We were at Para. Para is a large and flourishing commercial town, of forty or fifty thousand inhabitants, on the south side of the great estuary of the Amazon, and one hundred miles from the coast of the sea.

There are the remnants of several Indian tribes living around Para, who bring into its market fish and oysters, and fruits of fifty kinds, from the palms and other trees and shrubs of the forests. In the dense and lofty forests of palms on the islands and shores between Para and the ocean, we see again, as we saw at the mouth of the Orinoco, the Canoe Indians living in 'nests' built in the trees. These constructions, though exceedingly rude, are nevertheless comfortable and secure for the people who live in them, and whose modes, in many other respects, are equally curious.

These are very properly called Canoe Indians, for they live exclusively on fish and oysters; and to obtain them and to travel anywhere, and on any errand whatever, they must necessarily be in their canoes. They cannot step out of their houses except into their canoes. In their canoes they dart through the dense forests of lofty palms with a swiftness which is almost incredible. They never travel in any other way, and very many of them seldom set their feet upon the dry land.

These stupendous forests of palms (called miriti) constitute one of the curiosities of the Amazon, and perhaps of the world. Hundreds, and thousands, and tens of thousands of acres around the mouths of the Amazon and the Orinoco are completely covered and shaded by these noble trees; their trunks, almost perfectly straight and smooth, without knot or limb, rise like the columns of some lofty temple to the height of one hundred or more feet, and then throw out their graceful branches, somewhat in the form of an umbrella, which are interlaced together so thick that the sun seldom shines through them.

At low tide these trees may be said to be rising out of the mud, and at high tide they are rising out of the water. They are so far from the sea that no waves of the ocean, or even of the river, reach them; and the water of the rising tide creeps in and around them as quietly and unruffled as if it came out of the ground, and actually has that appearance.

At low tide the Indian's canoe lies in the mud, and he is as sure to be lying, and eating, and drinking, or sleeping in his wigwam of sticks and leaves. But when the tide rises, it lifts his canoe to the steps of his wigwam, when, with his gay red feathers in his head and his vari-colored paddle in his hand, his nets, his spears, and his black-headed little papooses in his canoe, he steps into it and darts off amidst the myriad columns of this mighty temple, echoing and re-echoing, as he glides, the happy notes of his song, and those of the thousand songsters above his head and around him.

How curious it is that a part of mankind should build their houses in the trees! These are, strictly speaking, odd people. You will recollect I told you of the Skin-builders, the Dirt-builders, the Bark-builders, the Grass-builders, and the Timber-builders, and here we have the Nest-builders! And what sort of builders shall we have next? We shall see.

In the neighborhood of Para, on the Rios Tocantins and Zingu, I visited a dozen or more tribes, and then, on a steamer, started to see others. Lay your map of South America on the table, and see what I had before me! Look at the rivers, and realize their lengths. I took the largest first, the Amazon—rode to Tabatinga, eighteen hundred miles, the western boundary of Brazil; and from that, between Peru and Ecuador, to Nanta, three hundred and fifty miles, at the mouth of the Yucayali, and yet four hundred miles farther, and leaving the steamer, crossed the Andes to Lima, the most beautiful city in the world!

But this is traveling too fast again. I passed several things on the way, and we will go back and take a look at them.

From Para, I started on the steamer *Marajo*, the second or third voyage she had made, and the first steamer that ever ascended that river. There were on board several Portuguese gentlemen from Rio de Janeiro, and several others from Para, with their families, forming together a very pleasing and agreeable traveling party no doubt, if one could have spoken their language.

The first day at noon brought us into the bay of the Amazon, with its hundred islands; and the second, to Santarem, at the head of tide-water.

Above this we began to stem the current, and, for the first time, had evidence that we were ascending a river; and for the first time, also, we were fully sensible of the majesty and grandeur of its movement.

I had a few months before crept and drifted along its shores and sluices in a humble craft, from the mouth of the Trombutas, without being able to see or to understand it. But we were now lifted upon the deck of a steamer, and stemming the current and viewing it on both sides at once, which gave me some basis for its measurement.

From the middle of the river the distance was so great that the forests on either shore settled into monotony and tameness; but with my knowledge of their actual grandeur, this only served to inspire me with the real magnitude and magnificence of the sweeping current intervening. But when the vessel was running near the shore, which was generally the case, to evade the strength of the current, no pen or pencil can describe the gorgeousness and richness of the overhanging and reflected forests that changed every moment as we passed.

Every length of the boat was in itself a picture to stop and look at; but why stop? For the coming one was just as beautiful. Conversation was at an end, for exclamations and interjections took its place. A never-ending mass of green, of yellow, white, and pink, and red; and that without monotony, unless, from the never-ending changes, change itself became monotony!

Here the rounded tops of the lofty trees, some white, some pink with blossoms, were crowding out their flowery heads amongst the mass of green, and extending their long branches down quite into the river, and a hundred twisting vines hung in knots and clumps, and festoons of parasitic flowers were jetting down from the tops of the highest trees—the overhanging, gorgeous, rolling, and impenetrable mass, sweeping the sides of the boat as we passed, seemed to be tumbling down upon us, while they hid from our view the lofty bank on which their stately trunks were standing.

And there, an opening! We see the high and sloping bank, spangled to the water's edge, and into it, with pink and purple flowers—and the graceful palmettoes, like a thousand open fans, leaning and bowing around; and above the bank, the straight and lofty trunks of palms and other stately forest trees, like the pillars of some mighty portico, supporting their dome of branches interlocked; and farther on, but a part of this, an 'upper forest.' The wind has done this. Huge trees have been uprooted, and, tumbling half-way down, have lodged their branches in the crotchets of others; falling vegetation has lodged on these until a super-soil has been formed; descending vines have taken root in them and clambered again to their tops, and interwoven and lashed the mass to the encircled trunks and branches; nuts and fruits have fallen on these and taken root, and trees and flowers are growing in a second forest some fifty or sixty feet above the ground!

And do these look like loathsome ruins—like a wreck—like a misfortune? No, they are rounded; they are hidden; they are looped, and festooned, and embraced with clinging and hanging vines, supporting bouquets of beautiful flowers and fig-trees bending with their blossoms and ripened fruit at the same time.

But how gloomy and desolate? Not so. This is Nature's temple; its roof is not tiles nor slates, but a bed of flowers! And man is its tenant. Blue curls of smoke are seen floating around amongst the trees, and from underneath, a hundred pair of black and sparkling eyes from behind the logs and trees, and a dozen or two of the bravest and boldest of both sexes come leaping to the brink of the bank, to salute us as we pass.

Man's abode! How splendid, how grand, how cheap, and how comfortable! Man wants but a roof in this country; the open air must be around him. How splendid a roof he has here, bespangled with flowers and dropping ambrosia! And how delicious the air that he breathes, rustling through the blossoms and spices with which he is encompassed.

We see hundreds of canoes as we pass on, gliding along the shores in different directions, filled with red heads and red shoulders, but when we get near them, they dart into the mass of overhanging branches and leaves, and disappear in an instant. Sometimes their villages stand upon the bank, and in hundreds they are yelling and saluting us as we are puffing along by them.

Obidos, at the mouth of the Trombutas, is where my friend Smyth and myself first launched out into the broad Amazon; a little Spanish town of one thousand five hundred or two thousand inhabitants. Our steamer was alongside and moored. Some passengers got out, and others came on board. The inhabitants were all upon the bank, and amongst them several groups of Indians, and all gazing in wonder at us. Here was work for my pencil, and groups of them were booked as I sat upon the deck. And just before the vessel was to start, as I was walking on the deck, a sudden outcry was raised amongst the squaws and then amongst the men, and all eyes were upon me, and many hands extended towards me.

It seems that amongst the crowd were a number of the Indians, men and women, whom Smyth and I had joined in the turtle-hunt six months before, who now were down in their canoes on a visit to Obidos, and who, having recognized me, were calling to me to come ashore and shake hands with them. This compliment I could not resist, nor could I deny myself the pleasure of shaking hands with these good creatures—these 'Amazons,' these 'Cannibals,' of the Trombutas.

I leaped ashore, to the great surprise of all the passengers, and of the captain also, and the boat delaying a little, gave me time for the interview. No one can imagine the pleasure which these poor people felt in discovering me, and then seeing me come ashore to shake hands with them. I told them I was glad to see them, and not now being quite so poor as I was when I was among them, if the captain would wait for me a few minutes I would make them some little presents.

I explained my views to the captain, and he granted me the time. I opened a box in my luggage, and supplying my pockets with a quantity of knives, fish-hooks, beads, etc., which I had laid in for such occasions, I went ashore and distributed them, when several of the men embraced me in their arms, and all, both men and women, shook me by the hand, wishing me farewell.

This scene excited the sympathies of the ladies and other passengers on board, who threw them many presents, in money and other things.

The boat was ordered to go ahead, and just as the wheels began to revolve, a little lad ran to the water's edge, and handed to the captain, who was standing on the wheel-house, a beautiful 'blow-gun' and made signs for him to hand it to me.

Oh, how pleasing such meetings are to me! How I love to feel the gladdened souls of native men, moved by natural, human impulse, uninfluenced by fashion or a mercenary motive! Mine, I know, has something native remaining in it yet.

Ten days from Para brought us to Nanta, having passed some fifteen or twenty small Spanish towns and missions, and at least one hundred encampments and groups of Indians on the islands and shores, who seemed to have got notice in some way of our approach, and had assembled to take a look at the boat, and salute it. They stared at us with uplifted hands, and raised their voices to the highest pitch, but fired no guns, for as yet they neither have them nor know the use of them.

From the immense numbers of Indians we saw gathered on the banks, it would seem as if the country was swarming with human inhabitants, while in the whole distance these interminable forests and shores showed us not a monkey, nor a parrot, nor a tiger! The former were led to the river-shore, no doubt, in the extraordinary numbers which we saw, by feelings of curiosity; whilst the latter, from fear at the puffing and blowing of the steamer, hid themselves in the forests in silence as we passed; but no doubt a grand chorus was constantly raised behind us after we had got by.

It is estimated that there are over one hundred tribes, speaking different languages, on the shores of the Amazon, from its rise at the base of the Andes, to its mouth; and at this point we have probably passed something like three-fourths of them. I could give the names of near one hundred tribes that I have already learned of in the valley of the Amazon, but the list would be of little interest here.

If it be true that there are one hundred tribes on the banks of the Amazon, which I doubt, we may easily get five hundred different names for them, and be ignorant of their own, their real names, at last.

Bands of the same great family or tribe are often improperly called tribes, and have languages very dissimilar, and therefore the endless confusion in classification.

There is a general system of teaching by the Catholic Missions throughout all parts of South America, to which all the tribes have had more or less access, and from which they have received more or less instruction in Christianity, in agriculture, and in the Spanish and Portuguese languages.

The soothing and parental manner of the venerable padres who conduct these missions is calculated to curb the natural cruelties of the savage, and have had the effect in all parts of that country to cut down the angles that belong to all natural society unaided by the advances of civilization.

These missions are everywhere; and around them, in their vicinity, always more or less extensive settlements of Spanish and Portuguese, called in the Spanish language Gauchos, who live by a mixed industry of agriculture and the chase.

This population mixes easily with the native races, and with this amalgamation ensues a blending of languages, which is one of the most extraordinary features to be met with in the country; and particularly so on the lower half of the Amazon and its tributaries, and also throughout the whole northern and eastern portions of Brazil, where the three languages—the Spanish, the Portuguese, and Indian languages—are all about equally mixed, and in such a way as sometimes to appear the most laughably droll and ridiculous, and at others, the most absurd and inexplicable of all jargons on earth.

This language, which they call Lingua Geral, is spoken by all, by Spaniards, by Portuguese, and by the Indians, much alike; and though it no doubt is a handy language for the country, it is exceedingly perplexing and embarrassing for the traveler, who may think that his Spanish and his French, which he has learnt for the occasion, are going to answer him through the country. He must employ an interpreter, or learn to speak the Lingua Geral, or be as mum as if he were in the deserts of Siberia.

At Tabatinga, eighteen hundred miles above Para, two steamers were building by Americans, who had brought the whole machinery from the United States complete and ready to be put in. These vessels were being built to run on the Amazon, and a few years will no doubt show us a fleet of these and other vessels at that place, which will be the great commercial depot of Western Brazil and Eastern Peru and Ecuador.

In the vicinity of Nanta are a great many Indian tribes, amongst which are the Zeberos, the Urarinas, the Tambos, the Peebas, the Turantinis, the Connibos, the Sipibos, the Chetibos, the Sensis, the Remos, the Amahovacs, the Antis, the Siriniris, the Tuirenis, the Huachipasis, the Pacapacuris, and at least a dozen others; their languages all dialectic, and their physiological traits and color altogether prove them to be only bands or sections of one great family, and that family only the fusion, perhaps, of Ando-Peruvian and Guarani.

It would be next to impossible for any stranger to trace the Amazon from its mouth to its true source in the space of his lifetime, and it would be ten times more difficult to trace the savage races in South America, through all their displacements and migrations, to their true fountain. Of the South American tribes there are none nearer approaching to their primitive state than many of the tribes about the heads of the Amazon; and amongst these I spent some time. They have forests full of game, and rivers full of fish, and all the varieties of palms with their various kinds of fruit; and also the immense plains or pampas, stocked with wild horses and wild cattle for food, and for their skins and hair, which are articles of commerce with them. From these combined advantages they insure an easy and independent living and have therefore the fewest inducements to adopt civilized modes of life.

XVIII

A RIDE ACROSS THE PAMPA DEL SACRAMENTO, and a passage of the Yucayali in a canoe, afforded me some of the loveliest views of country I ever beheld, and some of the most interesting visits I have ever made to Indian tribes; the shores of the Yucayali are not unlike those of the Trombutas—the animals, the birds, the trees, the flowers, everything the same.

The Connibos, of some two or three thousand; the Sipibos, of three thousand; the Chetibos, of an equal number, and the Sensis, inhabit its shores. These tribes are all much alike, and their languages strongly resemble each other, yet they are constantly at war, though only the river separates them.

The Connibos live upon the borders of the pampa, but build their villages in the edge of the forest. A village generally consists of but one house, but a curious house it is; it is a shed, and sometimes thirty or forty rods in length, constructed of posts set in the ground, to the tops of which are fastened horizontal timbers supporting a roof most curiously and even beautifully thatched with palm leaves. Houses in this country, I have said, have no sides, no walls, except those of the Gauchos, and the sides and partitions in those can be perforated with the finger, as they are but a web of palm-leaves.

The Connibo wigwam, or shed, contains sometimes several hundreds of persons, and the families are separated only by a hanging screen or partition, made of palm-leaves, suspended across the shed. Like all the tribes in the valley of the Amazon, they sleep in hammocks slung between the posts of their sheds, when at home; and when traveling, between trees, or stakes driven into the ground.

How curious are houses without doors, where, instead of walking in, we walk under! I have given an account of the Skin-builders, the Dirt-builders, the Bark-builders, the Grass-builders, the Timber-builders, the Nest-builders, and we now come to the Shed-builders! And if I have room enough, I intend to give you a brief account of the No-builders, the pigmies of the Shoshone race whom I found on the heads of the Colorado in North America, who build no houses, but creep in and sleep amongst the crevices of the rocks.

The Sipibos and Chetibos, though only separated from the Connibos by the river, have no communication with them except in warfare, and that is very seldom; each confining themselves in their canoes to their own shore; and their boundary line being so definitely established, it is less often passed over than those of tribes who have only an ideal line of division, which is most generally the case.

The Chetibos and Sipibos may properly be said to be Canoe Indians, their country being a dense and impenetrable forest, throwing them, from necessity, upon the river for subsistence and the means of traveling; and in their narrow and light little dugout canoes, they are indeed one of the prodigies of the world. When they all strike with their paddles at once, they may almost be said to bound over the waves. They ascend and descend the foaming rapids which in some places are frightful even to look at, and where they are at times entirely lost to the view from the foaming spray that is rising around them. They descend the Yucayali to Nanta, the Amazon to Tabatinga, to the Barra, and even to Para and back again, against a strong current for the distance of two thousand miles, in less time and with more ease than they could do it on horseback, provided there were roads.

The Chetibos are much like the Winnebago and Menomonie Indians on the shores of the great lakes in North America, and if placed by the side of them would scarcely be distinguished from them. Like all the Indians in this country they wear very little dress. The men always wear a flap or breech-cloth, and the women wear a cotton wrapper that fastens about the waist and extends nearly down to the knees. The necks and wrists of the women are generally hung with a profusion of blue and white beads, which have a pleasing effect, and also, in many instances, brass and silver bands around the ankles and around the head, fastening back the hair.

Both men and women daub and streak their bodies and limbs with red and white and black paint, much in the same way as the North American tribes. In this custom I see but little difference. The Connibos, the Remos, the Amahovacs, and all other tribes on the Yucayali and the Upper and Lower Amazon, have the same fondness for 'dress,' which is paint, according to his or her freak or fancy.

The Pacapacuris, the Memos, the Antis, and a dozen other small tribes, and the Connibos, who dwell around the skirts of the Pampa del Sacramento, lead a different life from the Canoe Indians I have just mentioned, and in appearance are more like the Sioux and Assinneboins on the buffalo plains in North America.

The Connibos interested me very much. They are one of the most curious, and ingenious, and intelligent tribes I met with. They seemed proud of showing me their mode of manufacturing pottery, which was in itself a curiosity, and in some respects would do credit to any civilized race. They have a place somewhat like a brick-yard on the edge of the prairie near their village, where the women mix and beat the clay with a sort of mallet or paddle, and afterwards mold (or rather model) it into jars for their turtle butter, and also into a hundred different and most ingenious forms—into pitchers, cups, pots, and plates; and what is actually astonishing to the beholder, these are all made in the most perfect roundness and proportion without the aid of a wheel, by the rotary motion of the hand and adjustment of the fingers and mussel-shells which they use in giving form.

After these are dried in the sun sufficiently, the painting operation begins, which is a curious scene, and performed by another set of artists, and some of them, evidently, with a talent worthy of a better place. With red and yellow, blue and black colors which they extract from vegetables, and brushes they make from a fibrous plant they get amongst the rushes at the river shore, these colors are laid on, and often blended and grouped in forms and figures that exhibit extraordinary taste.

Painted, they are then passed into the hands of old women, whose days for molding and painting have gone by, but who are still able to gather wood and build fires on the sands at the riverside where they are carried and baked; whilst the old women are tending to them, with hands clenched, they dance in a circle around them, singing and evoking the Evil Spirit not to put his fatal hand upon and break them in the fire. Those that come out without the touch of his fingers (uncracked) are then removed to the village and glazed with a vegetable varnish or resin which they gather from some tree in the forest.

This pottery, though it answers their purpose, is fragile and short-lived, being proof for a short time only against cold liquids, and not proof against those that are hot.

The sole weapons of these people, and in fact of most of the neighboring tribes, are bow and arrows, and lances, and blow-guns, all of which are constructed with great ingenuity, and used with the most deadly effect. My revolver rifle, therefore, was a great curiosity amongst them, as with the other numerous tribes I had passed. I fired a cylinder of charges at a target to show them the effect, and had the whole tribe as spectators.

After finishing my illustration, a very handsome and diffident young man stepped up to me with a slender rod in his hand of some nine or ten feet in length, and smilingly said that he still believed his gun was equal to mine; it was a beautiful 'blow-gun,' and slung, not on his back, but under his arm, with a short quiver containing about a hundred poisoned arrows.

The young man got the interpreter to interpret for him, as he explained the powers of his weapon, and which, until this moment, I had thought that I perfectly understood. He showed me that he had a hundred arrows in his quiver, and of course so many shots ready to make; and showed me by his motions that with it he could throw twenty of them in a minute, and that without the least noise, and without even being discovered by his enemy, whose ranks he would be thinning, or without frightening the animals or birds who were falling by them; and then there was the accuracy of his aim, and the certainty of death to whatever living being they touched!

This tube was about the size of an ordinary man's thumb, and the orifice large enough to admit the end of the little finger. It was made of two small palms, one within the other, in order to protect it from warping. This species of palm is only procured in certain parts of that country, of the proper dimensions and straightness to form those wonderful weapons. They are manufactured most generally, and the most extensively, by the Haycas and Zeberos tribes on the Amazon, more than two hundred miles from the Connibos, and two hundred miles above Nanta; and they are sold to the Connibos, as well as the Sipibos and all the other tribes in those regions, and also to all the tribes of the Lower Amazon, and even taken in large quantities to Para and sold in the market-place. The prices that these blow-pipes command in the country where they are manufactured are from two to three dollars; and on the lower Amazon, at the Barra, at Santarem and Para, from three to five dollars each.

Opening his quiver, the young man showed and explained to me his deadly arrows, some eight or nine inches in length. Some of them were made of very hard wood, according to the original mode of construction; but the greater and most valuable portion of them were made of knitting-needles, with which they are now supplied by the civilized traders. These are sharpened at the end, and feathered with cotton, which just fills the orifice of the tube, and steadies the arrow's flight. The arrows are pushed in at the end held to the mouth, and blown through with such force and such precision that they will strike a man's body at sixty yards, or the body of a squirrel or a small bird on the top of the highest tree.

The ends of these arrows, for an inch or more, are dipped into a liquid poison, which seems to be known to most of the tribes in those regions, and which appears to be fatal to all that it touches. This liquid poison dries in a few moments on the point of the arrow, and there is carried for years without the least deterioration. He explained to me that a duck, or parrot, or turkey, penetrated with one of these points, would live but about two minutes; a monkey or peccary would live about ten minutes; and a tiger, a cow, or a man, not over fifteen minutes. Incredible almost as these statements were, I nevertheless am induced to believe, from what I afterwards learned from other abundant information, that they were very near the truth. One thing is certain, that death ensues almost instantaneously when the circulation of the blood conveys the poison to the heart, and it therefore results that the time, instead of being reducible to any exact measure, depends upon the blood-vessels into which the poison is injected. If the arrow enters the jugular vein, for instance, the animal, no matter what size, would have but a moment to live.

The interpreter assured me that neither the bodies of birds or animals killed by these poisoned arrows were injured for eating, and that the greater part of the food of the Indians was procured by them; the poison being a vegetable extract, and the quantity at the same time so exceedingly small, that it becomes neutralized, so as not to interfere with digestive action.

I was anxious to witness some experiments made with it, and observing that these people had a number of young peccaries which they were raising for food, I bought one of them by giving the owner a couple of papers of Chinese vermilion, and allowing him the carcass of the pig to eat. He was much pleased with the arrangement, and brought the pig out. I got the young man to aim an arrow at the neck, explaining to him that I wished him to strike the jugular vein; but, missing that, it passed some five or six inches into the neck. The animal made no signs of pain, but stood still, and in two minutes began to reel and stagger, and soon fell to the ground upon its side, and in six minutes from the time the arrow struck it, it was dead.

I was then informed that there was another animal which I might like to kill. An immense rattlesnake had been discovered a few days before near their village, and as their superstitious fears prevent them from killing a rattlesnake, they had made a pen around it by driving a row of stakes, preventing its escape, until they could get an opportunity of sending it on some canoe going down the river, to be thrown overboard, that it might land on the banks of some of their enemies.

We proceeded to the pen, and having excited the reptile to the greatest rage, when it coiled itself up and was ready for a spring, I blew the arrow myself, and striking it about the center of its body, it writhed for a moment, twisting its body into a knot, and in three minutes, straightening itself out upon the ground, and on its back, was quite dead.

This might be considered a very fair test of the horrible fatality of this artificial poison; for I have often held the enraged rattlesnake down with a crotched stick until it has turned and bitten itself; and even then, excited to the most venomous pitch, and giving itself several blows, it will live some ten or fifteen minutes.

I bought the young man's blow-gun and his quiver of arrows, and I have also procured several others from other tribes, and several sacks of the poison, for experiments on my return, which may lead to curious and possibly important results. How awful and terrific would be the effects of an army of men with such weapons, knowing their powers, and skilled in the manner of using them!

This poison is undoubtedly a recent discovery. From the facts that I gathered in this and many other tribes, I learned that anciently the Indians went to war much oftener than they now do; that they then fought with lances, and shields, and large bows, but since the discovery of this poison for their arrows, they dare not come so near as to use those weapons; and that it had almost put a stop to warfare.

The young Connibo assured me that his tribe had resolved not to use these arrows upon any of their enemies, unless they began to throw poisoned arrows, and, in that case, to be ready to kill every one of them. And to convince me of the cruelty and horror of warfare waged with these weapons, he related to me, as matter of history, much as it seems to partake of the marvelous, that "some time after the poison was discovered, and these blow-guns were made, the war-parties of two neighboring tribes met in a plain, all armed with these weapons, and their bodies were afterwards discovered where every man was killed on both sides. Getting so near to each other, every man was hit; for each one, after he was hit, had time to strike his enemy, or half-a-dozen of them before he was dead."

Poisoning arrows has been a very ancient custom amongst savage tribes, and no doubt has been practiced for many centuries amongst the South American as well as amongst the North American races, and is too generally known and used to be any longer a secret; but the acme of poison, which seems to be that now used on the points of these little darts, I believe to be very different from that used by the same people on the blades of their lances and arrows, and to be a modern discovery.

This poison is no doubt a vegetable extract, or a compound of vegetable extracts; and though so extensively known and used by the Indian tribes, seems to be by them treasured as a secret so important and so profound as to have, so far, baffled all attempts to obtain it from them. It admits of no chemical analysis which leads to anything, except that it is a vegetable extract. That vegetable, and the mode of the extract, the analysis does not show.

Amongst the Macouchi and other tribes on the Essequibo, in Guiana, I obtained similar blow-guns, and, I believe, the same poison (though the color is different). The Indians there call it waw-ra-li. Many travelers, French, English, and German, have made great efforts to obtain the secret, and though some have thought themselves in possession of it, I still very much doubt the fact.

I, like many others, followed the phantom a long time, but in vain; and if I had found it, what good would it do? I don't wish to poison anybody; and game enough 'Sam' and I can always kill without it—powder and ball from Sam are rank poison.

Amongst the Chetibos, the Sensis, and other tribes, I had painted a considerable number of portraits, which surprised them very much, and gained me many compliments and many attentions as a great medicine man; and of the Connibos I had also painted several portraits, and passed amongst them for a wonderful man; but in the midst of all my success, my medicine met with a sudden reverse.

The Great Medicine, whom I had heard much of, and who at that time was absent, returned from a tour on the pampas with a party of young men who had been out with him to visit a neighboring tribe. He was an ill-looking, surly, wrinkled-up old gentleman. Of myself and my works he soon had a view, and from his people, no doubt, a marvelous account. He soon had his face painted black, and was parading about with his rattle in his hand, and singing a doleful ditty—his death-song, I was told; telling his people that this wouldn't do—that it was very fortunate for them that he had arrived just as he had—that here was something, to be sure, very wonderful, but that it would do them no good.

"These things," said he, "are great mystery; but there you are, my friends, with your eyes open all night—they never shut; this is all wrong, and you are very foolish to allow it. You never will be happy afterwards if you allow these things to be always awake in the night. My friends, this is only a cunning way this man has to get your skins; and the next thing, they will have glass eyes, and be placed amongst the skins of the wild beasts, and birds, and snakes. Don't hurt this man—that is my advice; but he is a bug-catcher and a monkey-skinner!"

One can easily see the trouble that was here brewing for me, and easily imagine, also, how quickly I lost caste from the preaching of this infallible oracle of the tribe, and how unavoidable and irrevocable was the command when I was informed that my operations must cease, and the portraits which I had made must be destroyed.

Those whose portraits I had made all came to me, and told me they would rather have them destroyed, for if I took them away they might have some trouble. I told them we would let them remain over another night, which would give them time to think more about it (give my pictures more time to dry), and if on the next day they still continued in their resolve, I would destroy them as they desired.

I had yet another motive for this delay—the hope of being able, by a little compliment and flattery, to get the old doctor to change his views, and to take up the right side; but in this I entirely failed, almost for the first time in my life. He had been to Para, or other places, where he had seen the stuffed skins in a museum, with glass eyes, and the poor old fellow had got the idea fixed in his mind that I was gathering skins, and that by this process the skins of his people would find their way there, and soon have glass eyes!

I luckily found in the bank of a little stream some white clay; and the next morning, when the Indians came in with the doctor, I had a good quantity of clay on my palette, mixed with water and some watercolors. I then said, "There are your portraits; I am very sorry that you don't let me have them to show to my friends amongst the white people; but you have resolved to have them destroyed. There are three ways—you may burn them! Or you may drown them! Or you may shoot them! You can destroy them in your own way. Your medicine man, who has frightened you about them, can tell you, most likely, which way will be the least dangerous!"

The old doctor lit his pipe, and they all sat down and smoked and talked a while, when he informed me that they were a little afraid to do either.

I then said there was another way I had, that of unpainting them, from which there could be no possible harm, but it required each one to sit a few minutes for the operation. This seemed to afford them a great relief, and in a few moments they were all unpainted, covered in with a thick coat of clay, which would perfectly preserve them until I wanted to see them again. All were satisfied. I took to my canoe and came off, all good friends.

From this I went west. I saw many Indians, many rivers, many rocks. I saw (and felt) the Andes, and entered Lima, on the Pacific, which I have before said is the most beautiful city in the world.

My tour was there half-finished; there will be a time and a book for the rest.

XIX

THE READER BEARS IN MIND THAT THE MAIN OBJECT of this work has been to convey, in a concise way, a general and truthful knowledge of the character, condition, and customs of the American Indian races. In order to prevent it from being tedious, I have thus far endeavored to weave into it such scenes and incidents which I have witnessed as were calculated to interest the reader, and at the same time help to illustrate the true character of these interesting people.

Leaving scenes and scenery now for a while, we will take a look at the Indians and learn more of them in a different phase. Everything, to be well understood, should be seen in different lights. We have seen how these people look and act in their own countries; we will now take a peep at them, mixing and mingling with the polished and enlightened of the world. We have seen them in the darkness of the wilderness; we will now see how they bear the light.

Whilst I was residing in London a few years since, with my whole Indian collection, and all the information which I had gathered in eight years' residence amongst them, there came to London two successive groups of Indians from North America, from two different tribes, and under the charge of two persons, their conductors, from the Indian frontiers, for the avowed object of acting out their modes before the English people.

In both instances I was applied to by the persons bringing them out to take the management of their exhibitions, which I did; which, no doubt, added much to their interest, as I was able to appreciate and explain all their modes. Their exhibitions were made both in England and France, and their mingling and mixing with all ranks and grades of society, to which I was a constant witness and interpreter, brought out points and shades in their character which I never should have learned in their own country; and I confess that until then, with all my study, I had but a partial knowledge of the character of these curious people, and that the rest of it, and even some of its most admirable parts, I learned when they were four thousand miles from their homes, and in the midst of the most enlightened society.

To give a brief account, then, of the rest of their character, as I learned it myself, I will here add a few extracts from my notes made at the time, some of which will be amusing, others will be met with surprise, and many will furnish convincing corroborations of the statements I made in the beginning of this book, that these people, in their native state, are endowed with a high degree of intelligence, of morality, of honesty, of honor, of charity, and religious sentiment. They exhibited at all times a strict adherence to decency, decorum, and social propriety of conduct, that not only excited the surprise, but gained for them the admiration and respect, of all who saw them.

No mode ever suggested itself to me while I was traveling amongst these people (nor could anything else have ever happened), so completely enabling me to learn the whole of their character; and there is nothing else on earth that I can communicate to the reader with so much pleasure, and with so much justice to the savage, in the remaining pages of this book, as the following brief account of incidents which many of the civilized world witnessed, and which all the civilized world ought to know.

The first of these parties consisted of nine Ojibbeways from Canada, whom I had the honor of presenting to Her Majesty the Queen and His Royal Highness the Prince Consort, in the palace at Windsor. They gave several of their dances before the royal party in the Waterloo Gallery, and afterwards sat down to a splendid dinner in an adjoining hall.

See the remarkable speech which the old chief made, as he stood before Her Majesty and all the household, which was interpreted to Her Majesty by their own interpreter, and which I wrote down word for word:—

"Great Mother, The Great Spirit has been kind to us, your children, in protecting us on our long journey here, and we are now happy that we are allowed to see your face.

"Mother, We have often been told that there was a great fire in this country, that its light shone across the great water, and we think we see now where that great light arises; we believe that it shines from this great wigwam to all the world.

"Mother, We have seen many strange things since we came here; we see that your wigwams are large, and the light that is in them is bright. Our wigwams are small, and our light is not strong. We are not rich, but we have plenty of food.

"Mother, My friends here and myself are your children; we have used our weapons against your enemies; our hearts are glad at what we have this day seen; and when we get home our words will be listened to in the councils of our nation. This is all I have to say."

The grace, and dignity, and perfect composure with which this old man delivered the above address before Her Majesty, amid the glare and splendor that was around him, seemed to excite the surprise and admiration of all.

His Royal Highness Prince Albert replied to him in a kind and feeling response, and handsome and genuine presents were made to them by Her Majesty. They gave their dances and other amusements in various parts of the kingdom.

After their return, another party of fourteen Ioways, from the Upper Missouri, arrived, in charge of a Mr. Melody, and under the sanction of the United States Government. This party, from a tribe living much farther west, and more completely in their native state and native habits, were a much better illustration than the first, and probably the best that ever has crossed, or ever will cross, the ocean for such a purpose. The names of this party were as follows:—

Jeffrey Doroway, Interpreter.

1. Mew-hu-she-kaw (the white cloud), chief, civil.
2. Neu-mon-ya (the walking rain), war-chief.
3. See-non-ti-yah (the blister feet), doctor.
4. Wash-ka-mon-ye (the fast dancer), warrior.
5. Shon-ta-y-ee-ga (the little wolf), warrior.
6. No-ho-mun-ye (the Roman nose), warrior.
7. Wa-ton-ye (the foremost man), warrior.
8. Wa-ta-wee-buck-a-nah (commanding general), boy.

Women.

9. Ruton-ye-wee-me (the strutting pigeon), wife of chief.
10. Ruton-wee-me (flying pigeon).
11. O-kee-wee-me (female bear).
12. Koon-za-ya-me (female eagle).
13. Ta-pa-ta-mee (wisdom).
14. _____ (papoose).

This party, when they arrived in London, took great pleasure in visiting my exhibition rooms and in seeing me, as I had visited that tribe some five or six years before, and had, in their own village, painted the portraits of the two chiefs of this party, and which were then hanging in my collection. I erected a strong platform in my exhibition room, on which these people gave their dances and other amusements before immense crowds of visitors assembled to see them.

On the first evening of their amusements they gave the war-dance, all dressed and painted like warriors going to war, and I stood by and explained all its features to the audience. In the war-dance, when the dance stops at intervals, it is customary for each warrior, in turn, to step forward, and, in a boasting manner, relate the exploits of his life—how he has killed and scalped his enemies in battle, etc. And in this dance, the old medicine man made a tremendous boast, brandishing his war club over the heads of his audience in a manner that caused great excitement in the crowd, and was followed by an enthusiastic applause. The old doctor was a bachelor, and had the most exalted admiration and respect for the ladies. And this compliment brought him again on to his feet at the edge of the platform, with his buffalo robe wrapped around him, and his right hand waving over the heads of the audience, when he began:—

"My friends, It makes me very happy to see so many smiling faces about me; for when people smile and laugh I know they are not angry."— (Immense applause and laughter, which lasted for some time.)

"My friends, I see the ladies are pleased, and this pleases me, because I know that if the ladies are pleased they will please the men."— (Great laughter and applause.)

"My friends, I believe that our dance was agreeable to you, and has given you no offence."— (Applause.)

"My friends, We have come a great way, over the great Salt Lake, to see you and offer you our hands. The Great Spirit has been kind to us. We know that our lives are always in his hands, and we must thank him first for keeping us safe."— (Applause.)

"My friends, We have met our old friend, Chippehola here, and we see the medicine things which he has done, hanging all around us, and this makes us very happy. We have found our chiefs' faces on the walls, which the Great Spirit has allowed him to bring over safe, and we are thankful for this."— (Applause and a "how, how, how," from the Indians; meaning "yes," or "hear, hear.")

"My friends, This is a large village; it has many fine wigwams; we rode in a large carriage (an omnibus) the other day, and saw it all."— (A laugh, and hear.)

"My friends, We came all the way from the ship on your great medicine road; it pleased us very much; and we were drawn by the iron horse. My friends, we think that before the trees were cut down this country was very beautiful. We think there were Indians and buffaloes in this country then."—(Applause.)

"My friends, We came very fast along the medicine road (from Liverpool), and we think we saw some quash-ee-quano* expand here [a medicinal herb, the roots of which the Indiana use as a cathartic medicine] but we were not certain; we should like to know. This is all I have to say."—(How, how, how, and great applause.)

An omnibus with four horses was engaged to give the party a drive of a couple of hours each day, by which means they were enabled to see every part of London and its suburbs, and also its institutions, into most of which Mr. Melody and myself accompanied them, that they might see and appreciate the benefits of civilization.

These poor people were much disappointed in not being able to see the Queen, as the party of Ojibbeways, their enemies, had; but they received many friendly invitations, where they were treated with great kindness. They were invited to a dejeuner at the mansion of Mr. Disraeli, near Hyde Park, where they all sat at a table splendidly set out, and at which the private friends of Mr. and Mrs. Disraeli were assembled. The most perfect decorum and apparent sangfroid attended all their motions and actions, and at parting, the war-chief said:—

"My friends,—The Great Spirit has caused your hearts to be thus kind to us, and we hope the Great Spirit will not allow us to forget it. We are thankful to all your friends whom we see around you also, and we hope the Great Spirit will be kind to you all.

"My friends,—We wish to shake hands with you all, and then we will bid you farewell."

INVITED BY MRS. LAWRENCE, OF BALING PARK, they partook of a splendid dejeuner on the beautiful lawn back of her mansion, at which H.R.H. the late Duke of Cambridge, the Duchess of Cambridge and the Princess Mary, the Duchess of Gloucester, and many other distinguished personages were present. The Duke of Cambridge carved the roast beef, and the lovely little Princess Mary and the Duchess of Cambridge, and Mrs. Lawrence carried round to them their plates of plum-pudding. After the fete, they gave several of their favorite dances, and taking their ball-sticks in hand, illustrated their beautiful game of ball on the lawn.

When the entertainments were over, and the Indians were about to depart, the war-chief stepped forward and addressed the Duke of Cambridge in the following words:—

"My great Father, Your face today has made us all very happy. The Great Spirit has done all this for us, and we are thankful to him, first, for it. The Great Spirit inclined your heart to let us see your face and to shake your hand, and we are very happy that it has been so."(How, how, how.)

"My Father, —We have been told that you are the uncle of the Queen, and that your brother was the king of this rich country. We fear that we shall go home without seeing the face of your Queen, except as we saw it in her carriage; but if so, we shall be happy to say that we have seen the great chief who is next to the Queen."(How, how, how.)

"My Father, —We are poor and ignorant people from the wilderness, whose eyes are not yet open; and we did not think we should be treated so kindly as we have been this day. Our skins are red, and our ways are not so pleasing as those of the white people; and we therefore feel the more proud that so great a chief should come so far to see us. This, my father, we never shall forget."(How, how, how.)

"My Father,— We feel thankful to the lady who has this fine house, and these fine fields, and who has invited us here today, and to all the ladies and gentlemen who are here to see us. We shall pray for you all in our prayers to the Great Spirit; and now we shall be obliged to shake hands with you all and go home."(How, how, how.)

H.R.H. the Duke of Cambridge then took the war-chief by the hand, and replied to him—"That he and all his friends had been highly pleased with their appearance and amusements, and most of all, with the reverential manner in which he had just spoken of the Great Spirit, before whom, whether red or white, we must all soon appear. He thanked the chiefs for the efforts they had made to entertain them, and trusted that the Great Spirit would be kind to them in restoring them safe to their friends again."

Very beautiful and liberal presents were then bestowed on them by the hands of the ladies, and the party took leave in their omnibus for London.

Let us turn back for a moment to this wonderful speech of the war-chief, and read it over again—to this concise, this appropriate, this reverential, this humble and eloquent address, from the lips of a wild man from the heart of the American wilderness— that no language, that no diction, and no study could improve—translated by one of the best interpreters, sentence by sentence, and written by myself, word for word, in my note-book as it was spoken.

What a beautiful illustration have we here, and how convincing, of the truth which should be learned as the basis of all human education, that nature has endowed man, even in his most ignorant wilderness state, with a knowledge of his Creator—of an Almighty Being on whom his existence depends, and to whom his daily thanks and prayers are to ascend!

And these are not the empty pretensions drawn out of them by the society they are in, but the sentiments that are daily uttered in the forests, and over the mountains, the lakes, and the rivers of their own countries, during all the days of their lives. I have seen them there, as the reader has learned, under all circumstances. Their speeches have been made to me, and I have heard them made a hundred times to others, and they always begin by thanking the Great Spirit first.

In councils, no man speaks without inviting the Great Spirit to witness what he is going to say, and to aid him in speaking the truth. Before eating, they invariably and audibly thank the Great Spirit for the food they are going to partake of.

These people have no churches or places of worship where they congregate together as white people do; but each individual has some solitary and sacred haunt where he occasionally goes for several days and nights together, without food, lying with his face in the dirt, as he is crying to the Great Spirit, even at the risk of his life from wild beasts and his enemies.

While these people were creating a great excitement in London, two Episcopal clergymen called on me one day and desired to know if they could have an opportunity of conversing with them on the subject of religion; to which I replied that I would do all in my power to bring it about. I mentioned the subject to Mr. Melody and his party, and they all agreed, and the day and hour were appointed. Apprehending the interesting and important nature of these conversations, I resolved to attend them, and with Jeffrey, the interpreter, to preserve the most perfect report of all that was to be said on both sides; which I did; and in each case (for there were ultimately several interviews) submitted my reports to the reverend gentlemen for their approval as to their correctness.

In the interview already appointed to take place, one of the reverend gentlemen, in the kindest and most friendly manner, explained to them the objects of their visit, and with their permission, gave them an account of the life and death of our Savior, and explained, as well as he could to their simple minds, the mode of redemption. He urged upon them the necessity of taking up this belief, and though it might be difficult for them to understand at first, yet he told them he was sure that it was the only certain way to salvation.

The war-chief, who was spokesman on most occasions, was all this time sitting and smoking his pipe, with his head cast down as he was listening; and having heard what the clergyman was anxious to explain, he handed his pipe to White Cloud, the chief, and with his arms resting on his knees, replied:—

"My friends, The Great Spirit has sent you to us with kind words, and he has opened our ears to hear them; which we have done. We are glad to see you and to hear you speak. As to the white man's religion, which you have explained, we have heard it told to us in the same way in our own country, and there are white men and women there now trying to teach it to our people. We do not think your religion good, unless it be so for white people, and this we don't doubt.

"My friends, The Great Spirit has made our skins red, and the forests for us to live in. He has also given us our religion, which has taken our fathers to the beautiful hunting-grounds where we wish to meet them. We don't believe that the Great Spirit made us to live together with the pale faces in this world, and we think that He has intended we shall live separate in the world to come.

"My friends, We know that when white men come into our country we are unhappy. The Indians all die or are driven away before the white men. Our hope is to enjoy our hunting-grounds in the world to come, which white men cannot take from us.

"My friends, You have told us that the Son of the Great Spirit was living on the earth, and that He was killed by white men, and that the Great Spirit sent Him here to get killed. Now, we don't understand this; this may have been necessary for white people, but the red men, we think, have not yet got to be so wicked as to require that. If it was necessary that the Son of the Great Spirit should be killed for white people, it may be necessary for them to believe all this, but for us, we cannot understand it.

"My friends, You speak to us of the Good Book which is in your hands. We have some of these in our village. We are told that all your words about the Great Spirit are printed in that Book, and if we learn to read it, it will make good people of us. I would now ask why it don't make good people of the whites living around us? They can all read the Good Book, and understand all that the Black-coats [missionaries] say, and still we find that they are not so honest and so good a people as our own; this we are sure of. Such is the case in the country around us, but here, we have no doubt but the white people, who have so many to preach to them, and so many of the Good Books to read, are all honest and good.

"My friends, In our country the white people have two faces, and their tongues branch in different ways. We know that this displeases the Great Spirit, and we do not wish to teach it to our children."

One of the reverend gentlemen here asked the chief if he thought the Indians did all to serve the Great Spirit that they ought to do, all that the Great Spirit required of them; to which the war chief replied:—

"My friends, I don't know that we do all the Great Spirit wishes us to do; there are some Indians I know who do not. There are some bad Indians as well as bad white people. I think it is difficult to tell how much the Great Spirit wishes us to do."

The reverend gentleman said: "That is what we wish to teach you; and if you can learn to read this Good Book it will explain all that." The chief continued:

"My friends, We believe that the Great Spirit requires that we should pray to him, which we do, and to thank him for everything we have which is good. We know that he requires us to speak the truth, to feed the poor, and to love our friends. We don't know of anything more that he demands. He may demand more of white people, but we don't know that."

The reverend gentleman, and several ladies attending them, here bestowed upon the Indians several beautiful Bibles, and other appropriate presents, and took leave.

OF REVEALED RELIGION THE INDIANS IN THEIR WILD STATE have no knowledge before it is explained to them. But of the existence of a God—a Supreme Being—whom they denominate the 'Great Spirit,' and of a 'world to come,' or a spiritual existence beyond the grave, they require no teachers; for the most ignorant of them all pray to the Great Spirit when they are in danger; and, when dying, paint their faces with their finest colors, and reach for their bows and arrows as companions to supply them with food on the "long journey that is to take them to their beautiful hunting-grounds."

We have had many reports from the American frontiers of tribes of 'heathens'—'heathen dogs,' so low in the scale of human nature as to have been "found without the belief in a God or a future state." Don't believe one word of these, for, from ignorance or a motive, I need not say which, every one of these are false.

Every American Indian, if he be not an idiot, has an intuitive knowledge of a Creator and belief in a future pleasurable existence;

and—happy people!—they have no metaphysics or sophistry of their own to induce them to believe to the contrary.

ONE DAY WHILST THEY WERE IN BIRMINGHAM, a miserable-looking woman, with her little child, both in rags, and begging for the means of existence, presented herself in front of the door, where the old doctor, of whom I have before spoken, was standing, whose pity was touched by the poor woman's appearance, and who beckoned her to come in by holding out and showing her some money, but which she was afraid to take.

The doctor went for one of the men in attendance, who assured the woman there was no danger, by which she was induced to enter the Indians' apartment, where the Indians were all seated on the floor, and all sympathizing with her miserable appearance. The war chief, getting Jeffrey to interpret for him, told her not to be frightened, for they were her friends; when the doctor walked up to her and put five shillings into her hand.

The war-chief then asked her some questions as to the causes of her becoming so distressed, which she explained. The Indians filled her apron with cold meat and bread, sufficient to last her and her child for several days. The kind-hearted old doctor then politely escorted her to the bottom of the stairs, and informed her by signs that, if she would come every morning at a certain hour, she would be sure to have food enough for herself and her little child as long as the party should remain in Birmingham; which was strictly performed by the doctor, and no doubt with an inexpressible satisfaction, as he found his patient every morning at the door and waiting for him.

It was thought by some friends, that if the Indians would give their exhibition for a couple of nights in the Town Hall, dividing the receipts with the two hospitals, their exhibition would be very popular, and it was agreed to. The profits of the two nights amounted to £145.12s. And the next day I was present when the chief handed to Mr. Joseph Cadbury, president of one of the hospitals, £72.16s.—one-half of the receipts; on which occasion Mr. Cadbury made some very feeling and friendly remarks, thanking them for the very handsome donation, and reminding them of the importance of sobriety and charity—recommending to them never to lose sight of them—which were two of the greatest virtues they could practice, and the most sure to gain them friends and happiness.

Though the war-chief, as I have said, was generally the spokesman on these occasions, it was left for the doctor to reply in this instance, and addressing himself to Mr. Cadbury, he spoke as follows:—

"My friend, —I rise to thank you for the words you have spoken to us. They have been kind, and we are thankful for them.

"My friend, —When I am at home in the wilderness, as well as when I am amongst the white people, I always pray to the Great Spirit; and I believe that the chiefs and the warriors of my tribe, and even the women also, pray every day to the Great Spirit, and he has therefore been kind to us.

"My friend, —We have this day been taken by the hand in friendship, and this gives us great consolation. Your friendly words have opened our ears, and your words of advice will not be forgotten.

"My friend, —You have advised us to be charitable to the poor, and we have this day handed you three hundred and sixty dollars to help the poor in your hospitals. We have not time now to see these poor people, but we know that you will make good use of the money for them; and we shall be happy if, by coining this way, we shall have made the poor comfortable.

"My friend, —We red men are poor, and we cannot do much charity. The Great Spirit has been kind to us though, since we came to this country, and we have given more than two hundred dollars to the poor people in the streets of London before we came here; and this is not the first day that we have given to the poor in this city.

"My friend, —We admit that before we left home we were all fond of fire-water, but in this country we have not drunk it, nor shall we— we know that it is a sin to drink fire-water, and your words to us on that subject are good. And if you can tell them to the white people who make the fire-water and bring it into our country to sell, then we think your words may do a great deal of good, and we believe the Great Spirit will reward you for it.

"My friend, —It makes us unhappy, in a country where there is so much wealth, to see so many poor and hungry, and so many as we see drunk. We know you are good people, and kind to the poor; and we give you our hands at parting, praying that the Great Spirit will assist you in taking care of the poor, and making people sober.

"I have no more to say."

Another incident relating to this subject is worthy of being recorded, and it is due to these poor people that such acts as the above, and the one to be related, should be made public.

At a subsequent time, while passing from Edinburgh to Dundee on a steamer, and when the captain was collecting his passage-money, there was a little girl in the fore-cabin, where the Indians were traveling, who could not pay her fare, as she had no money. She was in great alarm, and told the captain that she expected to meet her father at Dundee, and that he would certainly pay it as soon as she could find him. I was not on board at the time, but my men informed me that the captain was in a great rage, and abused the child for coming on board without the money to pay her fare, and said that he should not let her go ashore at Dundee, but that he should hold her a prisoner on board, and take her back to Edinburgh and put her in gaol.

The poor little girl was frightened, and cried herself almost into fits. The passengers, of whom there were a considerable number, all seemed much affected by her distress, and commenced raising the money amongst them for defraying her passage, giving a penny or two each, which, when done, amounted to only a quarter of the sum required, when the poor child's distress still continued. The kind-hearted old doctor, silently observing all this, went down below and related it to the party of Indians, and in a few minutes came up with eight shillings in his hand, much more than was necessary, and offered it to the little girl, who was frightened and ran away. The interpreter, however, prevailed upon her to take the money, assuring her there was no danger, when the doctor advanced and placed the money in her hand, saying to her, through the interpreter, and in presence of all the passengers who were gathering around, "Now go to the cruel captain, and pay him the money, and never be afraid of a man again because his skin is red; but be always sure that the heart of a red man is as good as that of a white man. And when you are in Dundee, where we are all going together, if you do not find your father, as you wish, and are amongst strangers, come to us, wherever we shall be, and you shall not suffer; and if money is necessary you shall have more."

THE END

THE LIFE OF JOHN WESLEY HARDIN

By John Wesley Hardin

I WAS BORN IN BONHAM, FANNIN COUNTY, TEXAS, on the 26th of May 1853.

My father, J. G. Hardin, was a Methodist preacher and circuit rider. My mother, Elizabeth Hardin, was a blonde, highly cultured and charity predominated in her disposition. She made my father a model wife and helpmate. My father continued to travel his circuit as a preacher until 1869, when he moved and located near Moscow, in Polk county, on account of bad health. In the same year he moved again, this time to Sumpter, in Trinity county, where he taught school. He organized and established an academy, to which institution he sent my elder brother, Joe C. Hardin, and myself. In the meantime my father was studying law, and in 1861 was admitted to the bar.

The war between the States had broken out at this time and while my father had voted against secession, yet, when his State seceded, he went with his State and immediately organized a company to fight and, if need be, to die for Southern rights. He was elected captain of this company, but resigned at the solicitation of the best citizens, Capt. Ballinger being elected to the command. So my father stayed at home because, as said the foremost men of the community, "You can be of more good use at home than off fighting Yankees."

Although I was but 9 years old at this time I had already conceived the idea of running off and going with a cousin to fight Yankees. But my father got on to the little game and put an end to it all by giving me a sound thrashing. Still the principles of the Southern cause loomed up in my mind ever bigger, brighter and stronger as the months and years rolled on. I had seen Abraham Lincoln burned and shot to pieces in effigy so often that I looked upon him as a very demon incarnate, who was waging a relentless and cruel war on the South to rob her of her most sacred rights. So you can see that the justice of the Southern cause was taught to me in my youth and if I never relinquished these teachings in after years, surely I was but true to my early training. The way you bend a twig, that is the way it will grow, is an old saying, and a true one. So I grew up a rebel.

In 1862 my father moved to Livingston, in Polk county, where he taught school and practiced law. In 1865 we again moved back to Sumpter; my father still teaching and practicing law, my brother and I being regular scholars. Our parents had taught us from our infancy to be honest, truthful and brave, and we were taught that no brave boy would let another call him a liar with impunity. Consequently we had lots of battles with other boys at school. I was naturally active and strong and always came out best, though sometimes with a bleeding nose, scratched face or a black eye; but true to my early training, I would try, try, try again.

We continued in Sumpter at school for some time, and of course I received the biggest part of my education there. I always tried to excel in my studies, and generally stood at the head. Being playful by nature, I was generally first on the playground at recess and noon. Marbles, rolly hole, cat, bull pen and town ball were our principle games and I was considered by my schoolmates an expert. I knew how to knock the middle man, throw a hot ball and ply the bat.

Of course we had examinations and school exhibitions, which were creditable to all concerned, but in 1867 an incident occurred which I think proper to relate. We were preparing for an examination when one of my schoolmates and myself had an almost fatal fight. His name was Charles Sloter, and as he wanted to be the boss among the boys, of course I stood in his way. In order to 'down' me he publicly accused me of writing some doggerel on the wall about one Sal, a girl scholar. It commenced, "I love Sal, and Sal loves mutton" and ended in some reflections upon Sal's personal attractions. I knew that he was the author of the poetry, and when he accused me of writing it I at once denied it and proved it up on him. He came over to my seat in the school room, struck me and drew his knife. I stabbed him twice almost fatally in the breast and back. A howl at once went up to expel me from the school, some even wanting to hang me. The trustees, however, heard the true facts in the case and instead of expelling me, completely exonerated me and the courts acquitted me.

I may mention here that poor Charley was long afterwards hung by a mob in an adjoining county

THE FIRST MAN I EVER SAW KILLED WAS TURNER EVANS and he was killed by old John Ruff in the town of Sumpter, Trinity county, Texas, in the year 1861. My father had just organized his company of soldiers to go to the seat of war at Richmond. I remember the day well. Ruff was a poor man and owed Turner Evans. Evans was overbearing and besides running an attachment on Ruff's property, annoyed him greatly in every way. Late in the evening Evans began to drink, and being rich and influential, had a crowd of hangers on around him. Fired by whisky he began late in the evening to go around town from store to store inquiring for Ruff, declaring that he would cane him wherever he found him. At last he found him in a small grocery store and at once commenced to curse and abuse him.

Ruff said: "Turner, you have ruined me financially and now come with your crowd to attack me personally. Go off."

Evans said: "I will, after I have caned you," and so saying he struck him over the head with his cane.

Ruff pulled a large Bowie knife and started for Evans. Evans' friends hit Ruff with chairs and tried to stop him, while Evans himself used his stick freely. Ruff, however, was by this time a determined and angry man, and cut at everybody that tried to stop him. He finally cut Evans down, and the sheriff appearing on the scene, Ruff was at once arrested. Evans' friends carried him off, but his wounds were fatal, the jugular vein being completely severed. He soon died and left a large family. Ruff, after lying in jail for several years, came clean. Reader, you see what drink and passion will do. If you wish to be successful in life, be temperate and control your passions; if you don't, ruin and death is the inevitable result.

IN THE FALL OF 1868, I went down to my Uncle's (Barnett Hardin) in Polk county, about four miles north of Livingstone. I was in the habit of making these trips, though I was then but 15 years old. This time they were making sugar and I took the trip to see them, carrying my pistol of course. I met a negro named Mage close to Moscow who had belonged to Judge Holshousen, a brother to my Uncle Barnett Hardin's wife.

I had a cousin named Barnett Jones who matched himself and me against this Moscow negro in a wrestling bout. The negro was a large, powerful man, and we were but two boys. Nevertheless we threw him down the first fall. He was not satisfied, so we threw him again, and this time scratched his face a little and made it bleed. Negro like, he got mad and said he could whip me and would do it. Barnett and others standing around stopped us from fighting. This seemed to make Mage all the more angry. He said he would kill me, and went after his gun. I went up to the house to get mine, too, but Uncle Barnett got on to the game and made me stay in the house, while that negro went around cursing and abusing me, saying "that he would kill me or die himself; that no white boy could draw his blood and live; that a bird never flew too high not to come to the ground."

Uncle Barnett then took a hand and ordered Mage off the plantation. The next morning I had to start home and go about seven or eight miles out of the way to deliver a message from my father to old Capt. Sam Rowes. About six miles from Capt. Rowes' place and eight from Judge Holshousen's, I overtook the negro Mage. He was walking and had a stout stick in his hand. A small creek ran to the east of the road, which made a sharp bend of about 100 yards, and from bend to bend ran a path.

Just as I overtook Mage he took the path while I stayed in the main road. He had gone about fifteen steps before he turned and saw me. He recognized me at once and began to curse and abuse me, saying that I was a coward for not shooting it out last night. I told him that I was but playing with him when I scratched him and did not intend to hurt him. He answered by saying that if he could but get hold of me he would kill me and throw me in the creek; that he believed he could outrun old Paint (the horse I was riding, and a very poor one), and catch me anyway. I told him to go his way and let me go mine, and whipped old Paint into a trot. Mage, seeing this, ran along the path to where it again met the main road and cut me off. He cursed me again and threatened me with death.

I stopped in the road and he came at me with his big stick.

He struck me, and as he did it I pulled out a Colt's 44 six-shooter and told him to get back. By this time he had my horse by the bridle, but I shot him loose. He kept coming back and every time he would start I would shoot again and again until I shot him down.

I went to Uncle Houlshousen and brought him and another man back to where Mage was lying. Mage still showed fight and called me a liar, if it had not been for uncle I would have shot him again. Uncle Houlshousen gave me a $20 gold piece and told me to go home and tell father all about the big fight; that Mage was bound to die, and for me to look out for the Yankee soldiers who were all over the country at that time.

Texas, like other States, was then overrun with carpet-baggers and bureau agents who had the United States army to back them up in their meanness. Mage shortly died in November 1868. This was the first man I ever killed, and it nearly distracted my father and mother when I told them. All the courts were then conducted by bureau agents and renegades, who were the inveterate enemies of the South and administered a code of justice to suit every case that came before them and which invariably ended in gross injustice to Southern people, especially to those who still openly held on to the principles of the South. To be tried at that time for the killing of a negro meant certain death at the hands of a court, backed by Northern bayonets; hence my father told me to keep in hiding until that good time when the Yankee bayonet should cease to govern. Thus, unwillingly I became a fugitive, not from justice be it known, but from the injustice and misrule of the people who had subjugated the South. I had an elder brother teaching school on Logallis Prairie, about twenty-five miles north of Sumpter, so I went up there intending in a few weeks to go to Navarro county where I had relatives.

So I stayed at old man Morgan's in an out of the way place and spent my time hunting wild cattle and game. In a little while the United States soldiers heard of my whereabouts and came after me. My brother, however, had heard of their coming and had told me. I soon was after them instead of they after me. We met in the bed of a deep creek and after a sharp fight two white soldiers lay dead, while a negro soldier was flying for his life. I ran up on him and demanded his surrender in the name of the Southern Confederacy. He answered me with a shot, when I brought him to the ground with a bullet from my Colt's 44. All this was kept very secret, and these soldiers were buried in the bed of the creek about 100 yards below where the fight took place. I knew they would cross the creek where they did so. I waylaid them, as I had no mercy on men whom I knew only wanted to get my body to torture, and kill. It was war to the knife with me and I brought it on by opening the fight with a double-barreled shotgun and ending it with a cap and ball six-shooter. Thus it was that by the fall of 1868 I had killed four men and was myself wounded in the arm. Parties in the neighborhood of the last fight took the soldiers' horses, and as we burned all their effects, everything was kept quiet.

IN JANUARY, 1869, I WENT WITH MY FATHER TO NAVARRO COUNTY and engaged in school teaching near Pisga. I had about twenty-five scholars, both girls and boys, from the age of 6 to 16 years. I taught school for three months at the old Word school house and when the term was out the school was offered to me again.

I HAD, HOWEVER, CONCEIVED THE IDEA OF BECOMING A COWBOY, and as my cousins were in the business. I began to drive cattle to shipping points. Of course in this kind of a life I soon learned how to play poker, seven-up, and euchre, and it was but a short time until I would banter the best for a game. I liked fast horses and soon would bet on any kind of a horse race, a chicken fight, a dog fight, or anything down to throwing 'crack-a-loo,' or spitting at a mark.

In those times if there was anything that could rouse my passion it was seeing impudent negroes lately freed insult or abuse old, wounded Confederates who were decrepit, weak or old. There were lots of those kind in the country in the sixties, and these negroes bullied both them and even the weaker sex whenever they had the advantage. Frequently I involved myself in almost inextricable difficulties in this way. Once I learned that in one of the eastern counties there was a most insulting and bulldozing negro bully who made it a point to insult these decrepit old men, and who paid no respect to white ladies.

In short, he was a terror to the community. I thought over this until I determined to see what could be done to stop him and his wickedness. I went to that neighborhood and found out when he was in the habit of going to town. I dressed myself as an old man and met him in the road. Of course when we met I would not give him the road and he at once commenced his tirade of abuse. I told him that I was old and feeble and lived in a distant country, but that I was a Southerner and did not want a big burley negro to treat me the way he was doing. This enraged him. He stopped his steers, jumped down off his wagon and commenced to pop his whip at me, calling me vile names and low down white trash. He popped me at last and I could not stand it any longer. I pulled off my mask, drew my six-shooter and told him to say his prayers. I told him I was going to kill him for his cruelty to white folks, but did not want to send him before his Maker without a chance to repent. He certainly prayed a prayer. "Jesus have mercy on dis bad nigger, and have mercy on all de poor white men and keep dis young white man from killing dis bad nigger." About this time my pistol went off and his prayer abruptly ended. The ball did not strike the negro, but it had the desired effect, for it reformed him completely. That negro afterwards became one of the best citizens of that county; became civil and polite and was never known to insult a white person, male or female, after that.

While living near Pisga, in Navarro county, I had made the acquaintance of nearly everybody there at that time. I knew the notorious desperado Frank Polk, who was finally killed at Wortham in Limestone county while resisting arrest after having killed the mayor of that town.

I knew the Newmans, the Tramels, the Rushings; the Andersons and Dixons were cousins of mine. I may mention here that I met Jim Newman quite lately and in talking over old times near Pisga in 1869, he asked me if I remembered how some fellow jumped when I shot at him. I told him, "Yes, I remember it." "Well," said Jim Newman, "I bet you at that time that you could not shoot his eye out, and we had a bottle of whisky on it; come in, now; it is my treat." I suppose I won the bet but did not recollect it after so many years. This same Jim Newman is now sheriff of Nolan county; his post office is Sweetwater.

Frank Polk had killed a man named Tom Brady and a detachment of Yankees came out from Corsicana to capture Polk and myself. They, as usual, failed on me, but got Frank. They carried him to Corsicana, where, after a long confinement, he finally came clean. At that time I had a cousin named Simp Dixon, who belonged to the "Ku Kluck Klan" and was sworn to kill Yankee soldiers as long as he lived. He had been raised in Northern Texas, but was forced to fly from there. His mother, brother and sister were tortured and killed by the United States soldiers because of their loyalty to the Southern cause. Simp, therefore, had good cause for hating the Yankees. There was a big reward for Simp and so, of course, I sympathized with him in every way and was generally with him. On one occasion in the Richland bottom a squad of soldiers ran up on us and a pitched battle immediately ensued. It was a free and fast fight. When the battle was over two soldiers lay dead. Simp killed one and I killed the other, while the rest escaped. Simp was afterwards killed by a squad of United States soldiers at Cotton Gin, in Limestone county. He was undoubtedly one of the most dangerous men in Texas. He was born in Fannin county in 1850 and was about 19 years old at the time of his death.

Late in the fall of 1869 my brother, Joe Hardin, came to see me and persuaded me to leave Navarro county, which I consented to do, and we went into Hill county, stopping a short time at Hillsboro with Aunt Anne Hardin and family and then going out some seven or eight miles into the county to Uncle Barnett Hardin's. We then went down the Brazos to some relatives of ours named Page, where I speculated in cotton and hides. I played poker and seven-up whenever I got a chance and once in a while would bet on a pony race. These races generally came off on the old Boles tracks near Towash. A man named John Collins had married a cousin of mine and I went into partnership with him. Things ran smoothly for some time and we were doing well until a tragedy occurred that forever dissolved our partnership.

I had been receiving letters from my father and mother urging me to quit my wild habits and turn to better ways. They wrote that they were going to move down to the Page settlement so that they could be with me. On the 24th of December my father came to see me and brought me good news from all the loved ones at home, and telling me that they had all moved to Navarro county. Next day was Christmas day and I borrowed my father's horse, a pretty good runner, to go to the grocery and the races at the old Boles tracks. Collins and I had matched some races to be run on that day, but of course we never told my father about this. There were a lot of Arkansas people there with horses; especially do I remember Hamp Davis and Jim Bradly. We came very near having a shooting match several times that day, as everybody in the '60s carried pistols, but all left the track apparently satisfied. Jim Bradly, whom I have mentioned above, was introduced to me as a desperado and a killer. I had been reliably informed that he was there for my especial benefit, but in those days an unknown desperado had as much influence on me as a snaffle bit on a wild horse. After the races about fifteen or twenty of us went to a grocery nearby kept by Dire & Jenkins; there was a gin there and one or two stores.

We soon got into a poker game. I had won $50 or $75 on the races and had $325 besides, thus having about $400 in all. At this time I was but 16 years old. It was arranged that Collins, my partner, was not to play, but Jim Bradly (the Arkansas bully) had borrowed his six-shooter. The game was composed of Jim Bradly, Hamp Davis, Judge Moore and myself. I knew afterwards that these three stood in against me but did not know this at the time. One thing, however, I did know, and that was how to protect myself pretty well from such fellows in a game of draw poker. I placed about $350 in gold in front of me and about $10 in silver. Bradly, on my left, placed in front of himself about $5 in silver and $20 in gold; Davis, on Bradly's left, about $10 in silver and $40 in gold, and Moore about $30 in gold.

The game proceeded quietly until about 12 o'clock at night, about which time I had won all the money. We were playing on a blanket in a small box house without a door but with a place open for a chimney in the north end. The house was about 13x14 feet and was situated about a quarter of a mile north from the grocery. The moon was shining brightly, and the night was clear and cold. I had won all the money on the blanket, as I said before, and all the players owed me. I had pulled off my boots and thrown them in the corner to my left next to Bradly, not suspecting that robbery was the intention of the game.

I was quietly fixing to quit the game unknown to the others and had put all the gold in my pocket, only having about $25 or $30 in front of me. Moore remarked that everybody owed Hardin. I said: "Yes," but Jim Bradly said no, and we left it to Moore and Davis to decide. They said, "Yes, you owe Hardin $5."

About this time we both got good hands and I bet him $5 on three aces. He made me put up the money but "called" me without putting up a cent. I said to him: "Now you owe me $10, let us settle up or quit." He said: "You are a g— d— liar and a coward," drew a big knife, and quick as a cat could wink made a grab for me, while Davis got my six-shooter in the corner. Collins then threw himself between Bradly and me and kept him from stabbing me to death.

This gave me a chance to get up and when I did Bradly drew his six-shooter and threatened to kill me if I did not give up my money. "Give me $500 or I will kill you, g—d— you," he said. Collins came to my rescue again and grabbed him, crying to me to jump out of the chimney opening or I would be killed. Out I went, barefooted on the frosty ground and ran out to our horses. Davis gave me a fearful cursing, calling me a murderer, a coward, a robber and saying he would get me before day.

Collins came out to where I was standing behind a tree and said: "John, let us go home; we are in a hell of a scrape." I said: "Where is your pistol?" He said: "Bradly borrowed it in the early part of the night."

"No," I said, "I am not going home and face my father in this condition; I want my boots, my money and my pistol. Don't be a fool, but take things coolly."

Collins went back to get my boots, which Bradly finally gave him permission to do. Bradly continued to abuse me and went to the grocery with his crowd, who by this time were all cursing me as a man who had been posing as a brave man, but who in fact was a coward and a damned rascal. As soon as I got my boots on I told Collins I wanted to go and see Moore, who had my money and pistol. He said he would go with me to his boarding house, as he knew the proprietor. We left our horses where they were and found Moore at the boarding house. He refused to give up either the pistol or the money without Bradly's consent. He agreed to go with Collins to see Bradly at the grocery about 100 yards off across the road in an easterly direction. When they got to the grocery and saw Bradly he was still cursing. He threatened Collins and swore he would kill me if he could find me. Moore told him I was at his boarding house after my pistol and money.

Bradly said: "Well, I'll go over there and fill him full of lead."

Meantime Collins had borrowed a pistol and persuaded Bradly to exchange telling him he was going home and wanted his own. John Collins bade him good bye and came back to the boarding house where I was. He wanted me to go home, but by this time Bradly had started over to where I was, swearing to kill me. The proprietor was trying to get me to leave, when I asked him for a pistol to defend myself with from robbery and death. He refused to do this, but Collins gave me his and said: "Now let us go to our horses." I said, "All O.K." and we started to go out of the gate and into the public road that lead to where our horses were.

Just as we got out of the gate we saw Bradly with six or seven others, including Hamp Davis, coming towards us, threatening to kill us, his crowd urging him on by shouting: "Go for him! We are with you," etc. I told John Collins to go in the lead. The gin was on the right, about fifty yards away, with a store about fifty yards from where we were standing. Bradly saw me and tried to cut me off, getting in front of me with a pistol in one hand and a Bowie knife in the other. He commenced to fire on me, firing once, then snapping and then firing again.

By this time we were within five or six feet of each other and I fired with a Remington 45 at his heart and right after that at his head. As he staggered and fell he said: "O, Lordy, don't shoot me anymore."

I could not stop. I was shooting because I did not want to take chances on a reaction. The crowd ran, and I stood there and cursed them loud and long as cowardly devils who had urged a man to fight and when he did and fell, to desert him like cowards and traitors. I went to my horse, rode over to Frank Shelton's, borrowed a gun, came back and demanded my money, but received no answer. I went on to where my father was at old Jim Pages' and got there at 2 a.m. I woke him up and told him what had happened. It was a great blow to him, for he had been counting on taking me back home with him. I told him I would go home anyway, but would keep on the west side of the Brazos river until the next night. I soon found out the situation was critical.

The whole country with the exception of a few friends and relatives, had turned out to hunt me; in fact, there was a regular mob after me, whose avowed purpose was to hang me. I had agreed with my father to meet him at a certain place on the night of the 26th, but they watched him so closely that he could not come. He had a trusted Masonic friend, however, named Martin, whom he sent to post me as to what was going on. Directly after Martin had left me a posse of some fifteen men ran up and surrounded me in a cotton pen. I told them that if they were officers to send one or two men and I would surrender, but I would not yield to a mob. They answered that I must give up or take the consequences.

I replied: "Consequences be damned. Light in if you think there is no bottom."

I commenced to pump lead at them and they cried, "Hold up." They then sent two men up to demand my surrender. When they came, I covered them with a double-barreled shotgun and told them their lives depended on their actions, and unless they obeyed my orders to the letter, I would shoot first one and then the other. They readily assented. "Tell your friends out there," I said, "that Hardin has surrendered and that they had better go home or meet you at old Jim Pages', that Hardin is afraid of a mob." They did so, and the crowd moved off toward Pages'. When they were out of sight I made both men with me lay down their arms. One had a double-barreled gun and two six-shooters; the other had a rifle and two derringers. They complied with my request under the potent persuasion of my gun leveled first on one and then the other. I then got on my horse and told those fellows to follow their pa's to Jim Pages' – that I would be along directly and to wait for me there. I reckon they are waiting for me there yet. I went off to the west, but soon changed to the east; went through Hillsboro and into Navarro county. There I saw my dear mother and my brothers and sisters. Soon after, my father came and brought me the news that they were hot after me and were going to Pisga hoping to find me there.

I got together three or four of my best friends and went to meet them. We met them on the west side of the Pinoak, about six miles from Pisga. They denied that they were after me. I told them to go back to Jim Pages' where I was going and where an arresting party was now waiting for me. I told them if they had a legal warrant to show it and I would give up. They said they had none. Thereupon one of my party took occasion to tell them they had gone far enough towards Pisga and that if they loved their wives and children to go back to Hillsboro. They went. I went back to Pisga, fixed up my affairs with Aleck Barrickman, started for Brenham on the 20th of January, 1870. I intended to visit my uncle Bob Hardin there.

About twenty-five miles from Pisga a circus was going on at a place called Horn Hill. One of the circus men had had a row with some of the citizens, resulting in some men being shot. We knew nothing about this and upon getting to town went to a hotel to get a bed. The circus people had all the beds engaged, so we could not get one. About 10 p. m. we went out to the circus camp fires. It was quite cold and while we were all standing round the fire I accidently struck the hand of a circus man who was lighting his pipe with a fagot from the fire. I begged his pardon at once and assured him it was a pure accident. He, however, just roared and bellowed and swore he would "smash my nose." I told him to smash and be damned; that I was a kind of a smasher myself. He said: "You are, are you?" struck me on the nose and started to pull his gun. I pulled mine and fired. He fell with a 45 ball through his head.

Barrickman covered the crowd until we could make a truce. I saddled our horses and we rode off, apparently to the north, but soon changed our course south. We met nobody who knew us, so after Barrickman had ridden with me about sixteen miles he returned back to Pisga and I went on to Brenham by way of Kosse, Calvert and Bryant. I was young then and loved every pretty girl I met, and at Kosse I met one and we got along famously together. I made an engagement to call on her that night and did so. I had not been there long when someone made a row at the door of the house. She got scared and told me it was her sweetheart, and about this time the fellow came in and told me he would kill me if I did not give him $100. I told him to go slow, and not to be in such a hurry; that I only had about $50 or $60 in my pocket, but if he would go with me to the stable I would give him more as I had the money in my saddle pockets. He said he would go, and I, pretending to be scared, started for the stable.

He said: "Give me what you have got first." I told him all right, and in so doing, dropped some of it on the floor. He stooped down to pick it up and as he was straightening up I pulled my pistol and fired. The ball struck him between the eyes and he fell over, a dead robber. I stopped long enough to get back most of my money and resumed my journey to Brenham.

I arrived there about the last of January, 1870, and went to Uncle Bob Hardin's, who was then improving his place. He persuaded me to farm with him and his boys, William, Aaron and Joe. All the money I had I gave to my aunt to keep for me. I thus became a farmer and made a good plough boy and hoer. I would often want to go to Brenham and did go with William or Aaron or Joe. I used to find it hard to get my money from my good aunt. I used to tell her I had to go to town to get me a pair of shoes or a hat and that she could not suit me if she went. On one occasion I won about $60 at roulette and when I brought my aunt the money she wanted to know where I got that money. I told her with a laugh that I had that money all the time. On another occasion Will and I rode our best horses to town and hitched them to the courthouse fence. When we got through "sporting" and came back for our horses we found them gone. They had evidently been stolen and though we rode a hundred miles or more we never laid eyes on those horses again.

I met a good many well-known characters on those trips to Brenham. I used to gamble a good deal and it was there I got the name of "Young Seven-up." I met Phil Coe first there in Brenham, that notorious Phil Coe, who was afterwards killed in Abilene, Kansas, by "Wild Bill." I stayed at my uncle's until the crops were laid by and though prospects were splendid, the country was getting pretty hot for me. The State police had been organized and McAnally had been placed on the force, so on consultation with friends, it was thought best that I should leave Brenham. I sold out my interest in the crop and again started on my roaming life. I first went to Evergreen, about 40 miles from Brenham. There were some races there and the town was full of hard characters. Bill Longley and Ben Hinds were there, as was also Jim Brown. In those days they gambled in the open air out in the streets when the weather permitted. Ben Hinds and I commenced playing "seven-up" on a goods box and I won about $30 from him, when I concluded to quit. He got mad and said if I was not a boy he would beat me to death. Ben was considered one of the most dangerous men in the country, but in those days I made no distinction in men as fighters. I told him I stood in men's shoes and not to spoil a good intention on account of my youth. He yelled at me: "You damned little impudent scoundrel, I'll beat hell out of you."

As he made for me I covered him with my pistol and told him I was a little on the scrap myself, the only difference between him and I being that I used lead. About this time a dozen men had gathered around. Some of them tried to catch me and others started to draw their pistols. I said: "The first man that makes a move or draws a gun I'll kill him." At the same time I drew my other pistol and made them all get in front of me, saying that I wanted no back action in this fight. You bet they got in front of me in short order. Ben then said: "Young man, I was wrong, I beg your pardon. You are a giant with a youth's face. Even if you are a boy I bow to you, and here is my hand in good faith." I answered: "I cannot take your hand, but I accept your apology in good faith." Ben said: "I will be your friend; don't be uneasy while you are here; Bill Longley will be at the races tomorrow, so stop over and we will have a good time."

Late that evening a dark looking man came to me and said: "My name is Bill Longley and I believe you are a spy for McAnally. If you don't watch out you will be shot all to pieces before you know it."

I said: "You believe a damned lie and all I ask is that those who are going to do the shooting will get in front of me. All I ask is a fair fight, and if your name is Bill Longley I want you to understand that you can't bulldoze or scare me."

Bill replied: "I see I have made a mistake. Are you here to see the races?"

I told him "not particularly." He invited me to stay over and see the horses. We went and struck a poker game going on in a crib. We both got into the game. Directly it came my turn to deal. I had three jacks to go on and raised $5. All stayed in and in the draw Bill drew three cards, while the other two players drew one apiece. I drew two and caught the other jack. Bill filled on aces. One of the other players made a flush and the other filled on queens. The flush man bet $5, the man with a full went $10 better. I studied a while and said: "You can't run me out on my own deal, so I go $10 better." Bill Longley said: "Well, stranger, you put your foot in it now; I go you $50 better." The man with a flush passed; the man with a queen full says: "Bill, I call a sight."

Bill says: "All right; how much money have you got?"
He counted out $45.
"Well, stranger," said Bill, "it's up to you. What do you do?"
I said: "What are you betting; wind or money?"
He said: "Money."
"'Tut it up," said I.

He went down in his pocket and pulled out four $20 gold pieces and took out a $5 gold piece.

I said, "All right," here is your $50 and I go you $250 better.

He said: "I go you; I call you."

I told him to put up the money. He asked me if his word was not good and I told him no. He went into his pocket again and pulled out eleven $20 gold pieces and asked me if I would credit him for the balance. I told him no.

"Well," he said, "I call you for $220."

I told him all right. "I reckon you have me beat."

He said: "I reckon so. I have got an ace full."

I said: "Hold on, I have two pair."

He said: "They are not worth a damn."

I said: "I reckon two pair of jacks are good," so the eventful game ended. I was ahead about $300.

Some way or another they all got on to my identity and they all treated me with a good deal of respect at the races the next day.

I went west and stopped at Round Rock in Williamson county to see my old school master, J. C. Landrum. I had been his pupil in the '60s at Sumpter. After this I concluded to go north from there as I had relatives in Navarro and Limestone counties. I naturally wanted to see them, even if I had to take risks in doing so. I still cherished the hope that the day would come when I could stand my trial and come clear. My father always told me that when the Democrats regained power I could get a fair trial, but I could never expect that under carpet-bag rule. Of course I had long ago concluded not to surrender for the present and whenever force was unlawfully employed to make me do so I met it with force, or else got out of the way.

IN AUGUST, 1870, I WENT TO NAVARRO AND STAYED AT PISGA, where I gambled a while. From there I went to Mount Calm, where my father was teaching school. There I peddled in hides and traded, making some money.

Soon after, I got a letter from my brother Joe, who was going to school at Round Rock to Professor Landrum. I also got one from the professor himself, both letters urging me to come up there and graduate with Joe. I went up there but only went to school for one day. The rewards that were offered for me made that country too dangerous a place for me to stop. I passed my diploma examination, however, satisfactorily, so Joe and I graduated together. My brother

Joe then went to Mount Calm, helped my father to teach school and became a lawyer. He afterwards moved out to Comanche in 1872 and there lived until he met his death at the hands of a howling midnight mob of assassins in June, 1874. I concluded to go to Shreveport, La., where I had some relatives, and on my way there I stopped at a town named Longview. There they arrested me for another party, on a charge of which I was innocent. The State police concluded to take me to Marshall, but I got out a writ of habeas corpus. I was, however, remanded to jail at Waco for some crime which I never committed.

I was put in an old iron cell in the middle of the log jail and nobody was allowed to see me. There were three other prisoners in there, and together we planned our escape. We were to wait until the food was brought in for supper and then we were to make our break. It was very cold weather when they first put me in jail and I had money with me to buy whisky and tobacco for us all.

Thinking they would soon be released they had offered to sell me a pistol, a 45 Colt with four barrels loaded. I unfolded my plan to them by which we could all get out. I was to cover the jailor as he opened the door and kill him if he did not obey orders. We were then all to rush out and stand the crowd off until dark would help us to easily get away.

They weakened, however, and so I bought the pistol for $10 in gold and a $25 overcoat. I had no idea when they were going to take me off, nor could I find out in any way. I tried to get them to go after my horse at Longview, but they would not do that.

One cold night they called for me and I knew what was up, and you bet I was ready for them. I found out that I was going because the negro cook only brought up three supper plates. When the prisoners complained that there were only three plates and four of us she said that "one of us was going to leave tonight." I prepared myself for an emergency. I had a very heavy fur coat, a medium sack coat, two undershirts and two white shirts. I hid the pistol, tied with a good stout cord, under my left arm and over it my top shirt. I put on the rest of my clothes to see how it looked. It looked all right, so I took off my coat and vest and went to bed.

When they came to wake me up I pretended to be awakened out of a sound sleep and to be very much surprised. They told me to get up and put on my clothes, that they were going to start for Waco with me. They told me I was wanted up there for killing Huffman in a barber shop. I appeared very much frightened and asked if there was any danger of a mob. Both Capt. Stokes and the jailer assured me that there was none. I then put on my vest and socks, putting a bottle of pickles in my overcoat pocket on the left side so as to make me look bulky. They searched me, but did not find any pistol. It was very cold and snow lay on the ground. They lead up a little black pony with a blanket thrown over him for me to ride 225 miles to Waco. I asked where my own horse and saddle was, and they told me at Longview. I tried to buy a saddle from the jailor, but he would not sell me one. I at last got another blanket and mounted my pony, my guard tying me on hard and fast.

So we started out of Marshall, they leading my horse. When daylight came they untied my legs and allowed me to guide the little black pony. If you had met our party that day you would have seen a small white man about 45 years old, who was a captain of police named Stokes, a middle weight dark looking man, one-fourth negro, one-fourth Mexican and one-half white. The former riding a large bay horse, the latter a fine sorrel mare and leading a small black pony with a boy 17 years old tied thereon and shivering with cold. They tried to frighten me every way they could. Stokes said they were going to shoot me if I tried to run off, and said that Jim Smolly would kill me any moment he told him to do so. I, of course, talked very humbly, was full of morality and religion and was strictly down on lawlessness of all kinds. I tried to convince them that I was not an outlaw and did not wish to escape anywhere. When we got to the Sabine river it was booming and we had to swim. They tied me on again and put a rope around my pony's neck.

Stokes leading, me next and Smolly bringing up the rear. The little black pony could swim like a duck and with the exception of getting thoroughly wet and cold, we got over all right.

We went on two miles out from the river and stopped for the night. Jim went to get some wood and fodder for our horses, while Capt. Stokes and myself started a fire and struck camp. We went to a house about 100 yards off and got an axe. We came back and he told me to cut some pine from an old pine tree. I assented, but made a complete failure with the axe as I was afraid my pistol might show. Jim soon got back, however, and we made a big fire, fed the horses, got supper, laid down and slept till morning, when we again started on our road to Waco.

When we reached the Trinity we found it out of its banks and dangerous to cross. We got the ferryman to ferry us over the main river, but when we began to cross the bottoms and the sloughs they tied me on the black pony again and kept me tied until we reached dry land. We went forward again and traveled until night, when we stopped and camped. Capt. Stokes went to get some corn and fodder for our horses. While he was gone Jim Smolly cursed me, as was his habit, and threatened to shoot me, pointing his pistol at me to scare me. Then he sat down on a stump near our horses, which were hitched to the body of the tree. I pretended to be going and got behind the little black pony. I put my head down on his back and meanwhile I untied the string that held my pistol. I kept one eye on him to see if he was watching me. When I got the pistol ready I rushed around on Jim and said: "Throw up your hands." He commenced to draw his pistol, when I fired and Jim Smolly fell dead, killed because he did not have sense enough to throw up his hands at the point of a pistol. I rode Jim Smolly's sorrel mare and rode to Mount Calm that night to my father's. Father gave me another horse and sent the sorrel mare back. This was in January, 1871.

I left my father's soon, bound for Mexico. I was going by way of San Antonio, but was arrested between Belton and Waco by men calling themselves police. They said they were going to take me to Austin, but night coming on, we stopped about ten miles from Belton. They agreed that one Smith should stand first guard, a man named Jones, second, and one Davis the last watch. They had a good deal of whisky with them and they all got about half drunk. I had concluded to escape on the first opportunity, so when we laid down I noticed where they put their shooting irons. I did not intend to sleep, but watched for a chance to liberate myself from unlawful arrest.

Jones soon dropped off to sleep and Davis soon followed; Smith sat up to guard me, but he forgot he was on duty or else was unconscious of the danger that threatened him and his companions. He began to nod, but once in a while he would roll his eyes around on me. Pretty soon he put his hand up to his head and his elbow on his knee and began to snore. I picked up Davis' shotgun and Jones' six-shooter. I fired at Smith's head and then turned the other barrel on Jones at once. As Davis began to arise and inquire what was the matter I began to work on him with the six-shooter. He begged and hollered, but I kept on shooting until I was satisfied he was dead.

Thus I got back my liberty and my pistols. I took an oath right there never to surrender at the muzzle of a gun. I never have done so, either, although I have been forced through main strength to give up several times since.

I went back by way of Marlin, in Falls county to tell them all good bye once more. I told my father what I had done and how those three men had arrested me while I was asleep. He said:

"Son, never tell this to mortal man. I don't believe you, but go to Mexico, and go at once. I will go part of the way with you."

I slept in the cellar that night and stayed in an old oat-house the next day. I started the next night and we went through Waco. This was about the 12th of January, 1871. My father went on with me as far as Belton and there we parted. I went on through Georgetown, through Austin, and thence through Lockhart to Gonzales. I had some relatives in the latter town and I concluded to stop over and see them.

These were the Clements; Jim, Manning, Joe, Gip, Mary Jane and Minerva. The girls were both married, the eldest to Jim Denson, the youngest to Fred Brown. They lived almost directly on my way from Gonzales to Hellena, an old and honored citizen showed me the way to my relatives' home.

My guide's name was Jim Cone. I told my relatives I was in trouble and on my way to Mexico. They told me I could go to Kansas with cattle and make some money and at the same time be free from arrest. I therefore concluded to give up my Mexican trip and went to work helping them gather cattle. We gathered mostly for Jake Johnson and Columbus Carol, who were then putting up herds for Kansas.

I thus soon got acquainted with the country on the Sandies, on Elm and Rocky and on the Guadalupe.

I had not been there long before the boys took me to a Mexican camp where they were dealing monte. I soon learned the rudiments of the game and began to bet with the rest. Finally I turned a card down and tapped the game. My card came and I said: "Pay the queen." The dealer refused. I struck him over the head with my pistol as he was drawing a knife, shot another as he also was drawing a knife. Well, this broke up the monte game and the total casualties were a Mexican with his arm broken, another shot through the lungs and another with a very sore head. We all went back to camp and laughed about the matter, but the game broke up for good and the Mexican camp abandoned. The best people of the vicinity said I did a good thing. This was in February, 1871.

When we were gathering cattle for the trail I was in charge of the herd with strict orders to let no one go into the herd. A negro named Bob King came to the herd, rode in and commenced to cut out cattle without permission. I rode up and asked him by whose permission he was cutting cattle in that herd. He said he did not have to have permission and asked who was the boss. I said:

"I am the man."

"Well," said he, "I have come to cut this herd."

I told him to keep out of it; that Clements would be here directly. He rode right into that herd and cut out a big beef steer. So I rode up to him and struck him over the head with my pistol and told him to get out of my herd. Although he had a six-shooter, he did not do anything, but begged my pardon.

About the last of February we got all our cattle branded and started for Abilene, Kansas about the 1st of March. Jim Clements and I were to take these 1200 head of cattle up to Abilene and Manning, Gip and Joe Clements were to follow with a herd belonging to Doc Burnett. Jim and I were getting $150 per month.

Nothing of importance happened until we got to Williamson county, where all the hands caught the measles except Jim and myself. We camped about two miles south of Corn Hill and there we rested up and recruited. I spent the time doctoring my sick companions, cooking and branding cattle.

About the fourth day we were there near Barnett Young's (a relative of mine) a big white steer of the neighborhood gave me considerable trouble. I could not keep him out of the herd, so I pulled my 45 and shot him, aiming to shoot him in the nose, but instead hit him in the eye. That ox gave me no more trouble, but his owner gave me no end of trouble in the courts. I think that ox cost me about $200.

After resting there about ten days all the hands recovered from the measles and the cattle and horses having improved so much in flesh we again started north.

After several weeks of travel we crossed Red River at a point called Red River Station, or Bluff, north of Montague county. We were now in the Indian country and two white men had been killed by Indians about two weeks before we arrived at the town. Of course all the talk was Indians and everybody dreaded them. We were now on what is called the Chisolm trail and game of all kinds abounded; buffalo, antelope and other wild animals too numerous to mention. There were a great many cattle driven that year from Texas. The day we crossed Red River about fifteen herds had crossed and of course we intended to keep close together going through the Nation for our mutual protection. The trail was thus one line of cattle and you were never out of sight of a herd. I was just about as much afraid of an Indian as I was of a coon. In fact, I was anxious to meet some on the war path.

There were lots of wolves in that country and I never heard anything like their howling. We killed a beef one night and they made the night hideous. I wanted to capture one, and in the early morning saddled my horse to see if I could not rope or kill one.

I struck out from camp and saw a big loafer about 200 yards from camp. He was about 200 yards away, but I turned Roan loose and pulling my pistol I commenced shooting. My very first shot hit him in his hip. I ran on to him and roped him. I pulled him to the camp, but the boys said that no wolf could enter camp and shot my rope in two. Mr. Wolf, however, ran the gauntlet and escaped. The whole outfit caught the wolf fever, which resulted in tired men and crippled horses. I also killed some antelope, running on them and shooting them from the saddle.

One morning on the South Canadian river I went out turkey hunting and killed as fine a gobbler as I ever saw. I went over to where he fell, picked him up and started for my pony. It was just about daylight, and when I got close to my pony I saw he was snorting and uneasy. I looked in the direction that he seemed to be afraid of and about twenty yards off I saw an Indian in the very act of letting fly an arrow at me, and quick as thought, I drew my pistol and fired at him. The ball hit him squarely in the forehead and he fell dead without a groan. I got away from there with my turkey as quickly as I could, went to camp and we all went to see the dead Indian. The boys wanted to take his bow and arrows as trophies, but I objected. We got a spade and an axe and dug a grave and buried the Indian with his bows and arrows, covering the grave with leaves to hide the spot from other Indians.

These Indians had established a custom of taxing every herd that went through the Nation 10 cents per head. Several other herds joined with us in refusing to pay this, and we never did, though many times it looked like war.

When we were crossing into Kansas, somewhere near Bluff Creek, we were attacked by a band of Osage Indians who would ride into the herd and cut out little bunches of cattle, sometimes as many as fifteen or twenty head at one time. It was straight-out robbery and I told the hands to shoot the first Osage that cut another cow.

ONE MORNING THESE INDIANS CAME TO OUR CAMP while I was away and scared the cook and hands almost to death. They took off everything they wanted to, including a fancy silver bridle of mine. I got back to camp about 10 a.m. and when I found out what had happened you bet I was hot. In a little while about twenty bucks came to the herd, rode in and commenced to cut out cattle. I rode up to where they were and saw a big Indian using my fancy silver bridle. I asked him how much he would take for it and offered him $5. He grunted an assent and gave me the bridle. When I got it I told him that was my bridle and someone had stolen it from camp that morning. He frowned and grunted and started to get the bridle back, and trying to pull it off my horse. I jabbed him with my pistol and when this would not stop him I struck him over the head with it. He fell back and yelled to his companions.

This put the devil in them. They came up in a body and demanded cattle again. I told him "no," as I had done before. An Indian rode into the herd and cut out a big beef steer. I told him to get out of the herd and pulled my pistol to emphasize my remarks. He was armed and drew his, saying that if I did not let him cut the beef out he would kill the animal. I told him that if he killed the animal I would kill him. Well, he killed the beef and I killed him. The other Indians promptly vanished. If they hadn't there would have been more dead Indians around that herd. The beef he had killed lay dead on the trail, so I mounted him by tying the dead Indian on his back and drove on.

When we had crossed into Kansas we felt better and safer. On reaching a place called Cow House, about twenty miles on this side of Wichita, a party of men interested in changing the trail from Wichita came out to the herd and induced us to go to the left of Wichita and cross the river about twelve miles above. They wished us to open this trail, as they were interested in building up a new town on the north bank of the Arkansas river. We followed a plough furrow on this new trail and these men furnished a guide. When we had crossed the river a delegation from the new town came out to meet us and invite all those that could leave the cattle to enjoy the hospitalities of the new town.

About sixty cow boys went to that town and it is needless to say filled up on wine, whisky, etc., some getting rather full. We all came back to the herd in a little while and started out again for Abilene.

We were now on the Newton prairie and my herd was right in front of a herd driven by Mexicans. This Mexican herd kept crowding us so closely that at last it took two or three hands to keep the Mexican cattle from getting into my herd. The boss Mexican got mad at me for holding, as he said, his cattle back. I told him to turn to the outside of the trail, as he did not have to follow me. This made him all the madder. He fell back from the front of his herd and quit leading the cattle. The result of this was that no one being in front of them they rushed right into my herd, so I turned them off to the left. The boss Mexican rode back up to where I was and cursed me in Mexican. He said he would kill me with a sharp shooter as quick as he could get it from the wagon. In about five minutes I saw him coming back with a gun. He rode up to within about 100 yards of me, got down off his horse, took deliberate aim at me and fired. The ball grazed my head, going through my hat and knocking it off. He tried to shoot again, but something went wrong with his gun and he changed it to his left hand and pulled his pistol with his right. He began to advance on me, shooting at the same time. He called up his crowd of six or seven Mexicans.

In the meanwhile Jim Clements, hearing that I was in a row, had come to my assistance. I was riding a fiery gray horse and the pistol I had was an old cap and ball, which I had worn out shooting on the trail. There was so much play between the cylinder and the barrel that it would not burst a cap or fire unless I held the cylinder with one hand and pulled the trigger with the other. I made several unsuccessful attempts to shoot the advancing Mexican from my horse but failed. I then got down and tried to shoot and hold my horse, but failed in that, too.

Jim Clements shouted at me to "turn that horse loose and hold the cylinder." I did so and fired at the Mexican, who was now only ten paces from me. I hit him in the thigh and stunned him a little. I tried to fire again, but snapped.

The Mexican had evidently fired his last load so we both rushed together in a hand to hand fight. The other Mexicans had by this time come close up and were trying to shoot me every chance they got. Jim Clements, seeing I had no show to win, rushed between me and the other Mexicans and told them not to shoot, but to separate us as we were both drunk and did not know what we were doing. Another Mexican who had not been there at the beginning of the fight then rode up and fired two shots at me, but missed.

We covered him with our pistols and he stopped. It was then agreed to stop the fight for a time, so the Mexicans went back to their herd. We were not fixed for that fight but wanted to be for the coming one. I had only an old worn-out cap and ball pistol and Jim Clements could not fight because his pistol was not loaded. This was the real reason we made a truce for the time. Jim and I went straight to camp and loaded two of the best pistols there. While we were doing this a message came from the Mexicans that time was up and they were coming. We of course sent the messenger back and told the Mexicans to keep off our herd and not to come around; that we did not want any more trouble.

Seven of them gathered on the west side of the herd and seemed to talk matters over. Presently the boss, Hosea, my old foe, with three men, came around to the east side where we were. I had changed horses, so I rode to meet him. He fired at me when about seventy-five yards away, but missed me. I concluded to charge him and turn my horse loose at him, firing as I rode. The first ball did the work. I shot him through the heart and he fell over the horn of his saddle, pistol in hand and one in the scabbard, the blood pouring from his mouth. In an instant I had his horse by the reins and Jim Clements had relieved him of his pistols and Hosea fell dead to the ground.

The other Mexicans kept shooting at us, but did not charge. They were in two parties, one about seventy-five yards to the south, the other about 150 yards to the west. We charged the first party and held our fire until we got close to them. They never weakened, but kept shooting at us all the time. When we got right on them and opened up they turned their horses, but we were in the middle of them, dosing them with lead.

They wheeled and made a brave stand. We were too quick for them, however, in every way and they could not go our gait. A few more bullets quickly and rightly placed silenced the party forever. The other party was now advancing on us and shooting as they came. We, therefore, determined to stampede the herd, which we did in short order by shooting a steer in the nose. This seemed to demoralize them for a while and they all broke to the cattle except one, who stood still and continued to use his pistol. We cross-fired on him and I ended his existence by putting a ball through his temples.

We then took after the rest, who now appeared to be hunting protection from other herders. We caught up with two of them and Jim Clements covered and held them while I rounded in two more. These latter two said they had nothing to do with the fight and that their companions must have been drunk. We let these two go to the cattle. A crowd of cow men from all around had now gathered. I suppose there were twenty-five of them around the two Mexicans we had first rounded up. We thus had good interpreters and once we thought the matter was settled with them, when suddenly the Mexicans, believing they 'had the drop,' pulled their pistols and both fired point blank at me. I don't know how they missed me. In an instant I fired first at one, then at the other. The first I shot through the heart and he dropped dead. The second I shot through the lungs and Jim shot him too. He fell off his horse and I was going to shoot him again when he begged and held up both hands. I could not shoot a man, not even a treacherous Mexican, begging and down. Besides, I knew he would die anyway. In comparing notes after the fight we agreed that I had killed five out of the six dead Mexicans.

Nothing of interest happened until we reached North Cottonwood, where we went into camp to deliver our cattle. We were now about 35 miles from Abilene, Kansas, and it was about the 1st of June that we all got word to come into Abilene, draw our pay and be discharged.

I HAVE SEEN MANY FAST TOWNS, BUT I THINK ABILENE BEAT THEM ALL. The town was filled with sporting men and women, gamblers, cowboys, desperadoes and the like. It was well supplied with bar rooms, hotels, barber shops and gambling houses, and everything was open.

Before I got to Abilene I had heard much talk of Wild Bill, who was then marshal of Abilene. He had a reputation as a killer. I knew Ben Thompson and Phil Coe were there and had met both these men in Texas. Besides these, I learned that there were many other Texans there and so, although there was a reward offered for me, I concluded to stay some time there as I knew that Carol and Johnson, the owners of my herd, "squared" me with the officials. When we went to town and settled up, Jim Clements insisted on going home, although they offered him $140 per month to stay. I continued in their employ to look after their stray cattle at $150 per month. Thus we settled our business and proceeded to take in the town.

Columbus Carol got into a fuss with a policeman that night at a notorious resort. Carson was the policeman's name, and he drew a pistol on Carol. I was present and drew mine on Carson, making him leave the place. I told him not to turn his head until he got to the corner of the next street and to go and get "Wild Bill," his chief, and come back and we would treat him likewise. But they never came back.

Next morning Carol and myself met Carson and Wild Bill on the streets, but nothing happened.

Jim Clements took the train and went back to Texas. Phil Coe and Ben Thompson at that time were running the Bull's Head saloon and gambling hall. They had a big bull painted outside the saloon as a sign and the city council objected to this for some special reason. Wild Bill, the marshal, notified Ben Thompson and Phil Coe to take the sign down or change it somewhat. Phil Coe thought the ordinance all right, but it made Thompson mad. Wild Bill, however, sent up some painters and materially altered the offending bovine.

For a long time everybody expected trouble between Thompson and Wild Bill and I soon found out that they were deadly enemies. Thompson tried to prejudice me every way he could against Bill, and told me how Bill, being a Yankee, always picked out Southern men to kill, and especially Texans. I told him "I am not doing anybody's fighting just now except my own, but I know how to stick to a friend. If Bill needs killing why don't you kill him yourself?"

He said: "I would rather get someone else to do it."

I told him then that he had struck the wrong man. I had not yet met Bill Heycox, but really wished for a chance to have a set-to with him just to try his pluck.

One night in a wine room he was drinking with some friends of mine when he remarked that he would like to have an introduction to me. George Johnson introduced us and we had several glasses of wine together. He asked me all about the fight on the Newton prairie and showed me a proclamation from Texas offering a reward for my arrest. He said:

"Young man, I am favorably impressed with you, but don't let Ben Thompson influence you; you are in enough trouble now and if I can do you a favor I will do it."

I was charmed with his liberal views, and told him so. We parted friends.

I spent most of my time in Abilene in the saloons and gambling houses, playing poker, faro and seven-up. One day I was rolling ten pins and my best horse was hitched outside in front of the saloon. I had two six-shooters on and of course I knew the saloon people would raise a row if I did not pull them off. Several Texans were there rolling ten pins and drinking. I suppose we were pretty noisy. Wild Bill came in and said we were making too much noise and told me to pull off my pistols until I got ready to go out of town. I told him I was ready to go now, but did not propose to put up my pistols, go or no go. He went out and I followed him. I started up the street when someone behind me shouted out:

"Set up. All down but nine."

Wild Bill whirled around and met me. He said:

"What are you howling about and what are you doing with those pistols on?"

I said: "I am just taking in the town."

He pulled his pistol and said: "Take those pistols off. I arrest you."

I said all right and pulled them out of the scabbard, but while he was reaching for them I reversed them and whirled them over on him with the muzzles in his face, springing back at the same time. I told him to put his pistol up, which he did. I cursed him for a long haired scoundrel that would shoot a boy with his back to him (as I had been told he intended to do me). He said, "Little Arkansaw, you have been wrongly informed."

By this time a big crowd had gathered with pistols and arms. They kept urging me to kill him. Down the street a squad of policemen were coming, but Wild Bill motioned them to go back and at the same time asked me not to let the mob shoot him.

I shouted: "This is my fight and I'll kill the first man that fires a gun."

Bill said: "You are the gamest and quickest boy I ever saw. Let us compromise this matter and I will be your friend. Let us go in here and take a drink, as I want to talk to you and give you some advice."

At first I thought he might be trying to get the drop on me, but he finally convinced me of his good intentions and we went in and took a drink. We went into a private room and I had a long talk with him and we came out friends.

I had been drinking pretty freely that day and towards night went into a restaurant to get something to eat. A man named Pain was with me, a Texan who had just come up the trail. While we were in the restaurant several drunken men came in and began to curse Texans. I said to the nearest one:

"I'm a Texan."

He began to curse me and threatened to slap me over. To his surprise I pulled my pistol and he promptly pulled his. At the first fire he jumped behind my friend Pain who received the ball in his only arm. He fired one shot and ran, but I shot at him as he started, the ball hitting him in the mouth, knocking out several teeth and coming out behind his left ear. I rushed outside, pistol in hand and jumped over my late antagonist, who was lying in the doorway. I met a policeman on the sidewalk, but I threw my pistol in his face and told him to "hands up." He did it.

I made my way to my horse and went north to Cottonwood, about thirty-five miles, to await results. While I was there a Mexican named Bideno shot and killed Billy Goran, a cow man who had come up the trail with me. He was bossing a herd then, holding it near by Abilene for the market. His murder by this Mexican was a most foul and treacherous one, and although squad after squad tried to arrest this Mexican, they never succeeded in either killing or arresting him.

Many prominent cow men came to me and urged me to follow the murderer. I consented if they would go to Abilene and get a warrant for him. They did so and I was appointed a deputy sheriff and was given letters of introduction to cattle men whom I should meet. About sunrise on the 27th of June, 1871, I left the North Cottonwood with Jim Rodgers to follow Bideno. Of course, we proposed to change horses whenever we wanted to. This was easy to do, as there were many horses around the herds and we knew they would let us have them when we explained our purpose. We hoped to catch up with him before he got to the Nation, and specially before he got to Texas. Off we went in a lope and got to Newton, about 50 miles away, by 4 p. m. I had learned of a herd there bossed by a brother of the dead Billy Goran and I sent a messenger to him telling him (the messenger) not to spare horseflesh. Goran came and one Anderson with him. I told him of his brother's death and we were soon on the trail with fresh horses and four instead of two in our party.

We had not as yet heard one word from Bideno. We expected to reach Wichita that night. About twelve miles from Newton, just about dusk, we came upon a herd bossed by Ben McCulloch, who was afterwards Assistant Superintendent of the Huntsville Penitentiary, while I was there. We changed horses again and took the trail, having as yet heard nothing of Bideno. We reached Wichita about 11 o'clock that night, having travelled 100 miles since starting. We concluded to rest until morning and then go on the south side of the river and make inquiry. I knew there were several Mexican herds near the river which Bideno might have gone to for a change of horses. We went next morning to these herds, going from one to the other, hunting for information. Finally we struck a Mexican who said that just such a man had stayed at his camp about 10 o'clock last night and had traded horses with one of his men early in the morning. He said the horse he had traded for was the best in camp. We were convinced that this must have been Bideno, so changing horses and flushed with hope we hit the trail again about 7 a.m. in a long lope.

We saw a herder about 8 o'clock who told us that two hours before he had seen a Mexican wearing a broad brimmed hat and going south in a lope, keeping about 200 yards from the trail. We were now satisfied we were on the right track and pulled out again, expecting to change horses at Cow House creek, about fifteen miles further on. We met a man near Cow House who told us that he had seen a Mexican wearing a broad brimmed hat and going south in a lope. When we got to Cow House we changed our horses at once and found that Bideno had done likewise an hour before. It was now about 10 o'clock, and hoping to overtake him before we got to Bluff creek, twenty-five miles off, on the line of Arkansas and the Indian Territory, we pushed our fresh horses to a fast lope. We heard from him several times, but he was always in a lope and always off the road.

After going about twenty miles we again changed horses, so that if we ran up on him our horses would be fresh. When we got to within two miles of Bluff creek the road forked. Anderson and I went through the city, while Rodgers and Coran took the other fork; all agreeing to meet in the Indian Nation on the other side of the creek.

Anderson and I, before going far got direct information that Bideno had just unsaddled his horse and had gone up town inquiring for a restaurant. We fired off our pistols and by this means got Coran and Rodgers to hear us and come back.

We soon got to Bluff, which was a town of about fifty houses. There were some bar rooms and restaurants in a line and we agreed to ride up like cow boys, hitch our horses and divide into two parties, each going into different places. Anderson and I went into a restaurant, but before we reached it we had to go into a saloon. I called for the drinks and took in the situation. I asked if we could get dinner and if a Mexican herder was eating dinner back there. They said there was; so I told my partner to get out his gun and follow me. We stepped into the entrance and I recognized Bideno. With my pistol by my side I said:

"Bideno, I am after you; surrender; I do not wish to hurt you and you shall not be hurt while you are in my hands."

He was sitting at the table eating and shook his head and frowned. He then dropped his knife and fork and grabbed his pistol. As he did it I told him to throw up his hands. When he got his pistol out I fired at him across the table and he fell over a dead man, the ball hitting him squarely in the center of the forehead.

Hearing the firing Coran and Rodgers rushed in also. Coran said: "I just want to shoot my brother's murderer one time. Is he dead?"

I told him he was, but he wanted to shoot him anyway. I would not let him, but he took his hat as a trophy.

In the meantime the waiter was jumping up and down, begging us not to kill him; that he was a friend of cowboys, etc. I quieted him by telling him if he did not get out he might, perhaps, get shot accidently, and he promptly acted on my suggestion.

We all went into the saloon and the bartender said: "Take what you want." We took some good whisky and he would not let us pay for it.

Quite a crowd had collected by this time and they all wanted to know what the shooting was about. I got outside the saloon and told the crowd how this Mexican had murdered a prominent cow man on the 26th at North Cottonwood; how we had followed him and demanded his surrender; how he had refused to give up and had drawn his pistol, when I was forced to shoot him. I then introduced John Coran, the dead man's brother. They all commended our actions and I gave those people $20 to bury him.

We started back to Abilene, rejoicing over our good luck. We reached Wichita that night, which was about fifty miles away. As we had ridden about 150 miles in 36 hours we all rested that night in Wichita.

There I told my companions my troubles in Abilene. We all agreed to go to Newton and thence to Abilene, where they were to stick to me against anything.

I had heard that Wild Bill had said that if I ever came back to Abilene he would kill me, so I had determined to go back there and if Bill tried to arrest me to kill him.

Well, we stopped next at Newton and took in that town in good style. The policemen tried to hold us down, but they all resigned—I reckon. We certainly shut up that town.

We went on to Abilene fearing nothing but God. While we were opening wine there, Wild Bill came in and asked me if I remembered our talk in the "Apple Jack."

"Well," said he, "you cannot 'hurrah' me, and I am not going to have it."

I told him, "I don't wish to hurrah you; but I have come to stay, regardless of you."

"Well," he said, "you can stay and wear your guns, but those other fellows must pull them off. You are in no danger here. I congratulate you on getting your Mexican. Come in and invite your friends. We will open a bottle of wine."

The boys had been watching us pretty closely and we all went into a room, they having their guns on. The marshal said nothing about their pistols then and after drinking a couple of bottles of wine left.

I then told my companions that Bill was my friend and had asked me to see that they took their pistols off. They asked me why I did not pull mine off. I told them that the marshal had not demanded that of me, but I knew he was our friend and would protect us all, and if he did not, I would. Well they said that if Wild Bill was all right with me they would go home, which they did.

Everybody in Abilene wanted to see the man that killed the murderer of Billy Goran and I received substantial compliments in the shape of $20, $50 and $100 bills. I did not want to take the money at first but I finally concluded there was nothing wrong about it, so took it as a proof of their friendship and gratitude for what I had done. I think I got about $400 in that way. Besides this, some wealthy cow men made up a purse and gave me $600, so altogether I got about $1000 for my work. I wish to say, however, that at the time I killed him I never expected to receive a cent, and only expected to have my expenses paid.

It was about the 2nd of July that John Goran, Jim Rodgers, Hugh Anderson and myself parted at Abilene. In a day or two Manning and Gip Clements came into Abilene and hunted me up. They found me with Jake Johnson and Frank Bell. To celebrate the meeting we opened several bottles of wine and then Manning said:

"Wes, I want to see you privately."

He, Gip and myself went up to my private room. Manning said:

"Wes, I killed Joe and Dolph Shadden last night, but I was justified."

"Well," said I, "I am glad you are satisfied, but I would stick to you all the same, even if you were not satisfied with your action."

Manning said that he was bossing a herd for Doc Burnett in Gonzales county and was driving them here. He had selected his own hands and had hired these Shadden boys. Everything had gone on smoothly until they crossed Red River. Then the Shaddens commenced playing off and refused to go on night duty. When they were ordered to do so they became insulting and demanded their time and money. When told they could quit they wanted pay for all the time had they gone through to Abilene. This, Manning refused to do, but offered to pay them for the time they had actually worked. He told them it was either this or leave camp or do night duty and stay. They stayed and did night duty. All the time going through the Nation they were trying to make the other hands dissatisfied and told them that they intended to kill Manning before they got to Abilene, where they knew that Jim Clements and Wes Hardin were and they would take Manning's part of course.

When they crossed the Canadian they gave up work entirely. Manning then offered them their full pay if they would leave. This they would not do, so he told Gip and the rest of the hands to watch them in word and actions. Manning actually would stay away from camp at nights to avoid trouble, as he knew they were fixing to kill him there. They began to talk about his cowardice in sleeping away from camp at nights. When the herd crossed the Arkansas, Manning told a friend of his that had their confidence too, that he was not going to sleep out of camp any longer.

The Shadden boys then said: "Well, if he comes back to sleep in camp at night we will kill him."

Manning was told of their intention and told his brother Gip in their presence to make down his bed in a certain place, which he did.

When they had gone. Manning told Gip what was up. Manning went on duty first that night himself and a hand came out to the herd and begged him not to go back to camp that night as these Shadden boys were sitting up waiting to kill him. Manning, however, took a friend and went to camp. He got there later than they expected and called out in a loud voice: "Gip, get up and go on herd." Gip said, "all right." Joe Shadden jumped up with his pistol, but Manning had on a slicker and also had his pistol in his hand. Manning fired first and put a bullet through Joe's head. Dolph, meanwhile, had fired at Manning, the hall going through his slicker and vest. Manning and Dolph Shadden then rushed together and scuffled, but Manning managed to fire, shooting him through the breast. He fell back on his bed, telling Manning he had killed him. Manning then turned the herd over to one of his hands, got his young brother Gip and came on here. When Manning told me this I said: "I have had a heap of trouble, but I stand square in Abilene. Wild Bill is my particular friend, and he is the one to help you here if papers come from Texas for you. Now, Manning, pull off your pistols until I see Bill and fix him."

I made Gip do the same thing. I then saw Columbus Carol and Jake Johnson and it was agreed that Columbus should see Wild Bill and square Manning Clements. But, unfortunately, Columbus got drunk and squared nothing. That evening we all dropped into a gambling hall and began to buck at monte. Wild Bill came in and said: "Hello, little Arkansaw." I said: "Hello yourself; how would you like to be called Hello!" Bill bought $20 worth of checks and lost them. Then he bought $50 and then $100. Manning and I walked out and went over to the American House to get supper. I had finished eating, but Manning and Gip had not, when in walked Wild Bill and McDonald. I knew in an instant that they had come to arrest Manning. Bill gave me the wink. In a few minutes he said: "How did you come out?" I told him about $25 ahead and asked him what he did. "I lost $250," said he. I told him I knew all the time he was playing the house's money when we had left. He laughed and said yes, that those fellows knew better than to refuse him. By this time Manning had finished eating and Wild Bill said:

"Are you through eating?"

Manning told him "yes," and he said: "I suppose your name is Clements. I have a telegram here to arrest Manning Clements; so consider yourself under arrest." Manning said "all right." I told Bill to let McDonald guard his prisoner a moment and told Bill I wanted to speak to him privately. I asked him if Columbus Carol had posted him.

"No," said he, "he is drunk. Why did you not post me yourself?"

I then told him that he had once promised to do any favor I asked of him; that Manning was a cousin of mine and that he relied on me for safety. I then asked Wild Bill what I could expect from him.

He told me he would turn him loose. I told him that was the only way of avoiding trouble. It was agreed that he should protect himself and his reputation as an officer by taking Manning to the Bull's Head saloon (Phil Coe's) and from thence to the lock-up. I asked him to tell me exactly what time he would turn him out and he said "12 o'clock." I then called Manning in and told him that Columbus had gotten drunk and had not posted Wild Bill and that in order to protect Wild Bill he must go to jail, but would be turned out at 12 m.

Wild Bill and McDonald then took Manning to jail, while I went to Jess McCoy and bought a horse and saddle for Manning to ride. By this time they had landed him in jail and Bill had sent for me to come up town. Jake Johnson was cutting up about the arrest and had a band of twenty-five Texans ready to liberate him. The police were also gathering at the jail. I took Jake off and told him that Columbus had gotten drunk and had not posted Bill. I explained it all to him and told him to bring his men up to Phil Coe's saloon and stay there. I went up to Phil Coe's and privately agreed to break open the jail at

12 o'clock if Wild Bill did not turn him loose at the appointed time. We went to work then and got fifty good men, stationing them in the back of the Bull's Head saloon, just across the street from the jail. I told Phil Coe that Wild Bill and I had agreed to meet at 8 o'clock to make a run or take the town in, so to speak, and it might be possible that I would not see him again before the play. I told Phil Coe that Wild Bill and I had set our watches together and so he and I also set ours together.

I agreed with Phil that he should get the key by 10 minutes to 12 and if at that time he had not gotten it to send me word. I told him where Wild Bill and I would be exactly at that time. I told him if I did not get word from him by 6 minutes to 12 I would kill Wild Bill, but whether he heard shooting or not to break open the jail if he did not get the key.

At 10 minutes to 8 by my watch I went to meet Wild Bill and we commenced to take in the gambling houses, etc. We began on monte and the banks we did not break, closed. Then we tried faro, and after a while they closed, too. Bill played the bluff racket and I bet with him, so where they paid him they had to pay me as well. I think we won about $1000 apiece that night.

On going over town we learned that a policeman named Tom Carson had arrested some female friends of ours and we determined to see them turned loose and to whip Tom Carson, although he was chief deputy of Wild Bill. We went to the calaboose and met Carson, but Bill did not say anything to him then, and called to the turnkey to bring the key. The prisoners got a hack and went home rejoicing.

Tom Carson asked Wild Bill what he did it for and Bill answered his question by knocking him down and then jumping on him with both feet. It was a bad beating up, for Wild Bill was a man 6 feet high and weighed 200 pounds. He was light complexioned, blue eyed and his hair hung down his shoulders in yellow curls. He was a brave, handsome fellow, but somewhat overbearing. He had fine sense and was a splendid judge of human nature. After this we again went up town and directly I asked Bill what time it was. He said, "15 minutes to 12," and handed me the key wrapped up in a piece of paper. I sent it at once to Phil Coe's at the Bull's Head saloon and sent word where Manning could find me. Manning soon joined me; we had some wine and then went to our horses.

We rode to Smoky river, where we got down and talked matters over. I had provided him with money and everything else necessary for the trip. It was agreed that we should meet again at Barnett Hardin's in Hill county, Texas, and that I should take care of his youngest brother, Gip, whom he left with me. We parted with this understanding and he went to Texas, while I went back to Abilene, reaching the town about 3 a.m.

IN THOSE DAYS MY LIFE WAS CONSTANTLY IN DANGER FROM SECRET OR HIRED ASSASSINS, and I was always on the lookout.

On the 7th of July Gip and I had gone to our rooms in the American hotel to retire for the night. We soon got to bed, when presently I heard a man cautiously unlock my door and slip in with a big dirk in his hand. I halted him with a shot and he ran; I fired at him again and again and he fell dead with four bullets in his body. He had carried my pants with him and so I jumped back, slammed the door and cried out that I would shoot the first man that came in. I had given one of my pistols to Manning the night before, so the one I had was now empty.

Now, I believed that if Wild Bill found me in a defenseless condition he would take no explanation, but would kill me to add to his reputation. So in my shirt and drawers I told Gip to follow me and went out on the portico.

Just as I got there a hack drove up with Wild Bill and four policemen. I slipped back and waited until they had gotten well inside the hotel and then jumped off over the hack. Gip came after me.

I sent Gip to a friend of mine to hide him. I hardly knew what to do. I was sleepy in the first place, and without arms or clothes. I knew all the bridges were guarded and the country was out after me, believing that I had killed a man in cold blood, instead of a dirty, low down, would-be assassin. I concluded to slip around and sleep in a haystack which I knew of. I heard them come and look for me, one remarking that he believed I was in that haystack and started to set it on fire. I crawled away into the haystack, knowing they would not set it on fire because it was too close to a store. If they had done so you would have seen a lad 19 years old in his night clothes crawling away from the officers and the fire in a hurry. I crawled to the edge of the stack after a while and saw two squads of police not far off.

I crawled to a cornfield in roasting ear, keeping the haystack between me and the police. Presently I saw a lone cowboy riding up within a few yards of me. I asked him if he knew me. He said he did. I put my hand to my side and told him to get down on the other side. He did it and I got up. The police saw this move and I turned my nag loose. The police were right after me and we had a hot race to the river, three miles off. I got there a quarter of a mile ahead and plunged my horse in. He swam like a duck and I got across in safety. They fired several shots at me from the other side and their bullets whistled unpleasantly close to me, so I soon put space between myself and pursuers. I went about a mile, when I looked back and saw three men coming at full speed, but I rode on and at that time few men could outride me. I weighed 155 pounds and was confident in myself, even though I was undressed and unarmed. I let that dun mare go a gait that I thought she could stand and that would put me in camp at least half an hour ahead of my pursuers. I looked back again and could see them coming about four miles off. It was about five miles to camp and downhill the most of the way, so I let her go and made it in about twenty minutes.

I was a sorry spectacle when I got to that camp. I was bareheaded, unarmed, red-faced, and in my night clothes. I went to work at once to meet my pursuers and got two six-shooters and a Winchester. The cook had prepared dinner and as I had eaten nothing since the evening before, I certainly relished it. The camp was right on the north bank of North Cottonwood and I dropped down under the bank while my pursuers rode up. Tom Carson and two others inquired of the cook where I was. He told them I had gone to the herd and asked them to get down and have dinner.

When they were eating I stepped up near them, but not near enough for any of them to grab me. I covered Tom Carson with my Winchester and told them, "All hands up or I'll shoot." All their hands went up, and I told the cook to relieve those gentlemen of their arms and told them that any resistance on their part would mean certain and untimely death. The cook did his work well, and I told them to finish their dinner, while I sat on a dry goods box with my Winchester in my hands.

When they were through I made Tom Carson and his two men pull off their clothes, pants and boots, and sent them all back in this condition to face a July sun for thirty-five miles on a bald prairie.

I waited out on Cottonwood several days until Gip Clements came out.

ON THE 11TH OF JULY, 1871, GIP AND I LEFT COTTONWOOD FOR TEXAS, well-armed and equipped in every way. We went by Emporia and Parsons and thence into the Nation.

One day we stopped for dinner with a trader who had a wagon drawn by a horse and a mule. He was a rough-looking fellow, heavy set, dark, and weighing about 180 pounds. He professed to be an expert shot and we commenced to shoot for a dollar a shot. In those days I was a crack shot, and I won several dollars. He then challenged me to shoot for $20. I did so and won easily. He then wanted to shoot for $50, which I again did and he again lost. He increased to $100, which I won. This made him wrathy and he wanted to fight. I told him he couldn't whip me and he called me a liar, drawing his pistol. I cocked mine in his face and Gip interfered by catching the trader's pistol, which alone prevented me from shooting him. Gip then took it away from him and he commenced abusing me and said if Gip would give him back his pistol he would kill me. Of course he knew that Gip would not do this. He kept cursing me and told me he could carry weight and whip my sort. I said:

"Old man, I don't want to kill you, but you have only yourself to blame if you make me do it."

I guarded him while Gip saddled the horses. All this time he was trying to get to the wagon where his Winchester was and I had to warn the old fool repeatedly to keep back or I would surely kill him. When Gip got the horses saddled I made him throw down the trader's pistol and guard him until I had gotten off about 300 yards. Then Gip bade the Indian trader farewell and we rode off, laughing, but glad we did not have to kill him.

Nothing of interest happened until we got to Barnett Hardin's on the 30th of July, in Hill county, Texas. There we met Manning Clements and after staying about a week we struck out for Gonzales county, where the Clements lived. We arrived at Manning's house on the 7th of August, 1871. The Shadden brothers, whom Manning had killed, had a brother and a brother-in-law living near there and we expected trouble, but soon after our arrival they concluded to move out.

E. J. Davis was governor then and his State Police were composed of carpet-baggers, scalawags from the North, with ignorant negroes frequently on the force. Instead of protecting life, liberty and property they frequently destroyed it. We all knew that many members of this State Police outfit were members of some secret vigilante band, especially in DeWitt and Gonzales counties. We were all opposed to mob law and so soon became enemies. The consequence was that a lot of negro police made a raid on me without lawful authority. They went from house to house looking for me and threatening to kill me, and frightening the women and children to death.

They found me at a small grocery store in the southern portion of Gonzales county. I really did not know they were there until I heard someone say:

"Throw up your hands or die!"

I said "all right" and turning around saw a big black negro with his pistol cocked and presented. I said:

"Look out, you will let that pistol go off, and I don't want to be killed accidently."

He said: "Give me those pistols."

I said "all right" and handed him the pistols, handle foremost. One of the pistols turned a somerset in my hand and went off. Down came the negro, with his pistol cocked, and as I looked outside I saw another negro on a white mule firing into the house at me. I told him to hold up, but he kept on, so I turned my Colts 45 on him and knocked him off his mule my first shot. I turned around then to see what had become of No. 1 and saw him sprawling on the floor with a bullet through his head, quivering in blood. I walked out of the back door to get my horse and when I got back to take in the situation the big negro on the white mule was making for the bottom at a 2:40 gait. I tried to head him off, but he dodged and ran into a lake. I afterwards learned that he stayed in there with his nose out of the water until I left. The negro I killed was named Green Paramoor and the one on the white mule was a blacksmith from Gonzales named John Lackey—in fact they were both from that town.

News of this of course spread like fire, and myself and friends declared openly against negro or Yankee mob rule and misrule in general. In the meantime the negroes of Gonzales and adjoining counties had begun to congregate at Gonzales and were threatening to come out to the Sandies and with torch and knife depopulate the entire country. We at once got together about twenty-five men good and true and sent these negroes word to come along, that we would not leave enough of them to tell the tale. They had actually started, but some old men from Gonzales talked to them and made them return to their homes. From that time on we had no negro police in Gonzales. This happened in September, 1871.

Soon after this I took a trip to see some relatives in Brenham, and nothing of interest happened until I returned.

A posse of negroes from Austin came down after me and I was warned of their coming. I met them prepared and killed three of them. They returned sadder and wiser. This was in September, 1871.

As my parents were still living in Limestone county at Mount Calm I concluded to go and see them. I went through Austin, through Georgetown, Belton and Waco, from thence to Mount Calm, where I found my parents well and glad to see me again. I stayed there until after Christmas and then went to Dallas. Returning to Mount Calm, I stayed there one night and went back south to Gonzales.

I got back the night Gip Clements married Annie Tennille and I enjoyed the supper and dance very much. My sweetheart, who was soon to be my bride, Jane Bowen, was there.

Nothing of importance happened until I married Jane Bowen, though we were expecting the police to come any time. They would have met with a warm reception in those times, when the marriage bells were ringing all around.

About two months after I married I had some business at King's ranch and went by the way of Goliad and San Patrico to Corpus Christi. At the latter town I stayed several days and then went out to King's ranch (sometimes called San Gertrudas). On my way out there, when about forty-five miles from Corpus Christi, I stopped to get my dinner and pulled off my saddle to let my horse graze. I looked around and saw two Mexicans coming towards me. They stopped about seventy-five yards away, got down and began to make coffee. This was evidently done to throw me off my guard, but it did not have the desired effect. I just saddled up my horse again and rode on, hoping to lose them. After I had gone about four miles I saw the same two Mexicans coming to meet me again. When they got about fifty yards away from me one got on one side of the road and the other on the other side to cross fire on me. I took them to be robbers, as they were. I spurred my horse out of the road and they immediately pulled their pistols and started out after me. I suddenly wheeled and fired quickly. I shot the one on my left off his horse and the one on the right soon quit the fight. Being in a strange country I put as much space between myself and the robbers as possible. I never did know whether I killed both Mexicans or not.

I was riding a splendid horse and got to Capt. King's ranch that night. I stayed there the next day, transacted my business and in company with Jim Cox I made my way to San Diego, stayed there overnight and then with Cox went on to Banquetto and stayed there a day or two.

There I got to thinking that I had one of the prettiest and sweetest girls in the country as my wife, who would soon be looking for me for I had promised to be gone only twelve days. The more I thought of her the more I wanted to see her. So one night about 10 o'clock I started from Banquetto for Gonzales county, 100 miles away.

I got home at about 4 a.m., but forever ruined a good horse worth $250 in doing so. The sight of my wife recompensed me for the loss of old Bob.

This was in May and I conceived the idea of going east with a bunch of horses. I commenced to gather them at once and in two weeks I was ready to go to Louisiana. I bid my angel wife good bye. It nearly broke my heart for she had implicit confidence in me and her hope and prayer was my safe return. This was about the 5th of June, 1872.

I concluded to go ahead of the herd to Eastern Texas, where I had some relatives. My herd was in charge of Jess and John Harper, who had been raised in Sabine county. Their father was living at Hemphill and was then sheriff of Sabine, so we agreed to meet at Hemphill, or rather, I agreed to wait for them there.

Nothing unusual happened on the trip except at Willis, where some fellows tried to arrest me for carrying a pistol, but they got the contents thereof instead. I stopped a week at Livingstone and stayed with my Uncle Barnett, Aunt Anne and my cousins. We all had a splendid time and then I went to Hemphill about the last of June.

I had a race horse at that time named "Joe," and he was hard to catch on a quarter of a mile. I soon matched a race with some parties from San Augustine in an adjoining county. I think the race was for $250 and we were to run 350 yards. I took Billy Harper and went twenty-five miles north to their tracks, won the race easily and got the money without any trouble.

It was now the 20th of July and expecting the horses soon, Billy Harper and I went back to Hemphill. I waited there for the horses and gambled, as much for past time as for money.

On the 26th of July I got into a difficulty with Sonny Spites, one of E. J. Davis' infamous State Police. It happened in this way: A man named O'Connor, returning from Louisiana was going back home to Austin and stayed one night near Hemphill. A State Policeman arrested him because he had on a pistol and brought him into Hemphill, where, on the policeman's bare statement the magistrate fined him $25 and costs, besides confiscating his pistol. I heard of the outrage and explained the case to the justice, who granted O'Connor a new trial and acquitted him. In the meantime the policeman had taken possession of O'Connor's horse and saddle and was already trying to sell them to pay the fine and costs, O'Connor being broke. I was in the front of the court house talking the matter over with O'Connor and some others when a small boy about 10 years old began abusing Spites for arresting O'Connor at his father's house. Spites came up and listened to him and finally told the boy if he did not shut up he would arrest him too.

The boy ridiculed him and defied him to do it, telling him that no one but a coward would arrest a poor traveler. Spites told him if he did not shut up he would whip him. The boy told him he was not afraid, just to go ahead and whip and arrest him. Spites got up to slap the boy, when I told him to hold on, that if he was in earnest to slap a man. He told me he would arrest me for interfering with him in the discharge of his duty. I told him he could not arrest one side of me, and the boy laughed. Spites started to draw a pistol. I pulled a derringer with my left and my six-shooter with my right and instantly fired with my derringer. The dauntless policeman ran to the courthouse and asked the judge to protect him. I learned afterwards that Judge O. M. Roberts was the man appealed to. I would not shoot a fleeing man, not even a policeman, so I jumped on a horse and rode around to where my own was at Dr. Cooper's. When I got there Billy Harper was leading my horse "Joe" out of the stable and Mrs. Cooper was bringing my saddle bags. I saddled Joe as quickly as possible and got my saddle bags on. (Mrs. Cooper was Billy's sister.) She cried out:

"Wes, yonder comes pa with some men; for God's sake don't shoot."

I told them good-bye and to get out of the way. Billy was trying to let down the bars and the sheriff and posse were right on me. I knew the sheriff was my friend, so I would not fire on him. I put spurs to "Joe" and went over the bars. Just as we went over two balls struck Joe in the neck, but we soon distanced them and went to a friend's house about two miles from town. I awaited developments there and sent for Billy Harper.

Billy came about dark and told me that Spites was not mortally wounded, only hit in the shoulder and scared to death. He said everybody approved of what I had done, and that Jess and John Harper had come with the horses. They were at Frank Lewis' with the herd, about seven miles from town, and were expecting me out tomorrow. This was about the 26th day of July, 1872.

On the 27th I went out to the herd and stayed there a few days. I sold my horses to the Harper Bros, and started back to Gonzales county, but expected to stop in Polk and Trinity counties on my way. Nothing unusual happened until I got within ten miles of Livingstone, in Polk county, where I stopped at a store and there being some gay fellows there, we soon made a race. The race was for $250, $100 being put up as a forfeit, and the distance being a quarter of a mile. The date of the race was the 30th of July. The men I had made the race with were named Hickman and I was told they intended to take the money whether they won or not. When the time came for me to put up the other $150 with the stake holder I told him what I had heard. His name was Dick Hudson and I told him I knew him when we had been boys together in Polk county. He said he knew me well, so I told him there was my money, but I wanted the other parties to understand that no man or set of men could lake my money without killing me unless they won it; that if these parties wanted a fight instead of a race they could not commence any too soon to suit me. After Hickman Bros. heard of this they altered their tone and wanted to draw down, but I would not draw. At 12 o'clock (the limit for putting up) I claimed and received the $350 without a murmur from the Hickmans.

My uncle, Barnett Hardin, lived only ten miles from there, so I went to his place on the 30th of July and hunted and fished for a week. After this Barnett Jones, a cousin of mine, and I went up into Trinity county, where we had some relatives and friends, getting to Trinity City on the 7th of August. We went to John Gates' saloon and ten pin alley, where I commenced to roll. Everybody beat me for the drinks and after I had lost a round or two a man named Phil Sublet and I matched a game for $50 in or out. We were to roll anything we wished, from a pony up. It was to be a ball game at $5 a ball. I beat him six straights and won $30 of the $50. He said:

"I am going to take my stake down."

I told him we had made the game for $50 and I reckoned he would have to have my consent first.

He said: "No, by God."

I told him that he could not get it unless the stake holder gave it to him after he had won it. He said I was a g— d— liar and put his hand to his pistol. I slapped him in the face and shoved a bulldog pistol at his head. Friends interfered and we made peace.

We then rolled another ball apiece and I beat him. Then I told him he could draw down the rest of his stake. Sublet thus having lost $35.

We then went out into the front room where the bar room was to have something to drink at my expense. While we were drinking Sublet slipped off and I missed him pretty soon. It flashed across my mind that he had gone off to get a gun, so I went behind the counter and got two six-shooters out of my saddle bags. I went to the front window, which opened to the south and was behind the counter. The saloon was a plank structure, 60x70 feet. It faced north and south and was about 20 feet wide. A front door from the south and front formed the entrance to the bar room. The bar counter was on the left as you went in. The bar was cut off from the alley by a partition with a door therein. There was a door that opened into the alley from the east about ten feet from the partition, and also a window opened on the south or front end of the saloon. I was at the window when John Gates, the proprietor, told me to go into the alley, that the fuss between Sublet and I was all fixed up. I reluctantly consented to go back into the bowling alley. When I got there I heard someone shouting out:

"Clear the way, I will shoot anyone that interferes with me. Come out, you g— d— s— of a b—."

He was in the streets south of the front door and was on his way round to the east door of the alley. I appeared at that door with my pistol and he fired one barrel of a shotgun at me. I thought I would kill him, but did not want to get into any new trouble so fired at him, not intending to hit him, and stepped back. As I did so a drunken man got up and caught me by the vest, saying that he and I could whip anybody. He had a big knife in his hand and I told him to turn me loose, but before he did it he pulled me into the middle or partition door. By this time Sublet had gotten in line with the door and as we darkened it he fired the other barrel of his shotgun at me. I knew I was shot, so I instantly took after him with my six-shooter, but he threw down his gun and broke for his life. I ran him through the streets and into a dry goods store. As we went through the store I fired at him but my pistol snapped and I found I had my pistol with the broken cylinder spring. My man was still on the run and I was getting weak from loss of blood. I fired again as he went out the door and the ball passed through his shoulder. I was gettin' mighty weak now, but staggered to the door as he ran, hoping to kill the man who I thought had killed me. He was about seventy-five yards away and I saw I could never kill him, so I turned to some friends who were near and told them:

"I am either killed or shot. If all the gold in the world belonged to me I would freely give it to kill him. I have one consolation, however, I made the coward run."

By this time my cousin, Barnett Jones, had arrived and as they were holding me up I recognized him. I told him to take a belt I had which held about $2000 in gold; to get my saddle bags, which had about $250 in silver, and give it to my wife in Gonzales county. I told him to tell her that I honestly tried to avoid this trouble, but when I was shot I ran my foe and made him pull his freight for his life.

Barnett, however, told me not to give up, that they were going to do all they could for me and that they would bring me to Dr. Carrington's office. The doctor called in another doctor, who, after examining me, decided to take the balls out. Two buckshot had struck me a little to the left of the navel. They had passed through my right kidney and had lodged between my backbone and ribs. Two others had struck my belt buckle, which was a big silver one, and that was what saved me. The doctors asked me if I thought I could stand the operation without opiates. I told them yes, that if I died I wanted my head clear. They placed me on my face and went to work with knife and forceps. They soon had the two buck shot out of me.

Dr. Carrington then told me that my wounds, ordinarily speaking, were fatal, but if I would be submissive there was a chance for me. I told him I would take that chance and obey his orders. Everybody thought I would die. I told my friends to cut the wires so that they could not send any papers from Austin for me. They placed me in an hotel and gave me the best of treatment.

About the 15th of August I was told that I had to move or be arrested. I had never gotten up out of bed, but the doctor told me if I was careful I could be moved, which my friends did, taking me to two miles east of Sulphur Springs. There the doctor visited me for several days, when it was again thought best to move me to Old Sumpter to Dr. Teagarden's. His son Billy, with whom I had been raised, was now with me. We got a hack and struck out for Sumpter, about twenty miles away. We started one night and got there before day. I received good treatment there and got along well, although I could not yet stand up well.

Everybody there tried to help me and everybody was my friend, but the infamous police were after me and there were several mischief makers meddling about me. My friends again thought best to move me out two miles to John Gates', where I did not stay long. I came back again to Dr. Teagarden's. About the 27th of August I again had to leave the doctor's house, and that in a hurry, too.

They brought my horse up to the back gate and got me on him. By this time I had so improved that I could walk from the house to the yard, but was very weak and sore and could not straighten up. In company with Billy Teagarden and Charley we eluded a posse of police and went over into Angelina county, where we had an old friend by the name of Dave Harrel. We got there about the last of August, 1872. The Teagardens returned to Sumpter.

After I had been at Harrel's for two days word came that there was a party of police coming to arrest me. I got a double barreled shotgun and resolved to sell my life dearly if they did come.

On or about the 1st of September two men rode up to the house, armed with Winchesters, and came in. They asked Mrs. Harrel if I was there, but she told them I was not. They cursed her for a damned liar and told her I was in the back room, but she denied them admittance.

I was in the back room all this time and heard all that was going on. I straightened myself up on my pallet and as they darkened the door I told them to hold up their hands; that they could not run over a woman and that I was going to protect that house. They turned around and left, saying they did not want to harm the woman, but were after John Wesley Hardin. They soon returned, but in the meantime I had sent for Dave Harrel, who was in the cotton patch nearby and he was saddling my horse to go to Till Watson's with me, about ten miles away.

The police by this time had opened the gate and were in the yard. Mrs. Harrel told them to get out of her yard and would not leave when we tried to get her to go to a neighbor's house.

These policemen came on with their Winchesters in their hands. I crawled to the back door and threw my shotgun to my shoulder as quickly as possible and fired, first at one then at the other. In the meantime I had received a shot in my thigh, but Dave Harrel brought me my horse and helped me on him. We got to Till Watson's about dusk.

I learned afterwards that a coroner's inquest was held over one of the policemen and that the verdict was "that he had met his death at the hands of an unknown party, from gunshot wounds."

I was now in a bad fix. I had a fresh wound which required immediate medical attention and my old wounds were giving me trouble again. I knew a mob were after me now, so I sent Dave Harrel to Rusk to tell the sheriff of Cherokee county, Dick Reagan, to come out and arrest me. I told him to tell the sheriff that there was a reward for me and I would surrender to him rather than be made the victim of mob law. I told him to tell him to bring medical aid, but that for all this I wanted one-half the reward.

He brought four men with him, but kept them in the dark and made them believe he would have trouble in arresting me. They came to Till Watson's about the 4th of September, 1872. They came into the house, the deputies remaining on the gallery. The sheriff came in and said:

"My name is Dick Reagan; I have come here to arrest you, as Dave Harrel told me you wished to surrender."

I told him yes, but a fair understanding made long friends. I told him I did not want to be put in jail; I wanted half the reward; I wanted medical aid; I wanted protection from mob law; I wanted to go to Austin as quickly as possible and from there to Gonzales.

He agreed to all this and said he would treat me right. He asked me where my arms were and I told him one of my pistols was in the scabbard and the other under my head. I reached for it, and as I was pulling it out to give it to him one of his men outside shot me on the right knee. I first thought, on the impulse of the moment, that I would kill the sheriff, but it flashed across me at once that it was a mistake and that in him was my only protection. The sheriff and posse were all very sorry that this happened and each seemed to vie with each other in making me as comfortable as possible. They got a hack and put pillows and bed quilts in it trying to make my journey easy.

WHEN WE GOT TO RUSK THEY PUT ME IN A PRIVATE HOUSE and sent for a doctor. They then took me to the hotel, kept by Dick Reagan on the corner of the square. Thus I arrived at Rusk about the 7th of September, 1872, with four bullet holes in me.

Many different and varied kinds of people came to see me, some of them expecting to see a man with horns on his head and were surprised when they saw me, saying, "He looks just like we' uns." They would ask me all kinds of questions; how many men I had killed; if I had ever killed a woman, etc.

Dr. Jimson soon got there and cleared out the room. They would come there day after day, however; some for curiosity and some for charity. I did my best to be polite to all callers.

Sheriff Reagan sent his son Dood to nurse me and he and I soon became chums. Mrs. Reagan was also very kind to me and seemed to never tire of fixing me dainty dishes to tempt a sick man's appetite.

I kept thinking of my wife in Gonzales, but never mentioned her name. I would ask the doctor every day when I could be moved. I knew I was charged with several capital crimes in Gonzales, but believed I could come clear if I had a fair trial there.

In putting down negro rule there I had made many friends and sympathizers and had made it a thing of the past for a negro to hold an office in that county.

Dick Reagan told me that whenever the doctor said I could be moved he would take me to Austin. We started for Austin on the 22nd of September, Deputy John Taylor going with the sheriff and I. On reaching Austin we stopped at a hotel and the next day they put me in the old jail down by the river. Barnhart Zimpelman was then sheriff there. Sheriff Reagan then went back to Rusk and I waited for him some time to come back with my horse "Joe" and $450 in gold for which I gave him an order on Till Watson. After waiting for his return several days, I concluded to see a lawyer, who got out a writ of habeas corpus and I was ordered to be carried to Gonzales.

We had a code of laws of our own in that Austin jail, in which there were always about twenty-five jail birds. Whenever a new prisoner was brought in we would all cry "fresh fish," and kangaroo court proceedings at once commenced. It was rarely the victim escaped without a fine or "shake." We would shake the "fresh fish" by getting hold of the corner of a blanket and tossing them nearly to the ceiling then letting them fall.

While in that jail I got acquainted with Burns and Kimble, who were afterwards hung for the murder of a peddlar.

Some friends in Austin, knowing I was wounded, frequently sent me meals from the hotels and I would always divide up with my fellow prisoners. One of the prisoners, an overbearing devil, one day said I was stingy about dividing up, and made a grab for some custard I was eating. I let drive at him with my boot, which was iron heeled, and sent him sprawling and bleeding to the floor. The jailor got mad about it and said he would put the man that did it in irons. I told him I was that man and explained the circumstances. He didn't iron me.

In a day or two four State Policemen started with me to Gonzales, and when we got to Lockhart they tried to make me ride a mule, as my horse was played out. My wounds were still painful and I did not like the looks of that mule. So one of the guards said he would let me ride his horse and he would ride that mule. Then a regular circus commenced and the mule threw that policeman so high and hard that everybody made fun of him. He soon traded it off for a horse.

When we reached Gonzales they had me shackled and chained to a horse, and the people there denounced such brutal treatment, saying that I had done more for the peace and welfare of the country than any other man in it.

Capt. Williams told the guards that they had just as well turn me loose as to leave me in Gonzales, but they put me in jail, where a blacksmith soon came and cut my irons off.

W. E. Jones was sheriff of Gonzales county then and told that my friends would soon be in to see me and to keep at and patient.

As well as I can recollect, on or about the 10th of October 1872, I cut into open daylight with a big saw, cutting through the iron bars on the south side. The guards on duty posted me when to work, as the saw made a big fuss. I got through late in the evening and waited until dark to leave the jail.

Manning Clements and Bud McFadden were there to see that I got off all right, and I rode Benny Anderson's iron gray horse home.

WHEN I GOT HOME I MET MY DARLING AND BELOVED WIFE. My neighbors and friends all came to see me and congratulate me on my safe return. I stayed at home and recuperated until January, 1873, when I began driving cattle to Indianola and shipping to New Orleans. Cuero was our nearest railroad, being twenty-five miles off, and about the 9th of April, 1873, I started there on some business connected with the shipping of cattle and to match a race with a certain party if I could do so. Just as I was about to start John Gay came to Manning Clement's house, where I happened to be, and told me they were opening a new road from Cuero to San Antonio by way of Rancho.

The road came by Manning Clements, and Gay told me if I would follow him across the prairie I would save time and get to Cuero any trouble. I got about eighteen miles from home, opposite the Mustang mot, when I saw a man riding a gray horse off to the right of the road about 200 yards therefrom. I saw he was armed with a Winchester and that he had two six-shooters on the horn of his saddle. He turned a little to the right, apparently looking for cattle, I suppose to put me off my guard, but it really put me on my guard. I checked up and he got down off his horse. I was now in the furrow leading to Cuero. I got down also, apparently to fix my saddle, but really to give him no advantage over me, for his arms and general appearance gave me the impression that he was either on the dodge or was an officer. He then mounted his horse and I did likewise, so we met face to face. We both stopped our horses and he said:

"Do you live around here?"

I told him I was traveling from San Antonio on my way to Cuero and "am trying to follow this furrow, which I am told will take me to Cuero." I asked him how far it was and he said about seven miles. Then he remarked that he had been over to Jim Cox's to serve some papers on him. "I'm sheriff of this county," said he. I had understood up to this time that Dick Hudson was the acting sheriff of DeWitt. I said:

"I suppose your name is Dick Hudson?"

He said no, but that Dick Hudson was his deputy and his name was Jack Helms.

I told him that my name was John Wesley Hardin. He says, "are you Wesley?" at the same time offering me his hand.

I refused to take his hand and told him that he now had a chance to take me to Austin.

"We are man to man and face to face; on equal terms. You have said I was a murderer and a coward, and have had your deputies after me. Now arrest me if you can. I dare you to try it."

"Oh," he said, "Wesley, I am your friend, and my deputies are hunting you on their own account, and not mine."

I had drawn my pistol by this time and he begged me to put it up and not to kill him. I said:

"You are armed, defend yourself. You have been going round killing men long enough, and I know you belong to a legalized band of murdering cowards and have hung and murdered better men than yourself."[1]

He said: "Wesley, I won't fight you, and I know you are too brave a man to shoot me. I have the governor's proclamation offering $500 for your arrest in my pocket, but I will never try to execute it if you will spare my life, I will be your friend."

I told him that his deputies were putting themselves to a lot of trouble about me and that I would hold him responsible for their actions. Well, I let him alone and we rode on together to Cuero. We separated about two miles from Cuero, agreeing to meet next day in town and come to an understanding.

Well, we met as agreed, and he wanted me to join his vigilante company, of which he was captain. I declined, because the people with whom he was waging war were my friends. I told him all I asked of him was that I and my immediate friends should be neutral. This was understood and we parted, agreeing to meet again on the 16th, he bringing one of his party, and I bringing Manning Clements and George Tennille.

I remained in town, finished my business and went to a bar room on the southwest corner of the square. I took a drink with some friends and then went into a back room where a poker game was going on and joined the play. It was a freeze out for $5 and I won the pot. We all went to the bar and a man named J. B. Morgan rushed up to me and wanted me to treat him to a bottle of champagne. I declined to do this. He got furious and wanted to fight, starting to draw a pistol on me. Some friends of mine caught him and I walked out, saying that I wished no row. I walked outside and was talking to a friend. I had forgotten all about Morgan when he came up again; told me I had insulted him and had to fight. He asked me if I was armed. I told him I was. He pulled his pistol half way out, remarking:

"Well, it is time you were defending yourself."

I pulled my pistol and fired, the ball striking him just above the left eye. He fell dead. I went to the stable, got my horse and left town unmolested.

The coroner held an inquest over his dead body, but what the inquest was I never learned. Afterward (about four years) I heard I was indicted for the murder of J. B. Morgan and about seven years afterward I entered a plea of guilty to the charge of manslaughter, getting two years in the penitentiary for it.

In the year 1878, and in fact previous to this date, there existed in Gonzales and DeWitt counties a vigilante committee that made life, liberty and property uncertain. This vigilante band was headed by Jack Helms, the sheriff of De Witt, and his most able lieutenants were his deputies, Jim Cox, Joe Tumlinson and Bill Sutton. Some of the best men in the country had been murdered by this mob. Pipkin Taylor had been decoyed by them at night from his house and shot down because he did not indorse the killing of his own sons-in-law Henry and Will Kelly by this brutal Helms' mob. Anyone who did not indorse their foul deeds or go with them on their raids, incurred their hatred and it meant death at their hands. They were about 200 strong at this time and were waging a war with the Taylors and their friends.

About the 1st of April, Jim Taylor shot Bill Sutton seriously in Cuero one night in a billiard hall. Such was the state of affairs when Manning Clements, George Tennille and myself went to Jim Cox's house to meet Jack Helms and Jim Cox, the acknowledged leaders of the vigilante band. When we got there they took me off and said they could and would work me out of all trouble if I would but join them. They said there were but two sides—for them or against them. I talked as if I would join them and they told me of a dozen or more of my friends whom they wished to kill, and who were the best men in the community, their sin lying in the fact that they did not endorse the vigilante committee's murdering. They told me they would have to do a whole lot of work to get me clear of all trouble, so I would have to do a whole lot for them, and they went so far as to say that if George Tennille and Manning Clements did not join them they would have to be killed. I told them then that neither George Tennille, Manning Clements nor myself would join them; that we wanted peace. I told them that I would not swap work with them, but that they and their mob must keep out of our country and let us alone. They agreed to this and said that they would let me know if any danger threatened me, but swore eternal vengeance on the Taylors and their friends.

When they had gone I told Manning and George just what had passed between us and George remarked that it would not be a week before the murdering cowards made a raid on us.

About the 23rd of April, 1873, Jack Helms and fifty men came into our neighborhood and inquired for Manning, George and myself. They insulted the women folks and Jack Helms was particularly insulting to my wife because she would not inform him of some of the Taylor party. We were all out hunting cattle at the time and when we came back and found out what had happened we determined to stop this way of doing, and sent word to the Taylors to meet us at the Mustang mot in order to concoct a plan of campaign.

There I met Jim, John, and Scrap Taylor, while Manning Clements, George Tennille and myself represented our side of the house. It was there agreed to fight mob law to the bitter end, as our lives and families were in danger.

A fight came off not long afterwards near Tomlinson creek, in which Jim Cox, one of the leaders of the vigilante committee, and Jake Christman were killed. It was currently reported that I led the fight, but as I have never pleaded to that case, I will at this time have little to say, except to state that Jim Cox and Jake Christman met their death from the Taylor party about the 15th of May, 1873.

On the 17th I was to meet Jack Helms at a little town called Albukirk in Wilson county. I went there according to agreement, a trusty friend accompanying me in the person of Jim Taylor. We talked matters over together and failed to agree, he seriously threatening Jim Taylor's life, and so I went and told Jim to look out, that Jack Helms had sworn to shoot him on sight because he had shot Bill Sutton and because he was a Taylor. Jim quickly asked me to introduce him to Helms or point him out. I declined to do this, but referred him to a friend that would. I went to a blacksmith shop and had my horse shod. I paid for the shoeing and was fixing to leave when I heard Helms' voice:

"Hands up, you d— s— of a b—."

I looked around and saw Jack Helms advancing on Jim Taylor with a large knife in his hands. Someone hollered, "Shoot the d___ d scoundrel." It appeared to me that Helms was the scoundrel, so I grabbed my shotgun and fired at Capt. Jack Helms as he was closing with Jim Taylor. I then threw my gun on the Helms crowd and told them not to draw a gun, and made one fellow put up his pistol. In the meantime Jim Taylor had shot Helms repeatedly in the head, so thus did the leader of the vigilante committee, the sheriff of DeWitt, the terror of the country, whose name was a horror to all law-abiding citizens, meet his death. He fell with twelve buckshot in his breast and several six-shooter balls in his head. All of this happened in the midst of his own friends and advisors, who stood by utterly amazed. The news soon spread that I had killed Jack Helms and I received many letters of thanks from the widows of the men whom he had cruelly put to death. Many of the best citizens of Gonzales and DeWitt counties patted me on the back and told me that was the best act of my life.

On the 18th of May, 1873, we got news of a mob of fifty men under the leadership of Joe Tomlinson who were coming into our neighborhood to kill and raid us in revenge. We concluded at once to go and meet them, and thirteen of us got together. It was about fifteen miles to where they were making their headquarters at Joe Tomlinson's place, four miles west of Yorktown. We found out that there were about fifty men in and around the house and that at night most of them slept on the galleries. We got there at 2 a.m. in the night of the 18th and agreed that we should slip up to the gallery and if we did this undiscovered to fire upon the sleeping mob. But the vigilantes' dogs soon announced our arrival and that game was up. We then sent runners to our friends for more help, detailing three men to do this. The remaining ten were to hold the enemy in the house until reinforcements came, when we would clean them out. Our forces began arriving about 4 p. m. and we were fixing to attack them when a party led by Deputy Sheriff Dave Blair made its appearance to relieve the Tomlinson party in the house. I took five men and headed them off in front of the house, and in fact, captured Blair right in front of his friends. When he declared that he was there to relieve Tomlinson I told him that was just what I was there to prevent and he had just as well commence work on me.

"Well," he said, "under the circumstances I won't persist, especially as all my men have deserted me."

Things began to get in shape for a good fight when some of the best citizens of the county came out to where we were preparing for battle. We had about seventy-five men and they had fifty. These men were the means of preventing a collision, and through their efforts a treaty was made which each and every one of both parties should sign. It was agreed that we should go to Clinton, the county seat of De Witt county, and have this arrangement recorded, which we did the following day, the 20th of May, 1873.

I RESUMED MY WORK AGAIN AND COMMENCED TO SHIP AND DRIVE CATTLE without anything tragical happening until December, 27th, 1873, when Wiley Prigon was attacked by four men and murdered in his store eight miles below Cuero. Prigon was a Taylor man and his murderers belonged to the Sutton gang. Thus was war stirred up between the two parties again.

They met this time at Cuero, each party trying to get the drop on the other. Shooting was the order of the day, but finally friends of both parties undertook to pacify them and an armistice was agreed to, both parties again signing articles of peace.

My wife and baby had taken a trip to Comanche to see my parents and my brother Joe's family.

On the 1st of January, 1874, leaving my cattle business in my father-in-law's hands, I pulled out for Comanche. Dr. J. Brosius went with me. At Austin I got sick and we continued our journey in a buggy. I met my wife and baby Molly in Comanche with my parents and brothers and sisters. I stayed there until the latter part of January and then, in company with my wife and baby, Dr. Brosius and Gip Clements, started home for Gonzales county by way of San Saba and Llano.

While in Comanche I had bought a racehorse named Rondo and I carried him with me on my way to Gonzales. I stopped at Llano and while there bought a herd of steers for the market and made a race for $500, which I easily won. So I journeyed on to Gonzales and reached home about the 15th of February. I then began gathering cattle for Kansas.

In the meantime the Sutton party had violated their pledges and on several occasions had turned our cattle loose.

In April, 1874, Sutton started some cattle north and he himself was going by rail to Wichita, Kansas. We had often tried to catch him, but he was so wily that he always eluded us. Jim Taylor had shot him and broken his arm in a saloon in Cuero. He had a horse killed under him in a fight on the prairie below Cuero and he had another killed while crossing the river below there. He was looked upon as hard to catch and I had made futile efforts to get him myself. I had even gone down to his home at Victoria, but did not get him.

In March my brother Joe and Aleck Barrickman came down from Comanche to visit me and after he had stayed several days I got him to go to Indianola, our shipping point. I told Joe that Bill Sutton was my deadly enemy and that he was soon going to Kansas by way of New Orleans. I told him to find out when Sutton would leave Indianola so that I could tell Jim Taylor and go at once to Indianola to kill him, as it was a life or death case whenever either I or Jim Taylor met him. So my brother and Barrickman went down there and attended to my shipping interests and in doing so got acquainted with Bill Sutton and found out when he would leave Indianola on the steamer Clinton. He let me know at once and I told Jim Taylor. Jim took Billy Taylor with him and went to Indianola. They went to my brother, who was boarding at Pat Smith's, who kept them informed as to when Sutton and party would board the Clinton. In the meantime he had hired two of the best horses in town for them to leave on. Besides that, there were six or eight brave men ready there who stood in with the play. The plan was to let Sutton and his crowd go aboard and then for Jim and Billy Taylor to follow and commence shooting, as soon as they saw them. Bill Sutton, his wife and Gabe Slaughter passed in at one of the dining hall doors. Jim and Billy Taylor met them and immediately began shooting. Sutton tried to draw his pistol, but failed, being pierced through the head and heart with Jim Taylor's bullets. Meanwhile a deadly fight was going on between Billy Taylor and Gabe Slaughter. Gabe Slaughter had found out that Jim Taylor was going to shoot Sutton and called out, "Look out, Billy," when Billy Taylor turned round on him, saying:

"Look out yourself, you d— s— of a b—."

He fired on Gabe Slaughter, who was drawing his pistol, and Slaughter fell with Sutton, a pistol in his hand and a bullet in his head.

The Taylor boys passed out of the Clinton on to the wharf and came up to the stock pens where my hands were branding cattle. There they got horses and came at once to Cuero, about sixty miles from Indianola, and from thence up to where I was branding cattle for the trail.

It was now April and I soon started my cattle for Wichita, Kansas, and put Joe Clements in charge. I was to receive the cattle in June at or near Wichita, but was not going with the cattle myself.

About this time my brother Joe and my cousin, Aleck Barrickman went home to Comanche and my wife and baby went with them to visit my parents there. It was understood that I should spend a week with them on my way up to Kansas.

Jim Taylor and I agreed to start another herd, as Ed Glover, Jim, Joe, Gip and Manning were all going up the trail, he (Jim) did not want to be left in that country by himself. In about two weeks we had complied with the laws and had started another herd of about 1000 head. We placed Dr. J. B. Brosius in charge with instructions to go by Hamilton, in Hamilton county, and they were there to send me word at Comanche, where I would be with my parents.

About the 23rd of April, 1874, Jim Taylor and I left Gonzales, bound first for Comanche and then for Wichita.

In the meantime Rube Brown had arrested Billy Taylor and had sent him at once to Galveston, so we never had a chance to rescue him. There was also a reward of $500 offered for Jim Taylor.

We got to Comanche on or about the 28th of April, having "Rondo" and two other racehorses with us. It was not long before I made two races to be run on the Comanche tracks on the 26th of May, 1874. I was to run "Rondo" against a mare that had beaten him before. My brother had a horse named "Shiloh" which I also matched, and a cousin of mine, Bud Dixon, matched a horse of his called "Dock."

The 26th of May was my birthday. About the 5th, Jim Taylor and I went with my brother and the sheriff's party some twenty miles into Brown county to get some cattle that belonged to my brother. The cattle were in possession of the Gouldstones and we got them and started back without any trouble. Night overtaking us, we stopped at Mrs. Waldrup's to pen our cattle. At the supper table Mrs. Waldrup told us how one Charles Webb, a deputy sheriff of Brown county, had come to her house and arrested Jim Buck Waldrup and had cursed and abused her. She had told him that no gentleman would curse a woman. Of course we all agreed with her. This is the first time I had ever heard of Charles Webb. There were present that night at the supper table Bill Cunningham, Bud and Tom Dixon, Jim and Ham Anderson, Aleck Barrickman, Jim Taylor and Jim Milligan (deputy sheriffs), Joe Hardin, Jim Taylor and myself. We were all first cousins to each other except Jim Taylor. There is no doubt but that we all sympathized with Mrs. Waldrup, who had been so abused by Charles Webb. On my trial afterwards for the killing of Webb the State relied on a conspiracy being formed at the supper table to kill Webb, and they used Cunningham to prove it, but they utterly failed, or else they would have broken my neck or found me guilty of murder in the first degree. The evidence that Cunningham gave on my trial was that my brother Joe (who was not indicted with me) had said: "We will get away with him at the proper time." That statement was an absolute lie. Cunningham was supposed to be our friend, but at my trial was looked upon as one of my brother's murderers and my enemy. But to return to my story.

We drove the cattle home next morning to Comanche and from that until the 26th but one more incident worthy of note occurred.

Henry Ware was a bully from Canada, and from some cause or other he disliked my brother Joe. He came to the herd one day (Jim Taylor told me this) and claimed a cow and my brother told him he could not get it. Ware persisted and put his hand to his Winchester, when my brother ordered him out of the herd at the point of a six-shooter, an order which, the Hon. Henry Ware promptly obeyed, and he did not get his cow.

The 26th of May saw a big crowd at the races, the news of which had been published all over the country. "Rondo" ran first and won easily. "Shiloh" came next and had a walk over. Next came "Dock," which was a close race, but he won by six feet. So I and my friends won everything in sight. I won about $3000 in cash, fifty head of cattle, a wagon or two and fifteen head of saddle horses. I set more than one man afoot and then loaned them the horses to ride home on.

I had heard that morning that Charles Webb, the deputy sheriff from Brown county, had come over to Comanche with fifteen men to kill me and capture Jim Taylor for the reward. I also heard that he had said that John Karnes, the sheriff of Comanche, was no man or sheriff because he allowed a set of murderers to stay around him, headed by the notorious John Wesley Hardin, and as he (Karnes) would not attend to his business, he would do it for him. I knew that Webb had arrested a whole cow camp a short time before and had treated a man whom he called John Wesley Hardin most cruelly, telling him he was afraid of his own name and jabbed him in the side with his gun, knowing positively that I was not in the country at that time. If I had been there I would have taught him a lesson sooner.

He did not make any breaks at the race tracks, but when we all came back to town he swore time and time again that he would kill me and capture Jim Taylor, and that this would be done before the sun went down. When I was told this I laughed and said I hoped he would put it off till dark or altogether.

We were all going from bar to bar, trying to spend some of the money we had won. I remember in one saloon I threw a handful of $20 gold pieces on the counter and called for the drinks. Some of my friends picked them up and thought I was drinking too freely and told me if any scrap came up I would not be able to protect myself. I assured them I was all right, but at last thought I had better go home to avoid any possible trouble.

I got Jeff Hardin, my little brother, to go to my brother Joe's stable and get his horse and buggy to drive out to my father's, who lived about two miles northwest from town. I bought such supplies as were needed at home and told Jeff to put them in the buggy and then to come up to Jack Wright's saloon on the corner, where Jim Taylor and myself would drive out to my father's.

We invited the whole crowd up to Jack Wright's to take a last drink. Frank Wilson, a deputy sheriff under Karnes, came up and locked arms with me just as I was going to drink and said:

"John, I want to see you."

I said all right.

This saloon was situated on the northwest corner of the square, the front facing the square to the east, with a door in front, and another door to the north near the west end of the saloon. Frank Wilson and I went out at the north door and then west for about ten steps, when I told him that was far enough and stopped on the back street west of the saloon. Frank said:

"John, the people here have treated you well; now don't drink any more, but go home and avoid all trouble."

I told him Jeff had gone for the buggy, and I was going as soon as he came. He says:

"You know it is a violation of the law to carry a pistol."

I knew now that he was trying to pump me, so I told him my pistol was behind the bar and threw open my coat to show him. But he did not know I had a good one under my vest. I looked to the south and saw a man, a stranger to me, with two six-shooters on coming towards us. I said to Frank:

"Let's go back to the saloon. I want to pay my bill and then go home."

We went into the saloon and we were stopped by Jim Taylor who said:

"Wes, you have drank enough; let us go home; here is Jeff with the buggy."

I said: "Let us go in and get a cigar, then we will go home."

About this time Dave Karnes remarked:

"Here comes that damned Brown county sheriff."

I turned around and faced the man whom I had seen coming up the street. He had on two six-shooters and was in about fifteen steps from me, advancing. He stopped when he got to within five steps of me, then stopped and scrutinized me closely, with his hand behind him. I asked him: "Have you any papers for my arrest?" He said: "I don't know you." I said: "My name is John Wesley Hardin." He said: "Now I know you, but have no papers for your arrest."

"Well," said I, "I have been informed that the sheriff of Brown county has said that Sheriff Karnes of this county was no sheriff or he would not allow me to stay around Comanche with my murdering pals."

He said: "I am not responsible for what the sheriff of Brown county says. I am only a deputy."

So Dave Karnes spoke up and said: "Men, there can be no difference between you about John Karnes," and said: "Mr. Webb, let me introduce you to Mr. Hardin."

I asked him what he had in his hand behind his back and he showed a cigar. I said:

"Mr. Webb, we were just going to take a drink or a cigar; won't you join us?"

He replied, "certainly." As I turned around to go in the north door, I heard someone say, "Look out. Jack." It was Bud Dixon, and as I turned around I saw Charles Webb drawing his pistol. He was in the act of presenting it when I jumped to one side, drew my pistol and fired.

In the meantime Webb had fired, hitting me in the left side, cutting the length of it, inflicting an ugly and painful wound. My aim was good and a bullet hole in the left cheek did the work. He fell against the wall and as he fell he fired a second shot, which went into the air.

In the meantime, my friends, Jim Taylor and Bud Dixon, seeing that Webb had taken the drop on me and had shot me, pulled their pistols and fired on him as he was falling, not knowing that I had killed him. Each shot hit him in the side and breast.

At my first attempt to shoot, Frank Wilson started to draw his pistol, but as soon as I had fired on Webb and before Wilson had time to draw, I covered him and told him to hold up his hands, which he did.

Several men were standing at the east end of the building next to the public square. When the shooting commenced they started to rush over to the saloon, but soon retreated.

I afterwards learned the plan was for Charles Webb to assassinate me and then for the crowd to rush up and with Frank Wilson's help to rush in and overpower Jim Taylor, thus getting the reward. They expected my relatives and friends to stand still while they did their bloody work. They believed they could not arrest Taylor without killing me, hence they attacked me.

The crowd outside ran back, as I stated above, and cried out:

"Hardin has killed Charley Webb; let us hang him."

The sheriff of the county, John Karnes, who was my friend came in with a shotgun and asked, "Who did this work?"

I told him I had done it, and would surrender to him if he would protect me from the mob. I handed him my pistol to show my good faith.

About ten men ran around the east corner and commenced firing on us and Jim Taylor. Bud Dixon and Aleck Barrickman drew their pistols and started to fire, when they ran back behind the corner. They were reinforced and charged again. John Karnes met them at the door and demanded that they disperse. They overpowered and disarmed him of his gun and were trying to get my pistol away from him. I told my friends that there was no protection for us there, and told Jim Taylor to come with me and the other two to go back west. So Jim and I ran across the street to some horses that were hitched nearby and as I ran I pulled my knife out of my pocket and cut the hitching ropes.

I now saw that my wife and sister Mat were in the crowd crying and looking down towards my brother's law office. I saw my father and brother Joe coming toward the scene with shotguns.

I concluded the best thing to do to avoid bloodshed was to get out of town. Jim Taylor wanted to charge the mob, but I said: "For God's sake, don't do that; you may hit the wrong one." (He told me afterwards he wanted to kill Henry Ware.) I caught his horse and kept him from shooting. We turned and went running out of town, the mob firing on us and the sheriff's party trying to protect us.

Dixon and Anderson, seeing we were safely out of town, got on their horses also and we met again at my father's where my father and brother joined us with the sheriff.

I was willing to surrender, but the sheriff said he could not protect me; that the mob was too strong and Charley Webb had been their leader. He advised me to stay around until the excitement died down and then come in and surrender.

So I went to some mountains about four miles off and next day my brother and some friends came out to see me and my party and by them I sent back the horses we had gotten out of town on and two pistols we had found in the saddle pockets.

At that time there were some companies of rangers there who were organized to keep the peace and protect the frontier from Indians. They took the place of the infamous State police. Bill Waller was their captain, and he wished to make himself famous at once. The sheriff told him he could and would arrest me whenever he was sure he could protect me.

He tried to get Waller to assist him in doing this, but Waller was really the captain of a "vigilante" band and would not do it. Even my father and brother told Waller that if he would himself guarantee me protection I would come in and surrender. Waller could guarantee nothing, but persisted in hunting me with his mob, composed of the enemies of all law and order. He aroused the whole country and had about 500 men scouting for me, whose avowed purpose was to hang me. Waller arrested my father and Barrickman's family and took them to Comanche to my brother's, where he put them under guard under the pretense of keeping them from giving me any information. They then arrested my brother, with Tom and Bud Dixon and placed them in the court house under guard. They also arrested Dr. Brosius, who had come to tell us that our herd was at Hamilton. In fact, there were squads of from 50 to 100 in each party hunting for me all over the country and instead of the excitement tiring out, it grew greater all the time. Once, two scouting parties met and fired upon each other, keeping it up for two hours until each drew off for reinforcements.

They had now cut me off from all communication with, my relatives and friends and were "brushing" the country for me.

About the night of the 1st of June, 1874, we camped about six miles west of Comanche in a valley close to a creek that had a large pool of water in it about two miles below. Water was very scarce and we got most of our water from this pool. The rangers found it out and we had several fights at or near the spring. On this night they found two of our horses. Jim Taylor, Aleck Barrickman, Ham Anderson and myself stayed together at night, but scouted in the day time, and I could not impress on Barrickman and Anderson the gravity of the situation. They could not understand how the feeling could be so bitter against us and they knew how well my father stood and that my brother Joe had a host of friends. They kept saying that there was no danger, and I could not even get them to stake their horses at night.

On the night of the 1st of January about 100 men in a party found their horses not far off. They caught the horses and camped on a hill in a clump of live oaks about 600 yards from where we were down in the valley. About 2 o'clock I got up and re-staked "Frank" and "Dock," mine and Jim's horses, and as I could not see the other horses I woke up Ham and Aleck and told them their horses were gone. They got up to hunt them and soon came back reporting the presence of the scouters and saying that there must be at least 150 of them. I thought they were waiting till day to attack so I concluded to move camp at once. The moon was shining brightly when we pulled out. Two men were on foot, packing their saddles simply because they were fools enough not to stake their horses when their lives were at stake. I told Ham and Aleck to go to a spot near a spring and we would go and get some horses from a place near there where Joe had some saddle horses running loose. So we parted, Jim Taylor and I going after the horses, Ham and Aleck going down the creek, their saddles and blankets on their backs. It was not long before we found the bunch of saddle horses, drove them to the pen and caught the two best.

We started back for the boys when I saw a man coming towards the pen. We saw he was lost. He got within ten steps of me when I threw my shotgun down on him and told him his life depended on his actions. The moon was shining brightly and Jim Taylor had caught his bridle. He said:

"John, for God's sake don't kill me."

I asked him who he was and he said:

"I am your friend, but I am a ranger. We found your horses tonight and knew you were close by. They sent me to Comanche for reinforcements. By daylight you will have 300 men around you and escape will be impossible. If they catch you they are going to hang you."

I then said to Jim: "We had better kill him; dead men tell no tales."

He said: "Oh, for God's sake, don't kill me; I'll never tell on you and will do anything for you."

After satisfying myself that he would do to trust I gave him a $20 gold piece to give to my wife and told him to tell her to go to Gonzales, where I was going to start for next morning. I told her not to be uneasy about me; that I would never surrender alive and that Jim and I had agreed to die together. That if either of our horses were shot down we would take the other up, but that we expected to be run up on before we got out of the country.

After many pledges of fidelity on his part we let him go and took the horses on to our companions. When we got there I told them that Jim and I were going to leave the country and if they wanted to go with us to say so quickly. They wanted us to stay and go to Bill Stones' house, a man whom they had lately helped out of trouble and whom they looked on as a friend. They said they had done nothing and no one would hurt them. So they said they would stay and go to Bill Stones'. I told them to leave the country as Jim and I were going to do; that they did not have to go with us, but to go anywhere, so that they got away from this country. I told them that Bill Stones would betray them if they went there; that these were no times to trust such men. They still said they were going, so I pulled out five $20 gold pieces and told them to divide it among them, and so we bade them good bye. It proved to be a last farewell. They went to Stones' who betrayed them and they were shot to death.

It was now daylight and Jim and I had to go out on the prairie to go the way we wanted to. To our right where we had camped the valley was full of men, so we turned to the left. The country was very rough and rugged, deep gulches making it almost impassable except at certain places. The rangers by this time had spied us and were after us, but as we were a quarter of a mile ahead we felt perfectly safe. We went on, crossing gulch after gulch, until we crossed a very deep one just before coming to the Brownwood and Comanche road. There was a long hill on the other side and just as we got to the summit we ran right upon Capt. Waller himself and 200 men. These were the reinforcements going out to meet the other rangers, who were now pursuing us. Capt. Waller ordered his men to halt and told us to surrender. I said, "Jim, look out! Follow me!" Putting spurs to "Frank" I went down the mountain, with Capt. Waller, his men and the bullets flying behind us.

Seeing that we must now meet our former pursuers, who were crossing the gulch at the only crossing, I said: "Jim, let us charge them and double them up as quick as lightning." So we wheeled again and Jim being ahead I told him to hold "Dock," as he was a fast quarter horse and my "Frank" was a mile horse. We were now charging uphill right among Waller's men, who were afraid to fire for fear of hitting each other. Often in that charge I would tell a man to drop his gun and he would obey me. Jim fired several shots and as we were passing out of the lines I saw a man aiming at him. I told him to drop his gun, which he did. We had passed out of the lines when someone upbraided him for his cowardice and he picked it up again and fired at us, hitting "Frank" in the hind leg but not hurting him enough to make him lame.

IT WAS NOW ABOUT 9 A.M. AND DRIZZLING RAIN. Capt. Waller apparently conceived the idea of running on us and turned his horse loose after us for that purpose. I told Jim to hold up as I wanted to kill him. I wheeled, stopped my horse and cocked my shotgun. I had a handkerchief over the tubes to keep the caps dry, and just as I pulled the trigger the wind blew it back and the hammer fell on the handkerchief. That saved his life. Waller checked up his horse and broke back to his men.

Jim and I went on about 200 yards further and got down to see what the damage was. We found that 'Frank' was shot, as were also our saddles and clothes, but that we were unhurt. The pursuing party fixing to surround us again, we got on our horses again and ran off from them. It seemed to me as if their horses stood still. We were riding racehorses. I had refused $500 for 'Frank' and $250 for 'Dock.' Good horse flesh is a good thing in a tight. [as George Catlin tells us, the Native Americans considered horse the best meat that nature had to offer and reserved it for special feasts ... as for Europeans and settlers ....

After running off from our pursuers we thought ourselves pretty safe, as they were behind us and we were riding good horses. In this, however, we were mistaken, for we presently came up on twenty-five men who were hunting us, but we got around them all right. We went boldly on, going around the town of Comanche and striking the Hamilton and Comanche road ten or twelve miles further on. It was raining hard and the country, as well as being rough, was covered with water, making the roads almost impassable. We thought we had done well, considering all this, to say nothing of the scouting parties we had to avoid.

We went on to Bud Tatum's, just eighteen miles from Comanche and we "hollered" and asked if we could stay all night. He told us to get down, and I laid my double-barreled shotgun down alongside of the fence, as I did not want to appear too heavily armed. After we had put up our horses and eaten supper I told the old man that we wanted an early start in the morning. He did not recognize us and promised to get us off early in the morning. He woke us up an hour before day and told us he had fed our horses. At the breakfast table he recognized me and asked me why I did not make myself known to him last night. I told him I did not want to alarm him. I was tired and did not want to take chances on his going and reporting me. He told us good bye and said:

"Don't be afraid of this old man. I am a friend of your father and brother Joe."

I got him to fix us up grub enough for a three day's tramp for two men. I told him to go out to the gate, get my double-barreled gun and give it to my brother next time he went to town. He told me he was going that day, so I laid out five $20 gold pieces and told him to give them to my wife.

Thus we stopped on the public road eighteen miles from Comanche that first night. Thirty rangers had passed by, going to Hamilton county to arrest the hands round our herd, but they never knew that we were at old Bud Tatum's. They had actually taken my brother's saddle horses, his racehorse and my wife's buggy horses and mounted them to help hunt us. Jim and I, however, did not propose to be caught like rats and made our way to Austin, arriving at Fancy Jim Taylor's on the night of the 5th of June.

He lived six miles northwest of Austin in the cedar brakes and we concluded to stay there and rest awhile.

On the night of the 17th, my cook, with Charley and Alf Day rode up and told us that thirty rangers had come out to the herd in Hamilton county, arrested the hands, had taken charge of the cattle and that they had barely escaped arrest. They had taken, they said, the rest of the hands to Comanche and held them there. On the 5th inst., they told me, the mob had hung my brother, Joe G. Hardin, Tom and Bud Dixon, my cousins, and had shot to death Ham Anderson and Aleck Barrickman on their pallets at Bill Stones'. Jim Taylor was sick and hardly able to ride, so we agreed to separate, as he wanted to go to Gonzales. Alf Day was his nephew and he went with him.

I went on the night of the 8th to the Colorado river with them and saw them safely through the city of Austin. I bade Jim Taylor good bye there for the last time and divided my purse with him, giving him ten $20 gold pieces to help him along.

I went back to Fancy Jim's, changed horses and with a friend, Rodgers, started back for Comanche.

We rode mostly at night and rested during the day. We got to old Bud Tatum's about sun down on the 10th and I sent Rogers up to Bud's to inquire into the situation. Bud had just come from Comanche and was loaded with information. He confirmed the report of the hanging and killing of my kinfolks. He said that any stranger going to Comanche was liable to be arrested and hung. He said to Rogers: "I would not go to town if I were you, but would go some other way unless you wish to be hung."

Now I was convinced that my brother and relatives had been foully murdered. Up to this time I could not even entertain the idea. I knew that up to the time I killed Webb, no living man stood higher in the estimation of his neighbors as a man or a lawyer than my brother Joe.

Nothing would do me now but to go to Comanche. My companion tried to dissuade me, but in vain. I told him we would go to father's that night, prowl around and see what we could learn.

About 12 o'clock we got to father's house. We unhitched our horses and unsaddled them back of the field. We then fed them and proceeded cautiously to the house. The last time we had been there was on the 30th of May, when thirty men were guarding the house and had fired on us. Talk about hearing bullets hiss and sing! The air was full of them that night, and they whistled over my head as they had never done before.

On this occasion we went to the well and began drawing water. I saw a man coming towards the well and waited until he got about ten steps from me, when I leveled my Winchester and told him his life depended on his actions. He said:

"For God's sake, John, don't shoot me. I am staying here on purpose to see you. Your father has me employed to do the work in the house and round the garden patch. Nobody suspects me. I gave your wife that $20 gold piece you gave me at the horse pen. They are well, but they have hung Joe, Bud and Tom and killed Ham and Aleck."

I said: "Hello, Dick; is that you?"

He said: "Yes."

"Let us shake hands," said I, and he came forward and proved to be the same Dick Wade whom Jim and I had arrested at the horse pens on the night of the 1st.

He then told me all about how the mob of 150 men had, on the night of the 5th, in the dead hours of midnight, come into the town of Comanche; had thrown ropes around the necks of Joe, Bud and Tom and had led them, bareheaded and barefooted, through the streets and out to some post oaks nearby, where they hung them until they were dead. He said that the next day old Bill Stones had led another band to his ranch and had shot to death Ham Anderson and Aleck Barrickman while they were sleeping on their pallets at his house.

I asked him where they buried Joe and he showed me where he lay buried near two live oaks. I stayed there by my brother's grave and sent Dick to town to see my father, but father would not let him awake my dear, sleeping wife, for he knew she would come to me, which meant death to me and all.

Father and Dick talked the matter over, but father thought it imprudent for him to come and see me. He told Dick to tell me that Jane and Molly, with Barrickman's family, were guarded to keep them from giving any possible information. "Tell him," he said, "that if they find out he is in the country they will kill me and wind up the family. Tell him not to surrender under any circumstances."

So Dick came back to my brother's grave at about 3 a.m. He told me all my father had said. Right there over my brother's grave I swore to avenge my brother's death, and could I but tell you what I have done in that way without laying myself liable, you would think I have kept my pledge well. While I write this, I say from the deepest depths of my heart that my desire for revenge is not satiated, and if I live another year, I promise my friends and my God to make another of my brother's murderers bite the dust. Just as long as I can find one of them and know for certain that he participated in the murder of my brother, just that and nothing more, right there, be the consequences what they may, I propose to take life.

It was now about 4 a.m. and whatever I was going to do had to be done quickly. I concluded to leave the country at once and go to Gonzales. If it had not been for my father, and the women and children I would not have left, but Waller had said that if I was seen in the country they would kill father and my little brother Jeff and wind up on the women and children. No one unless he had a heart as black and bloodthirsty as Bill Waller's could ever have made such a threat, or conceived such thoughts, so I woke my companion (from whom I had kept most of this news) and bidding Dick good bye, we saddled our horses. I saddled Frank and he saddled a mule. I then told Rogers just what was the matter; who I was and the extent of the danger. He said:

"Good God! I had no idea that you were John Wesley Hardin; all the money in the world would not have induced me knowingly to accompany you on such a trip, and here I am traveling to my grave with the notorious John Wesley Hardin at $2 a day."

I said: "You've got a pistol, haven't you?"

He said he had.

I asked him what he was going to do if a squad ran on us. He studied a while and said:

"Well, I hired for the trip and will go through. I will use the pistol for my boss if necessary."

We pulled out of Comanche about daylight and struck out for Lampasas on a straight line, over mountains and hills, when about 10 a.m. a scouting party ran on us. The mule had gotten leg sore and could not strike a lope. I would stop and let the party come up to within 200 or 300 yards of us, send a bullet from a needle gun over their heads, while my companion rode slowly along. Then I would catch up with him and again use my needle gun. We kept this up until it became monotonous. We then concluded to ride on together and if they ran on us, would fight it out together. At last we struck a creek and there we left our pursuers. We forged ahead until nearly sun down, when we began to get into the neighborhood of Lampasas. We saw a farm ahead and there we stopped, for "Frank" was almost as slow as the mule now. We rode up to the house to see if there were any horses hitched or staked which we could get. We saw an iron-gray horse staked in the field and we concluded to get him. The plan was for Rodgers to take "Frank" and the mule to Fancy Jim's near Austin and for me to go on. I went out to the field, caught the horse and saddled him. I bid Rodgers good bye and told him to take his time. I thought I had a good horse, but soon found out that I was wrong. It took me until nearly daylight to get to a friend's house about eighteen miles off. When I got to his house at daylight I found my nag had seen better days and was "stove up." I said to my friend:

"I am in a tight and this horse is not mine. I want you to send it back to the owner and tell him to charge it to John Wesley Hardin. I want your sorrel stallion. What is he worth?"

The owner said he did not wish to sell him much, but would take $250 for him. Well, I told him to catch him quickly and offered him the money. He told me to give it to the old lady. So I counted out to her thirteen $20 gold pieces. She said:

"John, I nursed you when you were a baby; take back this gold piece. I sympathize with you and want you never to stop killing those Comanche devils who hung Joe."

I told her I had plenty of money to do me and thanked her for her kindness.

By this time Mr. Nix had come with the sorrel horse and when I started out to him Mrs. Nix told me to wait for my breakfast, which I did.

While I was eating my breakfast Mrs. Nix went to my saddle pockets and put $250 in them, which I found afterwards.

In the meantime a squad of men came up to the house and I grabbed my Winchester and began firing at them from the window, when they broke and ran, but left one man on the ground with a bullet hole through his heart.

I bid my good friends goodbye, got on my sorrel horse and made my way to Fancy Jim's, where I rested several days.

In company with Charley, the cook, I then went to Gonzales, where I met George Tennille and others, who assured me of their lasting friendship and devotion. I heard from Jim Taylor, who was at Bill Jones' house.

I soon found out that I was not even safe in Gonzales county, and that a mob of seventy-five men under the leadership of Rube Brown and Joe Tomlinson now threatened me. Most of my friends were in Kansas, and with a few exceptions, those that remained were badly scared.

About the 20th of June I received a letter from Capt. Waller, who said he was going to send some prisoners to Gonzales and if they (the guard) were molested or the prisoners released, that he would kill my father and little brother, and probably my wife and child, whom he now held as hostages. These prisoners were men from my Hamilton herd. Their names were J. B. Brosius, Scrap Taylor, Tuggle and

White. I did not know exactly what to do. Of course I wanted to attack the guard, who were bringing my hands to De Witt, but still I knew that it meant death to my family. I concluded to keep quiet for a few days. I had about twenty men camped with me at Neal Bowen's, my father-in-law, on Elm creek, in Gonzales county. I finally came to the conclusion that I had better leave the country as soon as I could sell my cattle in Kansas. My money was running low, though I still had the $250 that Mrs. Nix had given me. I employed my father-in-law to go to Kansas, sell my cattle and return as quickly as possible. When the rangers got down to Chilton with my hands, they found that there were no charges against them, but learnt that the Tomlinson crowd were eager to kill them. They placed them in jail for that purpose, but nominally to hold them in event of some charges. On the night of the 30th of June these rangers turned over to the Tomlinson mob Scrap Taylor, Tuggle and White, who put them all to death by hanging. Dr. J. B. Brosius escaping. On the morning of July 1, 1874, these eighteen rangers, whose hands were still bloody with the blood of my friends, made a raid on me, but, after a skirmish, they got frightened and left on short order, leaving a dead ranger behind them. I then went towards Gonzales to see Jim Taylor, but got afraid of Bill Jones' intentions towards me and did not go there.

I went to Tip Davis' near Gonzales and stayed there two days. Then Mac Young and I bid our friends good-bye.

George Tennille went part of the way with us, and when we bid him good-bye it was for the last time.

Mac Young lived at Hempstead, and it was our intention to go there and take the cars for Kansas, shipping our horses also.

One evening about sundown we passed through Bellville, in Austin county, and went out to an old German's about two miles from town, on the Hempstead road. We had just stopped to get supper when a party under Sheriff Langhamer ran on us. It appeared that this old German had suspected us of being horse thieves and had sent to Brenham for officers to arrest us and had held back the serving of the supper until the sheriff and party arrived. They then told us that supper was ready, and as we sat at the table I heard someone open a cap box. I at once pulled one of my pistols out and put it in my lap, winking at Mac. About that time four or five men showed up with double-barreled shotguns, and I covered them with my six-shooter, demanding what they wanted. I told them if they did not at once turn their backs I would kill the last one of them, and when they turned to go I went, too, and Mac followed me into the corn patch.

After we had been down there several minutes I saw about twelve men coming towards us, about 50 yards off, and one man in front, about ten steps away. I told the man riding in front to halt those men or he was a dead man. He called to them and they halted. I asked him who he was and he said his name was Langhamer and that he was sheriff of the county.

By this time Mac and I both had him covered and I had his horse (they having cut us off from ours).

I said: "If you are sheriff, read your warrant for my arrest."

He said: "I have no warrant for you."

"Well," said he, "if you are a law-abiding man, give up, surrender to an officer."

He said: "I arrest you in the name of the State of Texas for unlawfully carrying arms."

I said: "You will play h— arresting me. I am a law-abiding citizen, and have as much right to carry arms while traveling as you have."

"Well," said he, "if you are a law-abiding man, give up your pistol."

By this time I was a little bit mad and told Mac to pull him off his horse, and if he resisted I would kill him.

Then he begged me not to kill him and said he would give up his horse and pistol. I got on and rode off safely, leaving Mac to the sheriff and posse, who arrested him on charge of carrying a pistol, for which he was fined $100, although he proved himself to be a traveler.

I rode on to my uncle's at Brenham that night, and in a few days Mac came up to see me, with his usual grin.

I abandoned my trip to Kansas as impracticable, and had sent J. D. Hardin of Brenham up there to help sell the herd. He came back in two weeks and brought me $500, saying that Bowen, my father-in-law, was not willing to sell yet. I wrote to Bowen to sell at once and come home, as I had determined to leave the country. Bowen soon did as directed and came home.

I again went to Gonzales county, saw him and settled all of my cow debts.

I was now about to leave, not because I was an outlaw, but because mob law had become supreme in Texas, as the hanging of my relatives and friends amply proved. I went to Brenham after my loving wife, who was as true to me as the magnet to the steel, met all my friends once more and settled my business there, preparatory to leaving the country.

Mac Young and I then went to New Orleans by land, and I there rejoined my wife and baby. Harry Swain and wife of Brenham (of which town he was marshal) accompanied them there. Harry had married Jenny Parks, and Hardin, a cousin of mine, Molly Parks; hence the friendship.

After stopping a week or so in New Orleans, my wife, baby and myself took the steamboat and went to Cedar Keys; then we went to Gainesville, and there I went into the saloon business.

I bought out Sam Burnet's saloon, and the first morning I opened, Bill McCulloch and Prank Harper, stockmen from Texas, walked in. I saw at once that both men recognized me, for I had punched cows with them both. We shook hands and they promised never to say anything about having seen me or knowing my alias. I had adopted the name of Swain, in honor of the marshal of Brenham, who was my friend and always had been.

I stayed in that business until the third day after I had opened, when the marshal of Gainesville, having arrested a negro, was attacked by a mob on his way to the jail. I ran up and asked Wilson if he needed help. He said: "Yes, I summon you, Swain, to assist me in my legal duties."

A big black negro asked me what I had to do with it, and I knocked him down. I shot another and told the rest to stand back. Just at that time Dr. Cromwell, a Kentuckian, came up with a double-barreled shotgun, and we landed that whole mob in jail, except the one I had knocked down and the one I had shot. This happened about the first of May, 1874.

A few days after this, the negro Eli, who had caused the above disturbance, attempted to rape a respectable white lady, for which he was arrested and placed in jail. Some of us went to that jail at midnight, set it on fire and burned Eli with it. The negroes were very much excited over the burning, but the coroner set everything all right by declaring that Eli had burned himself up in setting the jail on fire. The coroner himself, by the way, was one of our party the night before.

McCulloch and Harper soon came to me and offered to sell them out, as they had not yet done. I did so, and they went back home in January, 1875. I then sold out the most of my saloon and moved to Miconopy, eighteen miles from Gainesville, Fla.

There I set up another bar and traded in horses. I soon sold out, but, in the meantime, had gone to Jacksonville, Fla., and had entered into a contract to furnish 150 beef cattle to Haddock & Co., butchers.

It was not long before I had the beef cattle at Jacksonville, but Bill Haddock had just died. The firm refused to take the cattle, so I went into the butcher and liquor business. I sold out my saloon interests in May, 1875, finding that butchering and shipping cattle would consume all my time.

I CONTINUED IN THE CATTLE BUSINESS, BUTCHERING AND SHIPPING, until the middle of April, when two Pinkerton detectives came to Florida and found me out. In the meantime, however, I had gotten well acquainted with the sheriff and marshal and they were my friends and they "put me on" to the Pinkertons.

I at once concluded to leave Jacksonville, and a policeman named Grus Kennedy was to go with me. We went to New Orleans, intending to go to old Mexico, but the Pinkertons followed and came up on us near the line of Florida and Georgia. A fight was the natural result and two of the Pinkerton gang were killed. I escaped without a scratch.

It had been arranged that my wife and children were to meet me at Eufala, in Alabama, but on account of the fight with the Pinkertons I was behind time. When I arrived I found that my beloved wife had fulfilled her part of the engagement, as I saw her name, Mrs. J. H. Swain and children, on the hotel register. On inquiry I found that she had gone to Polland, Alabama, where she had some relatives. We had agreed on this plan in case I could not meet her. I took the night train for Polland, and there met my beloved wife and two children, Molly and John W. Hardin.

After stopping there about a week we concluded to go to Tuxpan, and we started for that place about the 20th of August, 1876. When we arrived at East Pascagoula we found that we would be quarantined as being from New Orleans, where yellow fever had broken out. So I stopped at Pascagoula to await the raising of the quarantine.

Then Gus and I went back to Mobile to play poker and cards and we were so successful as to win about $3500. We would go back and forward between Pascagoula and Mobile.

THE PRESIDENTIAL ELECTION WAS ON WHILE WE WERE IN MOBILE and on that day all the gambling fraternity there got on a high lonesome and took in the town.

One of our party got into a row and of course I took a hand. The row started in a house where I had ordered some wine, but instead they brought beer. I was mad at this and kicked the table over and the waiter yelled loud enough to awake the echoes. A row followed with Cliff Lewis, which soon became general. I did all in my power to stop it but failed. Our party got out in the streets and the party in the house (composed mostly of city police) began firing on us and advancing. We now answered their fire, and after killing two and wounding another, we drove them back into the house. No one saw me shoot except Gus and no one saw Gus shoot except me. We then ran down a street and I threw my 45 Colts over into a yard and told Gus to do likewise, as we expected to give up if we were arrested.

We went to a coffee house and ordered coffee. While drinking it four or five policemen came in and arrested Gus and myself. They took us to the lock up and told us we were arrested for murder. We of course denied being present at all while the shooting was going on. Finally, after spending three or four days in jail and spending $2500, we got a hearing and were discharged. The proprietors of the house testified that I had done everything possible to keep down the row and that Gus and I had left before the shooting took place. Gus had been arrested, to my surprise, for having pistols (which I had told him to throw away), three barrels of which had been discharged. Money, however, made this very easily explained in court.

I then went to Pascagoula, got my wife and children and went back to Polland, Alabama. We went out into the country south of Polland and stayed there with an uncle of my wife's.

Soon afterwards I concluded to go into the logging business and formed a partnership with a man named Shep Hardie, who was an experienced logger. We went west about sixty miles to the Stick river and began, doing well.

In the meantime, Brown Bowen, a brother of my wife's, under several indictments for murder, came to Polland. He wrote a letter home to my father-in-law, Neal Bowen, in Gonzales county on Elm creek, and said that my wife (his sister) joined him in sending love. At the time Neal Bowen received the letter, Lieutenant Armstrong of the rangers was situated at Cuero to see if he could detect my whereabouts. He had sent Jack Duncan, a special ranger, to my father-in-law's house. Jack pretended to be in some trouble and decided to buy a small grocery store from Neal Bowen, and went so far as to take stock.

One day Jack and Neal had gone to Rancho and Jack noticed that Neal got a letter which he put in his trunk when he got home. When Neal left the house Jack opened the trunk and got the letter that gave him the information he wanted, although he (my wife's brother) only stated that he had joined his sister in love to their father.

Neal answered the letter at once and in it mentioned some litigation which he was involved in over my property. He addressed the letter to me, J. H. Swain, Polland, Alabama, in care of Neal McMellon, sheriff of Escambia county.

Now Neal McMellon was a kinsman of my wife's and the letter Bowen wrote, which Jack got out of the trunk, mentioned this fact. When Neal had written the letter he asked the pretended storekeeper for an envelope, which he gave him, but secretly marked the envelope. Neal and Jack went to Rancho to get some supplies and mail the letter. Neal went to the post office with Jack and mailed the letter. Neal stepped out to buy supplies, when Jack told the postmaster he would like to get a letter back out of the office which he had just mailed and described it. He said he wished to make some alterations in it and the unsuspecting postmaster gave it to him. Jack opened the letter, stepped aside and read it. He saw at once that he had the information he wanted. He wrote to Armstrong to "come and get his horse." Armstrong came up to Coon Hollow, arrested the pretended storekeeper, placed him in irons and brought him to Cuero in a wagon.

When they got to Cuero they took the first train to Austin and consulted Dick Hubbard, the governor of Texas, as to extraditing me. After this they struck out for Polland, Alabama.

Jack came ahead and stopped at Pensacola junction, eight miles from Polland, about the 18th of July, 1877. I was at this time over on the Stick river, about sixty miles away, but Brown Bowen was in the vicinity of the junction and came there every day.

On or about the 19th of July Bowen got on a spree and got into a row with Mr. Shipley, the general manager of the railroad. He got the worst of the row and the next day came back to the junction, vowing vengeance. He said that when I came back I would wake things up; that I was not the peaceable John Swain everybody thought I was, but that I was the notorious John Wesley Hardin. Of course such talk as this inflamed the minds of Shipley and his friends.

About this time my partner and myself concluded to go to Pensacola to buy our supplies, and of course to play some cards. Now Shep was in the habit of going to Pensacola and blowing in his earnings. He was thus well acquainted and introduced me as his friend. We all soon got into a poker game, Shipley and I having a system understood between us which proved a winner. It was all I could do to keep Shipley from getting too drunk for us to win the money. About the 22nd of July I shipped some groceries to the Junction for home consumption from Pensacola. Thus Shipley was able to tell Jack Duncan where I was, and furnished him an extra train to go there at once. When he came he soon located me in the poker room, but was afraid to tackle me there. So after spending a night watching me without daring to make a break he went to the sheriff and told him that I would take the train that evening, the 23rd of July, 1877, and if he would arrest me alive he would give him $500. The sheriff consented to this, and in due time I went to the train with my friends, Shep Hardie and Neal Campbell, Jim Man and two or three others. At that time I was in the habit of smoking a pipe and we all took the smoking car, not knowing that I was soon to be attacked.

The car was standing close to the hotel, the gallery or portico of which ran parallel with the car. Duncan and the sheriff had placed twenty men in the rooms opening on this veranda to be ready for action in a moment's notice. Jack Duncan commanded these and they were stationed immediately above the car and within twenty-five feet of me, who, with my companions, was all unconscious of the impending danger. Armstrong was to work in the cars below, and took his stand in the express or baggage car next to the smoker. Finally I saw the high sheriff and deputies come through the car and pass out. Then another deputy came in whom I had played cards with and from whom I had won $150 or $200. He said:

"Swain, can't you stop over. I have got a roll here and if you can beat me you can have it."

I said: "Business before pleasure; I can't stop over."

"Well," said he, "we fellows played you for a sucker and got left. You seem to be a gentleman; come down again and we'll give you a nice game and won't play you for a green horn any more."

I told him I was very fond of the game and had been very lucky, and hoped at some future time to meet him and his friends over the green cloth. I told him it was a case of business before pleasure with me now and remarked that when I held a good hand I couldn't lay them down.

"Yes," said he, "and you seem to hold them oftener than anyone else I ever played with."

We said good bye and shook hands and I kept smoking my meerschaum pipe. In a minute the sheriff and a deputy (either of whom would weigh 170 or 180 pounds) came in at the door behind me and grabbed me, saying:

"Surrender! Hold up your hands."

I asked them what it all meant and appeared amazed. I hollered:

"Robbers! Protect me."

I wanted to throw them off their guard or a diversion for a second or two.

Had they done so I would have gotten my pistol. At this moment the deputy who had just bidden me good-bye came in and asked what was the matter. I said:

"You know I have done nothing; protect me."

He pretended to do so, but instead caught hold of my legs and threw me down in the aisle. A terrible struggle was now going on, and the party from the gallery fired a volley into the car. Jim Man, a young man 19 years old, jumped up and passed over me, struggling in the aisle, and rushed to the north end of the smoker where he was met by Armstrong and others, who shot him dead. He jumped out of a window and fell dead, pierced by several fatal balls. In the meantime I was fighting for liberty in the aisle with my three antagonists, who had been reinforced. They had me on my back, two or three men clinging to each arm, some on my breast, and others trying to catch my legs, which I was using with a vim. Once in a while they would hit me over the head with a six-shooter as the unequal fight went on. I would not surrender, or keep still. I swore I would never surrender at the point of a pistol and I was not going to do it now. At this time Armstrong rushed into the smoker with a drawn revolver and put it to my head and told me if I did not surrender he would blow my brains out. I said:

"Blow away. You will never blow a more innocent man's out, or one that will care less."

Someone else was trying to strike me over the head with a revolver when Armstrong called out:

"Men, we have him now; don't hurt him; he is too brave to kill and the first man that shoots him I'll kill him."

They finally bound me with my hands behind my back, with a big cable and then tied me to the seat of the car. I still had the stem of my pipe in my mouth and someone picked up the bowl, filled it, lit it and gave it to me to smoke.

When Jack saw I was fast he came down from his perch and slapped me on the back, saying:

"John, take a cigar. Oh yes," he said, "John Wesley Hardin, you are the worst man in the country, but we have got you at last."

I said: "Stranger, what asylum are you from?"

He said he was from Texas and was only feeling good over the capture of the notorious John Wesley Hardin. He said to Armstrong and others standing by:

"Have you taken his pistol?"

They replied no, that I had no gun. Jack Duncan said "That's too thin" and ran his hand between my over and undershirt, pulling out a 44 Colts cap and ball six-shooter, remarking to the others, "What did I tell you."

The train pulled out for the junction and I kept demanding to see the warrant for my arrest and by what legal right they had killed Jim Man and captured me. I told the sheriff that I wanted protection from these Texas kidnappers, but to all this they made no reply.

Oh, that was one time I wanted to die but could not. I remembered how my own brother and relatives had been led out of the court house at Comanche, bareheaded and barefooted, and hung by a mob. I felt as if a similar death awaited me, so I wanted to die now, but could not. I had the glad consciousness, however, of knowing that I had done all that courage and strength could do and that I had kept my oath never to surrender at the point of a pistol. Thus was my arrest accomplished on the 23rd of July, 1877.

We soon arrived at the junction and there I sent my loving wife some money. In the meantime my friends at Polland, eight miles away, had formed a rescuing party with the sheriff at their head and expected to legally release me when the train came through Polland, as it generally stopped there several minutes. But unfortunately the train passed through without stopping and they went on to Mobile, where they placed me in jail and went off to sleep.

THIS WAS NOW THE 24TH OF JULY AND I SENT FOR AN ATTORNEY. Young Watts came and after I had told him my case he took it. He guaranteed to release me for $500. He got out a writ of habeas corpus, and they were in the act of turning me loose when Jack Duncan and Armstrong came up and changed the whole business by securing a continuance. In the meantime Dick Hubbard of Texas had telegraphed to the governor of Alabama to hold me, as requisition papers were on the way.

On the night of the 24th these papers came and on the morning of the 25th we started for Texas. My wife and friends were still on the alert and a party of nine men were ready there at the depot to rescue me. But the wily Jack Duncan took a hack and carried me to a station several miles from Montgomery and we again took the train for Texas. He thus avoided a collision with my friends.

I knew my only hope now was to escape. My guards were kind to me, but were most vigilant. By promising to be quiet I had caused them to relax somewhat and they appeared anxious to treat me kindly, but they knew their life depended on how they used me. When we got to a little town, I think it was Decatur, we had to stop and change cars for Memphis. They took me to a hotel, got a room and sent for our meals. Jack and Armstrong were now getting intimate with me and when dinner came I suggested the necessity of removing my cuffs and they agreed to do so. Armstrong unlocked the jewelry and started to turn around, exposing his six-shooter to me, when Jack jerked him around and pulled his pistol at the same time. "Look out," he said, "John will kill us and escape." Of course I laughed at him and ridiculed the idea. It was really the very chance I was looking for, but Jack had taken the play away just before it got ripe. I intended to jerk Armstrong's pistol, kill Jack Duncan or make him throw up his hands. I could have made him unlock my shackles, or get the key from his dead body and do it myself. I could then have easily made my escape. That time never came again.

We again struck out for Texas and stopped at Memphis, where they put me in jail. We took the train again for Texas by way of Little Rock, and by this time our car was besieged by people who had read the account of my capture. It had been the same way at Memphis, where people flocked to the jail to see me in such numbers that it took a squad of policemen to keep them back. One man named Roe actually rode from Memphis to Texarkana to see me and his wish was gratified by these gallant officers, who brought him into the sleeper where I was trying to rest.

"'Why," he said, "there is nothing bad in your face. Your life has been misrepresented to me. Here is $50. Take it from a sympathizer."

I thanked him and he bid me good bye.

At every station on to Austin a crowd of curious people were at the depot to see me, but I was so well guarded that few succeeded.

When we got to Austin my guards learned that there was a tremendous crowd at the depot and so they stopped the train and took a hack for the jail. The crowd at the depot learned of the move and broke for the jail. The hack just did manage to get there first and they carried me bodily into the jail; so when the crowd arrived they failed to see the great curiosity.

I wrote to some of my relatives at once and to my friends, many of whom I had not seen for four years. Most of them responded and generously came to my assistance with influence and means.

I stayed in Austin jail until the latter part of September and then a company of rangers (No. 35) commanded by N. O. Reynolds and accompanied by Sheriff Wilson and his deputies escorted me to Comanche.

The reason I was guarded by such a strong escort was because they were afraid that the brutal mob who had hung my relatives would hang me.

After traveling several days we reached Comanche, about 160 miles from Austin. Of course our military appearance created interest in every town through which we passed. I rode in a buggy with Sheriff Wilson, the most of the company in front and the lesser part bringing up the rear. We camped out every night and my escort did everything in their power to make me comfortable, except that they kept me securely shackled and cuffed. On arriving at Comanche my escort marched up, waited for me to be carried into the jail, as I was too heavily shackled to walk. Reynolds placed a guard around the jail and went out to see what the situation was. He soon found that feeling was very violent against me and that there were 200 men camped two miles from town for the purpose of hanging me.

The sheriff had summoned thirty-five citizens to guard me in the jail. Knowing the situation, and feeling somewhat interested, I told Lieutenant Reynolds to put the citizens outside of the jail yard to guard me and his men inside if he wished to save me. He wisely did this. My idea was that if the mob made an attack on the jail the citizen guard would assist them and if they were inside they would overpower the rangers, which they could not do if they were separated.

The brave Reynolds told me that if the mob attacked me or the jail he would arm me and let me out to rough it with him and his men. He would also arm the men in jail, of whom there were ten or twelve. He gave this out publicly and the mob never came, but I received anonymous letters saying that if I put off my trial or got a change of venue they would make a demand for me.

As I did not have the confidence in the rangers I should have had I announced ready for trial. I considered a "demand" equal to a delivery to the mob, for I had wrongly no confidence in the rangers. I remembered how my own brother and relatives had been hung by a mob and when there was a company of rangers in the town at the time and ten of them actually on duty.

I employed to defend me S. H. Renick of Waco, T. L. Nugent of Stephenville and Adams of Comanche. Either from fear of the mob or some other unknown cause my counsel allowed the State to put in evidence my character to influence the jury without raising any objection. The very judge himself was disqualified and biased. He had actually given counsel to Frank Wilson about my arrest just before the killing of Webb. He was plainly disqualified. They never allowed any evidence of my escape to be brought up, although I could easily have shown that I gave up to the sheriff in good faith and only escaped when the mob disarmed the sheriff, fired on me, and finally hung my brother and cousins.

The State tried to prove a conspiracy, but utterly failed in this, hence the prosecution ought to have fallen through. The State proved themselves that Charley Webb had fired at me twice before I drew my pistol or that I drew and fired as he was shooting his second shot.

The simple fact is that Charles Webb had really come over from his own county that day to kill me, thinking I was drinking and at a disadvantage. He wanted to kill me to keep up his name, and he made his break on me like an assassin would. He fired his first shot at my vitals when I was unprepared, and who blames a man for shooting under such conditions? I was at a terrible disadvantage in my trial. I went before the court on a charge of murder without a witness. The cowardly mob had either killed them or run them out of the country. I wasn't to trial in a town in which three years before my own brother and cousins had met an awful death at the hands of a mob. Who of my readers would like to be tried under these circumstances? On that jury that tried me sat six men whom I knew to be directly implicated in my brother's death. No, my readers, I have served twenty-five years for the killing of Webb, but know ye that there is a God in high heaven who knows that I did not shoot Charles Webb through malice, nor through anger, nor for money, but to save my own life.

True, it is almost as bad to kill as to be killed. It drove my father to an early grave; it almost distracted my mother; it killed my brother Joe and my cousins Tom and William; it left my brother's widow with two helpless babes; Mrs. Anderson lost her son Ham, and Mrs. Susan Barrickman lost her husband, to say nothing of the grief of countless others. I do say, however, that the man who does not exercise the first law of nature—that of self-preservation—is not worthy of living and breathing the breath of life.

THE JURY GAVE ME TWENTY-FIVE YEARS IN THE PENITENTIARY and found me guilty of murder in the second degree. I appealed the case. The rangers took me back to Austin to await the result of my appeal. Judge White affirmed the decision of the lower court and they took me back to Comanche in the latter part of September, 1878, where I received my sentence of twenty-five years with hard labor.

While I was in that Austin jail I had done everything in my power to escape. The cells were made of good material and in fact the jail was a good one, with one set of cages on top of the other, separated by sheet iron. I soon got so I could make a key that would unlock my cell door and put me in the run-around. I made a key to unlock that and now all I had to do was to climb to the window and saw one of the bars. I could then easily escape. But some "trusties" found out the scheme and gave it away to the jailor, who placed a guard inside the jail day and night. Thus it became impossible for me to do the work in the window though I had the key to the cell and the run-around.

There were from sixty to ninety prisoners in that jail all the time and at least fifty of these stood ready to inform on me any time. There was the trouble about getting out.

In that jail I met some noted men. Bill Taylor, George Gladden, John Ringo, Manning Clements, Pipes and Herndon of the Bass gang, John Collins, Jeff Ake and Brown Bowen.

After receiving my sentence at Comanche they started with me to Huntsville, shackled to John Maston a blacksmith of Comanche convicted for attempting to murder and under a two years' sentence. This man afterwards committed suicide by jumping from the upper story in the building to a rock floor, where he was dashed to pieces. Nat Mackey, who was sentenced for seventeen years for killing a man with a rock, was chained to Davenport, who had a sentence of five years for horse stealing. Thus there were four prisoners chained by twos in a wagon and guarded by a sheriff and company of rangers. Of course great crowds would flock from everywhere to see the notorious John Wesley Hardin, from the hoary-headed farmer to the little maid hardly in her teens.

On one occasion a young lady told me she had come over to where we were passing the day before and would not have missed seeing me for $100. I asked her if she was satisfied now. She said:

"Oh, yes; I can tell everybody I have seen the notorious John Wesley Hardin, and he is so handsome!"

I said: "Yes, my wife thinks so."

When we got to Fort Worth the people turned out like a Fourth of July picnic and I had to get out of the wagon and shake hands for an hour before my guard could get me through the crowd.

We stopped at Fort Worth all day and all night and then took the train for Huntsville. We arrived there on the 5th of October, 1878, and crowds would come all along the route to see us, especially at Palestine. I was astonished to see even the convicts in stripes gazing at me when we got inside the walls of the penitentiary.

Then they gave me a breakfast of coffee, bacon, bread and molasses, shaved me smooth, cut my hair and weighed me. I tipped the scale at 165 pounds. Then they gave me a bath and took down all the scars and marks on my body. They asked me what my occupation was and assigned me to the wheelwright's shop.

I knew there were a heap of Judases and Benedict Arnolds in the world and had had a lifelong experience with the meaning of the word treachery. I believed, however, that in jail even a coward was a brave man, so I went to work to plan my escape.

I found out where the armory was, about seventy-five yards off from the wheelwright's shop, and concluded to undermine towards it. A carpenter's shop, the superintendent's and director's office had to be undermined before we got there. I took into the conspiracy about seventy-five of the best men, mostly life and long term men. Only those who were to do the actual work were let into the plan, the rest were to blindly trust me to say the word and then follow me. The plan was to reach the armory by the underground passage and there wait until the guards came in to put up their guns and went to eat their supper.

We would then seize the guns, demand a surrender, take the prison and liberate all who wished to go except the rape fiends. I perfected my plans about the 1st of November and we began to tunnel towards the armory. We had to tunnel through five brick walls twenty-four inches thick. This we easily did for we had saw bits, chisels and almost every tool adapted to such work. We were working from the wheelwright's shop and while one would work the others would watch. We used a small rope or cord as a signal. If the man working wanted any tools, he would give a signal. By pulling the rope we would find a note on the end of it telling anything he wished to say.

So we finished our work quickly and about the 20th of November we were waiting for the guards to put up their guns before cutting through the pine floor. These guards were in the habit of taking outside the walls from 100 to 150 to work on the outside, and it was when these guards came into their supper that we intended to make our break. Meanwhile several life convicts rushed to the superintendent's office, told him of the conspiracy and how near it was being executed. The superintendent arrested me and nine others, putting us in irons. I denied all knowledge of the armory conspiracy, they put me in a dark cell on bread and water for fifteen days, with a ball and chain attachment.

There were twelve of us doing the tunneling. Two told it to the authorities and "on pressure" nine others owned up. I am certain two long time men were pardoned. Bill Owens and Bill Terril from Waco, the latter having a twenty-five year sentence. I believe that three others got their time cut for the same reason—betraying the plot.

When they took me out of the dark cell they put me to work in the factory. I was now "celling" with a lifetime man named John Williams and he was turnkey on our row. He was in with me on the tunneling scheme and had played traitor, although I was not aware of it.

I now conceived the plan of making keys to all the cells on our row in which there were some eighteen or twenty cells all locked with padlocks. I soon had the keys ready and also had impressions of the keys to the outer gates of the prison and had made keys to them which worked well.

For some time I had been able to dispense with my ball and chain. I had cut the brads off that held the shackles together and had put on instead a bolt with a tap to it, which I could unscrew at will.

On the 26th of December I gave John Williams the keys to see if they would work and he said they worked like a charm. I intended on the night of the 26th to unlock my door and then all the other cells, muzzle the guard, unlock the main prison door and then gate after gate to freedom. I determined to resist all opposition and had two good six-shooters that a trusty had brought in to me for that purpose.

That evening I was suddenly arrested and locked up. They searched me, found my keys and also the bolt in my shackles; in short my cell mate had betrayed me and the game was up. That night about twenty officers came in and tied my hands and feet. They jerked me down upon a concrete floor and stretched me out upon my face. Two men got hold of the ropes that held my hands and two more of the ropes that held my feet. Then the underkeeper, West, took a strap about 20 inches long and 2 ¼ inches thick. It was attached to a handle about 12 inches long. He began to whip my naked body with this instrument. They were now flogging me and every lick left the imprint of every lash, of which there were four in this whip, consisting of thick pieces of thick harness leather. I heard someone say: "Don't hit him in the same place so often." At last the superintendent said, "that will do," after they had hit me thirty-nine lashes, the limit.

My sides and back were beaten into a jelly, and still quivering and bleeding they made me walk in the snow across to another building, where they placed me in a dark cell and threatened to starve me to death if I did not reveal the plot. I told them I would tell them nothing; that I meant to escape and would kill them in a minute if they stood in my way. They left me there for three days without anything to eat or drink, and on the fourth day I was carried to another cell in a high fever and unable to walk. I stayed there for thirty days.

About the first of February, 1879, they took me out and put me to work in the wood shop. All this time I was plotting and scheming to get away, but my fellow convicts always gave me away and generally got some privilege for doing so. I was not able to do the work in the wood shop and was in a row all the time with the guard, who had orders to watch and work me. He did not work me much for when he told me to take hold of a plank I told him I couldn't without hurting myself and would refer him to the doctor. He would sometimes report me, but that did no good as I would sooner have taken the punishment than worked there.

In June, 1879, I was put to work in the boot and shoe shop at my own solicitation and soon became one of the best fitters and cutters they ever had.

By this time I began to realize how much of a traitor the average convict was to his fellow. I concluded to try bribing a guard, which I succeeded in doing. Jim Hall, the man who killed Marshal Gosling, was in this plot. Well, to cut a long story short, we got out into the prison yard, when thirty armed men arrested us and took us to the dark cells. This plot was also given away by a convict.

They flogged me again, but not so cruelly as before. I concluded I could make no play that the officers would not get on to and was more cautious from that on. My desire to escape was as strong as ever.

I was getting along tolerably well for a man in prison and began reading a good deal. I managed my work so as to make it very light, and took up arithmetic and mathematics as a study. I went through Stoddard's arithmetic and Davies' algebra and geometry; the balance of my time I devoted to history.

One night the officers came to my cell and told me to come out. They tied me and flogged me again for some imaginary crime and flogged about thirty others for nothing. They may have done this to scare me.

Now I wanted to get away worse than ever before. I became more and more prudent in my actions and conversations and began getting along all right once more.

I HAD NOW BEEN WORKING IN THE SHOP SINCE JULY, 1879, and this was 1883.

Then three other convicts and I conceived the idea of attacking the southwest picket with pistols and trying to climb the walls, but we had finally to give this up because we could not get the fire arms. Still & Co. were running a saddle shop in the walls and this shop ran close to the picket spoken of. Eugene Hall was working in this shop and Still & Co. were constantly receiving boxes of material by express. Eugene Hall and I were friends and he was as anxious to escape as I was. Every Sunday we would compare notes. I asked him one Sunday if he had a friend outside who could be induced to box up some arms and send them to us. He said he thought he had. I told him to tell his friend to box them up in a black box and send them by express to Still & Co. We knew we could see if the black box came when the whistle blew and we all went out to dinner. We intended to get the guns and fight our way out. Hal's friend weakened, however, and that game was up for the present.

In the meantime Bud Bohannon had been assigned to Still & Co., and not trusting the man very much, but knowing he wanted to escape, I told Hall to approach him and see if he favored my plan, but telling Hall not to mention my name. Bohannon liked my plan and at once began to execute it. Of course I was in the play, but talked to no one but Hall on the subject. On the Sunday before it was all to come off I saw Hall and told him that I would take one six-shooter and throw down on the guard from the southwest window of the shop and tell him that his life depended on his actions. If he did not obey I would kill him, the distance being only about ten yards. I then wanted him and his pals to go up a ladder, take him and his arms away and await me at the picket. Then we were to go to the State stable, get horses and leave. Of course, I said, we may have the guard to kill and we are very apt to have some fighting to do, but we can do it so quickly that not even the prisoners need know it, much less the town. This was my plan.

Bohannon wanted to attack the gate keeper and make him open the gate. This was not feasible. Then he wanted to climb the walls with ladders at a place not practicable. Besides all this he wanted to go and hunt up other men to make the play after he and Hall got the guns.

I told Eugene Hall I would have no more to do with it unless the men who were in the play would watch the express wagon and go at once to Still & Co.'s to get the pistols. They must then attack the southwest picket. Hall told me that Bohannon would not do that, so I drew out of it.

Sure enough when the time came I saw the black box come in and in a few moments Bohannon came by me and offered me a pistol. I declined it. I saw three or four convicts out in the yard rushing here and there aimlessly. They went to the gate, but the gate keeper, being on the outside, got out of their way. They had no certain plan of action and fired several shots either in the air or at the pickets. They finally surrendered before reaching the walls. Of course they whipped them.

I kept on working in the shoe shop until the fall of 1883, when I was taken sick with an abscess in my side and had to give up work. I had been shot in 1872 in my side and this was the wound that became affected.

The officials made fun of me and treated me cruelly. I was denied a place in the hospital, but had a nurse and was permitted to stay in my cell. For eight months it looked as if I never would get well, but finally I began to slowly improve and when I was able to walk, Assistant Superintendent Ben McCulloch wanted me to go to work again, but I refused because I was not able to do so.

After a few days he locked me up on bread and water. When he turned me out I went to work in the tailor shop. They put me to work making quilts. I got the guard and foreman to give me a certain task and got permission to read when I had finished it.

I was now a constant reader. In the years 1880, 1881, 1882, I had studied theology and had been superintendent of our Sunday

School. We had a debating society there, of which I was a member and had been president.

IN 1885 I CONCEIVED THE IDEA OF STUDYING LAW and wrote to the superintendent asking for his advice about what to read in order to have a practical knowledge of both civil and criminal law. He referred this letter to Col. A. T. McKinney, of the Huntsville bar. In a few days I received the following letter:

Huntsville, 6th May, 1889.

Hon. Thos. J. Goree:

Dear Sir—Replying to your favor covering note of Mr. John Wesley Hardin, I beg to state that applicants for license under the rules of the Supreme Court are usually examined on the following books:

Blackstone's Commentaries, 4 vols.
Kent's, 4 vols.
Stephens on Pleading, 1 vol.
Storey's Equity, 2 vols.
Greenleaf on Evidence, 1 vol.
Parsons on Contracts, 3 vols.
Daniels on Negotiable Instruments, 2 vols.
Storey on Partnership, 1 vol.
Storey's Equity Jurisprudence, 2 vols.
Revised Statutes of Texas, 1 vol.

For a person who desires to pay special attention to criminal jurisprudence, I would advise him to read Walker's Introduction to American Law, 1 vol., and Bishop's Criminal Law, 2 vols., before reading the course recommended by our Supreme Court.

These books (except the Revised Statutes) can be obtained at about $6 per volume from T. H. Thomas & Co., of St. Louis. The Revised Statutes can be obtained from the secretary of State, Hon. J. M. Moore, Austin, Texas, for $2.60.

Yours truly, A. T. M'KINNEY.

The Death of Hardin

The *El Paso Daily Herald* of August 20th, 1895, gives the following account of the killing of Hardin:

"Last night between 11 and 12 o'clock San Antonio street was thrown into an intense state of excitement by the sound of four pistol shots that occurred at the Acme saloon. Soon the crowd surged against the door and there, right inside, lay the body of John Wesley Hardin, his blood flowing over the floor and his brains oozing out of a pistol shot wound that had passed through his head. Soon the fact became known that John Selman, constable of Precinct No. 1, had fired the fatal shots that had ended the career of so noted a character as Wes Hardin, by which name he is better known to all old Texans. For several weeks past trouble has been brewing and it has been often heard on the streets that John Wesley Hardin would be the cause of some killing before he left the town.

"Only a short time ago Policeman Selman arrested Mrs. McRose, the mistress of Hardin, and she was tried and convicted of carrying a pistol. This angered Hardin and when he was drinking he often made remarks that showed he was bitter in his feelings towards young John Selman. Selman paid no attention to these remarks, but attended to his duties and said nothing. Lately Hardin had become louder in his abuse and had continually been under the influence of liquor and at such times he was very quarrelsome, even getting along badly with some of his friends. This quarrelsome disposition on his part resulted in his death last night and it is a sad warning to all such parties that the rights of others must be respected and that the day is past when a person having the name of being a bad man can run rough shod over the law and rights of other citizens. This morning early a Herald reporter started after the facts and found John Selman, the man who fired the fatal shots, and his statement was as follows:

"I met Wes Hardin about 7 o'clock last evening close to the Acme saloon. When we met, Hardin said:

"You've got a son that is a bastardly, cowardly s— of a b—."

"I said: "Which one?"

"Hardin said: 'John, the one that is on the police force. He pulled my woman when I was absent and robbed her of $50, which they would not have done if I had been there.'

"I said: 'Hardin, there is no man on earth that can talk about my children like that without fighting, you cowardly s— of a b—.'

"Hardin said: 'I am unarmed.'

"I said: 'Go and get your gun. I am armed.'

"Then he said, 'I'll go and get a gun and when I meet you I'll meet you smoking and make you pull like a wolf around the block.'"

"Hardin then went into the saloon and began shaking dice with Henry Brown. I met my son John and Capt. Carr and told them I expected trouble when Hardin came out of the saloon. I told my son all that had occurred, but told him not to have anything to do with it, but to keep on his beat. I also notified Capt. Carr that I expected trouble with Hardin. I then sat down on a beer keg in front of the Acme saloon and waited for Hardin to come out. I insisted on the police force keeping out of the trouble because it was a personal matter between Hardin and myself. Hardin had insulted me personally.

"About 11 o'clock Mr. E. L. Shackleford came along and met me on the sidewalk. He said: "Hello, what are you doing here? "

"'Then Shackleford insisted on me going inside and taking a drink, but I said, "No, I do not want to go in there as Hardin is in there and I am afraid we will have trouble.'

Shackleford then said: "Come on and take a drink anyhow, but don't get drunk.'

Shackleford led me into the saloon by the arm. Hardin and Brown were shaking dice at the end of the bar next to the door. While we were drinking I noticed that Hardin watched me very closely as we went in. When he thought my eye was off him he made a break for his gun in his hip pocket and I immediately pulled my gun and began shooting. I shot him in the head first as I had been informed that he wore a steel breast plate. As I was about to shoot the second time someone ran against me and I think I missed him, but the other two shots were at his body and I think I hit him both times. My son then ran in and caught me by the arm and said: 'He is dead. Don't shoot any more.' I was not drunk at the time, but was crazy mad at the way he had insulted me.

"My son and myself came out of the saloon together and when Justice Howe came I gave my statement to him. My wife was very weak and was prostrated when I got home. I was accompanied home by Deputy Sheriff J. C. Jones. I was not placed in jail, but considered myself under arrest. I am willing to stand any investigation over the matter. I am sorry I had to kill Hardin, but he had threatened mine and my son's life several times and I felt that it had come to that point where either I or he had to die.

(Signed.) JOHN SELMAN."

Frank Patterson, the bartender at the Acme saloon, testified before the coroner as follows:

"My name is Frank Patterson. I am a bar tender at present at the Acme saloon. This evening about 11 o'clock J. W. Hardin was standing with Henry Brown shaking dice and Mr. Selman walked in at the door and shot him. Mr. G. L. Shackleford was also in the saloon at the time the shooting took place. Mr. Selman said something as he came in at the door. Hardin was standing with his back to Mr. Selman. I did not see him face around before he fell or make any motion. All I saw was that Mr. Selman came in the door, said something and shot and Hardin fell. Don't think Hardin ever spoke. The first shot was in the head.

(Signed.) F. F. PATTERSON."

DAYS ON THE ROAD

CROSSING THE PLAINS IN 1865

By Sarah Raymond Herndon

DEDICATED TO THE PIONEERS OF MONTANA AND THE 'GREAT WEST,' WHO CROSSED THE PLAINS IN WAGONS.

We Start

AS I SIT HERE IN THE SHADE OF OUR PRAIRIE-SCHOONER, with this blank book ready to record the events of this our first day on the road, the thought comes to me:

"Why are we here? Why have we left home, friends, relatives, associates, and loved ones, who have made so large a part of our lives and added so much to our happiness? Are we not taking great risks, in thus venturing into the wilderness? When devoted men and women leave home, friends and the enjoyments of life to go to some far heathen land, obeying the command: "Go, preach my Gospel, to every creature," we look on and applaud and desire to emulate them. There is something so sublime, so noble in the act that elevates the missionary above the common order of human beings that we are not surprised that they make the sacrifice, and we silently wish that we, too, had been called to do missionary work.

But when people who are comfortably and pleasantly situated pull up stakes and leave all, or nearly all, that makes life worth the living, start on a long, tedious, and perhaps dangerous journey, to seek a home in a strange land among strangers, with no other motive than that of bettering their circumstances, by gaining wealth, and heaping together riches, that perish with the using, it does seem strange that so many people do it.

The motive does not seem to justify the inconvenience, the anxiety, the suspense that must be endured. Yet how would the great West be peopled were it not so? God knows best. It is, without doubt, this spirit of restlessness, and unsatisfied longing, or ambition—if you please—which is implanted in our nature by an all-wise Creator that has peopled the whole earth.

This has been a glorious May Day. The sky most beautifully blue, the atmosphere delightfully pure, the birds twittering joyously, the earth seems filled with joy and gladness. God has given us this auspicious day to inspire our hearts with hope and joyful anticipation, this our first day's journey on the road across the plains and mountains.

It was hard to say good-bye to our loved and loving friends, knowing that we were not at all likely to meet again in this life. I felt very much like indulging in a good cry, but refrained, and Dick and I were soon speeding over the beautiful prairie, overtaking Cash, who had lingered behind the others, waiting for me.

"A penny for your thoughts, Cash?"

"I was wondering if we will ever tread Missouri soil again?"

"Quite likely we shall, we are young in years, with a long life before us, no doubt we will come on a visit to Missouri when we get rich."

We were passing a very comfortable looking farmhouse, men, women, and children were in the yard, gazing after us, as we cantered past.

"Don't you believe they envy us and wish they were going, too?"

"No, why should they?"

"Oh, because it is so jolly to be going across the continent; it is like a picnic every day for months; I was always sorry picnic days were so short, and now it will be an all-summer picnic."

"I wish I felt that way; aren't you sorry to leave your friends?"

"Of course I am, but then I shall write long letters to them, and they will write to me, and I will make new friends wherever I go, and somehow I am glad I am going."

After we came within sight of our caravan we walked our ponies, and talked of many things, past, present, and future. When within a mile or two of Memphis our first camp was made. Our six wagons, with their snow-white covers, and Mr. Kerfoot's big tent, make a very respectable looking camp.

As we were provided with fresh bread, cake, cold chicken, boiled ham, pickles, preserves, etc., supper was quickly prepared for our small family of four, and we enjoyed it immensely. Then comes my time to write, as I have promised friends that I will keep a journal on this trip. Mr. Kerfoot thinks the Government is going to smash and greenbacks will not be worth one cent on the dollar, so he has turned all his money into gold coin, and stowed it into a small leather satchel—it seems quite heavy to lift or carry.

As Mrs. Kerfoot was sitting on a camp-chair near our wagons, Mr. Kerfoot came toward her, saying, "Here, mother, I want you to take care of this satchel, it is all we will ask you to do, the girls will cook and wash dishes, the boys take care of the stock, and I will oversee things generally, and we will do nicely." She accepted the responsibility without a word, and as he walked away she turned to me, and said, "I wish it was in some good bank, I expect nothing else but that it will be stolen, and then what will become of us?"

While I have been writing Neelie (Cornelia) and Sittie (Henrietta) have been getting supper for a family of twelve, no small undertaking for them, as they have been used to servants and know very little about cooking.

When everything was ready, Neelie came to her mother exclaiming, "Come, mamma, to supper, the first ever prepared by your own little girl, but not the last I hope, see how nicely the table looks, Emma and Delia picked those wild flowers for you, how brightly the new tinware shines, let us imagine it is silver and it will answer the same purpose as if it were."

Her mother smiles cheerfully, as she takes her arm. Cash sneers at Neelie's nonsense— as she calls it. Mr. Kerfoot nods approval, as Neelie escorts her mother to the table. When all are seated Mr. Kerfoot bows his head and asks God's blessing on the meal.

Everyone seems to enjoy this picnic style of taking supper out of doors, and linger so long at the table, that Neelie has to hint that other work will have to be done before dark. When at last the table is cleared, she says to Emma and Delia, "Don't you want to help me wash these nice, bright dishes and put them away?"

They are always ready to help Neelie, and the work is soon done. Amid laughter and fun they hardly realize they have been at work. Mr. Kerfoot insists that we women and the children must sleep in houses as long as there are houses to sleep in. Mother and I would greatly prefer sleeping in our spring-wagon, to making a bed on the floor in a room with so many, but as he has hired the room we do not want to seem contrary, so have offered no objection. The boys have carried the mattresses and bedding into the house, and Neelie has come for me to go with her to arrange our sleeping-room. So goodnight.

Through Memphis

WE WERE UP WITH THE SUN THIS MORNING AFTER A NIGHT of refreshing and restful sleep. Neelie and I commenced folding the bedclothes, ready to be sent to the wagons, when she startled me with a merry peal of laughter, "Look here, Miss Sallie, see ma's treasure, she has left it on the floor under the head of her bed. Don't say anything, and I will put it in the bottom of a trunk, where it ought to be, and we will see how long it will be before she misses it."

She thought of it while at breakfast, and started up excitedly, "Neelie daughter, did you see that precious satchel?"

"Yes, ma, I have taken care of it, and put it where it will not be left lying around loose anymore."

"Thank you, my dear, I am glad you have taken care of it."

"Why, mother, I did not expect you to carry that burden around on your arm by day, and sleep with it at night. I only intend for you to have entire charge of it, and put it where the rest of us do not know the hiding place, so that when we are obliged to have some, we will have to come to you to get it. And then give it sparingly, for much, very much depends upon what is in that satchel."

We came to Memphis about nine A.M.

Court was in session, several friends and acquaintances, who were attending court, came to the wagons to say good-bye. Mother's brother, Uncle Zack, was among them. He said, "Remember, when you wish yourselves back here, that I told you not to go."

"Yes, we will when that time comes and send you a vote of thanks for your good advice," I replied.

Cash, Neelie and I have been riding our ponies all day. We are stopping in a beautiful place for camping, near the farmhouse of a Mr. and Mrs. Fifer. They are very pleasant elderly people, who have raised a family of six children, who are all married, and gone to homes of their own. It is a delightfully homey home, yet it seems sad that they should be left alone in their old age. We will sleep in the house again tonight, I shall be glad when we get to where there are no houses to sleep in, for it does not seem like camping out when we sleep in houses. Cash and Neelie want to sleep in the tent, but their father says no, and his word is law in this camp.

Brother Hillhouse discovered very early this morning that the tire on one of the wheels of the ox-wagon was broken. He started off ahead of the rest of the wagons to find a blacksmith shop and get it mended by the time we would overtake him. It was ten o'clock when we came to the shop, near a flour-mill. There was a very bad piece of road before we crossed the creek, a deep ditch had been washed out by the spring rains. I waited to see the wagons safely over, when someone came beside my pony with outstretched hand saying, "Good-morning, Miss Raymond, I see you are in earnest about crossing the plains."

"Why, how do you do, Mr. Smith? Am glad to see you, of course I am in earnest about crossing the plains, but where did you come from? I supposed you would be at the Missouri River before this time, have you turned back?"

"Oh, no, we are waiting for better roads and good company."

"Come, go with us, I will promise you good company, and the roads will improve."

"Where are Cash and Neelie? I have not seen them."

"They did not stop, when I waited to see the wagons over the difficulties."

"Then I have missed seeing them; was in the mill when they passed. Remember me to them. We will start again tomorrow, and will overtake you in a few days, perhaps."

"Hope you will, good-bye until we meet again."

"Farewell, may you enjoy as pleasant a trip as you anticipate."

"Thank you," and waving him good-bye, I spoke to Dick, and he cantered up the hill past the mill and the wagons. I soon caught up with Cash and Neelie.

"Guess who I saw at the mill?"

"Did you see anyone we know?"

"Yes, an especial friend of yours, Cash, Bob Smith, of Liberty."

"Oh, dear, I wish I had seen him. Was Thad Harper with him? Are they going back home?"

"No; they are waiting for better roads and good company. I did not see Thad Harper. Bob said they will overtake us in a few days."

"I hope they will, they would be quite an addition to our party."

"Yes, but they won't; do you suppose they are going to let us see them cooking and washing dishes? Not if they know themselves. Then they would have to play the agreeable once in a while, and that is what they are not going to do on a trip of this kind. I do not expect to see them, they would rather stay where they are another week than join our party."

"I believe you are right, Neelie, for he did not say good-bye as if he expected to see me very soon."

When it was time to stop for lunch, we found a very nice place and waited for the wagons. While at lunch we saw an emigrant wagon, drawn by three yoke of oxen, coming up the road, and were somewhat surprised to see it turn from the road and come toward our camp. It proved to be Mr. John Milburn, of Etna, and his sister Augusta. They have traveled in one day and a half the distance we have been two and a half days coming.

Miss Milburn is a very intelligent, well-educated young lady, some two or three years my senior. We are not very well acquainted with her, but have met her frequently, and have known of her several years. She is an active member of the Presbyterian Church at Etna. She has her little nephew, Ernest Talbot, with her. He is seven years old, her sister's dying gift, a very bright child and considerably spoiled, but dear to his auntie's heart as her own life. They have started to Montana to get rich in the gold mines. Mr. Milburn leaves a wife and two small children with his widowed mother, to watch, and wait, and pray for his success and safe return home.

We crossed the dividing line—though we did not see it—between Missouri and Iowa soon after noon, and it is very probable some of us will never tread Missouri soil again. As we were coming through Stilesville, a small town this side the line, there were several loafers in front of a saloon who acted very rudely, to say the least.

We distinctly heard such remarks as the following, "Whew, what pretty girls, and how well they ride—Missourians I'll bet."

"Say, boys, let's try our luck; maybe we can each hook a pony tonight?"

Mr. Milburn's team is so tired out with such fast driving that we have stopped earlier than usual, and I have had more time to write. We are only two or three miles from Stilesville. The weather is perfect; we will sleep in the wagons tonight. Mr. Kerfoot thinks it necessary to guard the camp. I believe it an unnecessary precaution, for if those loafers at Stilesville had meant mischief they would not have expressed themselves so freely. However, Ezra and Frank Kerfoot (Mr. Kerfoot's nephews), Sim Buford, and Brother Hillhouse, will take turns standing guard, each one for two hours.

Oh, how we did sleep last night, dreamless and sound. Our first night in the wagons was undisturbed and sweet. We were up with the birds making ready for an early start. Mother prepares breakfast, while I roll up the beds and cover closely to protect them from the dust; one of the boys milks the cows, while I assist mother, and when breakfast of hot biscuit, ham and eggs, applesauce, coffee, and breakfast-food (which I should have mentioned first), is over, I strain the milk into an old-fashioned churn that is big at the bottom and little at the top, cover closely and fix it in the front of the freight wagon, where it will be churned by the motion of the wagon, and we have a pat of the sweetest, most delicious butter when we stop in the evening that anyone ever tasted. Mother washes the dishes, we prepare lunch for our noon meal, I stow it in the grub-box under the seat in the spring-wagon, the boys take the pipe off the little sheet-iron stove, empty the fire out and leave it to cool, while I am putting things away in the places where they belong. It is wonderful how soon we have learned to live in a wagon, and we seem to have an abundance of room.

When horses are harnessed, oxen yoked and everything ready to start, we girls proceed to saddle our ponies; some of the boys usually come and offer assistance, which is politely declined, as we are going to wait upon ourselves on this trip.

The wagons start, leaving us to follow at our leisure. We don our riding-habits, made of dark-brown denim, that completely cover, and protect us from mud and dust, tie on our sun-bonnets, mount our ponies unassisted, and soon overtake and pass the wagons.

We started this morning at seven o'clock. It is delightful riding horseback in the early morning.

Bloomfield, Iowa

WE WERE ON THE LOOKOUT FOR BLOOMFIELD, about ten o'clock we could see the spires and steeples glittering in the sunshine. When we reached the suburbs we stopped to wait for the wagons.

When we reached the business part of the city, I dismounted and made ready to do some shopping, as a few necessary articles had been forgotten when purchasing our outfit.

"Aren't you going with me, girls?"

"Oh, dear, no; not in these togs, short dresses, thick shoes, sun-bonnets, etc."

"I think we appear much better in our short dresses, thick shoes, and sun-bonnets than we would in trailing skirts, French kid shoes, and hats of the latest style, especially as we are emigrants, and not ladies at home. However, I do not wish you to suffer mortification on my account, some one of the boys will go with me."

"May I go, Miss Sallie?" Ezra asked.

"Certainly, and thank you."

We called at two drug stores, one grocery and several dry-goods establishments, and made several small purchases. The clerks seemed quite interested, and asked numerous questions. Some wished they were going, too; others thought we had a long, hard journey before us.

When we came back, they were waiting for us. I gave the satchel containing the purchases into mother's care, mounted Dick, and we were soon on the way. About a mile from Bloomfield we stopped for lunch of sandwiches, gingerbread, cheese, fruit and milk.

We all have such ravenous appetites, the plainest food is relished and enjoyed, as we never enjoyed food before. If anyone suffering from loss of appetite, or insomnia, would take a trip of this kind, they would soon find their appetite, and sleep the night through without waking.

Brother Winthrop wanted to ride Dick this afternoon, so I took passage with mother and drove the horses until I began to nod, when I gave the lines to her and climbed back into the wagon for an afternoon nap. I woke up as we were driving into Drakesville, a small but very pretty town. Mother and I talked the rest of the afternoon, she enjoys this life as much as I do; we built air-castles for our future habitation; I trust there was not enough selfishness in the building material to hurt us if they tumble about our ears.

Mother seems happier than she has since the war commenced, and our eldest brother, Mac, went into the army. We stopped for the night earlier than usual, about five o'clock. We are camping in a lane near a farmhouse.

Our little sheet-iron stove is taken down from its place on a shelf at the back of the freight wagon. Mother gets dinner and prepares something for lunch tomorrow, at the same time. The boys buy feed from the farmers, as the grass is not long enough to satisfy the horses and cattle. I write as long as it is light enough to see.

The young people complain about my taking so much time to write, but since I have commenced I cannot stop. I am thinking all the time about what things are worth recording.

After dinner mother washes the dishes and makes all the arrangements she can for an early breakfast. She thinks I am another "Harriet Beecher Stowe," so she is perfectly willing to do the work in the evening and let me write. Oh, the unselfishness of mothers. I do my share, of course, mornings, and at noon, but evenings I only make the beds in both wagons.

We have white sheets and pillow-cases, with a pair of blankets, and light comforts on both beds, just the same as at home, and they do not soil any more or any quicker, as we have them carefully protected from dust.

I had been writing a little while after dinner, when Frank stepped up with a basket of beautiful red-cheeked apples in his hand, not a wilted one among them.

"Where shall I put them?"

"Oh, Frank, how lovely they are. Where did you get them? Thank you so much; they are not all for me?"—as he emptied the last one into the pan. "Are all the others supplied? This seems more than my share."

"Yes; they are for you, we bought the farmer's entire stock; the others are supplied, or will be without you giving them yours."

He had just gone, when Sim Buford came and threw half a dozen especially beautiful ones into my lap.

"Thank you, Sim, but I am bountifully supplied, don't you see?"

"So you are, but keep mine, too; I can guess who it was that forestalled me." Laughing as he walked off.

So we are feasting on luscious apples this evening, thanks to the generosity of our young gentlemen.

WE CAME THROUGH UNIONVILLE AND MORAVIA TODAY. Have traveled farther and later than any day yet. It was almost dark when we stopped, and raining, too; to make a bad matter worse, we are camping in a disagreeable muddy place, and have to use lanterns to cook by.

We were obliged to come so far to get a lot large enough to hold the stock. We will be glad to sleep in the house tonight.

Mrs. Kerfoot is homesick, blue and despondent this evening; she has always had such an easy life that anything disagreeable discourages her. Perhaps when the sun shines again she will feel all right.

This morning dawned clear and bright; all nature seemed refreshed by yesterday's rain, and we started joyfully on our journey once more. We came through Iconium early in the day, are camping in Lucas County, near a beautiful farmhouse. We expect to stay here until Monday, as we do not intend to travel on Sundays.

It is a beautiful moonlight night, someone proposes a walk. As Cash is giving Winthrop his first lessons in flirtation, they, of course, go together; Sim and Neelie, Miss Milburn and Ezra are the next to start, and Frank is waiting to go with me. Hill stays in camp, in conversation with Mr. Kerfoot and Mr. Milburn.

He is more like an old man than the boy that he is, not twenty yet. After we had gone a short distance, Miss Milburn asked to be excused, and returned to camp; Ezra, of course, going with her.

We walked on for a mile or more, enjoying the beautiful moonlight, and having lots of fun, as happy young people will have. When we returned and I had said good-night to the others, I climbed into the wagon to finish my writing for the day by the light of the lantern.

The front of Mr. Milburn's wagon almost touches the back of ours, forming an angle. I had been writing a few moments when I heard sobbing. I was out in a jiffy, and had gone to the front of their wagon without stopping to think whether I was intruding. "May I come in?" I asked, as I stepped upon the wagon-tongue.

"Oh, yes, come in, Miss Sallie, but I am ashamed to let you see me crying, somehow I could not help it. I felt so lonely and homesick."

"I am sorry you feel lonely and homesick. Did any of us say, or do anything this evening that could have hurt you?"

"Oh, no; not at all, only I always feel that I am one too many, when I am with you all; you seem so light-hearted and happy, so free from care, so full of life and fun, that I feel that I am a damper to your joyousness, for I cannot get over feeling homesick and sad, especially when night comes."

"How sweetly Ernest sleeps, and how much he seems to enjoy this manner of life."

"Yes; he is a great comfort to me, as well as a great care. He is dearer to me than to anyone else in the world; his father seems to be weaned from him, since they have been separated so long. He has not seen him more than half a dozen times since his mother died. I feel that he is altogether mine. May God help me to train him for Heaven. He will never know what I have sacrificed for him. I have a mind to tell you, if you care to hear, why I am here, and why I am not happy."

"It may perhaps relieve you, and lighten the burden, to share it."

And then she told me what I will record tomorrow, for it is almost midnight, and mother has been asleep for two hours, and I must hie me to bed.

"Of course you have heard about my engagement to Jim Miller. I know it has been talked about."

"Yes; I have heard the matter discussed."

"We have been engaged two years, and were to be married next month. He insisted that I must give up Ernest to mother. I felt that I would be violating a sacred trust, and that mother is too old to have the care of such a child, and I told him so. We quarreled, and while I was feeling hurt and indignant, I told Brother John I would go with him to Montana. He gladly accepted my offer, and his wife was so glad John would have someone to take care of him if he got sick. So here I am and I know I ought not to have come, for Jim Miller is dearer to me than my own life."

"I am so sorry for you, yet I believe that in some way it will be for the best, you know the promise, 'All things work together for good, to those who love the Lord.' "

"I will try to believe it. You have done me good, Miss Sallie. I am glad you came. Come again."

I LEFT CAMP VERY EARLY, and walked on alone, that I may write to Brother Mac before the wagons overtake me. I am seated in a comfortable fence corner, and here goes for my letter:

Lucas County, Iowa, May 8, 1865.

Dear Brother:

We were delayed several days after the time set for starting, when we wrote you to meet us at Council Bluffs by the 10th. We thought I would better write, that you may know we are on the way, and hope to meet you by the 15th or the 16th. You must possess your soul with patience, if you get there before we do, and have to wait. I could write a long letter, I have so much to tell you, but will wait until we meet. Mother seems in better health and spirits than she has since you went into the army. We are enjoying the trip very much, and I find myself feeling sorry for the people that have to stay at home, and cannot travel and camp out. Good-bye until next week.

With sincerest love,

Your sister, Sarah.

The wagons are coming in sight, just as my letter is finished and addressed, and ready to mail at the next post-office. My pony is in harness today, as one of the work horses is a little lame, so I will have to ride in the wagon or walk. As the morning is so fine I will walk until I begin to tire.

Cash joined me in my walk, and we walked until noon. How wisely planned are these physical bodies of ours, how easily inured to the burdens they must bear. Before we started on this trip, such a walk as we took this morning would have completely prostrated us; now, we did not feel any inconvenience from the unusual exercise.

Frank invited us, Cash and I, to ride in his wagon this afternoon. We accepted the invitation, and made an emigrant visit. He had arranged his wagon for our convenience and comfort, and we spent a very pleasant afternoon. Frank mailed my letter at Charaton, and on his way back bought candy and nuts for a treat for his visitors, which we, of course, enjoyed exceedingly.

I should not care to ride in an ox-wagon all the way across the plains, but for half a day, once in a while, it is a pleasant change, especially when so delightfully entertained. The afternoon passed quickly. We are camping near a large party of emigrants, some of the men came to our camp. They look tough; they are from Pike County, Missouri, on their way to Oregon.

A very cold day for this time of year, too cold to think of riding horseback, so we all took passage in the wagons. As we have plenty to read, and lots of visiting to do, it is no hardship to ride in the wagon for a day.

The boys have made a splendid camp-fire, and we are getting thawed out, cheered, and ready for a jolly evening. There was just one stunted oak left standing, away out here in this great expanse of prairie—for our especial benefit, it seems. The boys cut it down, and taking the trunk for a back-log, the top and branches to build the fire, we have a glorious camp-fire away out here in Union County, Iowa. It is surprising to find Iowa so sparsely settled, we travel sometimes half a day and do not see a home. There are always a few farms near the towns. The settlements are the only breaks in the monotonous landscape.

Oh, the tedious, tiresome monotony of these vast extended prairies: To look out and away, over these seemingly endless levels, as far as the eye can reach, and see only grass, grass everywhere, with beautiful prairie flowers, of course, but the flowers cannot be seen in the distance. No earthly consideration would induce me to make a home on any of these immense prairie levels. How my eyes long for a sight of beautiful trees, and running streams of water; how delightful to stroll in the woods once more.

The Icarian Community

BROTHER HILLHOUSE'S BIRTHDAY. He is twenty years old. We made a birthday cake for him last night. We divided it into twenty pieces at lunch today, and there was just enough to go around and leave two pieces for himself. The girls say we must have some kind of a jollification tonight. I hope they will leave me out, for I want to write about the "Icarian Community." We came through Queen City this morning, and this afternoon came to a town of French people, called "The Icarian Community."

But why Icarian? I cannot understand, for certainly they did not impress me as high flyers, neither as flyers at all. They seemed the most humdrum, slow-going, even-tenor, all-dressed-alike folks I have ever seen. Every dwelling is exactly alike, log-cabins of one room, with one door, one window, a fireplace with stick chimney. I rode close by the open doors of some of the houses, and tried to talk with the women, but we could not understand each other at all. The floors, windows and everything in the houses were scrupulously clean, but not one bit of brightness or color, not a thread of carpet, or a rug, and all the women's and girls' dresses made of heavy blue denim, with white kerchiefs around the shoulders and pinned across the front of the waist, the skirt above the ankles, and very narrow and heavy thick-soled shoes. The men and boys all looked alike too, but I did not observe them closely enough to describe them.

There are several large, long buildings, one with a large bell in belfry on top of building. They are dining-hall, town-hall, school-house and two others. I did not learn what they are used for. All the buildings are one story, of the plainest architecture, for the one purpose of shelter from sun and storm. There is not a thing to ornament or beautify, not a shade-tree or flower, yet everything—men, women, children, houses, yards and streets—are as clean as they can be made.

They are peaceable, law-abiding citizens, live entirely independent of the people of adjoining neighborhoods. They are supposed to be wealthy; the town is the center of well-cultivated and well-stocked farms.

The principle upon which the community is founded is "Brotherly Love," a sort of cooperative communism, in which all things are the common property of all. They live upon what their farms produce, have vast herds of cattle and sheep, a fine site for their town, and seem the picture of contentment, which is better than riches.

We stopped within sight of Quincy, and another camping outfit. We soon learned they are Mr. Harding and Mr. Morrison and family, from Lewis County. We are acquainted with Mr. Harding and have often heard of the Morrisons.

Mr. Morrison and Mr. Harding came over, and the men have had a sociable, gossiping time this evening; the men can surpass the women gossiping any time, notwithstanding the general belief to the contrary. The young folks have been playing games to celebrate Hillhouse's birthday. They had hard work to get him to join them.

WE DROVE ONLY UNTIL NOON, and stopped to stay over Sunday, so that we can do our washing and baking, without violating the Sabbath. We do not have collars and cuffs, and fine starched things to do up, but we have a great many pocket handkerchiefs, aprons, stockings, etc. We have pretty bead collars made of black and white beads, tied with a ribbon, that always look nice and do not get soiled. We are in a beautiful grove of trees. The boys have put up a swing. There is nothing in the way of play that I enjoy as I do a good high swing. There are plenty of boys to swing us as high as we want to go. I fear the Sabbath will be desecrated with play tomorrow, if not with work, for the temptation to swing will be hard to resist.

The horses went off two or three miles last night, the men were all off bright and early this morning hunting them. Mr. Kerfoot found them, and came back about nine o'clock. By the time they were all here the morning's work was finished and we were ready—for what?

A day to spend in rest and service for the Master? Oh, no. A day spent in swinging, frivolous conversation, and fun. I am ashamed to tell it, but it is nevertheless true, and I believe we all thought less about a service of worship than we did last Sunday. It is so hard to get right, if we do not start right.

We have visitors in camp tonight, two gentlemen from Clark County, neighbors of the Kerfoots—Mr. Suitor and Mr. Rain.

They started for the gold mines in Montana two or three weeks ago. After reaching the Missouri River they heard such frightful stories of Indian depredations being committed on the plains that they sold their outfit for what they could get, and are returning home on horseback. Poor fellows, how I pity any man that has so little grit. I should think they would be ashamed to show their faces to their neighbors, and say, "We were afraid, so we came back home."

I believe Mrs. Kerfoot is the only one of our party who would be willing to turn back, and perhaps she would not if it were put to the test. We would not like to be scalped and butchered by the Indians, but it does seem so cowardly to run away from a possible danger. "The everlasting arms are underneath." God can, and will, take care of us as well on the plains as anywhere. He is leading us through unknown paths. We can trust Him. Heaven is as near one place as another.

Our second Sunday has not been much of an improvement on our first. The first we worked, today we have played. The boys swung us all morning, until we were ready to "holler nuff." We had Sunday dinner between two and three o'clock, then we wrote letters to friends at home, read until sleepy, took a nap of an hour, then Mr. Suitor and Mr. Rain came, and we listened to their frightful stories of what the Indians are doing to emigrants.

I left them in disgust, to come and record our misdoings of this, our second, Sunday on the road. It is almost bedtime, and I must make the beds, for we are early to bed and early to rise while on this trip.

ALAS, ALAS! HOW CAN I WRITE THE DISASTROUS HAPPENINGS OF THIS DAY? My hand trembles and my pencil refuses to write intelligibly when I attempt to record the sad, oh, so sad, accident that has befallen us. We parted from our visitors this morning, and started on our way, feeling rested and glad to be journeying on again. How little we knew of what a day would bring forth. We stopped for lunch at noon in a little vale, or depression, on the prairie, but where there was no water. Just as we had finished our lunch, Neelie came, she said, to see if we could make an exchange for the afternoon, her mother riding with mine, and I with the young folks in the family wagon.

Of course it was soon arranged, and I told her I would come as soon as I helped mother put things away. (We sometimes visit in this way.) Mrs. Kerfoot soon came around, and when everything was ready I started to go to their wagon. It was the last one in the train. As I was passing Mr. Milburn's wagon he called to me to "Come and get a drink of water." He had taken a long walk, and found clear, pure water, not very cold, but much better than none at all. I gratefully accepted a cup. He and his sister then invited me to ride with them. I told them of my engagement with Neelie, and, of course, they excused me. Oh, that I had accepted their invitation; just such a little thing as that might have prevented this dreadful accident. Such great events turn on such little hinges sometimes.

About three o'clock in the afternoon, as we were plodding along after the fashion of emigrant teams, we young people in the last wagon, having a jolly sociable time, with song and laughter, fun and merriment, the front wagons stopped. Ezra, who was driving, turned out of the road and passed some of the wagons to see what the trouble was. Mr. Kerfoot came running toward us, calling to Neelie, "Get the camphor, daughter, Mr. Milburn has shot himself somehow, and has fainted."

Ezra got out to go with him and Neelie asked, "Shall we come, too, papa?"

"No, my daughter, you girls would better stay here, your ma and Mrs. Raymond are with Gus, and they will know what to do."

Before he had finished what he was saying they were running to the place of the accident. We could only wait, hoping and praying, oh, so earnestly, that it might not prove so serious as Mr. Kerfoot's manner and tone caused us to fear. Afterward, Winthrop came to us; he was pale, with compressed lips, and sad eyes; he came up close, leaned upon the wagon wheel, and said in a low tone, "He is dead." Oh, how dreadful. We all left the wagon and went to the front as fast as we could.

I have gathered from witnesses the following account of how it happened. There was a flock of prairie chickens ahead of the wagons to the left of the road. Mr. Milburn and several of the boys took their guns and were going to try to thin their number. The wagons had not halted, but were moving slowly on, the hunters had gone on a little in advance of the wagons, they tried to fire all together, one of the boys snapped two caps on his gun, it failed to go off, so he threw the gun into the front wagon, and took his whip, in disgust. The wagon had moved on to where Mr. Milburn was standing with his gun raised; there was a shot, Mr. Milburn dropped to his knees, turned and looked at his sister, saying, "Gus, I am shot." And fell forward on his face. She was in the next wagon.

Gus screamed, jumped from the wagon, ran to her brother, and raised his head in her arms. All who were near enough to hear her scream ran to them and she said, "John has hurt himself with his gun and has fainted, bring restoratives quick."

In a few seconds, there were half a dozen bottles, with brandy, camphor, ammonia there, and every effort was made to restore him, but all in vain. He died instantly and without a struggle.

When Mr. Kerfoot knew he was dead, he looked for the wound and found a bullet-hole between his shoulders. Just then one of the boys picked up his gun where he had dropped it and exclaimed, "It was not this gun that did the mischief, for it is cold, and the load is in it."

On looking around to find where the deadly shot had come from, someone took hold of the gun in the front wagon. "Why, this gun is warm. It must have been this gun went off."

"Oh, no; it could not have been that gun, for there was no cap on it," said the boy who had thrown the gun there.

Circumstances proved that it was the gun without a cap that did the fatal shooting. I would have supposed, as the boy did, that it was perfectly harmless without a cap. I have heard it said, "It is the unloaded gun, or the one that is supposed to be unloaded, that generally does the mischief." No doubt the hammer was thrown back when he threw it in the wagon.

On investigating we found a rut in the wheel-track just where he fell. It is possible that when the front wheel dropped into the rut with a jolt the hammer fell, igniting the powder, either by the combustible matter that struck, or by the flash occasioned by the metal striking together.

Mr. Milburn was not opposite the wagon when he raised his gun to shoot, but the wagons were moving slowly and the front one came up with him as he was taking aim, and that was why Gus thought it was his own gun. She saw the smoke rise, he stumbled and fell to his knees, she called to him. "Why, John, what made you fall?"

He looked around at her and said, "Oh, Gus, I am shot." The last words he spoke.

How hard to be reconciled to such a dispensation when such a little thing could have prevented it, only one step in either direction, or the gun pointed the other way. Why, oh, why, has this awful thing happened?

The poor boy seems to be as heart-stricken as Gus. In her unselfish grief she has been trying to comfort him.

I have read of a minister of the Gospel "who dreamed that he died; after entering the gates of Heaven he was led into a large empty room, on the walls of which his whole life was spread out as a panorama. He saw all the events of his life, and many that had been hard to understand in his lifetime were here made clear, and through it all the guiding, protecting hand of God had been over him." Perhaps Mr. Milburn is saved from a worse fate.

We were about three miles from Frankfort when the accident happened. We came on here as soon as possible—a sorrowing, and oh, so sorrowful, procession now. It does not seem that we can ever be the merry party that we have been. Winthrop had been riding Dick; he stood there, ready, saddled and bridled when Mr. Milburn fell; Frank mounted my pony and rode as fast as he could go to Frankfort to get a doctor.

Mr. Milburn was dead before he was out of sight. We met them as we came. A room has been rented and Mr. Milburn prepared for his last long sleep. The people of Frankfort are very kind, and sympathetic.

THE FUNERAL SERVICES OF THE PRESBYTERIAN CHURCH were held at two o'clock this afternoon, a resident minister officiating. Mr. Milburn was very nicely laid away, and his grave marked and enclosed with a neat, strong fence before Gus and I left the cemetery. The people have been so very kind. The funeral was largely attended for a stranger in a strange place. There is no telegraph office here, so we have had to write letters instead of sending telegrams.

I believe Gus's plans are to go on with us to the Missouri River, sell her outfit, and return home by steamboat down the Missouri River, up the Mississippi to Canton, where friends will meet her and go with her to Etna.

The friends that stayed with us Sunday night told us that the authorities are not allowing emigrants to take the northern route, because of the Indian depredations that have been committed on that route. That if we went to Council Bluffs we would have to come down the river to Platsmouth to get on the southern route. So we changed our course accordingly.

We came through Whitecloud, Glenwood and Pacific City today. At Whitecloud I made a few purchases, traded with a little German merchant who crossed the plains a year ago; he says we have a delightful trip before us. He expects to go again to the Rocky Mountains, and make his home there, as soon as he can sell out and settle up his business here.

Just before we came to Glenwood, as the girls passed on their ponies, Gus said to me, "Sallie, go ride your pony, too; you have not had a ride for several days. Pardon me if I have been selfish in my great sorrow."

"No, Gus, I would rather stay with you than to ride Dick, as long as you need me."

"Thank you, dear; your company has been very grateful to me, but now I would really enjoy seeing you ride through Glenwood."

To please her, and myself, too, I soon had saddled and mounted Dick and overtaken the girls. As we were riding through Glenwood a photographer sent a messenger to request us to, "Please stop five minutes and let him take our picture." We rode to the position indicated, doffed our sun-bonnets, and looked as pleasant as we could. We did not wait to see the proof, and I expect he was disappointed.

Pacific City is on the Missouri bottom, or lowlands. Above the town are the highest bluffs I have ever seen. We hitched our ponies and climbed to the top. The view was magnificently grand, the sun sinking in the west, the river could be seen in the distance, with large trees on the banks, the lowland between the bluffs and the trees was dotted with cattle and horses grazing, here and there a pond or small lake with its waters shining and sparkling in the glimmering sunset, the city below us in the shadow of the bluffs. Everything was so sweet and peaceful, we were more than paid for our climb. The wagons had passed before we came down, so we mounted and hastened to overtake them before driving into camp.

On the Banks of the Big Muddy

OUR JOURNEY ACROSS IOWA AT AN END, we are on the banks of the Big Muddy, opposite Platsmouth. We will stay here until Gus's things are sold, and we have seen her off on the steamboat. I stay with her nights, and this afternoon is the first time I have left her since the 15th.

We have had a very, very busy day. Mr. Kerfoot has sold Gus's wagon and team (three yoke of oxen) for $550, a good price everyone says. More than they cost them, I believe. The freight will be sold at auction. We have all helped with Gus's suit and it is almost finished. Hillhouse went up to Council Bluffs this morning, expecting to bring Brother Mac back with him. Instead of finding him he got a letter—also the one I wrote a week ago—saying he was not coming. He has decided to study medicine and will come west when he is an

M.D. We are disappointed, of course, yet perhaps it is for the best—we must try and believe so anyway. Most perfect weather.

The Morrison and Harding outfit have come, also several other families from Lewis and Clark counties. The Kerfoots are acquainted with some of them. They had heard of the sad accident. Some of them were friends of Mr. Milburn.

Mr. Thatcher and his wife came to call upon Gus this afternoon, and invited her to their home in Platsmouth to stay until she takes the steamboat for home. Mr. Thatcher and Mr. Milburn have been friends for years. She accepted their invitation and will go there tomorrow.

As the people from different camps were sitting around an immense camp-fire, not far from our wagons, someone proposed music. Some of the men in Mr. Clark's camp are fine musicians, they brought their violin and flute, and gave several instrumental pieces, then some familiar songs were sung and someone started Just Before the Battle, Mother. They had sung two verses when I heard a shriek from Gus's wagon. I hastened to see what was the matter. "Oh, Sallie, tell them to please not sing that, I cannot bear it. Dear Brother John used to sing it so much. It breaks my heart to hear it now."

I sent Winthrop, who had followed me, to ask them to stop singing. Poor Gus, she was more overcome than I have seen her since her bereavement.

Mr. Kerfoot, Cash, Neelie, Ezra and I came with Gus to Platsmouth. She said good-bye to mother, Mrs. Kerfoot and the others this morning. All were sorry to part with her. She has become very dear to us all. Gus's freight was brought over in the wagon and sold at public auction and brought good figures, thanks to Mr. Thatcher, who, when he saw anything going below its real value, bid it in himself. He has a grocery store. He and Mr. Kerfoot have attended to all business transactions for Gus, so that she has not been bothered at all, and have done better for her than they could have done for themselves.

Mr. and Mrs. Thatcher, Cash and I came with Gus and Ernest to the steamboat. We parted with them about nine o'clock on board the "Sioux City." Dear friend, I have become greatly attached to her, in the three weeks we have been so intimately associated. May God grant her a quick and safe journey home. We cannot hope it will be a happy one.Note. —Miss Milburn and her lover were married about six months after her return, and have lived happily, etc.

Cash and I came directly to camp, after saying good-bye to Gus; found everyone busy getting ready for an early start tomorrow. We have been here almost a week, yet I have not had time to try the fine swing the boys put up the next day after we came here until this afternoon. The camps that were here over Sunday are all gone except those that will travel with us. It is probable there will be half a dozen more camps here before night. It is surprising to see what a great number of people are going west this Spring.

We hope to start very early tomorrow morning. I trust our party will not be so much like a funeral procession as it has been since the 15th. Vain regrets cannot remedy the past, and I believe it is our duty to be as cheerful and happy as possible in this life.

We were up with the earliest dawn, and our own individual outfit ready for a very early start, yet it was the middle of the forenoon before all the wagons were landed on the west bank of the Missouri. It takes a long while to ferry fifteen wagons across the river. We girls rode our ponies onto the ferryboat. They behaved as if they had been used to ferryboats all their lives. As we were waiting near the landing a stranger came, apologized for speaking to us, and asked, "Are you going to Montana?"

"No, sir, our destination is California, or Oregon; we are not fully decided which."

"Oh, you ought to go to Montana; that is the place to get rich."
[This man is mentioned here because of what happened to him before he reached his journey's end.]

He told of his marvelous success in that country since 1863; the Indians were mentioned. He spoke of them with such contempt; said he would rather kill an Indian than a good dog. Says he left a wife and six children in Iowa, the oldest boy about fourteen who wanted very much to go with his father, but his mother needed him. Last night he came into his father's camp. He had run away from home; says he is going to Montana too. His father told it as if he thought it smart and a good joke. What sorrow and anxiety his poor mother is no doubt suffering.

Cash, Neelie, Sim Buford, Ezra, Frank, Winthrop and I while waiting in Platsmouth went to a photographer's and had our pictures taken; tintype, of course, all in one group, then each one alone, then Sim and Neelie together and Cash and I on our ponies. We only came five miles after our rush to get an early start. There are nine families and fifteen wagons in our train now. Miss Mary Gatewood has a pony for her especial use, so there will be four of us to ride horseback. There are enough wagons now to make quite a respectable corral. I did suppose, as we had been resting so long, we would make a long drive. Feed for the stock is very good here, and as it is fifteen miles to the next good camping place, where there is plenty of water and feed, it has been decided that we stay here until tomorrow. The boys have put up the inevitable swing, and we have concluded "that what cannot be cured must be endured." So we will make the best of it, but certainly at this rate we will not reach our destination before it is cold weather.

OH, DEAR; HERE WE ARE YET, ONLY FIVE MILES FROM PLATSMOUTH. Morrison and Harding have lost two fine cows, half a dozen men have been hunting them all day, but without success. There is not a doubt but that they have been stolen. Our stock will have to be herded, hereafter, to guard against thieves. We have spent the day reading, writing, sleeping, swinging, and getting acquainted with our neighbors.

The Morrison family wagon is just in front of us, and the Kerfoot's just behind, so we are to have the most pleasant neighbors possible to camp next to us. Mrs. Morrison is almost as pretty as Cash, although the mother of four children; she is so bright and cheerful, so full of life and fun, she will be great on a trip like this.

Mr. Morrison has an impediment in his speech, and when he is excited—like he is this evening, because they cannot find their cows—he stutters dreadfully, and will say, "Or sir, or sir, or sir," until it is hard to keep from laughing. In ordinary conversation and when not excited, he talks as straight as anyone. He seems so fond and proud of his wife and children I like him. Neelie and Sim, and Frank and I took a stroll this afternoon in search of wild flowers. They are few and far between, yet we enjoyed the walk through the woods in this lovely springtime weather.

We came fifteen miles, are camping on a high rolling prairie, not a tree or shrub within sight; we are near a neat white farmhouse. Everything seems to be very new, but does not have that "lick and a promise" appearance that so many farmhouses in Nebraska have. Things seem to be shipshape, the house completed and nicely painted, a new picket-fence, and everything on the place— barns, henhouse, etc., all seem well built, as if the owners are expecting to make a permanent home. I would prefer a home not quite so isolated and far away from anywhere. There do not seem to be any women about the place, perhaps they are coming when everything is ready for their comfort.

Traveled all day, and made a long drive without meeting anyone or passing a single habitation. We are camping near—what the people west of the Missouri River call—a ranch. There is a long, low log-cabin, with dirt roof, a corral, or enclosure for stock, with very high fence, and two or three wells of water in the vicinity, and that is all. No vegetable garden, no fields of grain, nor anything to make it look like farming. I think it is a stage-station, and the people who occupy do not expect to stay very long.

There are three other camps near, the people of the other trains are having an emigrant ball, or dance, in a room they have hired. They sent a committee with a polite invitation to our camp for us to join them, which was as politely declined. They are strangers, and the conduct of some of the women is not ladylike, to say the least.

We girls were riding in advance of the wagons when we saw a long freight train coming. We stopped to let our ponies graze until they would pass. I glanced at the driver on the second wagon and recognized an acquaintance. "Why, girls, that is Kid Short," I exclaimed.

He looked at me so funny, and began to scramble down from his high perch. "Why, Miss Sallie, I could not believe my eyes at first. Where did you drop from?" shaking hands with each of us.

"Didn't drop from anywhere; have been thirty days getting here by the slow pace of an ox-train. Sim Buford and some more boys that you know are with the train you see coming."

He soon said good-bye to us, spoke to a man on horseback, who dismounted, gave him his horse and climbed to the seat Mr. Short had vacated in the front of the freight wagon, drawn by eight mules, while Kid hurried off to see the boys. He and Sim have been neighbors, schoolmates, and intimate friends all their lives. Sim says Kid is homesick and expects to go home as soon as he can after reaching Omaha. He has been freighting from Omaha to Kearney, and has been away from home since last fall. We are camping near another station, with the same trains we camped near last night not far off.

We are camping in the valley of the Platte. We are obliged to stop at the stage-stations to get water for ourselves and the stock from the wells. The water is very good, clear and cold. The same trains that have been camping near us since we left Ashland are here again tonight. Two of the women called upon us a while ago. We were not favorably impressed. They are loud, boisterous and unladylike; they speak to strange gentlemen with all the familiarity of old acquaintances. According to Thackeray, they are "Becky Sharp" kind of women.

Our little village on wheels has stopped near a large two-story log-house that was built in the early fifties for a wayside tavern; there are fifteen rooms; there are frightful stories told of dark deeds having been committed under that roof, of unwary travelers homeward bound from California that never reached home, but whether true or not I cannot say. The people of the other trains are having a dance in the large dining-room of the old house.

As Ezra and I were riding in front of the train we came to where a man was sitting on the ground hugging his knees, two men were standing near trying to talk to him, seemingly. As we rode up one of them came toward us, saying, "That is an Indian, over there." We rode close to him, and Ezra said, "How," but he did not even grunt. He was very disappointing as the "Noble Red Man" we read about. He wore an old ragged federal suit, cap and all. There were no feathers, beads nor blankets. He was not black like a Negro, more of a brown, and a different shade from the mulatto. He was ugly as sin.

On the Banks of the River Platte

HERE WE ARE ON THE PLATTE WITH ABOUT TWO HUNDRED WAGONS in sight. We are now on what is known as "The Plains." My idea of the plains has been very erroneous, for I thought they were one continuous level or plain as far as the eye could reach, no hills nor hollows, but it is nothing else than the Platte River Valley with high bluffs on either side. There is some timber on the banks, but the timber of any consequence is on the islands in the middle of the river, out of reach of the axe of the emigrant. This is the junction of the roads from St. Joe and Plattsmouth, and that is why there are so many wagons here tonight. Surely, among all these people there must be a minister of the Gospel, so perhaps we will have public worship tomorrow. Our trip grows more interesting, even Mrs. Kerfoot seems interested, as so many people are going West, it must be the thing to do.

We are organized into a company of forty-five wagons, a captain and orderly sergeant have been elected, and hereafter we will travel by system. Mr. Hardinbrooke is our captain. He has gone on this trip before; he is taking his wife and little girl with him to Montana. A Mr. Davis is our orderly sergeant.

We are now coming into a country infested with Indians, so it is required by Government officials that all emigrants must organize into companies of from forty to sixty wagons, elect captains and try to camp near each other for mutual protection. The grass for stock is unlimited. About twenty of the wagons in our train are freight wagons, belonging to the Walker Brothers, Joe and Milt. Joe has his wife with him. Milt is a bachelor; their sister, Miss Lyde, and a younger brother, De, are with them. They are going to Montana. We have been introduced to Mr. and Mrs. Hardinbrooke, and to the Walkers and their ladies. They are pleasant, intelligent people, and will add much to the pleasure of our party, no doubt. Frank and I went horseback riding this afternoon to the station to get some good water from the well. I cannot drink the river water. No public worship today, although there were so many of us here.

We were awakened at an early hour this morning with a bugle call. Three companies were organized yesterday; there were about twenty wagons that were not asked to join either party, so they pulled up stakes and left while Frank and I were away. The strange women were of the party; they must be some miles ahead by this time, and I hope they will stay ahead. When our long train of wagons are stretched out upon the road, we make a formidable looking outfit for the Indians to attack. As far as the eye can reach, before us and behind us, there are wagons, wagons, wagons; some drawn by oxen, some by mules, and some by horses. All fall into the slow, sure gait of the oxen. There are whole freight trains drawn by oxen; there are more ox teams than all others. After our evening meal, a number of us started for a stroll along the bank of the river. Before we reached the river, we were met by a perfect cloud of mosquitoes that literally drove us back. I never came so near being eaten up. There is a strong breeze blowing toward the river, which keeps them from invading the camps, for which I am thankful, otherwise there would be little rest or sleep for us tonight. They are the first mosquitoes we have seen on the road.

There is such a sameness in our surroundings that we seem to be stopping in the same place every night, with the same neighbors in front and back of us, and across the corral. When we organized, Mr. Kerfoot's wagons were driven just in front of ours and Mr. Morrison's just behind ours, so we have the same next-door neighbors, only they have changed places. We are in the central part of the left-hand side of the corral. The wagons occupied by the Walkers and Hardinbrookes are just opposite in the right-hand side of the corral. We always stop in just this way, if only for an hour at noon—which we do every day for lunch, and to water the stock. When we halted today, the rain began to pour, the stock scattered in every direction. When it stopped raining, the cattle could not all be found in time to start again this afternoon, so we only made half a day's drive. It has commenced raining again, and promises a rainy night. It is not very pleasant camping when it rains, yet it would be much more unpleasant if it did not rain—to lay the dust, refresh the atmosphere, and make the grass grow.

When the captain finds a place for the corral, he rides out where all can see him, and gives the signal, the first and central wagons leave the road; the first to drive to where the captain stands, the other and all behind it cross over a sufficient distance to form the corral by the wagons stopping, so as to form a gateway, for the stock to pass through, turned so that they will not interfere with each other when hitching. The next wagon drives to position, with the right-hand side of cover almost touching the left-hand or back, outer edge of the wagon in front, with tongues of wagons turned out, so that all can be hitched to at one time. In this way the entire corral is formed, meeting at the back an oblong circle, forming a wall or barrier, the cattle cannot break through. The horses are caught and harnessed outside the corral, but the cattle have to be driven inside to be yoked.

WE CAME THROUGH A LITTLE TOWN—VALLEY CITY. There is a very pretty attractive looking house near the road. Cash and I had come on ahead of wagons. Our inclination to enter that pretty home was irresistible, so we dismounted, took off our habits, hitched our ponies, and knocked at the door. A very pleasant lady opened the door and gave us hearty welcome. We told her frankly why we came. She laughed, and said, "I have had callers before, with the same excuse, but you need not apologize, I am glad my home is attractive to strangers."

The gentleman of the house is postmaster, and has his office in the room across the hall from the parlor. While we were there the coach arrived, and the mail was brought in. He did not know we were there, and called to his wife to "Come see this mail." We went with her, and oh, such a mess. They had emptied the mail-sack on some papers that had been spread upon the floor, and such a lot of dilapidated letters and papers I never saw before. I picked up a photograph of an elderly lady, but we could not find the envelope from which it had escaped.

Perhaps some anxious son, away out in the mines, far from home and friends and mother, will look in vain for mother's pictured face, and be so sadly disappointed. I am so sorry for the boy that will miss getting his mother's photograph. She looks like such a sweet, motherly mother. A great many of the letters were past saving; if the owners had been there they could not have deciphered either the address or the written contents, for they were only a mass of pulp; the postmaster said it was "Because they send such old leaky mail-bags on this route; those post-office folk seem to think any old thing will do for the West, when we ought to have the very best and strongest, because of the long distances they must be carried." All that could be, were carefully handled and spread out to dry; still, they would reach their destination in a very dilapidated condition.

We have made a long drive, are within four miles of Fort Kearney. There are a great many wagons within sight besides our own long train, whichever way we look we can see wagons. The road from Kansas City comes into this road not far from Valley City, and there are as many, or more, coming that way as the way we came. People leaving war-stricken Missouri, no doubt. I have never seen a fort. I do hope Kearney will come up to my expectations.

I was disappointed in Fort Kearney, as I so often am in things I have formed an idea about. There are very comfortable quarters for the soldiers; they have set out trees, and made it quite a pretty place, away out here in the wilderness, but there is no stockade, or place of defense, with mounted cannon, as I had expected.

Sim and I rode horseback through the fort while the wagons kept the road half a mile north of the fort. Only a few of us came by the way of the fort. A soldier gave us a drink of water from a well by the wayside. He seemed a perfect gentleman, but had such a sad expression. We were told that these soldiers were in the Confederate service, were taken prisoners, confined at Rock Island, and enlisted in the Government service to come out here and fight Indians. They are from Georgia and Alabama.

Two families have joined our train and come into corral on the opposite side, just behind the Walkers: Mr. and Mrs. Kennedy—a newly-married couple—and Mr. and Mrs. Bower, with a daughter fourteen and a son five. We only came one and a half miles west of the fort near Kearney City. I do not understand why we have made such a short drive, for the boys say the feed is not good, it has been eaten off so close.

WE WERE OBLIGED TO LEAVE CAMP AND TRAVEL TODAY, the first Sunday we have hitched up since we started. It was a case of necessity, as there was not feed for our large herds of cattle and horses. We made only a short drive, just to get good feed for the stock.

We are camping near a station that must seem like a military post, there are so many soldiers. Several soldiers came to our camp this afternoon; they confirmed what we heard yesterday. They are Confederate soldiers, they were prisoners, and their homes are in far-away Georgia and Alabama, and they are desperately homesick. It is a distressing sickness. I have been so homesick that I could not eat or sleep, and a cure was not effected until I was at home again. Then how nice it did seem to be home, and how good everything tasted. I do hope this cruel, homicidal war will soon be over, and these fine-looking Southern gentlemen will be permitted to go to their homes and loved ones, who, no doubt, are waiting and longing for their return. My heart aches for them.

We stood by the graves of eleven men that were killed last August by the Indians. There was a sort of bulletin-board about midway and at the foot of the graves stating the circumstances of the frightful tragedy. They were a party of fourteen, twelve men and two women, wives of two of the men. They were camped on Plum Creek, a short distance from where the graves are. They were all at breakfast except one man who had gone to the creek for water, he hid in the brush, or there would have been none to tell the tale of the massacre.

There had been no depredations committed on this road all summer, and emigrants had become careless and traveled in small parties. They did not suspect that an Indian was near until they were surrounded, and the slaughter had commenced. All the men were killed and scalped, and the women taken prisoners. They took what they wanted of the provisions, burned the wagons and ran off with the horses.

The one man that escaped went with all haste to the nearest station for help. The soldiers pursued the Indians, had a fight with them and rescued the women. One of them had seen her husband killed and scalped and was insane when rescued, and died at the station.

The other woman was the wife of the man that escaped. They were from St. Joe, Missouri.

Ezra met with quite an accident today; he went to sleep while driving the family wagon—he was on guard last night—the horses brought the wheel against a telegraph pole with a sudden jerk that threw him out of his seat and down at the horses' heels— a sudden awakening—with a badly-bruised ankle.

We are in the worst place for Indians on all this road. The bluffs come within half a mile on our left, and hundreds of savages could hide in the hollows; the underbrush and willows are dense along the river banks. There is an island, about a mile in length, that comes so near this side in many places that a man could leap from bank to bank. The island is a thick wood, a place where any number of the dreaded savages could hide, and shoot down the unwary traveler with the guns and ammunition furnished them by the United States Government.

How I would like to climb to the top of those bluffs, and see what is on the other side, but the captain says, "Stay within sight of camp." And I must obey.

A Narrow Escape

CASH, NEELIE AND I CREATED QUITE A SENSATION THIS MORNING. We waited, after the train had started, to mount our ponies as we usually do. Cash and I had mounted, but Neelie led her pony, and we went down to the river to water them, Neelie found some beautiful wild flowers, and she insisted upon gathering them. Of course we waited for her. The train was winding round a bend in the road, and the last wagons would soon be out of sight. We insisted that she must come. "The train will be out of sight in five minutes, and we may be cut off by savages in ambush."

She did not scare worth a cent. She led her pony into a little hollow to mount when we saw two men coming toward us as fast as they could ride. Cash rode at an easy canter to meet them, while I waited for Neelie, who was deliberately arranging her flowers so that she would not crush them.

"Those men are coming after us, perhaps there are Indians around."

She took her time, just the same.

When the captain saw that the train would soon be out of our sight, he went to Mr. Morrison, who was on horseback, and said, "Ride quietly back and warn those girls of their danger, there are Indians around. They have been seen by the guard, on the island, and by the herders, in the hollows of the bluffs this morning. They would not be safe one minute after the train is out of sight."

They had kept it quiet, as they did not wish to cause unnecessary alarm, for they knew there was no danger, for the Indians knew they were being watched, and besides we are too many for them. Mr. Morrison started, but not quietly; he snatched off his hat, whipping his horse with it, passed Mr. Kerfoot's wagon as fast as his horse could go. Mr. Kerfoot asked, "What is the matter?" Someone said, "Indians!"

He wound the lines round the brake-handle, leaped from his high seat on the front of the wagon, grabbed the first horse in reach, snatched Mr. Gatewood's boy out of the saddle, jumped on the horse and came tearing toward us, lashing the horse with his long whip—his hat flew off soon after he started, but he did not know it. He passed Mr. Morrison, and meeting Cash, he stopped long enough to bring his whip over her horse's haunches with all his might, and sent her flying toward the train. He next met me —for I started, when I saw them coming, and was perhaps a hundred yards ahead of Neelie— and stopped and said, "Miss Sallie, do you know that we are in the very worst Indian country there is on this road?"

He did not wait for a reply, but went on to Neelie, who was looking all about to see the Indians. He gave her pony a cut with his whip, as he had Cash's, and we went flying over the ground, Neelie's merry laughter pealing forth. Mr. Kerfoot did not speak to either of us. Mr. Morrison had turned back with Cash, and scolded all the way, she said he stuttered and stuttered, until she had hard work to keep from laughing. The captain had stopped the train, and we were greeted with loud cheering and hurrahs.

There was considerable joking about our being anxious for an adventure, and the young men were profuse in their declarations about what they would have done if we had been captured by the Indians. Everyone laughed about our "narrow escape," as they called it, except Mr. Kerfoot; he was pale and trembling. It is a shame that he should have been so unnecessarily frightened by our thoughtlessness, and I believe he thinks it was my fault. I wonder what he would have thought if I had left Neelie to come alone?

ONE OF THE MEN FOUND THE SKULL OF A HUMAN BEING TODAY while we were stopping at noon. It seems horrible to think of one's bones being scattered about in such manner. There is a storm coming; a storm on the plains is something to be dreaded, especially a wind-storm. Old men who have been freighting across the plains for years, say they have seen wagons upset with three tons of freight in a wind-storm. I am more afraid of a wind-storm than of Indians. The boys say I am not afraid of Indians at all.

The storm came with great violence last evening; we saw it coming in time to be prepared for it, so there was no damage done. The rain came down in torrents, and made the roads as hard and smooth as a floor, not any mud. It has been fine for horseback riding, everything seems so fresh and clean and pure, and not too warm. Mr. Milt Walker joined us about an hour before camping time. He seems a very pleasant gentleman.

WE HAD A STORM LAST NIGHT, MUCH MORE TERRIFIC than the night of the 14th, yet there was no harm done, more than to frighten some of the women and children. For my part I enjoyed the coming of the storm exceedingly. I never witnessed a storm-scene so sublimely grand. Oh, for the pen of an artist, that I might picture the majesty and grandeur of the coming of that storm.

Nellie Bower has a pony, and rides with us sometimes. She is a very mature young lady for her age, and very pleasant company. Neelie and I were riding together this morning, while Cash and Nellie Bower rode a short distance ahead. We had been on the road about half an hour when Dr. Fletcher and Milt Walker rode up, requesting the pleasure of our company, in a very formal manner. Of course we smilingly bowed assent, and the doctor rode with Neelie, and Milt with me. It is the first time there has been any formality in our pairing off while riding. The boys sometimes ride with us, but they come informally, we ride as we please, and stop and climb into the wagon when we please, without saying by your leave.

I am sorry any such formality has been commenced, for when I want to lope off, and be by myself, I want to feel free to do so, rather than to be constrained to entertain a beau, as we did this morning. Of course. Dr. Fletcher and Mr. Walker have not gone with us thus informally. I presume we succeeded in entertaining them, for when the train turned out for noon, each gentleman looked at his watch and wondered "If it could be possible it is noon?"

Dr. Fletcher is stepbrother of the Walkers —his mother and their father being married. He is physician for our train; an intelligent, handsome man, below medium in size. I think he must be dyspeptic, for he is always finding fault with everything. He seems to admire Neelie very much. We came through Cottonwood this morning. Stopped at noon where the feed is fine, so it has been decided that we stay here until tomorrow. The sky has the appearance of another storm this evening. We have had a busy afternoon.

The bluffs near here are quite high and abrupt. I climbed to the top this morning. I seemed to be away up yonder, when looking down at our corral the people looked like midgets. The bluffs are 150 feet high. I received a beautiful bouquet of wild flowers this evening, but do not know who sent it. The boy said, "A gentleman sent it." But he either could not, or would not, tell what gentleman. Perhaps the one that sent it thought I would know instinctively, but I am certainly in the dark.

Two gentlemen took lunch at our table this afternoon; they are father and son. Hillhouse met them out on the road; they asked him, "Do you know where we can get something to eat? We have had nothing since a very early breakfast."

He brought them to our wagons, and we soon had a lunch ready for them. Their name is Reade, the father's hair and whiskers are as white as snow, otherwise he is not an aged-looking man. They asked questions, and when they found we had not fully decided upon our destination, they insisted that Montana is the place for us. They have been there and are going again with freight. They belong with the Irvine train. Each train goes by the name of its captain, ours is known as "The Hardinbrooke train." Then there is the McMahan train, and the Dickerson train, that always camp within sight of us, for mutual protection. We have not met any of the people from the other trains. The Irvine train—which is very large—are some miles ahead of us. The Reades were hunting cattle, had been as far back as Cottonwood, but without success. The son had a long talk with the boys before leaving camp. After he had gone, Hillhouse came around and took a seat on the wagon-tongue, near where I was engaged in the interesting occupation of the week's mending. I said, "Mr. Read thinks Montana the place for us."

"Yes, so do the Walkers, and Mr. Hardinbrooke, and Mr. Morrison, and everyone else that are going to Montana."

"Well, why not go there?"

"I do not like for you and mother to go there, for it will be rough living I expect, but I intend to go as soon as you are settled somewhere near Mr. Kerfoot's folks."

"Just listen to the boy. Mother come here for five minutes, do. What do you think this boy is saying? That he is going to Montana when we are settled in California, or some other place."

"Well, if he is going to Montana, we are going, too. How many women are on their way there in these trains? I reckon it will not be any worse for us than it will be for them."

"All right, if you are both willing to go to Montana, we will change our plans accordingly. It is not as far as California."

And I know he is glad. So it was settled then and there that Montana will be our destination.

We Decide to Go to Montana

WE STARTED VERY EARLY THIS MORNING, as soon as light, about four o'clock. I think the most of the women were yet in bed. It was a glorious morning, and I did so enjoy my early ride on Dick. We had not been on the road very long when Frank joined me. I told him, "We had decided to go to Montana."

He was silent a moment, then said, "It is the place to go. I do hope we can persuade Uncle Ezra to go there, too."

"I hope he will decide to go with us, for it would be hard to part with all of you now. It would seem almost like leaving home again."

We halted at nine o'clock, had breakfast at ten, started again at twelve. Stopped again at four, and are camping on Fremont's Slough.

We are camped on the banks of the South Platte. The men have driven the stock across to an island. I do not know if it is because they are afraid of the Indians stampeding them, or that the grass is better. If there should be danger, I presume they would not tell us. There is a town of prairie dogs near; several of us went to make them a visit, but the boys had been there with their guns shooting at the little things, and frightened them so they would not come out, although we waited in silence until almost dark. I shall make another effort to see them very early in the morning before the boys are awake. I have heard they are early risers, that they come out to greet the rising sun. We met an acquaintance today—Will Musgrove—he is on his way to Central City, Colorado. He is night herder for a freight train. The most casual acquaintance seems like an especial friend, when we meet, away out here, so far from home, or anywhere else.

Winthrop was quite sick last night with cramp colic. I was up with him the latter part of the night, so was dressed and ready for my visit to Prairie Dog Town at an early hour. The little fellows were up, standing at their doors, and greeted me with a welcoming bark. Some of them turned and darted away, no doubt to tell others we had come, for they immediately came back to peep out at us and bark and chatter, as if carrying on a lively discussion. They seemed perfectly fearless as long as we kept our distance, but if we tried to get a nearer view, they whisked away, and were gone in an instant; then they would send out two or three scouts, and if we had gone far enough away, they would come again to their doors. They have been well described by many writers. Cash and Frank joined me, while at Prairie Dog Town.

I rode horseback this morning, and Milt Walker rode with me. Winthrop is about well this evening. His was the first sickness we have had. Will Musgrove came up with us while we were halted for noon—his train is a short distance behind—he rode with me in the wagon all afternoon, and drove the horses, and mother rode Dick. We had a long talk about friends at home. He took dinner with us, and then said good-bye, and we will see him no more, for we will travel faster than the freight train.

Mr. and Mrs. Morrison are large-hearted, cheerful people, who seem to be always happy and trying to make others happy. Mrs. Morrison learned that Miss Lyde Walker has her guitar, and sings beautifully, so she invited her to come to their tent and help to entertain a few friends. It was a very pleasant diversion. While Lyde was singing, the men and boys from all over the corral came near to listen. When she sang The Cottage by the Sea, both inside and outside the tent, there was great applause that terminated in an encore. But no, she would not sing anymore; she murmured something about the rabble, and laid her guitar away.

If I was gifted with a talent, with which I could give pleasure to people, I would certainly do so whenever opportunity was afforded. I would be glad to promote the happiness, and dispel as much sorrow as possible, in this sorrowful world.

WE CAME THROUGH A PLACE CALLED STAR RANCH, or Old California Crossing. We are camped twelve miles below Julesburgh. Mr.

Reade called this evening; we told him we had decided to go to Montana. He seemed as pleased as though personally interested.

Says the Irvine train is only half a mile ahead tonight, and invited us to go with him to call upon the young ladies. We, with one accord, asked to be excused. We all felt that we are not in calling costume.

We are camping in Colorado. Came through Julesburgh, a rather insignificant-looking place, to have such notoriety as it has in the newspapers. We met a company of soldiers with about twenty Indian prisoners. They were captured at Fort Laramie, and they are taking them to Fort Kearney. The soldiers had a fight with about one thousand Indians three weeks ago. There were no soldiers killed, though a number were seriously wounded, and they lost a good many horses. There were squaws and papooses with the prisoners, though not captives.

The Indians in the fight were Sioux and Cheyennes; they all look alike to me. They were the most wretched-looking human creatures I ever saw, nothing majestic, dignified, or noble-looking about any of the Indians I have seen. An ex-Confederate soldier gave me my information about the fight. There are a great many Southern soldiers on this route. We passed another newly-made grave this afternoon. Mr. Reade called this evening.

I WAS CAUGHT IN A HAILSTORM THIS MORNING. I was half a mile from the wagons, on a high bluff, looking over the river, watching the storm coming. I did not realize that it was so near, but all at once it came down pell-mell and gave me some pretty hard knocks. Dick seemed in a hurry to get to the train, and I let him go. We seemed to fly over the ground through the storm, but we had the benefit of it all, for it stopped just when we reached the wagons.

I unsaddled Dick and turned him out, while I took passage in the wagon, changed my wet clothes for dry ones and wrapped in a shawl to keep from taking cold. When the teams were being hitched up at noon, Hillhouse said to me, "Dick has not had water; you would better ride to the river and give him a drink."

The river was half a mile from the road, but in sight all the way. Dick cantered to the watering place, drank all he wanted, and we started back when I saw someone coming toward me. I will not say who it was because of what followed.

"I thought you were getting too far behind for safety."

"Oh, there isn't any danger; you need not bother about me."

"Bother? Oh, no." And then came a declaration that about took my breath. At first I felt that I would like to box the presumptuous boy's ears. Then I wanted so much to laugh. But when I saw how desperately in earnest he was I thought, perhaps, I have been to blame for not seeing how things were tending. I was perfectly amazed; such a thought never occurred to me.

Our ride back to the train was rather embarrassing to me. I tried to make him see the comicality of the whole business, but he would not see it. We passed a station where the Indians had burned all that would burn, but these adobe, dirt-roof houses, or cabins rather, would not make much of a blaze I imagine. Inside one of the cabins—or what was left of it—were two dead Indians that had been killed in the fray.

MR. READE CAME WITH SIX YOUNG LADIES TO CALL UPON US THIS MORNING, also one gentleman from the Irvine train. They had gone down into their trunks and were dressed in civilization costumes. They were Misses Nannie and Maggie Irvine—sisters—their brother, Tom Irvine, Miss Mollie Irvine, a cousin—Miss Forbes, and two other young ladies, whose names I have forgotten. They are all very pleasant, intelligent young people. The trains are keeping as close together as possible, for protection, for the Indians are on the warpath. Every station and ranch-building that we are passing these days has been destroyed.

Mr. and Mrs. May—a newly-married couple that came into our train at the junction of the roads—are both musicians; several of our young men have fine voices, and with Lyde's guitar, and Mr. May's violin we have had an enjoyable musicale away out here in the wilderness. If the Indians had been within listening distance it would be interesting to know what impression the music made upon their minds, as "Music hath charms, etc." The music this evening has been the happiest feature of the day, for I have had to ride in the wagon all day. One of the big horses went lame this morning, so Dick was put in harness and the dear little fellow has worked all day. He looks funny beside the big horse; the harness had to be taken up to the last holes to make it fit him. I would not enjoy taking this trip without a saddle-horse or pony to ride. I must be more generous hereafter and let Lyde and Mrs. Kennedy and other ladies that have no horse ride Dick oftener than I have been doing. I have not fully realized how very tiresome it is to ride in the wagon all day, and day after day.

I have always supposed that good water would be very scarce on this road; we have not found it so, there are always from one to three wells at the stage-stations, with excellent water, free for all—thanks to Uncle Sam for this provision for our welfare. In some places wood is very scarce and must be hauled long distances; we cooked dinner this evening with wood hauled from near Cottonwood. Cedar logs are fastened under the wagons, lengthwise between the wheels; as there are no stumps or rocks in the road they carry all right, when there is no wood to pick up the log is taken down, a piece cut off and split up for use. It is surprising with what a little bit of wood one can cook a meal on these sheet-iron stoves.

AMONG THE MEN WHO ARE DRIVING FOR THE WALKERS is an eccentric old bachelor named Fogy; he is very bashful when in the presence of ladies. I have often heard it said that men cannot drive oxen without swearing; it is a mistake. I have seen a whole lot of ox-driving on this trip, and today I heard the first profane oath since we left the Missouri River. It would have been funny if it had not been shocking. We have traveled all day where the bluffs come close to the river, the road is very uneven, little hills and hollows, in some of the hollows there is mud. Mr. Fogy admires Neelie very much (at a distance, of course), we often hear the extravagant compliments he pays her, and his regrets about that troublesome if.

Soon after the start this morning, Neelie and I rode to the front to escape the dust and sand that were flying; as we came near the front wagon we were startled by hearing a terrific oath. The wagon had stuck in the mud and would, of course, stop the entire train. Mr. Fogy was the driver. He was greatly embarrassed and distressed when he knew we had heard him swear, and stopped stock still and let the wheels sink into the mud so that they had to double teams to get them out. He afterward told some of the boys he was effectually cured of swearing; that he never felt so cheap in his life, and if he is ever tempted to swear he knows the remembrance of that moment will check him. We had a refreshing shower about two o'clock, that laid the dust, cooled the air, and made everything sweet and fresh. We hoped and expected to have a pleasant afternoon, after the rain there was a calm—not a little tiny breeze or breath of air—it was just suffocating, and then came a cloud of buffalo-gnats that almost devoured us, so that horseback riding was an impossibility.

The Mountains in Sight

WE COULD SEE THE MOUNTAINS, as the sun was sinking behind them; they were plainly visible though one hundred miles away. It does not seem possible they are so far away. Long's Peak and others near it are the points in sight. They look very much as I have imagined mountains would appear in the distance.

Mr. Walker is my informant as to names of places, distances, etc. He has been over the road and seems to know all about it. We usually ride some hours in company each day, so I have fine opportunities for asking questions, and he seems a willing instructor. He never broaches the sentimental, has never paid me a compliment in words I am glad to say, for since my late experience I would hesitate to ride with him were he not the sensible man that he is. We crossed a small stream today that was bridged and had to pay fifty cents toll for each wagon; the ford had been spoiled, or we could have crossed without the bridge.

We stopped at noon where the road forks, the left-hand road goes to Denver. Mr. and Mrs. May, and Mr. and Mrs. Kirkland and children took the left-hand road, as they are going to Denver. Mr. May's brother, George, goes on to Montana on horseback; he will leave us in the morning and depend upon reaching stations, or emigrant camps, for food and shelter nights. I do hope the Indians will not get his scalp.

We have been feasting on antelope, the first that any of our party have killed. It is fine, much better than venison—but then I never ate venison when I was so hungry for fresh meat—we do get so tired of cured meat. We see no game except antelope and jack rabbits. The great herds of buffalo—that we read about—have not been in sight as yet.

Mr. Morrison's four-horse team ran away this afternoon with Mrs. Morrison and the children in the wagon. I had been riding with them since noon, had just left the wagon. When all the horse teams were driven out of ranks and down to the river for water, the lead horses took fright at an ant-hill—the ant-hills are big as a chicken-house—and started to run. There were several men near who caught and stopped them just as the forewheel went over the bank of the river.

Mr. Harding was driving; he tried to rein them away from the river but they were right on the verge when stopped, one moment more and there would have been a serious accident. Mrs. Morrison did not scream nor try to jump out, neither did she allow the children to, but sat quite still and acted like the sensible woman that she is.

We are only six miles below the crossing of the South Platte.

We were awakened this morning at the first peep of dawn by the sound of the bugle call. Soon the teams were hitched, corral broken, and we were journeying to the crossing of the river, where we were driven into corral again. While we were getting breakfast the men were raising the wagon-beds and fixing them upon blocks as high as the wheels, and binding them tight with ropes to the coupling poles and lower parts of the wagons, ready to ford the river. They had a top-heavy appearance, as if the least jolt would topple them over. Some of the women were very nervous about riding in wagons set up on stilts, and felt quite certain somebody would be drowned. Wagons were crossing when we drove into corral, of course we had to wait our turn—first come, first served. Some enterprising young men have the blocks and ropes there to rent, at a very reasonable hire, too, for they might have asked what they would, we had no choice but to use them.

The river is half a mile or more wide, about half way over there is a large freight wagon stuck in the quicksand, just below the track of the wagons; it has been there since yesterday; it is slowly, slowly sinking, and cannot be gotten out. It has been unloaded and left to its fate, it seems a signal of distress to warn drivers to keep farther up the river and avoid the quicksands.

I drove the horse team over, and Hillhouse rode Dick and directed our going. The wagons of our train were all over and in corral by two o'clock without accident or mishap. Wagons have been crossing all day, and this evening we are a considerable town of tents and wagons; more than two hundred wagons within sight on the north side of the South Platte, at the eastern extremity of Fremont's Orchard—though why it is called an orchard I cannot understand, for there is certainly no fruit, neither promise of fruit about it, mostly quaking-asp and Cottonwood, I think. Our corral is just to the left of where the wagons drive out, and near the bank of the river. Hillhouse has crossed the river on Dick at least twenty times today; he seemed to know just how to help and has been in constant demand, so he and Dick are thoroughly tired out tonight. We will stay here over Sunday, and hope to have religious services tomorrow as there are several preachers with us. I have not met any of them except Brother Austin who preached for us last Sunday.

Cash is much better, able to be out, though quite pale and weak. The mountains looming up in the distance seem to be the goal to which we are tending, and now we seem to make some progress every day for we are certainly nearer than when we first saw them on the twenty-ninth of June. Before they came in sight we did not seem to make any progress, but traveled day after day, and seemed to camp at night always in the same place; there was such a sameness in the landscape. In the early morning when the sun shines upon the snow-capped mountains the effect is thrilling; they seem to be the great altars of earth raised up to Heaven for the morning sacrifice.

IT IS WONDERFUL, WONDERFUL TO BEHOLD how this town of tents and wagons has sprung up since yesterday morning when there was no sign of life on this north bank of the South Platte, and now there are more than one thousand men, women and children, and I cannot guess how many wagons and tents. The wagons have been crossing all day, the last one has just been driven into corral at sunset.

I was sitting on the bank of the river watching with anxiety the wagons as they ploughed through the deep waters—for the ford has washed out and the wagons go in much deeper than when we crossed yesterday—when a gentleman came and introduced himself as Dr. Howard, physician for the McMahan train. He said, "Miss Raymond, I have known you by sight since we camped at Kearney, and now as I have an errand for an excuse I hope to become better acquainted."

I could not imagine what his errand could be, for he talked of other matters for fifteen minutes or more, then said, "Miss Raymond, I have been directed to your wagons for the best and most wholesome bread that is baked on this road. Captain McMahan's nephew, Robert Southerland, has been very sick but is now convalescing and needs nutritious and wholesome food to help him gain strength. I came to ask you for a piece of good bread."

Of course I gave him a loaf, and said, "Come get more when that is gone." He thanked me profusely.

There has been no serious accident nor any lives lost, although thousands of cattle, hundreds of horses, and more than a thousand human beings have crossed the river since yesterday morning.

Oh, for the pen of a Dickens to describe this wonderful scene, which no one ever has or ever will see again, just as it is. The moon is at the full and shining brightly as there is not a cloud in the sky, the camp-fires do not glow as they do dark nights. The men are building a great bonfire in the middle of our extemporaneous town.

There is to be a praise and thanksgiving service for our safe conduct through the deep waters and our protection from the Indians. The people are beginning to gather near the bonfire and I must go, too.

The scenes in this great expanse of low, level land on the north side of the Platte in the early hours of this morning is hard to describe. Corrals and camps here, there and everywhere. Cattle and horses being driven into corrals to be harnessed and yoked, men and women cooking by camp-fires and on stoves, everybody seemed to be in a great hurry, all was animation and life, men riding after horses, oxen and mules; yelling, hallooing and calling, but not a profane oath did I hear. Among so many children, we rarely ever hear a child cry, and never hear a woman scold.

Our train was the third to break camp and file into the road this morning. The place that knew us yesterday will know us no more forever. Our town of tents and wagons that was teeming with life this morning is this evening deserted, silent, and uninhabited. We have folded our tents and driven or rode away. I did not mount immediately, but led Dick by the bridle, and gathered a magnificent bouquet of the most beautiful wild flowers. I had loitered by the way and did not notice that I was getting far behind our train, when I looked up and saw only strangers in the train that was passing. I thought it was time to mount, threw the bridle over Dick's head, while arranging my flowers, so that I would not crush them. I saw a gentleman in the train throw down his whip and start toward me, as if to assist me in mounting. I waited until he was quite near, then placing a hand on either horn I sprang lightly into the saddle, turned and waved my bouquet toward him as Dick galloped off. Such a cheer as the men in the train did raise, and then such merry laughter; it was fun to hear them.

Dr. Howard says it was Colonel Woolfolk —a gallant young widower—and the men that witnessed it guyed him unmercifully on having been snubbed. We came to the western extremity of Fremont's Orchard, ten miles, and stopped for lunch. Then came the Sand Hills, where all the heaviest wagons had to double teams to get through. The captain came on four miles and selected a camping ground, and we drove to our places, to wait for the heavy wagons to get through the sand.

Hillhouse, and several others, who came on with us, went hunting for antelope. We have been feasting on antelope for several days; it is fine, but if I could have my choice I would rather live on ham and bacon all the while than to have our men go hunting in this Indian country. Since we have crossed the Platte we have no protection from the soldiers, as there are no stations on this side the river.

We suffer agony when our boys are away from camp guarding stock or hunting. I have no fears for myself nor any of us while we are all together in corral; but just a few away by themselves, how easily they might be cut off. There were Indians seen this morning by men looking for feed for the stock. It is almost dark and the boys have not come. I think the captain is getting anxious; he keeps looking in the direction the boys have gone. Ten P.M. The boys have just come with one antelope. They lost their bearings and came to the river, one mile or more above camp, and that was what kept them so late. When we scolded, they said they were obliged to stay to get at least one antelope for our Fourth of July dinner tomorrow.

We Celebrate the Fourth

WE MADE CORRAL AT ELEVEN A.M., the captain announcing, "That we will stay four hours." I do not know if we stopped so soon, because it is the Fourth, or because it is so intensely warm, and the sun beams so hot, or because it was such a delightful camping-place. Whatever the cause, there we rested beneath the shade of large cottonwood trees, and it was so pleasant.

We had dinner at two. Our bill-of-fare —oyster soup, roast antelope with oyster-dressing, cold beans warmed over, dried fruit sauce, and our last cake and custard for desert. We used the last of our eggs, which were packed in salt; it is surprising how nicely they have kept. I believe they would have kept another month. We had a very enjoyable feast, with an abundance of lemonade without ice. The boys put up a large swing on two large cottonwood trees; two could swing at once, with lots of strong arms to send us away up high. We began to file into the road at three P.M. Our fun was all too short. Dr. Fletcher rode with Neelie, and Milt Walker with me.

Here is where we would have crossed the South Platte—if we had not forded it at the east end of Fremont's Orchard—on Lathan's Ferry. If all those wagons had crossed on the ferry it would have been a big pile of money for the ferrymen, for they charge one dollar a team.

We passed a squalid-looking Indian village today; it was just teepees and huts. Oh, dear, but they do look so uncomfortable. We are at the mouth of the Cache la Poudre —where somebody cached their powder. The water is so very clear and cold; it seems so nice after the muddy Platte. As there are no stations on the north side of the river, there are no wells. The Cache la Poudre is supplied by springs that flow from the snowcapped mountains that seem to be right over there.

As we were passing another Indian town I peeped into two or three of their dwelling-places. They are desolate-looking homes; no sleeping-places, no tables, chairs nor any furniture, just some rolls of blankets and buffalo robes, some camp-kettles, and that was all. There were squaws and pappooses innumerable squatted around on the outside of their teepees, the squaws making moccasins, or decorating them with beads. When we said "How," they grinned and held up two fingers, indicating they wanted two dollars for a pair. We did not purchase.

We are camped at the foot of the Black Hills. They seem like immense mountains to me. There are four large corrals near the little village of La Porte. We rushed through with dinner, then Mrs. Hardinbrooke and I started for the top, taking our note-books with us. Before we had gone far, Winthrop and Frank joined us. Frank brought his gun; I do not know if he expected to find Indians or antelope up here. After much puffing and blowing, climbing and clambering, we reached the top. Oh, it is magnificently grand. If only I could make a pen-picture of this scene that others might realize it, as I do.

The mount upon which we stand is shaped like the quarter of a ball or globe miles and miles in diameter and circumference; we having climbed up the outside of the quarter to the top edge are looking down a steep precipice—the perpendicular side of the quarter. When a stone is thrown over, it takes it twenty-five seconds to reach the bottom, where the Cache la Poudre River runs at the base of the precipice.

How easy to step off into eternity from this place. I would not like to live near here, lest I might be tempted to do it some time. The valley over there looks as if—away back in the ages past—another quarter of the great ball that had been separated from this quarter, had been lifted by giant hands and carried away, leaving the most picturesque valley that I have ever beheld. There are three prosperous-looking farms in sight, a large herd of cattle grazing, and a beautiful grove or park at the northern end of the vale. West of the valley, and opposite where we stand, are peaks much higher than this; behind which the sun is sinking. The setting sun has crowned the mountain-tops with a crown of glory and brightness. The moon is rising out of beautiful, white fleecy clouds in the east. It is lovely beyond description.

How beauteous is this earth.

How bright the sky, How wisely planned by him Who reigns on high.

The sun is gone, night is coming; we must go, for we are at least one and a half miles from camp. I fired Frank's gun before starting; I aimed at the river, and hit the mark. How weak and insignificant these words seem when compared with the reality.

THE SCENIC BEAUTY OF THE ROUTE we have come over today was ever changing. We were either coming through a narrow canyon, across a beautiful vale, climbing or descending a steep hill or mountain.

We are camping in a beautiful basin surrounded on all sides by high hills, and where the grass is plentiful. There is only one other train with us, but then it is the McMahan train, and they are all such fine-looking young men—and of course they are brave —that I always feel safe when they are near. Our captain has forbidden our going out of sight of camp. There are canyons in all directions; how I would like to explore.

Hillhouse and Sim Buford gathered some wild currants while herding; they will pass for fruit, but they look better than they taste. We have made sauce of them; with lots of sugar and cream they look inviting, and the boys seem to like them; very few will satisfy me. We can always have cream for breakfast, as the milk stands overnight, and a pat of the sweetest, most delicious butter every evening, when we travel, as the milk is churned by the motion of the wagon. Fruit is very necessary on this trip, because of the alkali in the water, dust, and air we breathe, to keep us in health.

I was up very early this morning; I cannot spend precious time in bed after daylight while we are camping in this delightful place and have this perfect weather. I led Dick to the spring for a drink, bathed my face and hands in the cool water, picked a bouquet for the breakfast-table, and returned to camp to find the girls in bed. They missed a glorious sight by not seeing the sun rise.

Mother and Mrs. Hardinbrooke went with me to the top of the hill nearest camp this afternoon. They picked flowers and enjoyed the view for a while, then returned to camp, leaving me to come later. I sat on a large flat rock, just below the top, as mother said, "The Indians could see me so much farther if on the very top." I promised her I would not go out of sight; that if an Indian carried me off they could see him and know where I had gone. I did so enjoy the quiet of this Sunday afternoon; I had Mrs. Prentiss's delightful book, "Stepping Heavenward," to read, and time passed so quickly the sun was setting before I thought of going back to camp. Some of the boys laughed and said, "We were watching, and if an Indian had put in an appearance we'd have settled him; we knew you would not see him until he had you." I thanked them for their watchfulness.

Just when we had mounted our ponies for our morning ride, Mr. Walker came and asked us to go with him to the top pi a mountain we could see far ahead and to the right of the road. He said, "The prospect is very fine, indeed, from that mountain-top. I was there two years ago."

Cash and Neelie were included in the invitation, also Mary Gatewood, but their fathers would not let them go. So Nellie Bower and I were the only ones who were allowed to accept his invitation. We rode our ponies until the ascent became too steep, and then dismounted and climbed. It was a hard climb, but we were amply paid. The view was magnificently grand. We found Mr. Walker's name where he had cut it in the soft stone two years ago, and we left our names, with date and former place of residence, cut in the stone. There were hundreds of names there, but I looked in vain for a familiar one. I wonder if anyone that we know will find ours? We passed the graves of two men this morning who had been killed by the Indians. What a sad fate; God forbid that any of our men or boys should die such a death.

We are camping near a military post— Virginia Dale. It is just as beautiful as the name would imply. There are soldiers here for the protection of emigrants passing through these hills and mountains. Cash and I were riding with the captain when we came to the station. The officer in charge came out to speak to the captain and asked some significant questions, "How long have you been in the hills?"

"Two days and nights."

"Where have you camped?"

"In that basin about eighteen miles back. We stayed over Sunday."

"Have the Indians troubled you?"

"We have seen no Indians."

He seemed greatly surprised, and said, "There has been no train come over that road within the last month without trouble, especially where you stayed over Sunday. Did not you notice those canyons in every direction? The Indians could surround you before you could know there was one near. The hills are full of Indians."

He told the captain where to camp, and where to send the stock for safety and protection. The captain thanked him, and we were starting on when the McMahan train came in sight.

"Ah, ha!" he exclaimed, "I see now why you have not been molested. Just keep that train in sight, and you need have no fear of Indians." And he just doubled up laughing until it was embarrassing to us.

"But why? Why will that train be a protection more than another?"

"Don't you see that portable engine lifted away up there, and all those iron pipes? The Indians think it is cannon or some sort of machinery invented for their destruction; no doubt they believe it could kill them by the hundreds, though the mountains stood between it and them."

So that is why we have not been molested. We have heard of depredations before and behind us, but we have not seen an Indian. Blessings on the McMahan train; I hope we will not lose sight of it while we are in this Indian country.

We have passed through some very narrow canyons today, where there was barely room for one wagon to pass. Great rocks were hanging overhead on one side, with a rushing stream beside and just below the road on the other. There are beautiful waterfalls in the canyons. I was standing watching one of the highest, waiting for the wagons to pass. The last one had gone when Mr. Morrison came and peremptorily commanded me to "Come on. Miss Sallie. The I-I-I-Indians will c-c-c-carry you off some of these days," he stuttered. Of course I went.

The captain's orders are, "Do not leave camp this evening." We were only just corralled when I saw Lyde Walker climbing a nearby mountain. It is the first time I have known her to leave camp since we came into the Black Hills; she is very much afraid of Indians. When she came back I asked, "Why, Lyde, did you not hear the captain's order that we were not to leave camp this evening?"

"Oh, there is no danger when the men are on guard and watching. It is when they feel secure and are not looking out for them that I am afraid. Indians do not molest people when they are expecting them."

Laramie Plains

THE SOUNDING OF THE BUGLE and the echo that reverberated through the mountain gorges this morning was enchantingly sweet, and must have driven slumber from every eyelid. We left the hills at noon and are camping on Laramie Plains. We came over some very steep, rocky roads before we reached the plains. I watched the wagons anxiously as they descended the steep, rocky mountain-side, bounding and bumping against the big rocks, expecting and dreading an upset, but all landed safely on level ground at last, and I gave a sigh of relief and thanksgiving. We have not had an uncomfortably warm night all summer, but while we have been coming through the hills the nights have been really cold, so that we have slept under blankets and comforts, like winter-time. There is no sickness in camp at all; it is marvelous how very well we are. I hope it will continue so.

We crossed the Big Laramie River just before noon. Had a good crossing; the water is clear, the bed of the river is covered with gravel, the banks are low, and the water is not very deep. I rode across on Dick; the water just came to my stirrup. We will stay here until tomorrow, as there is no water for fifteen or twenty miles, and we cannot go so far in half a day. We young people planned a fishing expedition for this evening, but the mosquitoes are so thick on the bank of the river we had to give it up. Some of the boys went seining; Brother Winthrop was among them, so we will have fish for breakfast tomorrow morning.

The mosquitoes have not disturbed our rest at night, yet they have several times been very thick on the banks of the rivers, but have not been troublesome in camp. Perhaps the smoke keeps them away. The McMahan train keeps with us, so we are safe. Dr. Howard rode with us this morning; he is a widower.

We passed two large ponds of alkali this morning. The water had dried up, and the alkali was two or three inches thick all over the pond; it looked like ice, until we came very near. Mrs. Hardinbrooke had a sick headache this afternoon; I took care of little Annie that she might not disturb her mother. She is a dear, sweet child and seems fond of me. There was a rather serious accident as we were driving into corral. Mr. Hazel wood's horses were frightened and ran away, upsetting the wagon and smashing it up considerably. Mrs. Hazelwood, her sister, and two children were in the wagon; Mrs. H. was considerably bruised, the others were not hurt. Dick drank alkali water this evening. I have been feeding him fat bacon; no doubt the grease and alkali have turned to soap before now in his stomach, and soap is not poison, so he will not die this time, and I will take better care of him the next time we are near alkali.

The men were until almost noon repairing the broken wagon. An accident that happens to one is assumed by all until results are overcome. As we were ready for the start, a little girl ran among the oxen to catch her pet crow; an ox kicked her on the forehead and cut a gash that had to have a few stitches and be bandaged, so we were delayed again. When order reigned once more we crossed the Little Laramie. It is very much like the Big Laramie, only not so wide nor deep; I rode Dick over, and then came on ahead of the train, keeping within sight. When we had traveled about an hour the rain came down. I was likely to get very wet before our wagons came, for they were among the last in the train; I took the saddle and bridle off Dick, sat down on the saddle to keep it dry, and to wait for the wagon. I was resigning myself to a drenching when Mr. Grier, driver of the front wagon, came and spread a great big rubber coat over me, so that I was completely sheltered and was hardly damp when our wagons came.

Then mother drove the horses close up to the wagon in front I tossed my saddle and bridle in, hopped up on the tongue of the wagon before the wagon behind got close up, and we started without stopping but the one wagon. We could not stop until we came to feed for stock, so we were obliged. to travel in the rain. We drove into corral about four P.M., and are again quite near the mountains. There are more pleasant things than camping in the rain. The water is so impregnated with alkali I fear it will cause sickness; the stock are in greater danger than we, for we can guard against it.

As I climbed out of the wagon this morning I saw the most beautiful rainbow I ever looked at. The bow was complete, the colors dazzlingly bright and just as vivid in the center as at the ends. It was not raining in camp, but raining hard on the mountain-side. The rainbow was so near we might easily have reached the end and "found the pot of gold." The rain came down all morning; we did not break camp until ten o'clock and then made only a short drive. We are camping among the hills once more, with not another train in sight. The McMahan train is behind us, but we do not know how far away they are, so we are glad to wait until they catch up. There is a mountain near that I would like to climb, but it is against orders.

WE ARE ALL HERE; ALTHOUGH SOME of the women last night seemed to think there was small chance of our seeing the light of this morning's sun. Had we known that the McMahan train was within calling distance —just a hill intervening—perhaps we would have rested easier and slept more soundly. It is considered a very dangerous place where we were last night and where we have traveled today. Although it is Sunday, I am sure there is not one in camp that would have voted to stay there to rest. We have heard horrible stories of the depredations that have been committed along this road and in these mountains within the last month. We saw with our own eyes—just before we came to Rock Creek—a station that had been burned and all the inmates killed or taken prisoners; there were none to tell the story of the fight, although the bodies of all who were known to be there were not found. The buildings were not all burned, the fire either went out, or was put out by the rain, after the Indians left. They have been repaired, and soldiers stationed there now. We saw at the same station a coach that had been riddled with bullets; it was found on the road about a mile from the station, without horses, driver or passengers.

It is supposed the Indians killed the driver, took the horses, and it is not known yet whether there were passengers or not, the coach being so riddled with bullets; it is feared there were passengers. A guard of soldiers go with the coaches we meet, or that pass us now. We crossed Rock Creek on a toll-bridge, and had to pay fifty cents toll for each wagon.

Just after we crossed the bridge, and where there is a sudden turn in the road, as it winds around the mountain, we saw where two men had been killed and two wagons burned last week. The tire became loose on a wheel of the next to the last wagon in a freight train, the men stopped to tighten it, while the rest of the train moved on, not thinking of danger, and was out of sight in a few minutes. An hour later some of the men came back to see what kept them. There they were—dead and scalped—the horses gone, and wagons on fire. The Indians had taken all the freight they could use, piled wood under the wagons, and set it on fire. We saw quantities of white beans scattered over the ground, also the irons from the wagons.

We are within sight of Elk Mountain and seemingly quite near it. Sim and Hillhouse picked a nice lot of gooseberries while stopping at noon. I have been sitting in the wagon, picking off stems all afternoon; they also brought a bucket of snow. It is really refreshing, and such a novelty to have a snowball to eat in July. The gooseberries are quite plentiful around here. Cash and I went with Hillhouse and Sirti to pick some this evening, but a shower drove us to camp; the boys stayed and picked as long as they could see. If we had time, we could gather gooseberries enough to supply the train for a month. They are very fine and large; they are certainly an acceptable addition to our bill-of-fare, where a sameness of diet is unavoidable. I shall always consider them a fine fruit hereafter.

About an hour after we drove into corral the McMahan train came, and their corral is quite near. We are so glad they are here; we feel safe when they are near.

SUCH A COLD, RAINY, DISMAL DAY AS THIS HAS BEEN. It has rained without stopping from early morn until now, and it is almost sundown. This is the first all-day rain we have had this summer. It has rained all night several times, but that is not so bad.

Since we have been in this Indian country the tents have not been put up; everyone seems to think it safer in the wagons than in tents outside the corral, so we have had to sit in the wagons all day. I have read, sewed, written, picked over gooseberries and ran through the rain and visited some, yet the day has seemed long. The herders have to take the stock two miles away to find feed, so we are consumed with anxiety, notwithstanding we know our Father's care is round and about us, and He can and will protect us. When we came here we could see Elk Mountain, but now it is enveloped in clouds, entirely hidden from view. It is not pleasant camping when it rains all day long.

The wagons started soon after daylight, before we were out of bed. We had been on the road a little while when I heard Hillhouse call to Brother Winthrop—who was driving our wagon—"Oh, just look, Wint. Isn't that a grand sight?"

I knew there was something to see, so I was soon up and dressed and sitting with Winthrop. I shivered with cold until my teeth chattered, but was well repaid for any inconvenience by the grandeur of the sight I looked upon. Why try to describe or picture anything so entirely impossible? The masses of fleecy white clouds, with the brightness of the morning sun shining upon them as they floated around and over the top of the mountain, made an ever-changing, beauteous panorama that I cannot describe. As the clouds rose higher and higher, they seemed to mass over the top of the mountain, as in benediction, glittering in the sunshine until they seemed to melt away.

I waited until the sun had warmed the air, then mounted Dick for my morning ride. The McMahan train broke corral and drove into line just behind our wagons. I had only just started when Dr. Howard rode up on his pony Joe and requested the pleasure of riding with me. The doctor is a very pleasant, cultured gentleman, and is very fond of his pony, yet Joe cannot be compared with Dick for beauty, neither for easy gait. Why, Dick is the most beautiful pony on this road. He is a bright bay with long and heavy black mane and tail, and his gait is as easy as a cradle. I can ride all day and not be tired at all. While his horse—well, I will not describe him. It might hurt the doctor's feelings.

We came to the foot of Elk Mountain, on the Medicine Bow, about nine o'clock. We find plentiful and excellent feed for the stock, so the captains have announced, "We will stay here until tomorrow."

THE DOCTOR THANKED ME FOR THE PLEASURE our morning ride had afforded him, and asked, "Can we not make up a party to climb Elk Mountain after breakfast?"

"I hope so. I will ask some of the young people."

About ten o'clock a few of us commenced the climb. Lyde Walker, Nellie Bower, Cash and Neelie, Sim Buford, Brother Hillhouse, Dr. Howard and myself. We were well paid for the effort; we found beautiful wild flowers, and some wild strawberries not five feet from a snow-bank. The snow is in a ravine on the north side where the sun does not shine. The berries and flowers are on the bank of the ravine, high enough to catch the rays of the sun, facing the south. The view was fine; we could see a large white lake far away to the west. Dr. Howard said it was alkali.

We passed the alkali lake this afternoon. It was a strangely beautiful sight—the water as white as milk, the grass on the border intensely green. I always thought grass would not grow where there is alkali, but it is certainly growing there; the contrast of white and green was vivid. The wind was blowing the water into little glittering, dancing skipping wavelets; the sight was so unusual that it was fascinating, though the water is so dreadfully poisonous.

There are several musicians in the McMahan train; Lyde says they serenaded me last night. She says they stood between our two wagons. I think she is trying to tease me.

"Ask Dr. Howard, if you do not believe me. He was one of them."

"Oh, no. I would be ashamed to acknowledge I did not hear them, and would feel like a dunce if they had not been there."

Dr. Howard gave me the bouquet he gathered on Elk Mountain, which was most beautifully arranged, and asked me "To keep it until it falls to dust." I have put it between the leaves of a book and will perhaps never think of it again.

We came through Fort Halleck today. There were eight wigwams, or teepees, at the east end of the town; the squaws wore calico dresses and hoops. I believe they were more comical-looking than in their blankets. I fail as yet to recognize "The noble red man." They are anything else than dignified; they seem lazy, dirty, obnoxious-looking creatures.

Cash and I made a few purchases at Fort Halleck. I paid eighty cents for a quire of writing paper, and Cash paid fifty cents for a can of peaches. Mrs. Morrison is on the sick-list today, and Delia Kerfoot has a very sore mouth—scurvy, the doctor says, caused by the alkali in the dust and air. Neelie and Frank are both complaining.

We Cross the North Platte

THE GROUND WAS COVERED WITH A WHITE FROST THIS MORNING, and it is freezing cold. Mrs. Morrison and Frank are better; Delia's mouth is healing. Neelie continues to drag around; she will not acknowledge that she is sick enough to go to bed, but she certainly looks sick. I wish they would call Dr. Howard; somehow, I have more faith in him; perhaps because he is older and more experienced.

We are on the banks of the North Platte; arrived about three o'clock, did not stop for lunch at noon. We came ahead of the other trains, which will be here tonight. We will have the privilege of crossing first in the morning.

The men have taken the herds five miles away to get good feed. They are in danger from Indians. The captain called for volunteers. My brothers both offered to go, but the captain said, "Only one of Mrs. Raymond's boys must go."

Hillhouse said he would be the one. He was on guard last night, too.

We are in no danger here, for there are several trains here now and there will be more tonight. Oh, the anxious watching, the prayerful longing for day that we must endure this night, because of loved ones exposed to danger. What a precious privilege that we can go to the Mercy-seat with the assurance that if we ask aright our petitions will be granted. How do people live without Christ and a Mercy-seat? What can they do, when suffering anxiety, grief, or bereavement, if they cannot go to Jesus with their sorrows? Precious Savior, what a refuge in time of trouble, what a joy to carry everything to God in prayer.

The McMahan train is near. Dr. Howard has been here; he begged me to let him see my diary. I asked to be excused.

The night passed without alarm, and we are all here; I am thankful. Some of the men in our train were afraid to risk fording the river, and paid four dollars per wagon to be ferried over on a rickety old ferryboat that looked more dangerous than driving over.

Hillhouse and Winthrop were both engaged with the ox-team, Winthrop on the seat and Hillhouse riding Dick. When they drove into the river I motioned to mother to keep quiet and drove the horse-team right in behind them. The current is very swift; they had all they could do to keep the oxen from going with the current, and did not know I had followed them until they came out on an island in the middle of the river. Hillhouse smiled a sickly little smile, and said, "You should not have tried that."

Dr. Howard stood near, holding his pony by the bridle. He complimented me on my skill in driving, and said, "I saw you drive in that swift and treacherous river with bated breath, but soon saw that you knew what you were doing, yet I rode Joe in just behind you to be ready for emergencies."

"Thank you for your thoughtfulness. I will not halloo until I am out of the woods —the other side is to be crossed yet."

Hillhouse said, "You would better wait on the island, and I will come back and drive your wagon over."

But of course I could not do that, after all the complimenting I had received. I drove in—with fear and trembling—for there lay a big freight wagon upset in the middle of the stream. It was more difficult than the first side, the banks higher and steeper, and the water deeper. We got over without mishap; the doctor came on his pony just behind us. I wandered off alone after lunch and climbed to the top of a nearby mountain. I found there a large pyramid of loose stones that looked as if they had been piled there by travelers, each one contributing a stone.

I selected a snow-white stone from the mountain-side and added to the pile. There is another town of wagons being made on the west side of the North Platte. The wagons have been crossing all day, and are crossing yet. Hundreds of wagons have been driven over that turbulent and rushing river, and not a serious accident occurred.

I have been on the lookout for the Irvine train, but it is not here. I think it is ahead of us, and we will not see the young ladies or Mr. Reade again on this trip, yet as we are all going to Montana we may perhaps meet again.

WE ARE WITHIN SIGHT OF PINE GROVE in Wyoming Territory.

Neelie was very much better this morning; almost well, she said at noon, and rode her pony this afternoon. I was riding with her when I noticed a heavy rain-storm coming. I begged her to come on and not risk getting wet.

"Oh no, Miss Sallie; I don't want to ride fast. This air is so delicious, and I think I want to ride alone for a while; you go on, and I will come very soon."

I saw it was useless to urge her. I am always careful not to expose myself unnecessarily to a drenching, so I raced on to our own wagons and had barely time to unsaddle Dick and turn him loose when down came the rain in torrents. I was so anxious about Neelie and expected her to come tearing through the rain. I looked from the back of the wagon and saw her coming—plodding along at the same slow gait, as if she did not know it was raining. When the rain was almost over she came along—drenched, of course. She laughed at my look of dismay and paid no heed to my scolding. Mother and I both urged her to go quickly and change her wet garments for dry and warm ones. She got off her horse and climbed into the wagon.

When we stopped I went around to see how she fared. She sat in the wagon with a blanket-shawl around her, and the wet clothes had not been changed for dry ones. She was shivering with cold.

"Oh, Neelie, my precious girl, I am afraid you have killed yourself."

"Oh, no, Miss Sallie; I am not so easily killed as all that."

"But, Neelie, you have been sick for a week, and now to get this drenching. I fear the consequences."

The family do not appear at all anxious, so there is nothing I can do but hope and trust that her naturally strong constitution may bear even this strain. I advised her to go to bed, drink hot tea, and get into a perspiration. I doubt very much if she will do it.

Milt Walker is on the sick list, too. Hillhouse went to bed with a severe headache last night, but a night's rest has entirely restored him.

We crossed three very muddy streams today, the first muddy water we have seen since leaving the South Platte. Since coming to the mountains, the water has been as clear as crystal until today; perhaps we are coming into mining country. We stopped quite early this afternoon; the McMahan train has passed and gone out of sight. I hope they will not go too far, and that they will lend us protection with their portable engine and other machinery.

WE PASSED THE SUMMIT OF THE ROCKIES TODAY, and are camping on the western or Pacific slope tonight. The ascent has been so gradual we should not have known when we reached the top but for the little rivulets running in different directions. Quite on the summit and very near to each other we saw two little rivulets starting on their way; one to meander toward the Pacific, while the other will empty its confluence into the Mississippi, and thence on to the Gulf. Just a scoopful of earth could change the course of either where they started—from the same spring really. As it is, how widely different the scenes through which they will pass. So it is with human lives—a crisis is reached, a decision is made, and in one short hour the whole trend of our life is changed with regard to our surroundings, associates, environments, etc.

We came through Bridger's Pass today, crossed a toll bridge near Sulphur Springs, and had to pay fifty cents toll for each wagon. The streams are all muddy that we have crossed today. We saw two beaver dams; they look like the work of man with shovel and trowel. We are camping two miles west of Sulphur Springs.

We are camping near another muddy creek near a station that was attacked by Indians ten days ago; they wounded one soldier very severely and ran off with nine horses.

After we were in corral, while waiting for the stove to be set up and the fire to be made, I was sitting in mother's camp-chair idling and thinking, when Neelie came to me. She dropped upon the grass beside me and, laying her head in my lap, said, "Oh, Miss Sallie, I am afraid I am going to be sick in spite of everything, and I have tried so hard to get well without sending for the doctor."

Dr. Fletcher is desperately in love with her and tried to tell her so one day not long ago, catching her hands while talking, which she resented as a familiarity, and has not spoken to him since. She told me about it the evening after. It happened at noon. I told her I believed he was sincerely in earnest and that she had wounded him deeply.

She told me what she had done to try to cure herself; the medicine she has taken is enough to kill her. I called mother and told her what Neelie had told me. Mother said, "You poor child, you do look sick, indeed; you must go to bed and send for the doctor right away." I went with her to the wagon, helped her to get ready for bed, and told Cash to send for Dr. Fletcher. She said she would as soon as Bush—her brother—came.

After dinner I went again to see Neelie; the doctor had not yet come, but Bush had gone for him. I stepped upon the tongue of the wagon and could, with difficulty, restrain an exclamation of disgust. Neelie interpreted my expression and said, "Cash just would do it; said I was looking so like a fright."

Cash had powdered and painted Neelie's pale face and crimped and curled her hair— and made her look ridiculous—trying to hide the sick look from the doctor. I did not answer Neelie, but went and scolded Cash; in a low tone she said, "She was so dark around the eyes, her lips blue, and her cheeks so pale I could not bear to have Dr. Fletcher see her looking so homely. She has told you about their little love-tiff?"

"Yes, but don't you suppose he can see through that paint and powder? I am afraid he will think Neelie did it, and she will appear ridiculous in his eyes." I saw the doctor coming, so came away. As I was sitting here writing, he came a while ago and said, "Miss Raymond, will you sit with Miss Kerfoot tonight and see that she has her medicine strictly at the right time?"

"Certainly I will. Is she very sick, doctor?"

"She is in a much more serious condition than she or the family realize. It would not be wise to alarm her, but the family ought to know she will need very careful attention. I will tell them tomorrow. You need not sit up after the last dose of medicine is given, which will be at midnight. I think she will rest better if everything is quiet, and the lights out."

I know from the doctor's tone and manner he thinks Neelie dangerously ill. The doctor gave me directions about her medicine, and I went immediately to her wagon.

LAST EVENING AS I WAS ON MY WAY to sit with Neelie I met Ezra. He said, "Miss Sallie, Sim is quite sick; very much like Cousin Neelie is, I think. I wonder if we are all going to be sick?"

"Oh, no; I hope not. I am very sorry Sim is sick."

When I left Neelie—a little after midnight—sleeping quietly, to come home, I noticed a light in the wagon that Sim and Frank occupy. I did not awake this morning until everything was ready for a very early start. Mother had kept my breakfast warm by keeping the stove until the last minute. I sat in the wagon and ate my breakfast after the train had started. When through I climbed out and went to see how Neelie was. I found her feverish and restless; her symptoms unfavorable.

Oh, the dust, the dust; it is terrible. I have never seen it half as bad; it seems to be almost knee-deep in places. We came twenty miles without stopping, and then camped for the night. We are near a fine spring of most excellent water—Barrel Spring it is called. I do not know why; there are no barrels there. When we stopped, the boys' faces were a sight; they were covered with all the dust that could stick on. One could just see the apertures where eyes, nose and mouth were through the dust; their appearance was frightful. How glad we all are to have plenty of clear, cold water to wash away the dust.

Neelie is no better. Such a long drive without rest and through such dust was enough to make a well person sick. I fear the consequences for both Neelie and Sim, for Sim is a very sick boy. Hillhouse told Sim last night that we would take him with us and take care of him, if he wanted to come and Mr. Kerfoot would let him. He wants to come, of course; so he sent for Mr. Kerfoot this morning to come to his wagon, as he wished to see him on business.

Mr. Kerfoot came, and Sim asked to be released from his contract to drive through to California. Mr. Kerfoot asked, "Why do you want to leave us?"

"I believe Montana is the place for a young man to go, and besides I am very sick and can have better care with the Raymonds than I can here, for Neelie needs all your attention."

"I reckon your chances are as good as the rest of us have." And walked off.

Frank came for me, and I went to see Sim; he is very sick, has a high fever and coated tongue. He asked me to see Mr. Kerfoot. Frank went with me. Mr. K. seemed to know what we came for; he was scarcely civil. I put the case plainly, and said, "We must take care of Sim, either with or without your consent; we owe it to his father and mother, and to himself, to see that he is taken care of. He cannot be taken care of where he is."

After rearranging the boys' wagon and making room for Sim's bed and other belongings; Ezra, Frank and Hillhouse helped him to the wagon and put him to bed, while I went to the McMahan train, which was quite near, and asked Dr. Howard to come and prescribe for him. The doctor came, bringing the medicine with him. He says it is mountain fever.

The separation of the train is being talked of, and is no doubt absolutely necessary, for the herd is so large it is hard to find pasture for them all together. When the division is made, those going to California will form one corral, and those bound for Montana will form another. This will separate us from Mr. Kerfoot's family; I do hope we will not have to part while Neelie is so sick. I do so want to help take care of her.

Among the families that came into our train at Kearney was a family of four young ladies and their father—a widower—named Ryan. Sue, Kate, Mary and Maggie are their names. Mr. Ryan told some of the young men that he was taking his daughters to the west, where there are more men and fewer women, so they could have a better chance to get good husbands than in Missouri. It has been a good joke among the boys, and some of them have tried to be very gallant to the young ladies—as they are on the market.

George Carpenter, a driver for Hardinbrooke and Walker, when the train separated this morning, pretended to go into hysterics. He had a fit on the inside of the corral when Mr. Ryan drove off with the other half of the train. Mr. Kerfoot did not know he was fooling, and ran to his assistance; the captain passed, took in the situation and smiled. Mr. Kerfoot knew then it was a hoax, and it made him so mad he declared he would not stay in a train where the captain would smile at such conduct.

The doctor had said to him, "It is necessary that I see Neelie several times during the day, and you will be taking great risk if you leave the train until she is much better." He had decided to stay, and join the others any time before they came to the California road, west of Green River. He was so mad at the captain for smiling at Carpenter's nonsense, and because he did not rebuke him, that he made the boys bring in the horses and cattle and hitch up as quickly as possible. In an hour after the others started they had followed. Mr. Kerfoot did not say goodbye to anyone. I do hope Neelie will not suffer for his crankiness.

We are now a corral of twenty wagons, the greater number freight wagons; they are in corral on the opposite side, while the families are all on our side. The Hardinbrookes, Walkers, Bowers, Kennedys, Morrisons, Currys—a family of five—Mr. and Mrs. Baily and their daughter, about ten years old, and a widowed sister of Mrs. Baily and her little girl, about the same age as her cousin, are with us at the back end of the corral. I do not know these people, only just to speak when we meet, but they now help to form our corral.

We came only two or three miles after the train separated, just far enough to get out of the dust. Mr. Kerfoot's family and ours have been almost as one family since we have been on the road, and I have become greatly attached to all of them and especially to Neelie. She is the dearest, sweetest girl, so very unselfish, and always ready to help any and every one that needs help. There is not one in the family but could be spared better than Neelie except, of course, her father. They all love her so, and depend upon her for everything. She is a precious daughter, a darling sister, and a true friend.

Sim is very much better; he has some fever, but not so high a temperature as yesterday. Dr. Howard is very attentive. He says it is mountain fever that Sim and Neelie both have. Dr. Fletcher called him to see Neelie; he says she is a very sick girl, but not worse than Sim was when he first saw him. Her temperature is not so high.

I wonder if mountain fever is contagious, or what it is that causes it? It seems the air is so pure and invigorating one could not get sick at all. I never felt better in my life, and mother seems so well. I am afraid it is the sameness of diet and poor cooking that is making Mr.

Kerfoot's folk sick. The bread they make is hard as brick-bats when cold.

We Overtake the California Train

WE CAME UP WITH THE OTHER HALF OF THE TRAIN about ten o'clock, and have traveled in company the rest of the day. We have separate corrals about two hundred yards apart; the stock is not herded together.

Neelie has been restless with high fever and flighty when she dozes; with eyes half open, poor girl she is certainly very, very sick.

We are near a delightful spring, cold as ice, and clear as crystal. I went to the spring to bathe my face and hands, and brush my hair. Mr. Kerfoot and Frank came for water. Mr. Kerfoot said, "Miss Sallie, why don't you and your folks come and go to California, where you started to go?"

"Why, Uncle Ezra, you know the reason. We think Montana the better place for the boys to get a start, and we want to do the best we can for them."

"Tut, tut; wealth is not the chief thing in life. You can make a living anywhere, and Montana is an awful place. Why, the only law they have is mob law, and if a man is accused of crime he is hung without judge or jury."

"Notwithstanding, there seems to be a great many nice people going there, and I am not in the least afraid of my brothers being accused of crime."

"I do believe you will regret going to Montana, and I also believe it is all your doing that you are going. I think it is very unkind of you to leave us now when Neelie is so sick and needs you so much."

"We are not leaving you, Mr. Kerfoot; it is you leaving us against the doctor's orders, too."

I made a great mistake saying that, he fairly raved; he was so angry, actually beside himself with rage. He said very unkind things without the least foundation or truth in them, and which I will try to forget. I am so sorry for him. I did not answer a single angry word, and I am glad I did not. But Frank did; he was about as angry as his uncle was, and talked manfully in my defense. He gave his uncle the lie, and clenched his fists and seemed ready to fight.

I ended the embarrassing scene by walking away. Mrs. Hardinbrooke was waiting for me; we climbed to the top of a very steep point, which was hard to climb, and we were out of breath when we reached the top and were glad to sit and rest. The view was fine, the evening pleasant, and we were glad of each other's companionship, but we did not talk. I think Mrs. Hardinbrooke attributed my silence to anxiety about Neelie, and she was not far from the truth.

Neelie was very much better this morning; her fever gone, she was very weak, but was free from pain. Her medicine had the desired effect. She had rested quite well last night—better than since she has been sick— and all her symptoms are favorable.

The doctor seemed greatly encouraged and told Mr. Kerfoot that if they would stay here until Monday he felt sure Neelie would be out of danger and they could move on without any risk of doing her harm. He did not dream that Mr. Kerfoot would again disregard his advice. Neelie continued better until noon, then someone proposed moving on a half day's drive, thought it would not hurt her if they made only short drives at a time.

Mr. Kerfoot listened, and finally consented. He is very much afraid of Indians, and in a few days we will be out of the Indian-infested country. The doctor is very much out of patience with him, told me he gave Mr. Kerfoot a piece of his mind.

You must make big allowance for the poor man. He does not realize that he is endangering Neelie's life; he cannot believe it possible that such a calamity as Neelie's death can befall them while he is trusting in a merciful Father above. Yet I do wish someone might have exercised authority and prevented their going.

Sim is very much better, improving rapidly. Mr. Walker is able to be around once more. I wonder if he had mountain fever?

I have been trying to get the dust out of our wagon this afternoon; it was hard work taking everything out and cleaning off the dust. Lyde Walker pleasantly entertained us this evening with songs accompanied with guitar. The wagon the Walkers occupy is just in front of ours since the separation.

We came fifteen miles today, but have not overtaken the California train. It must be that Neelie is no worse, and their traveling yesterday did her no harm, or they would have waited over today; we shall hope so anyway.

Dr. Howard rode with me this morning. We are traveling on Bitter Creek, which is considered the very worst part of all the road. I had heard so much about the desolateness of this part of the country that

I expected to find a barren waste. It is not so bad as represented. There are long distances where there is not sufficient pasture for the stock, but in places the feed is plentiful. The captain and two or three men are off the road the greater part of the day hunting pasture; we stop when they find it at whatever hour it may be.

Monday, July 31. We came twelve miles, passed one station; it was built of stone and seemed a very comfortable place. Mrs. Hardinbrooke has been quite sick today. I have taken care of little Annie. We have not had any word from Neelie. I trust that no news means good news. Sim was able to sit up in the wagon for a while this afternoon. I think with care he will be well in a few days. We have had delightful weather, since we passed the summit. The roads are quite dusty, but not like they were before we came to Barrel Springs. The water in Bitter Creek is not so nice as the mountain streams and springs, but it is not bitter, as I thought it would be from its name.

WE ARE AT POINT OF ROCK, the place is rightly named; one who never saw them could hardly imagine such enormous piles of rock; they are high as mountains, with scarcely any dirt among them, the sides are smooth and even, the stone is soft like slate or sandstone, and the whole face of the enormous pile, as high as man can reach, is literally covered with names, dates, and places of former residence from all over the United States. I looked in vain for some familiar name. I left my name in a conspicuous place, so if any of my friends look for my name they will not be disappointed. There are springs flowing from the clefts in the rock; and oh, with what pleasurable anticipation did I hasten to partake of the pure water, as I, of course, supposed it was.

I had been riding with the captain as he came ahead to find a camping place when the train came. I rode to our wagon, got a cup and crossed Bitter Creek to get a drink of nice, cold spring water. I took one swallow. Oh, oh, oh; the horrid stuff. I was glad there was no one with me to see the face I made. I think I never swallowed a more disagreeable dose. It was the strongest sulphur-water I ever tasted. In my haste and eagerness I did not notice that the atmosphere was impregnated with sulphur, and the sulphur formations around the springs, because they were covered with dust.

The wind is blowing as cold as Greenland. I expect we will have to go to bed to keep from freezing. Mrs. Hardinbrooke is no better; her symptoms are the same as Sim's and Neelie's were at first, and we fear she is taking the fever. Dr. Fletcher thinks Neelie must be better, or we would have heard, as Mr. Kerfoot said he would send back for him if she got any worse.

WE HAD A VERY COLD NIGHT; there was ice a quarter of an inch thick this morning. Several head of Hardinbrooke's and Walker's cattle were missing this morning; the men have been hunting them all day, they were found this evening in a canyon four miles from camp; there were the tracks of two horses, with shoes, that had driven them there. The Indians do not shoe their horses, so there must be thieves besides Indians in this country. And here we are another whole day's drive behind the other half of our train. Oh, I wonder if it will be possible to overtake them now, before our roads separate entirely. They must be at least two days ahead of us, if they have not been delayed.

The mountains in this region are very barren, composed of sand and rock, principally.

It comes nearer being desert than anywhere on the road. We have traveled all day, and have come only thirteen miles. The road has been very rough indeed. I rode in the wagon the greater part of the day, so I could take care of little Annie Hardinbrooke; her mother is very sick. I have thought so much about Neelie, whenever the wheels would strike a rock, or jolt down into a rut; how she must have suffered, if in pain or fever; how hard it must have been for her.

Lyde says Dr. Fletcher is very impatient and cross, because of the delay; he threatened to take a horse and go horseback yesterday, when he found the train would not move. She thinks he is very anxious about Neelie, and very much in love.

The wolves howled around our camp all last night and kept Caesar—our watch-dog—barking; so we could not sleep. Have made only a short drive, and are camping at Rock Springs, where the road forks. The men are not agreed as to which road to take; the upper—or right-hand road—is the shortest, but the lower is best supplied with pasture and water. If we take the upper road we cannot hope to see our friends again, so Dr. Fletcher and I want to take the lower road, for we still hope that we may overtake them.

Mrs. Hardinbrooke is very sick; I fear we are going to have another case of serious sickness in our camp, I have taken care of Annie again today, which seems to be the most efficient service I can render, as Lyde and Mrs. Joe Walker take care of Mrs. Hardinbrooke when her husband cannot be with her. He takes all the care of her at night, and a most excellent nurse he seems to be. Sim is quite well, only pale and weak.

THE DECISION WAS MADE IN FAVOR OF THE LOWER ROAD. As the train was rolling out I had just mounted my pony, when Dr. Fletcher came and asked me to ride with him. He has never seemed to care for my company, nor I for his until since we have been so anxious about Neelie. Our anxiety has been a bond of sympathy, and we have rather enjoyed each other's society. We had gone a short distance ahead of the train when we saw someone coming horseback. I soon saw that it was Frank. We hurried on to meet him. He shook hands without speaking. I asked, "How is Neelie?"

"She is very low. I came after you, doctor. Our camp is about four miles from here; we have waited two days for you, and thought you would certainly come yesterday. When you did not come, we thought you must have gone the upper road, and I was going back as far as the first station to inquire if you had passed. I am glad, indeed, to meet you, but greatly fear you will not be in time to save Neelie."

The doctor asked two or three questions, excused himself and rode away at a gallop, leaving Frank and I to follow, while I plied him with questions, which he answered patiently. He then said, "Neelie was much better for a day or two after we left you; we all thought she was getting well; she spoke of you every time I saw her, and wondered why you did not come. Since the fever came back I have not talked to her at all. Part of the time she has been delirious, and when conscious she was too weak to talk."

Oh, dear. I do so want to see her and help take care of her.

A Fatal Shooting

WE RODE A WHILE IN SILENCE, then Frank said, "That is not all the bad news I have to tell. Miss Sallie,"

I looked up quickly and asked, "What else has happened, Frank?"

"Frasier was shot and killed day before yesterday evening."

"Oh, Frank; how did it happen?"

"Hosstetter did it, but I think he was not much to blame."

Frasier is the man who spoke to Cash, Neelie and I, as we were watching the wagons ferried across the Missouri River, whose son ran away from his mother, and home, to come to his father, and go with him to Montana. Frasier had teams and wagons for freighting, and Hosstetter some capital to invest in freight, to take to Montana. Frasier advised the purchase of flour, and he would freight it to Virginia City for fifteen dollars per cwt. He said flour was worth fifty and sixty dollars per hundred in Virginia City. (So it was in the Spring of 1864, and as high as seventy-five and one hundred dollars per hundred, which was the cause of a bread riot in Virginia City.)

No doubt Frasier was honest in his advice, and would have invested in flour for himself. He charged more freight than was right, for ten and twelve cents is the prevailing price; but then Hosstetter should have found that out for himself. When he found he had been imposed upon and learned that flour is retailing at Virginia City for $15 per hundred, he was angry, dissatisfied, and perhaps quarrelsome. Frasier was no doubt very aggravating. They had quarreled several times, and the evening of the 3d, Frasier was heard to say to Hosstetter in a threatening tone:

"You may consider yourself lucky if you ever see Montana. You need not expect to get any of this flour. It will take it all to pay the freight."

It was getting dark, and Frasier stood with one hand on a wheel as he talked. He then got into the wagon and out again, with something in his hand, which Hosstetter thought was a revolver in the gathering darkness. He came back to the wheel where he had been standing when he made the threat, and Hosstetter thought he had come to shoot him, and fired twice, as he thought, to save his own life. Frasier fell, shot through the brain, and died instantly.

Then it was found he had a hatchet in his hand, and had come to tighten a tire on the wheel, which he had found loose when he laid his hand on it. Frasier's eldest son of fourteen years is here. There are five children and their mother at home. Hosstetter has three children and a wife. Eleven innocent persons to suffer, no one knows how intensely, for that rash act.

Frasier's son knelt beside his father's dead body, and placing his hand on his breast, he swore a fearful oath that he would have but one purpose in life until his father's death is avenged. Oh, what a shocking ambition for so young a boy.

Frasier and Hosstetter have traveled and camped near us all the way from Plattsmouth. When the train was organized they came into it; when it was divided they went with the others as there were not so many of them, and the herd was smaller.

By the time Frank and I had discussed the direful circumstances connected with Frasier's death, in the presence of this greater calamity Neelie's sickness did not seem so sad an affliction as it had before, for she is not dead, and while there is life there is hope.

We came in sight of three corrals about eight o'clock, camping near together.

EVERYTHING HAD A FUNEREAL APPEARANCE. Men stood around in small groups talking earnestly in a low voice, whittling sticks, the incessant occupation of most men when trying to think.

Those with whom we are acquainted bowed as we passed them, without speaking. I was soon off my horse and ready to see Neelie, while Frank took Dick to hitch him for me.

As I approached the tent where Neelie is, Mrs. Kerfoot came to meet me.

"How is she, Aunt Mildred?" I asked anxiously.

"We think perhaps she is better now. She is quiet and resting easy, but she has had a very restless night, and the doctor says she must be kept perfectly quiet; not the least excitement."

She had led me away from the tent while talking. I saw in a flash what she meant. I was not to see Neelie.

"After we left you she kept asking about you, and when you did not come, we thought perhaps you had gone the short cut, and so we told her you had gone the short cut to Montana, and we would not see you anymore. She seemed grieved at first, but became reconciled to what could not be helped, and now, if she should see you of course it would excite her, and I know you would not do anything that might harm her, or make her worse."

"Oh, no; of course not."

Emma, Delia and Juddie had come to where we were talking. I kissed them all, said good-bye, and came away, with a heavy heart.

I unhitched Dick and, leading him by the bridle, went on in advance of the trains, selected a place for the corral, unsaddled Dick, and waited for the wagons. I did not have long to wait, and the captain was so good as to corral on the place I had selected.

I had a motive in being in advance of the other trains. I hoped to get Hillhouse and mother to consent to pull out of corral and go on if the train did not move. We are not in any danger from Indians now, and we can go alone if no others choose to go with us. I cannot bear to stay here and not see Neelie.

We could not move today, but Hillhouse says we will tomorrow morning. The men from these four trains elected judge, jury, prosecuting attorney and lawyer for the defense, and have tried Hosstetter for murder. The jury brought in a verdict of "Not guilty." He shot in self-defense, as Frasier had threatened to kill him.

Hillhouse served on a jury, the first time in his life. He is only twenty. They buried Frasier yesterday. Lyde and I visited his grave this afternoon. Hosstetter seems very remorseful; blames himself for being so hasty.

WE WERE UP BRIGHT AND EARLY THIS MORNING.

I climbed into Mrs. Hardinbrooke's wagon to tell her good-bye, kissed little Annie as she was sweetly sleeping. Mrs. H. seemed sorry to have us go. I met Dr. Fletcher as I was leaving Mrs. Hardinbrooke and asked about Neelie.

"She is very low, indeed. Of course, while there is life we may hope; but if she lives they will have to stay here a week or ten days."

I did not tell him we were leaving, but said good morning, and went to find Lyde. She was worried and anxious about Milt. He has been staying behind the train to drive lame oxen almost every day since he has been well enough. He is usually in camp by 10 P.M. Last night he did not come. She said, "Brother Joe is quite sick, too. I wonder what will happen next?"

"Oh, Lyde, no very serious calamity has happened to you or yours, nor me or mine. Let us not borrow trouble, but hope for the best. Milt will be here in a little while. I know he is able to take care of himself, and he is going to do it."

We Leave the Train

THE WAGONS HAD STARTED, so I mounted Dick and was off. As I came into the road I looked back, and saw Milt coming in sight, driving his lame oxen. I left the road once more and went to Frasier's grave. His son has set it with prickly pears, so closely that it will make a pretty mound if it grows, and will be a protection from wolves, unless their hides are thick and tough. Poor boy, he must have been seriously scratched while transplanting the prickly things, but perhaps it was a relief to his mental suffering, to bear physical pain while trying to do a last something for his poor father.

I spent a dreary morning. I feel the parting with our friends so distressingly. It is not likely we will meet again in this life. I think Sim is feeling blue over it, too.

We met a squad of soldiers from Green River going to arrest Hosstetter, and take him to Port Bridger for trial. They say his trial was not legal. He and all the witnesses will have to go by the way of Fort Bridger, and will perhaps be detained for some time. I do hope for his own and his family's sake he will be cleared. The upper road from Rock Springs goes by the way of Fort Bridger, I think, for the soldiers spoke as if it was not on this road.

We arrived at Green River about three o'clock. The river is about as wide, deep and swift as the North Platte, yet I have not dreaded any of the rivers we have crossed as I did dread to ford this one. Perhaps it was because there are so few of us, for in numbers there is a feeling of security, even in crossing deep and dangerous streams. We crossed without accident or loss, and are camping on the west bank of Green River. When we first came to the river, one of Mr. Curry's boys exclaimed:

"Well, this river is named right. If I had been going to name it, I believe I would have named it Green River, too, for it is green."

The water is very clear, yet the river has a bluish-green appearance. I do not understand why.

There are several corrals along the river, but the people are strangers, so we feel very much alone. There is a station here and soldiers' tents within sight. We are camping on blue grass, with the mountains very close. They are the highest I have seen. I would like to climb to the top, but mother says there are too many soldiers and strangers around.

At the foot of the mountain, a little way from our camp, there is a graveyard with about a dozen graves. It is a beautiful spot, with the mountain for an enduring monument. Several of the graves have been made this year, with names and dates quite distinct on the plain pine headboards. Others are entirely worn or washed off by the relentless hand of time and storm. It seems that Bitter Creek was too much for the weak or frail constitutions. Like Moses, they were permitted to look upon the better land before they died.

The soldiers brought Hosstetter here in the night, and I suppose the witnesses came too. I wanted to go to the station to see if I could hear anything from Neelie, and the rest of the sick folks, but mother did not want me to go where there are so many soldiers, so I did not go. We started very early this morning and have driven about twenty miles. Are camping on Black Fork, where the horses and cattle are just wading in fine pasture right around camp.

We ascended a mountain this morning that was seven miles from base to summit, the way the road is. We had toilsome climbing, and I guess the teams found it a hard road to travel before we reached the top. I came on in advance of the wagons, sometimes riding and sometimes leading Dick where it was very steep, and had time to enjoy the magnificent scenery that lay spread out on all sides. The snowy range could be seen in the distance, glittering in the morning sunshine. The wild currants are here in abundance. I am going fishing with the boys, so I must be off.

WE CAUGHT FISH ENOUGH FOR BREAKFAST LAST EVENING, and gathered currants enough for sauce, but I spoilt the sauce by putting the sugar in, when I put them on to cook, they hardened and were not fit to eat. I have been experimenting today and have succeeded in making a nice cobbler.

I did not sweeten at all before baking, but made the sauce sweet enough to sweeten all. I also made a fine sauce by cooking the currants only a very few minutes, and putting in the sugar after they were cooked. We will have currant dumplings for dinner tomorrow. We have picked a lot, enough to make sauce and pies and other good things for a week. The currants are a beautiful fruit, and some are as large as small cherries. We are waiting at Camp Plentiful, in the hope that some of the wagons from the train will drive in before night.

There are three wigwams within sight of our camp. Sim and Hillhouse went hunting today. On their way back they stopped at the wigwams and found them occupied by white men with squaws for wives. Ugh!

Somehow I felt a little suspicious of those white men living with squaws, and feared some of our horses might be missing this morning, but my suspicions were groundless. Our horses and cattle were all here, well fed and ready for a long drive. We were off bright and early, without seeing anyone from the train.

We passed the Bridger Road, where our friends going to California will turn off, so we are not likely to see them again, perhaps for years, perhaps never again in this life.

There is a very fine ranch at the junction of the roads, where we stopped at noon. Two men from this ranch visited our camp this evening. They were rather fine looking, genteel in appearance, dressed in civilization style, but for some unexplainable reason, I was afraid of them. They tried to be very cordial and polite. They engaged Sim in conversation, and plied him with pertinent questions, such as:

"Who owns those big American mares?" (referring to our horse team).

"They are the property of a widow."

"Whose bay pony is that?"

"It belongs to the widow's daughter."

"Who is the owner of that chestnut sorrel?"

"Mr. Curry, father of those boys playing over there."

They asked many more questions. Where we came from? Where we are going? What we expect to do, etc.

Sim answered them patiently and civilly. He thinks they are horse thieves, but hopes they will not be mean enough to steal from a widow. As if horse thieves care who they steal from. No doubt, their ranch is stocked with stolen horses and cattle, for they have things as they choose away out here, where there is no law, except the law of might.

God's Word says, "As the partridge sitteth on eggs, and hatcheth them not; so he that getteth riches, and not by right, shall leave them in the midst of his days, and at his end shall be a fool" (Jer. 17: 11).

We are camping on Ham's Fork, where the currants and fish are very plentiful, and the pasture very fine. We had our currant dumplings for dinner. They were lovely. No one can imagine how we appreciate this fruit by the wayside, except those who have been deprived of the strawberries, raspberries, blackberries and cherries, each in their season, and confined to the sameness and tameness of diet, which people making this trip are necessarily confined to. This fruit would seem inferior among other cultivated fruits, but where it is, it seems a luxury provided for our benefit.

Thursday, August lo. We went fishing at noon. It is such fun to fish in water so clear that we can see the fish biting at the hook. They do not seem at all afraid, and sometimes there will be two, three, or four grabbing at the hook at the same time. Such shoving, pushing and crowding as they all try to get the tempting bait. How eager and unsuspecting they are. Soon the strongest or fleetest, or rather the most unfortunate one seizes it. Away goes bait, hook and all, and then out comes a fish on dry land. I give a shiver of pity for the unlucky fish, as I call to the boys: "I have another."

It does seem such a cruel thing to take them from their pleasant home in the deep, clear, cool water. But then, "Life is sustained by death." And thousands upon thousands of lives are taken daily to nourish and sustain human life. We are in a beautiful place, where all things necessary for camping are plentiful, and we are all alone, no corral within sight; the first time we have been entirely alone.

IT WAS CONSIDERED UNNECESSARY FOR ANYONE to stand guard last night, as we had come two days' travel from where the suspicious characters live. So all went to bed, retired early, slept soundly, and even neglected to put Caesar's rug in its usual place—under our wagon—so he went into the tent with Mr. Curry's boys to find a comfortable bed, leaving the camp entirely unguarded. One of our big horses wears a bell. I was awakened in the night by hearing an unusual rattling, and the horses came galloping up to the wagons. Dick whinnied. I raised the wagon cover and spoke to him, and he commenced cropping the grass. The other horses were in sight, but not eating. They seemed frightened, and just then Caesar came tearing out of the tent and ran toward the road barking fiercely. The moon was shining brightly. I looked out at the back of the wagon, but could not discover anything wrong, but evidently there was something wrong, for Mr. Curry's horse was gone this morning.

Mr. Curry, Sim and Hillhouse have been hunting the horse all day, but without success, except to find certain evidence that it had been stolen. They found the camp-fire, where three horses had been tied for some time. They then found where four horses had traveled, so they concluded there were three men after the horses.

The boys think it was the merest accident that our horses are not gone too, but I believe it was providential care that kept them for us. Mr. Curry is anxious to stay and try to recover his horse. I believe, as the boys do, that it will be a waste of effort, for if men are mean enough to steal a horse they will manage to keep it. But we do not like to offer too many objections, as it might seem like selfishness on our part, as we are not the losers.

Oh, dear, why don't people be good, and do as they would be done by? How much happier this world would be if there were no thieves nor wicked people in it. I know it is hard for Mr. Curry to give up his fine horse without making an effort to get it back. Yet I feel sure he will not get it. For if he found it he could not force the thieves to give it to him.

It was decided this morning that Hillhouse, Sim and Mr. Curry would go in pursuit of the horse thieves. Sim is just recovering from a severe sickness, and is not able to go on such a trip, but he positively refused to stay in camp and let Hillhouse and Mr. Curry go without him. I believe it will prove a wild goose chase, so mother and I exacted a promise from Hillhouse that he will not stay away tonight. We are looking for him. It is getting dark. Surely they will not leave us here in this wilderness with only two boys and Caesar for protection. If we are left alone, I shall take my turn, with Winthrop and Alex. Curry standing guard in camp. Sim rode Dick this morning, the others walked. What they expect to do if they find the thieves (which they are not likely to do) I do not know.

Mr. and Mrs. Kennedy, Mr. and Mrs. Bower, Nellie and Alton, and Mr. Grier's teams passed here today. They left the train the next morning after we did. The train had not started then. They said Neelie was about as when we left, and Mrs. Hardinbrooke was no worse.

Hillhouse came in about an hour after dark. He was very tired and hungry; had walked since early morning until he started back at three o'clock. He tried to prevail upon Sim to return, and let him go on with Mr. Curry if he must go. But Sim would not listen to such a proposition, although he is still weak from his late sickness. Mr. Curry thinks he will find his horse at the ranch near the junction, although the trail they were following led away from, instead of toward it. If he finds it, he will go back to the train and get the men to help him get it either by fair means or by force.

He then proposed that they keep Dick, but they said he would not reach camp before midnight on foot and he might lose his way, but Dick would take him the shortest route if he would just let him go his own way, which he did, and he brought him safe about an hour after dark.

I am so sorry for Mrs. Curry. She tries to be brave for her children's sake, but anyone can see she suffers, and Alex says she does not eat at all, just takes a cup of tea once in a while.

Another day has come and gone, and the wanderers have not returned. Hillhouse said he did not expect them today, but would look for them tomorrow, for they will not have anything to eat after today, and will be obliged to leave the foot hills and come to the road, whether they find the horse or not, to get something to eat.

A party of emigrants stopped near us today at noon, and one of the men came to our camp. We, of course, asked if they had seen the Hardinbrooke train. They passed the train Sunday. They were still where we left them at the west end of Bitter Creek. He saw and talked to the captain, who told him to tell us, if he caught up with us, "The sick folks are all better, and they expect to come to Green River Monday." They may catch up with us yet.

I do not know what we would do with ourselves if it were not for the currants. We are making jelly, and as it takes lots of currants to make a little jelly, we have not suffered from enforced idleness, with our suspense and anxiety.

There are three varieties of currants here. The yellow ones are not very plentiful. They are the largest and best. I have made a pickle jar full of the loveliest jelly. It is the color of gold and as clear as crystal. The red currants are very plentiful and more like the tame currants, though they do not yield as much juice.

We gather the bushes by the armful, and carry them to camp, and sitting near each other, we pick off the currants.

Though we do not talk much, we like to be near each other. Another day and they have not come, and another night of anxiety before us.

The Wanderers Return

I WAS AWAKENED VERY EARLY THIS MORNING, as soon as it was light, by hearing Hillhouse bustling about making a fire in the stove, as if in a hurry for his breakfast. I dressed as quickly as possible, and hastened out to see what it meant—for it was only four o'clock. When I asked for an explanation, he said:

"I am going to hunt those men. I can't stand this any longer. I have laid awake almost all night thinking about them."

"What can you do? You will be lost yourself."

"No danger of that. I will go back on the road as far as Green River, get some of the soldiers and some of the boys that know them, and we will hunt until we find them, or know what has become of them. I may meet them on the road and return tonight, but I will not come until I bring them with me, or know their fate."

I could not object to his going, but oh, how my heart sank at the thought.

We made all haste to get breakfast, and Hillhouse was all ready to start when Mrs. Curry and the boys came out. Mrs. Curry seemed both glad and sorry he was going, said she hardly knew which. I had supplied him with pencil and paper, and he promised to send us word every opportunity. He mounted Dick and rode away without saying good-bye.

He had gone almost out of sight. One moment more and a bend in the road would hide him from our view. When, lo, there is a gun fired not far off.

My thought was Indians, and I looked to see if Hillhouse was hurt. He was waving his hat furiously and came tearing back to camp. Then I heard Mrs. Curry cry out:

"Oh, it is my husband." And she dropped in a heap on the ground, and cried out loud.

They were plainly visible by that time, coming over the hill and down to the creek and through it, before anyone could show them where they could cross without getting wet.

All was excitement for a while. The meeting between Mr. Curry and his family was very touching, indeed. I think Mrs. Curry had about lost all hope of ever seeing him again.

How famished and worn out they did seem to be. Sim was utterly exhausted. I do not believe he could have gone another half mile. We gave Sim a bowl of bread and milk, and a cup of coffee. Then the boys helped him to bed in our wagon, because it is on springs and we expected to start before he waked. Within one hour after they reached camp Sim was sleeping the sleep of exhaustion. We did not ask any questions, nor let him talk at all, before he went to sleep.

Mrs. Curry prepared the best breakfast the camp could afford for her husband, and as the family had not breakfasted, they all sat down together. She came for Sim to take breakfast with them, but he was sound asleep, and I would not have had him awakened for the best breakfast ever prepared. Perhaps Mr. Curry can stand eating such a meal after starving so long, but I believe it would kill Sim in his weak condition, for he is not fully recovered from his recent illness.

We made all haste to start once more, and by eight o'clock were on the way. We had left the camp where we spent five such anxious, distressful days. Sim did not awaken until after ten o'clock. We gave him some fish and bread and milk, which we had ready for him.

When he had eaten, he lay in bed and told mother and I the following narrative of what had befallen them since they left camp:

"After Hill left us that first afternoon, we walked on as fast as we could, as long as we could follow the trail. Then made a fire, ate some supper without anything to drink. We had not seen water since noon.

"We rolled up in our blankets and lay down with our feet to the fire and tried to sleep. I am sure I did not sleep an hour, I was so tired and nervous. As soon as it was light enough to see, we were up and ate a dry breakfast, for we could find no water in the vicinity. We were soon following the trail. Before night we had eaten all our grub, and found no water. Oh, what would I have given for a cup of cold water? It seemed that we must find water or perish. We dragged on as long as we could see; then lay down and slept from exhaustion. When we awoke it was light.

"I was so weak that Mr. Curry had to help me to get on my feet. I declared I could go no further. Mr. Curry prevailed on me to try, for we must be near Green River. I made a desperate effort, and dragged on for half a mile perhaps, Mr. Curry carrying my blanket, when I positively could go no further, and told Mr. Curry to go on and leave me and try to save himself. Mr. Curry was desperate. He said: 'I must find something to eat.' He covered me with the blankets and went to look for some kind of game.

"When he had gone about a hundred yards he saw a bird about the size of a partridge sitting on a limb ready to be shot. He took careful aim and shot its head off. He hastened back to where I lay, made a fire, skinned the bird, and held it on a sharpened stick before the fire and roasted it thoroughly. I would have eaten it when half done, but Mr. Curry would not let me have it until well cooked, for fear it would make me sick.

"I never tasted fowl that tasted so good as that did, although we ate it without salt. After eating I felt better, and made another effort to move on. We had gone only a little way when Mr. Curry stopped, listened a moment, and exclaimed: 'There, hear the rushing of the river?'

"I could not hear it at first, but soon I heard the glad sound too. It gave us courage, and with renewed energy we pushed on, and before eleven o'clock we reached the river. We slacked our thirst, cautiously, at first, then had a bath and were refreshed.

"While I rested on the bank, Mr. Curry looked up and down the river for the trail, which had gone into the river. He did not find it. We then started for the road, which we came into in about an hour, just below the ranch at the junction.

"A party of emigrants had stopped for noon, who gladly gave food and refreshment to us weary wanderers. While I was resting, Mr. Curry investigated the ranch, looked among the horses in the pasture, peeped in stables, but did not find his horse.

"After Mr. Curry had given up getting his horse he was all eagerness to get back to his family, but considering how very weak I was, he consented to stay with the kind people we had fallen in with until morning, so we traveled with them, and I rested in a wagon all afternoon.

"At the first peep of dawn Mr. Curry was up and awakened me. I felt refreshed and ready for our early walk. Mr. Curry explored the grub-box, found some bread and meat, which he appropriated, leaving greenbacks to pay for our entertainment.

"We expected to reach camp by ten o'clock P. M. but I gave completely out, and we were obliged to lie down and rest when about five miles from camp. I slept until awakened this morning before it was light by Mr. Curry, who was so anxious to be on the way I wondered that he let me sleep so long.

"We came over the foot-hills, instead of by the road, and saved about a mile in distance. We saw Hill riding away from camp and felt sure he was starting to try and find us. Mr. Curry fired his gun to attract his attention, and you know the rest."

He turned over and went to sleep again, and slept until we stopped for noon. We made a long drive today and are camping at the foot of Bear River Mountain.

Bear River Mountain

I AM ON THE SUMMIT OF BEAR RIVER MOUNTAIN, in the border of a beautiful grove of pine and quaking-asp, near a spring of the most delicious ice-cold water. I must be some miles ahead of the wagons that I left toiling up the steep mountain side. Yet I do not feel that I am alone. Oh, no. I feel that God is here in his might, majesty, power and glory. I feel His nearness now, and as I gaze from these dizzy heights upon the country spread out beneath my feet, I am lost in admiration, the scene is so grand, so magnificent, that I forget my own vanity and nothingness. I feel that I am standing upon an altar raised by Nature's grateful hand up to Nature's God, and that I could offer myself a willing sacrifice.

This is emphatically one of the high and sacred spots of earth. How manifold, how wonderful are the works of Nature: Everywhere something worthy of our highest admiration is presented to view; everywhere do we see the manifestation of an invisible and omnipotent Creator. The terrific storm, the broad prairies, the majestic forest, excite within our bosoms emotions of awe and admiration, yet there are no places on earth that I have seen which have a tendency to inspire me with such tender feelings, such elevated, pure, holy thoughts as mountains.

Oh, it seems that one could never sin, or have an evil thought, in such a place as this. Behold the mountains as they stand upon their broad bases, contemplate them as they rear their snowy tops in awful, majestic grandeur above the clouds, view them as you will, and they ever present the same untiring pleasure to the mind.

Men and women will travel thousands of miles and make the greatest exertion to climb the rugged steeps of mountains, to enjoy for one short hour the charming prospect. I have wondered at this sometimes, as I have read of their hazardous exploits in trying to obtain a point where they could have the finest view, but I never shall again.

A country destitute of mountains may be fertile and productive of all that conduces to human happiness, yet it will lack the essential of attractive moral grandeur.

It may enchant the imagination for a moment to look over prairies and plains as far as the eye can reach, still such a view is tedious and monotonous. It can in no wise produce that rapturing delight, that pleasing variety of the sublime and beautiful of landscape scenery which mountains afford.

Let those whose tastes are on a level with the ground they tread feel proud of and admire their prairie fields, but give to me a mountain home.

The wagons are almost at the top, and as mother has driven up the steep ascent, I will drive down the western slope, and have mother ride Dick, and enjoy the delightsome scenery as we descend the mountainside, which looks very steep from here.

We were all the evening crossing the mountain, and it was a hard drive. We are camping at the foot of the mountain near a spring in Bear River Valley, within calling distance of the Chilicothe train.

We passed two freight wagons on the mountain-side that were rather badly smashed up. One had upset, and crackers in a broken-up condition, and other debris from family groceries were scattered about.

We learned that the wagons are Dr. Yager's, and he has gone somewhere to get the wheels mended. We are quite disappointed that he is away, for Sim is not so well as he was yesterday, has had fever and been flighty and in a stupor this afternoon. He needs medical treatment, and we hoped to have Dr. Yager prescribe for him.

We passed eight graves on the mountain, one a young lady twenty years old from Monroe County, Missouri. A beautiful resting place for the dead. Mrs. Yager is quite sick, and seems sadly disheartened. Thinks crossing the plains and mountains in a wagon (they have a very comfortable carriage) is a sad, discouraging, never-to-be-repeated experiment. I am sorry she could not enjoy the fine prospect on the mountain-top, for she is a lady who would appreciate such grandeur to the fullest under favorable circumstances. We reached level ground without accident, and were glad to come up with friends we had met before on the road.

WE LEFT THE CHILICOTHE TRAIN THIS MORNING. As it will take all day to get the wagons mended, they cannot start today. We came on to Bear River, reached here a little after noon, and will stay here until tomorrow.

We crossed a toll bridge on Smith's Fork, and met Captain Hardinbrooke's brother at the bridge. He is going to meet the train. He did not know of Mrs. Hardinbrooke's illness. He asked very especially and with some confusion, "Is Miss Walker well?"

Ah, I think I know who he is going to meet, and understand some things that have not been very clear to me before. "Ah, ha, Miss Lyde, you have guarded your secret well, but see if I have not guessed it now?" Well, he is very nice looking, and if he makes as good a husband as his brother, he will no doubt be worth coming to Montana for. I wish you joy, and that I may be present at the wedding festivities.

The boys have gone fishing, all but Sim. Poor boy he is too sick again. I feel very much out of patience with Mr. Curry because of the tramp he led Sim when in so weak a condition.

We passed a grave this morning that was made yesterday for a young mother and her new-born babe. Oh, how sad. With what an aching heart must that husband and father go on his weary way, leaving his loved ones by the roadside.

We crossed another toll bridge. It seems to me that emigrants are greatly imposed upon by these men who claim toll. They throw a very poor excuse of a bridge across a stream that could be easily forded if let alone, but they spoil the crossing by digging ditches and throwing in bush and timbers to obstruct the fording, then build a cabin, close to the bridge, and squat to make a fortune by extorting large toll from emigrants, who have not the time to stop and contend for, their rights. It seems a shameful business.

While stopping at noon we saw a company of Indians coming down the road toward our wagons. My first sensation was fear, but upon reflection I knew that is not the way they go on the warpath, and by the time they reached camp I was ready to say "How," and try to talk to them. There was one that could understand English and talked quite well.

They are Bannocks, the tribe that was conquered in Idaho some years ago. Their chief was with them. He held a stiff neck and tried to look dignified, and only looked ridiculous. They are going on a buffalo hunt. It seems that the whole tribe is going, squaws, pappooses and all.

We have been meeting them all afternoon and are camping with them all around us tonight. They all seem to want my pony. I have been asked at least twenty times this afternoon to "Swap." I gave all the same answer, "No swap." Why, I would not give my Dick for twenty of their ponies.

The squaws and pappooses are around our camp tonight begging biscuit. They are the greatest beggars I ever saw. I do wonder if they are hungry?

We crossed the steepest, straight up and down mountain today that we have crossed yet. It seemed that the wagons would turn a somersault as we were making the descent.

Sim was too sick to sit up, and he would slide down in a heap, bed, bedclothes and all, against the seat and grub-box. We stopped twice to have him helped back into place. When we reached level ground he was all piled up again. Poor Sim, he is very sick. I do wish we could come across a physician. We have administered simple remedies, but seemingly without effect. There is an old lady ninety-three years old in a train camping near us tonight. She is cheerful as a lark, sings sometimes, and is an incessant talker.

She says she is going to Oregon, where she expects to renew her youth. She looks very old and wrinkled in the face, but is very active in her movements, and not at all stooped. The people she is with are not at all refined or cultured, but I do like to talk to the old lady, she is so quaint. It makes mother seem quite a young woman to see her with an old lady more than forty years older than she is. Why, she seems just in the prime of life, and we had thought her growing old.

Since we crossed the last steep mountain the horse flies have been very troublesome, the first that have bothered us all summer. I wonder if the Indians brought them?

We came through two villages today; they are about five miles apart. The first Bennington, the last Montpelier—pretty large names for such small places. They are Mormon towns, although this is Idaho Territory. The women appeared sad and sorrowful enough to be the wives of Mormons. I did not see one of them smile. Our wagons were thronged with women and children selling butter, eggs, cheese and vegetables. They sold eggs at seventy-five cents per dozen, butter seventy cents per pound, cheese fifty cents, potatoes twenty-five cents, and everything else in proportion. The prices seemed enormous to us, but I presume we would have purchased if they had been double what they were, for we are about starved for such things. Just think of spending a whole summer without garden productions.

This is a beautiful valley. Too good to be possessed by a community of bigamists. What a stigma upon the Government of these United States that whole communities are allowed to live criminal lives with impunity. I wonder how many are paying the penalty for bigamy in the penitentiaries of the United States? What is crime in one place, under the same Government, I would think, would be crime in all other places, if the one did happen to be an isolated case, while the other is in large numbers, or wholesale. I suppose I am not well enough versed in law and politics to understand why it is crime in one place and not in the other. We are camping eight miles from Montpelier. Sim is much better today.

HERE WE ARE AT SODA SPRINGS. I am surprised to see so small a town, for it is quite an old place for this western country, at least ten or fifteen years old, and does not have a post-office. The town is beautifully situated, the landscape views are glorious. The soda springs are bubbling up out of the ground in many places in this vicinity, and I expect there will be a city here some day. There are medicinal springs here that possess wonderful curative properties, or people think they do. We wanted Sim to test them, but he said: "I am getting well as fast as possible, and I don't care to drink that nauseous water. I prefer the pure, unadulterated snow water from the mountain springs."

This is the junction of the Oregon and Montana roads. There are three camps within sight of us.

As we drove into the road this morning there was a train of eight wagons came into line just behind our wagons, and have traveled with us all day, stopping at noon when we did, and they are camping near us tonight, though we have separate camps. They are from Missouri, and are going to Virginia City. They seem to think as we all came from the same State, and our destination is the same place, that of course there is a bond of fellowship that is mutual, but to be frank, I must confess I do not care to go into a strange place in their company, for I fear we would be judged by the company we keep, and I think it would not be very favorable, so we will try to get away from them as soon as possible.

The weather is perfect. This is a beautiful valley. The men say the land is extremely rich. We are camping on the Blackfoot. We have not been able to shake our Missouri friends.

We came to a toll bridge over the Blackfoot this morning, where the toll was one dollar per team, and fifty cents for horseback riders. There had been an excellent ford just below the bridge. The men collecting the toll had spoiled it by digging ditches on both sides near the bank. The water was clear, and they were plainly visible. Hillhouse mounted Dick to see if we could ford it. One of the men screamed out at him: "You will mire your horse if you try that."

"I'll risk it." And he rode in below where the ditches were dug. The pony's feet were not muddy. Hillhouse found we could easily ford the creek below the ditches, which we did without accident.

It does seem a shame that we should have to pay toll for crossing a stream like that, after fording South Platte, North Platte and Green River.

The Missourians refused to pay the exorbitant price, and offered them fifty cents per wagon. They swore they would not take a cent less than one dollar. But the travelers were too many for them, and they drove over and did not pay a cent. The toll men were fearfully angry, and made great threats, but the men dared them to do their worst and laughed at them.

I do hope we will get ahead of these people tomorrow. They are not the kind of people I like to travel with.

We have met as many as twenty men today going back to the States from the Virginia City mines. George Mays was with them. I mentioned about his leaving the train to go through on horseback, expecting to get his meals at stations and emigrant trains, when his brother with his bride went to Colorado. Says he worked just one day and got five dollars for it, and took the back track the next day.

"Mining is the only work a man can get to do, and it would kill an ordinary man in less than a week."

He is distressingly homesick. He is going to Denver to his brother.

We were up at the first peep of dawn, had breakfast, and were hitching up to start, when the folks in the eight wagons began to emerge and light their camp fires, so we have left them some, distance behind. We have been meeting men all day returning from the mines. They give a doleful account of the hard times in Montana. They say: "There are a few fortunate ones who are making money like dirt, but they are the exception, about one in a hundred."

One man was very anxious to buy Dick. I told him: "This pony is not for sale," and rode away before he could say anything more. The boys say we have met as many as two hundred men today returning from the mines. I believe we are all somewhat discouraged this evening. We have always heard such flattering reports from Alder Gulch and Virginia City.

We have overtaken Mr. Grier, Mr. Bower and Mr. Kennedy. Some of Mr. Bower's cattle have eaten a poisonous herb—wild larkspur, I believe it is. One ox has died and several are poisoned, but will not die. They got the poison weed the day before yesterday, when they stopped at noon. I am glad we have overtaken them, but sorry for their misfortune. Hillhouse has just now come in, and says Joe, one of our big white oxen, is poisoned. He came for remedies and to sharpen his knife to bleed him. No doubt he got the poison the same place Mr. Bower's cattle did when we stopped for noon. Sim, Hillhouse and Winthrop have gone to his relief.

Later.—The boys came back very much discouraged after working an hour, and said: "The blood will not flow, and he is swelling frightfully. I fear he will die, for when the blood will not run and the animal begins to swell, they cannot be saved."

Mother said: "We will not let him die without further effort, at least. Come on, Sarah, let us try what we can do for him."

We melted a quart of lard and put it in a long-necked bottle (that we had brought for the purpose of drenching horses or cattle), cut up a lot of fat bacon into strips, put on our big aprons, and taking a bucket of cold water, we were ready. Hillhouse said: "Don't give him water." I answered, "You never mind, who is doing this?"

We were not long finding poor Joe. He seemed to be suffering dreadfully. His nose was as hot as fire. It actually burned my hands when I took hold of it to drench him with the lard. He seemed to know we were trying to help him, and did not resist at all when I put the bottle in the side of his mouth to pour the lard down his throat. He looked at us with his great, soft, patient eyes in such a docile, knowing manner, I felt sure he would not bite me, so I put my hand away down his throat to make him swallow the strips of fat bacon. He swallowed them as patiently as if he knew what they were for. We then bathed his nose with the cold water, without letting him drink any, and before we came away he seemed relieved, and the swelling had stopped and he breathed much better. I believe he will live.

JOE DID NOT DIE. This morning when Hillhouse went to see about him, expecting to find him dead, he was grazing, and seemed as well as ever, except his nose, which looks as if it had been scalded.

We came to Snake River ferry this morning, six miles from where we camped last night. We paid eight dollars for our outfit crossing on the ferry. As Nellie Bower and I were standing on the bank of the river watching the wagons being ferried over, holding our ponies by their bridles, a gentleman came near. Lifting his hat and bowing politely, he said to me: "I will give one hundred dollars in clean gold dust for that pony."

"This pony is not for sale, sir, at any price."

We came from the ferry about two miles, and stopped for lunch. I told Hillhouse what the man said.

"If I were you, I would certainly sell him, so many seem to want him. He will very likely be stolen."

"Oh, I can't sell my pony."

After lunch the men folks went to fish in Snake River. They had been gone but a few minutes, when the man that wanted Dick rode into camp. He rode straight to our wagons, and said:

"I will give you one hundred and ten dollars for that pony."

I had begun to relent somewhat. I felt that it would not do to be sentimental under existing circumstances. We had spent almost all our money for toll, ferrying and other expenses on the road. It might prove to be a serious matter to be in a strange place without money, and if we fail to get employment we will be obliged to sell something, and there is nothing we can spare so well as Dick. I knew the man had offered all and more than I could expect to get for him.

But as Hillhouse was gone fishing and I could not think of selling my pony myself, I said to the man:

"My brother is not here, and I cannot let him go."

"Tell your brother to bring him to the ferry, and I will send you the pay for him."

"I think you need not expect him, for I am sure he will not come."

He went away without Dick, and Hillhouse did not take him back, so I have my pony yet. We came five miles and camped, as too long a drive is not good for the poisoned cattle. I wish there was a longer distance between us and the man that wants my pony.

Mr. Grier sold his riding horse at the ferry. He says:

"There is a party of half a dozen gentlemen going to the States horseback. They are all supplied, except the man that wants your pony. He has waited, trying to find a horse with an easy gait, and Dick is the only one that has suited him. Oh, he will be back again, Miss Raymond, and make another offer, and if you do not let him have him, I don't know what he will do, for he seems determined to get him."

If he does come I will not dare to refuse him, but I do hope we are out of reach of temptation. Dick is as fat as when we started. I comb and brush him every day, and he shows his keeping. He always looks nice and sleek. He is a bright bay, with heavy black mane and tail.

IT WAS SCARCELY DAYLIGHT WHEN that hateful man was here again after Dick. I had just finished dressing when Hillhouse came to the wagon and said:

"Shall I let Dick go?"

"Do as you think best." And I threw myself on the bed for a good cry. I had not stopped crying when he came back, and throwing a buckskin purse into my lap, said:

"There is your pony." There was one hundred and twenty-five dollars in gold dust in it. I sobbed out loud. Hillhouse looked at me with contempt in his expression, but said nothing. I could not help crying.

I know he would never sell anything that he loved, and I love that pony. I let the purse roll out of my lap down into the bottom of the wagon, and have not touched it yet. Of course, I knew the wagon-bed was tight, and there is no danger of its being lost. We came to Silver Lake today. We are having a fine shower of rain, which we were needing very much. It was some time coming, so we had dinner over and were ready for it when it reached us.

We have traveled today over Snake River desert, nothing but sand and sagebrush. We watered at noon at a toll well, called Hole-in-the-sand, and paid ten cents a head for watering stock. I wonder what we will have to pay toll for next?

We are camping on Camel's Creek. There is a family camping near us from Bannack, going to the States. The lady is a sister of Mr. Esler, one of the quartz kings of Montana, so she says; I presume everybody knows about him, but I must confess I never heard of him until now.

His sister is taking his motherless babe back to its grandmother. Mr. Esler's wife died more than a month ago. The babe is about four months old, and as sweet as can be. I could not keep my hands off it, and that is how I came to get acquainted with its auntie. She is a great talker, seems to think I am going to Montana husband-hunting, and volunteered a deal of advice on the subject, especially I must not tell that I am from Missouri, as Missourians are below par in Montana. She is from New York. Oh, dear, it makes one tired to see a full-grown woman so frivolous.

We watered the stock at noon at Hole-in-the-rock. Didn't turn them out to graze, as there was nothing for them to graze on.

Mr. Bower has lost another ox, and was obliged to buy a yoke of oxen to get his wagons over the ranges. There are two mountains to cross before he reaches his home in the Madison Valley, fifteen or twenty miles the other side of Virginia City. Of course, he had to pay a most exorbitant price. Joe, our ox that was poisoned, seems as well as ever, except his nose has peeled off as if scalded into a blister.

We are camping at the foot of the last range we will cross before we reach our destination.

Mrs. Kennedy and I have become quite well acquainted the last few days. She was a bride of only a few days when they started to the West. Her husband drives one of Mr. Bower's teams. They are going among strangers, to make them a home and fortune. She is a very intelligent and well-educated young woman. I do not know her husband very much.

MOTHER'S BIRTHDAY. She is fifty-three years old. We have not been able to celebrate it especially, yet she is not likely to forget it, though spent in climbing a Rocky Mountain range. We have been now four months on this journey. Have lived out of doors, in all sorts of weather. It has been very beneficial to mother. She was looking frail and delicate when we started, but seems to be in perfect health now, and looks at least ten years younger.

I have not heard her utter one word of complaint, either of physical suffering or outward discomfort, such as the heat or cold, mud, dust, rain, nor any of the things that make camping out disagreeable, and so many people grumble about. "What can't be cured, must be endured," is her motto, and the one care has been that we all keep in good health, and she would ask nothing more.

We are camping in Pleasant Valley, a depression right on top of the mountain, just large enough for a good-sized ranch. It is a beautiful place, the scenery is magnificently grand. There is a fine grove of beautiful trees at the lower end of the vale. The sides and upper end are hedged in by straight up and down hills or mountain-sides, about fifteen feet high. The grass is a luxuriant green and very plentiful.

There is a station here, occupied by a family that used to live in Virginia City. They have two very bright little girls, who have spent the early evening hours with us. They are perfect little chatterboxes to talk. They have a married sister living in Virginia City, the wife of a Mr. Wheeler, who is a candidate for some office. The little girls had forgotten whether for sheriff or Member of Congress.

As we were descending the mountain we met a freight train loaded with people returning to the States. After we had passed them about half a mile, Hillhouse was walking in front of the wagons, and found a miner's shovel. It is bright and shining, but not new. It is worn off some. The men tell Hillhouse it is a good omen, that he will make money by the shovelful. He laughed, and said: "I reckon I'd better keep it, then, to shovel it up with."

When I awoke in the night I heard the rain pattering on the wagon-cover. This morning the mountains were all covered with snow, and presented a magnificent picture. Those nearest our camp are covered with pine trees of an intensely dark green. The snow on the boughs and beneath the trees glittered in the sunshine. The scene was constantly changing, as the warm sun melted the snow from the boughs, and before night it was all gone except on the highest peaks, where it stays all summer.

The roads have been sloppy and muddy today, though the water has all run off or evaporated, so that it is comparatively dry where we are camping, notwithstanding there was so much snow and water on the ground this morning. It is too cold for comfort this evening. We are hovering around the stove with our shawls on.

Sweet Water Canyon

WE CAME THROUGH A DEEP, DARK CANYON this morning, and passed the grave of a man that was robbed and murdered last week. It is the deepest and darkest canyon we have traveled through. Ten men have been robbed and murdered in it in the last two years. We were in no danger of being molested. Only men who have their fortunes in gold about their person are intercepted, robbed and killed. How awful it seems. Why will men be so wicked?

In several places in the canyon the road has been widened with pick and shovel, perhaps two or three days' work done, and we had to pay ten dollars toll for our two wagons passing over it. We stopped at noon on Black Tail Deer Creek. Are camping on the Sweet Water, about twenty-five miles from Virginia City. This is a beautiful place. There are fine large trees along the creek, high mountains around a lovely dale. It is just large enough for a fine farm. There is a deserted cabin here, where someone commenced improving a farm, became home-sick and discouraged, and left it for someone else.

We are camping within seven miles of Virginia City, near a freight train of about fifty wagons, with from seventy-five to one hundred people all together, men, women and children, returning to the States.

To hear these people talk of the disadvantages and disagreeable things with regard to life in Montana, would have a tendency to discourage one, if it were not so palpable that they are homesick, and everyone knows that when that disease is fairly developed, everything is colored with a deep dark blue, and even pleasant things seem extremely disagreeable to the afflicted person. The ladies seem to have the disease in its worst form, and of course they make the gentlemen do as they wish, which is to take them home to mother and other dear ones.

We have had a very pleasant day, about as pleasant as the day we started on this journey, the first day of May. It is cheering that the first and last days of our journeying should be so lovely. After four months and four days of living outdoors we are all in the most robust health. Yet we shall be glad to have a roof over our heads once more, even if it is a dirt roof.

Here we are camping in the suburbs of the city, in Alder Gulch, where the miners are at work. How I wish my descriptive powers were adequate to making those who have never seen gulch-mining see as I see, and realize the impression made upon me as I first looked into the gulch at the miners at work. There is a temporary bridge (very shaky) across the gulch that wagons may pass over. Standing on this bridge, in the middle of the gulch, looking up and down, and even beneath my feet, the scene is a lively one. So many men, it seems they would be in each other's way. They remind one of bees around a hive. And such active work. It seemed that not one of that great multitude stopped for one instant shoveling and wheeling dirt, passing and repassing each other without a hitch. It made me tired to look at them. The ground is literally turned inside out; great deep holes and high heaps of dirt. The mines are said to be very rich.

2 P.M.—We dined at noon today. Had beefsteak at fifty cents per pound and potatoes at twenty-five cents. I do not know if the price had anything to do with it, but it certainly tasted better than any I ever ate before.

I interviewed a woman—or rather she interviewed me—that lives near where we are camping. She said her name is Neihart. Her husband is a miner and earns seven dollars per day. Judging from the manner in which they seem to live, they ought to save at least five of it. I presume I did not make a very favorable impression, for after I came back to camp she called across the street to her neighbor—so we could hear what she said:

"Some more aristocrats. They didn't come here to work. Going to teach school and play lady," with great contempt in her voice.

I laughed at the first impression made, and tried to realize that teaching is not work.

The End of Our Journey

MRS. CURRY, SIM, HILLHOUSE AND I are going to town as soon as Mrs. Curry is ready. We held a council whether we should get out our street suits and last summer's hats, or go in our emigrant outfits, sunbonnets and short dresses, thick shoes and all. Decided in favor of the latter. No doubt the people of Virginia are used to seeing emigrants in emigrant outfits, and we will not astonish them.

Evening.—We were not very favorably impressed with Virginia City. It is the shabbiest town I ever saw, not a really good house in it. Hillhouse and I, after hunting up and down the two most respectable looking streets, found a log cabin with two rooms that we rented for eight dollars per month. Mrs. Curry did not find a house at all. We thought as so many were leaving there would be an abundance of vacant houses, but there were enough living in tents to fill all the houses that were vacated.

Mr. Curry's folks and Mr. Kennedy's will go to Helena. Mr. Bower has a ranch on the Madison Valley. Mr. Grier will stay here for a time, anyway.

The cabin is on the corner of Wallace and Hamilton Streets, next door to the city butcher. The cabin has a dirt roof. There is a floor in it, and that is better than some have. It is neat and clean, which is a comfort.

We found quite a budget of letters at the post-office, the most important of which are from brother Mac and Frank Kerfoot. Mac's letter:

Cincinnati, August 10, 1865.

Dear Mother, Sister and Brothers:

It is with fear and trembling that I pen this letter. I have not heard from you for more than a month, telling me you had decided to go to Montana. The papers are full of accounts of Indian depredations. I have realized to the fullest extent that Hope deferred maketh the heart sick. In your last letter you had decided to go to Virginia City, so I will direct this letter to be held until called for. I am glad you are not going any farther West. I cannot conceive why you wanted to go to that far off wild Western country. I do wish you had stopped at Omaha, or St. Jo, or even Denver. It would have been better than Montana. With sincerest love to all,

Your son and brother,

Mac.

But oh, the sad, sad news comes in Frank's letter. Neelie is dead. Oh, the anguish of soul, the desolateness of heart, that one sentence gives expression to. Frank's letter:

Green River, Wyoming Ter., AUG. 18.

Dear Miss Sallie,

I write to tell you of our very great sorrow. Precious Neelie is gone. We are all sorely bereaved, but how Uncle Ezra's family can ever get along without her, I cannot see. Any member of the family, except uncle, could be spared better than Neelie. She got very much better, and the doctor said if uncle would stay there another week, he was sure Neelie would be well enough to travel without danger of a relapse, but if she had another relapse she could not be saved.

The Hardinbrooke train left Monday morning. Mrs. Hardinbrooke was much better. The Gatewoods and Ryans stayed with us. Neelie was much better. She sat up in bed some. That night Uncle Ezra did not sleep at all, he was so afraid of Indians. The next morning, as Neelie had a good-night's rest, and was feeling stronger, nothing else would do but we must move on to Green River, where the soldiers are. We started about nine o'clock, and drove twenty-five miles without stopping. It was very hot and dusty. Uncle drove the family wagon and watched Neelie carefully. After a time she seemed to be sleeping quietly, so he thought she was all right. But it was the sleep from which there is no waking in this life.

Dr. Howard and Dr. Fletcher were both at Green River, and they both worked all night trying to arouse her, but without success. At early dawn Neelie's sweet spirit took its flight, and we are left desolate.

Miss Sallie, do you remember Carpenter? the young man that made Uncle Ezra so mad by pretending to go into hysterics when the Ryan girls were leaving the train? When he heard that Neelie was gone, he went out on the mountain and found a large, smooth, flat stone, white as marble, but not so hard, and engraved Neelie's name, age, and date of her death on it, to mark her resting place. He worked all day upon it, and at the funeral he placed it at the head of her grave, and if you ever go over this road it will not be hard to find Neelie's grave. We gathered wild flowers and literally covered her grave with them.

Darling Neelie, our loss is her gain, for we all know that she was an earnest, devoted Christian. We will start on our now sorrowful journey tomorrow. I wish you were here to go with us, but hope you will be successful where you are, and happy too.

Mrs. Hardinbrooke was much worse after they came here. That hot, dusty drive was hard on well people; for sick people it was terrible. When Neelie died she was very low, but she has rallied, and the rest of the train will move on tomorrow. But Mr. Hardinbrooke will stay here with his wife until she is entirely restored, and they will go to Virginia City on the coach. All send love to you all. Aunt Mildred asked me to write you.

Very sincerely your friend,

Frank.

I believe I am homesick this evening. It is so dreary to go into a strange place and meet so many people, and not one familiar face. But I must not complain, for we are all here, not even Caesar missing. My heart aches so for the Kerfoots. I do not know how they can bear this terrible bereavement under such trying circumstances.

Mr. Curry's folks have started to Helena. Mr. Bower's to the Madison Valley, and Mr. Kennedy with them, to drive his team, leaving Mrs. Kennedy with us until tomorrow, when they will take the coach for Helena.

We moved into our cabin this morning. It does not seem as much like home as the wagons did, and I believe we are all homesick if we would acknowledge it.

The boys found a checkerboard nailed on the window where a pane of glass was broken out. We pasted paper over the place. They made checkermen out of pasteboard, and Sim and Winthrop are having a game. Hillhouse is reading the Montana Post. Mother is making bread, and initiating Mrs. Kennedy into the mysteries of yeast and bread-making.

As Hillhouse was on his way to the butcher shop, he passed an auction sale of household goods. The auctioneer was crying a beautiful porcelain lamp. He stopped to make the first bid. "One dollar" he called. There were no other bids and he got the lamp—his first purchase in Virginia City. (He has it yet.)

When he brought it home, with the meat he went to get, mother said: "What is the use of the lamp without the chimney?"

So he went to purchase a chimney after dinner and coal oil to burn in the lamp. He had to pay two dollars and fifty cents for a chimney, and five dollars for a gallon of coal oil, so our light is rather expensive after all. And thus ends our first day in Virginia City, and brings Crossing the Plains and Mountains in 1865 to an end.

THE END

Printed in Great Britain
by Amazon